RAILWAY&
TRAMWAY
TICKETS

MALAGA BOOKS

RAILWAY&
TRAMWAY
TICKETS

GORDON FAIRCHILD&
PETER WOOTTON

LONDON
IAN ALLAN LTD

Back cover:
In 1964, British Railways Board modernised the booking hall at London's Liverpool Street station. (*Above*) The interior in December 1963, immediately before reconstruction, showing, left to right, Main Line Ticket Office and Continental Ticket & Information Bureau. (*Below*) The newly modernised interior late in January 1965, showing ticket printing machines and five-service counter.

Front cover:

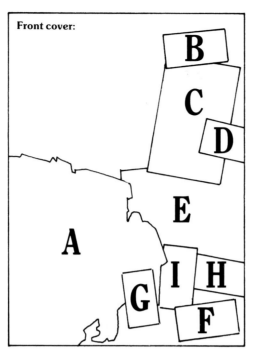

First published 1987

ISBN 0 7110 1701 8

Published by Ian Allan Ltd, Shepperton, Surrey; and printed by Ian Allan Printing Ltd at their works at Coombelands in Runnymede, England

Dedication
For all the many friendly collectors whose exchanges have created and sustained our personal collections over many years.

Royalties from the sale of this book have been donated directly to the charities named below.

The Woking Homes
(Registered Charity No 200346)
The Woking Homes were founded in London in 1885 to provide care for fatherless children of London & South Western Railway Company employees. In 1908 the Homes moved to Woking, where an orphanage for 250 children was maintained. In 1947, facilities were provided for the residential care of retired staff from British Rail's Southern Region. Since 1984, the facilities have been available to all current and retired staff of British Rail and Associated Transport Industries. Residential care is provided for up to 12 children, either long or short term, to deal with the particular needs of a shift industry.

The Foundation for Ephemera Studies
(Registered Charity No 287771)
The Foundation exists to encourage the conservation and study of ephemera — the 'transient minor documents of everyday life'. It is concerned with the function of these fugitive items as evidence of the spirit of the period that produced them. The range of subject matter is wide. It covers printed and handwritten items from laundry lists to proclamations, from workhouse dietaries to travel tickets. The Foundation is a registered educational charity. It initiates research projects in the field of ephemera studies and it has custodianship of a notable ephemera collection, a body of material available for study and, by special arrangement, reproduction for publication.

The charity seeks funding for its operations from bequests, endowments etc, and welcomes offers of ephemera — singly or as collections — for consideration for inclusion in the Collection. The Trustees would like to express their appreciation of the kindness of the authors of this book in making over a portion of the royalties from its sale for the furtherance of the Foundation's work.

A (main photo)
Interior of Maryland, LNER booking office taken four days before closure in October 1947. Note Edmondson ticket tubes on either side of serving window, with drawers below for bulk stocks; at far left is the then current timetable book.

B (red star ticket)
A distinctive Nottingham (Victoria) pre-1923 station Platform Ticket.

C (serial 5013)
A reminder of continental through-coupon booklets of pre-Grouping days. Note the endorsement extending validity from 17 to 25 days, and reference to a 'Mr Fisher's Party' as passenger(s).

D (serial 11)
Typical of Great Central Railway pre-dated Cheap Excursion tickets in the early years of this century. Ticket #11 has the date Nov.13.09 and although properly issued and more than once inspected on the day, survived INtact and now, IN perpetuity.

E (serial 80340)
Members of many national and international legislatures are permitted concessionary or free travel. On 10 April 1924 Members of Parliament in Britain were granted free travel for journeys to and from London, and elsewhere on Parliamentary business. Today Members may make unlimited journeys to and from London and their constituency free of charge by rail, or air if the distance warrants. In recent years Members' spouses have similarly been granted up to 15 trips per year, and each of a Member of Parliament's children under the age of 18 have the same allowance.

The illustration shows a Rail Travel Warrant provided by British Railways Board at the House of Commons. This must be exchanged for a valid travel ticket before commencement of the journey concerned. Special thanks are conveyed to the two Members, and Official concerned.

F (serial 00000)
An uncommon French National Railways through ticket to Jersey specifying the route though not the company or vessel making the sea crossing. The serial number and matching *000 printed* fare suggest this may have been a 'proof' ticket prepared in isolation from regular stock. Printing is known to have been late in 1938, less than a year after formation of *Société Nationale des Chemins de fer Francais*.

G (serial 99991)
Breakfast coupon: from a Great Western Railway stitched *carnet* available for steamer across the Irish Sea; train Rosslare to Dublin and return; supper on board steamer back to Fishguard.

H (serial 370)
Ireland's Great Northern Railway operated an electric tramway on the Hill of Howth from 1901 until closure in 1959. This ticket represents a railway round trip with a ride on the tramcar.

I (serial 578)
This brightly coloured card dated 1898 was issued at Bonar Bridge (later Ardgay) on the pre-Grouping Highland Railway, north of Inverness. For the journey to London's Euston station, one Bicycle was charged 6/6d (32½p).

Contents

Acknowledgements

The authors are grateful to the following for assistance which has included much essential local research, provision of tickets, general advice, or permission to copy and quote:
Joseph Canfield, the late W. Ivor Grantham, the late John C. Hanbach, Mrs Agnes Hanbach, Max Ruh, Robert Saxon.

Thanks are also due to the following for important assistance:
Alderney Railway Society, American Antiquarian Society, Australian Railway Historical Society, the late André Beauvais, The Boots Company plc, Maurice I. Bray, The British Library, Yorkshire, British Railways Board, Dee Brown, Chatto & Windus Ltd, The *Daily Mail*, Dundee District Council, East Sussex Library Service, Dr R. S. B. Hamilton, Kent & East Sussex Railway, Lancaster City Museums, London Underground Ltd, The Patent Office, London, Sheila Pamphilon, Philadelphia Department of Records, Royal Society for the Prevention of Cruelty to Animals, William Donald Schaefer Esq (Mayor of the City of Baltimore), Gerrit C. van Straaten, White Mouse Editions Ltd, Peter H. Williamson, The Administrator of Woburn Abbey.

Special appreciation is extended to:
Roger Atkinson OBE, David L. Curson and Mrs Hilary Howarth for their help with aspects in which they are acknowledged experts.

Spring 1987   *G.H.I.F.*
                                                          P.H.W.

Abbreviations

BR	British Rail(ways)
BRB	British Railways Board
BStW	Baker Street & Waterloo Railway
BTC	British Transport Commission
CIE	Coras Iompair Eireann (Irish Transport Company)
CL	Central London Railway
CTC	Croydon Tramways Company
GC	Great Central Railway
GE	Great Eastern Railway
GLC	Greater London Council
GN	Great Northern Railway
GW	Great Western Railway
IE	Iarnrod Eireann (Irish Rail)
IOW	Isle of Wight Railway
KES	Kent & East Sussex Railway
L&Y	Lancashire & Yorkshire Railway
LBSC	London Brighton & South Coast Railway
LCC	London County Council
LCD	London Chatham & Dover Railway
LE	London Electric Railway
L&G	London & Greenwich Railway
LGOC	London General Omnibus Company
LMS	London Midland & Scottish Railway
LNER	London & North Eastern Railway
LNW	London & North Western Railway
LPTB	London Passenger Transport Board
LRT	London Regional Transport
LSW	London & South Western Railway
LT	London Transport
LTE	London Transport Executive
LTS	London Tilbury & Southend Railway
LUL	London Underground Ltd
Met	Metropolitan Railway
NB	North British Railway
NCB	National Coal Board
NCC	Northern Counties Committee
NE	North Eastern Railway
NS	North Staffordshire Railway
PLA	Port of London Authority
R&C	Rye & Camber Tramway
RCH	Railway Clearing House
REC	Railway Executive Committee
SE	South Eastern Railway
SEC	South Eastern & Chatham Railway
SR	Southern Railway
USRA	United States Railroad Administration
WL	West London Railway

Introduction

The collecting mania is an ancient one. Sometimes it stems from a simple love of possessions and sometimes from the more creditable desire to preserve for the future things that could easily be lost for ever. The 6th century Saxon chieftain acquired beautiful jewellery in life and hoped that in death it would be placed in his grave and so travel with him to *Valhalla*. The 18th and 19th centuries saw the rise of the curio hunter. As a result the manufacture of china and other domestic trivia became a major industry and its resale after a few years a profitable enterprise.

The ephemerist is seeking not so much objects that will appreciate in value as paper throw-aways and minor transient documents that have served their functions and would otherwise be destroyed and discarded. Retained they record a particular era or illustrate a popular activity. Some may be reminiscent of a political, religious or commercial success now long gone from headlines. One can collect bonds and share certificates, passports, theatre bills and cigar bands, borne along by some industry or activity of their time. Items such as the indenture and the slave poster have an intrinsic story to tell. Some collectibles must be formed into groups or whole collections before they will adequately relate their history or merit conservation. A random selection from the huge family of collectible printed ephemera might include invitations, maps, timetables, currency notes, ocean liner menus, chemists' labels, cigarette cards and matchbox labels. Equally, billheads and QSL cards form into historically important collections at the hands of their respective devotees.

Of all printed collectibles the postage stamp enjoys the most widespread and internationally popular following, albeit stoked by commercialisation. Philately knows no national boundaries. Stamps tell us something about almost every facet of human knowledge and provide an excellent insight to political geography and to momentous events the world over.

Railway and Tramway tickets have many of these attributes also. When it comes to recording the changing face of world politics, the rise and fall of a transport empire or usage in the terminology of six continents, tickets are surprisingly informative. Often visually attractive, they are of a convenient size for sorting and graphic display by professional archivists and hobbyist collectors alike. More than this, railway and tramway tickets often achieve a highly personal appeal. 'Some were used by my Grandfather'; 'That one came from Aunt Gertie's sole journey abroad' and 'I bought this one to see the homecoming of Her Majesty', are typical comments accompanying a contribution to a collection.

Collecting the world's passenger tickets has become a pastime in its own right. The hobby has 'arrived'. It presents a unique opportunity to acquire knowledge while relaxing with a display of printed throw-aways which have, happily, escaped conventional (and very final) disposal at a local railway station or tramway depot. The ticket is a window through which to view a bygone company, thereby to live a little with nostalgia. A residual element of romance resides in the ticket that brought one home from war or even from an enjoyable but otherwise almost forgotten holiday in a far-off county. Some collectors view their tickets as a microcosm of history or geography. They see them as descriptive of the story of a line or as evidence of the existence of stations and tram routes renamed, relocated or closed many years before. Still more devotees enjoy tickets for what they tell of the kind of traffic carried, the social aspect and the category of person who may have presented them at busy barriers. A successful connoisseur writing in 1898, commented 'To travel with a passenger ticket and then to add it to a collection is one of the few instances of the commonly disputed possibility, of eating our cake and having it thereafter'.

The object of this book is to enthuse and assist the potential collector, whether he has long been a general transport enthusiast or only recently taken to the rails. Perhaps also the hitherto detached general reader, who may already have a liking for browsing through the showcases of any and every hobby, will commence a collecting activity that he will discover to be both informative and entertaining.

Few published books are of direct assistance to the collector of tickets. The only published work to grapple with the subject in depth and offer profuse illustrations of more than one national source, is *Passenger Tickets*[1] by the late Professor Lionel Wiener. This work, prepared for the use of professional transport administrators, was itself an extract from other works by the professor and appeared in instalments up to July 1947. It may never be equalled. After a full 40 years it remains an outstanding production, but sadly it is long out of print.

A great deal has been written regarding the history and development of railway and tramway tickets, their universal acceptance in all imaginable guises and of course their utilitarian application to the collection of fares and charges. There seems however, to have been scant rendering of the rôle of tickets as pieces of ephemera representing moments of history encapsulated in print. The Chapters which follow are intended to demonstrate both the archival and entertaining character of this studious and steadily expanding hobby of ticket collecting.

Before proceeding into the detail of 16 chapters and the romance of several hundreds of fares, a selection of tickets is reproduced (Page 9) to bring together England, Ireland, Scotland and Wales. **Items 1 to 8** span the period between 1870 and 1950: they represent travels of people and parcels, a tram rider and two holders of subscription tickets; they record an international trip by rail-cum-boat and the journey made by one dog. An unusual, stout, oval-shaped card, thin receipt-type forms and conventional pasteboard tickets combine to complement a fine linen form of yesteryear.

Above:
Thomas Edmondson (1792-1851), Quaker, Ticket Pioneer. *A modern impression by Sheila Pamphilon.*

5

Ticket for Live Stock, to be subject to the Conditions on Back of this Ticket.

THE LEVEN & EAST OF FIFE RAILWAY COMPANY.

TICKET FOR HORSES, CARRIAGES, AND DOGS.

No. **69** Date, _11 / 10_ 186_

_____ o'Clock Train.

From _Leven_ to _Edinburgh_

£ _____ s. _____ D.

Horse at

Carriage at

Dog _1_ at

Name, _____

_____ Booking Clerk.

N.B.—Received the annexed Ticket, subject to the Conditions expressed thereon.

DOGS are not allowed to be taken by the Trains unless Booked and Paid for. They are not allowed to be taken into the Carriages, and they must be provided with Collars, Chains, and Muzzles.

1

Cb 1555

OUTER		INNER
Beatrice Street		Beatrice Street
Green Street		Green Street
West Street		West Street
Causeway Avenue		Causeway Avenue
Howley Lane	TRANSFER 1¼d. WARRINGTON Corporation Tramways	Howley Lane
Mill Lane		Mill Lane
Longford Street		Longford Street
Marsh House Lane		Marsh House Lane

AUTO-TICKETS LTD, BIRKENHEAD

6

The Glasgow Tramway & Omnibus Co., LIMITED.

PREPAID PARCEL
Not exceeding 7 lbs.

2d.

No. **18777**

SPECIAL CONTRACT.

The Company will endeavour to forward all Parcels promptly, but it must be distinctly understood that they will not hold themselves responsible for the loss or detention of any Parcels. Parcels are sent solely at sender's risk.

8

MAWDDWY RY

Issued subject to the conditions in the Time Tables of the respective Co. over whose Lines this Ticket is available.

THIRD CLASS

DINAS To
ABERANGELL

Aberangell Fare -/4

7399

3

Ulster Transport Authority

ONE WEEK. 2nd. CLASS.

Marino & Belfast

8 JAN 1949

Expires _____

Subscriber _____

For conditions of issue see back.

2

G. N. R.
SINGLE JOURNEY
Available for ONE WEEK from Date of issue

LEEDS (T.O.) to
LEEDS (T.O.) LEEDS (T.O.)
Grimsby via Oxcroft & Retford & from Grimsby to

HAMBURG
HAMBURG HAMBURG
BY G. C. RY. CO'S BOAT.
14s. 3d. Third Class & Steerage 14s. 3d.
SEE CONDITIONS ON BACK.

337 337

England, Ireland, Scotland and Wales.

4

86 _Only one to travel at a time_

This Ticket will be Forfeited if Transferred

Waterford and Central Ireland Railway.

SUBSCRIPTION TICKET _Second_ CLASS.

For _Three_ Month

Between _Ballyragget_ _Kilkenny_ Stations.

Available on and from _July 1 900_

Up to and including the _30th September 1900_

Holder's Name and Address in full, _Miss E. or Mrs. Meredith Ballyragget_

Amount, £ _Paid_

Signature of _Secretary_

per _____

For Conditions on which SUBSCRIPTION TICKETS are granted, see other side.

7

F **4629**

The Rhondda Tramways Company Ltd

Up **4d** Down

Treherbert and Market Square Tonypandy

Crown Hotel, Trealaw and Station Road Dinas

St Peter's Church and Station Road Porth

Bodringallt Colliery and Ystrad

This Ticket is only available by the Car upon which it is issued, and must be shown on demand

This Ticket must be punched opposite the Section to which the Passenger is entitled to travel. Subject to the Company's Bye-laws.

Williamson, Manager, Ashton

CHAPTER 1

Mr Edmondson's Wonderful Invention

Five generations of travellers have thought of a railway ticket as a piece of pasteboard 2¼in long and 1¼in wide. Most have been aware that George Stephenson (1781-1848) invented the railway engine and perhaps many vaguely thought that he also produced the ticket at the same time. In fact, this came about 12 years after the opening of the Stockton & Darlington Railway and three years before the world's first adhesive postage stamp, and with no influence from Stephenson.

The early 19th century was the heyday of the stagecoach. The coach passenger paid his fare and supplied his name at the company's office and was booked for a specific coach, as the holidaymaker must book for a motor-coach excursion today. Sometimes the stagecoach passenger would be given a receipt (deemed most important in America until about 1839) for his money on a scrap of paper or perhaps something similar to the early United States ticket illustrated as **Item 9**. More importantly his name and the details of his journey were placed on a waybill. In Britain this document was supplied to the guard or driver as his instructions for the trip. He would hold a modest roll call at each stage and personally ensure that his passengers were picked up and set down at the places of their choice.

William Chaplin (1787-1859), a prominent figure among stagecoach[2] operators, was one of the first to realise that the industry could not compete with the railway. His coaching business was at the height of its success in the very years when the first ticket-related patents were being considered. As soon as he saw the way things were going, Chaplin invested in and later joined the London & South Western Railway. By 1843 most major British stagecoach lines were reduced to feeders or severely truncated.

Just as the builders of the first railway coaches had nothing to copy but the stagecoach, so the first passenger booking clerks knew no other way than that of the coach proprietor. The waybill was still supplied to the guard and the roll call held at each station. The differences were that there were far more passengers to cope with, advance bookings were no longer essential and the guard might be handed a separate and hurriedly prepared waybill at each station.

It was in 1837 that the recently appointed master of Milton (now Brampton) station on the Newcastle & Carlisle Railway began to consider the mounting problem. Thomas Edmondson (1792-1851) was a Quaker, a native of Lancaster and then aged 45. At his station the passenger received no ticket. The fare money was simply handed by the stationmaster to the guard. Edmondson's principal concern seems to have been that there was no simple check between the fares collected and the cash handed to the guard. The integrity of the staff was the company's only safeguard. In the periods between trains, he started writing out little receipts on a sheet of card which he cut with scissors. These stated the names of the two stations concerned and the fare and were numbered by hand. By keeping a record of the numbers, he could easily calculate how much to hand to the guard. It was clear to Edmondson that if the passenger surrendered the tiny piece of card at his destination, his right to travel would be established and further documentation avoided. His employers seem to have been impressed by his ingenuity and even spoke of promotion but they did not bring themselves to introduce the system throughout their railway.

In the meantime, Edmondson made further progress with his idea and created a basic printing press for his tickets, operated by inserting a piece of card through a slot near the base and striking the top with a mallet. He was able to exhibit his models to the public in the summer of 1838. Interest soon spread beyond the Newcastle & Carlisle Railway which had opened three years before. Captain Laws, an official of the Manchester & Leeds Railway, visited him at Milton to see his system at work and was sufficiently impressed to offer him a post in Manchester at twice his existing salary.

Edmondson left Milton early in 1839, took a post with the Manchester & Leeds, and witnessed its opening in July that year. He seems to have enjoyed considerable freedom with his new employers and continued to invent and produce more sophisticated machinery for printing and also dating tickets and patented it in his own name. After almost two years he left the company on excellent terms to set up his own printing business in Manchester. His former employer now became a principal

9

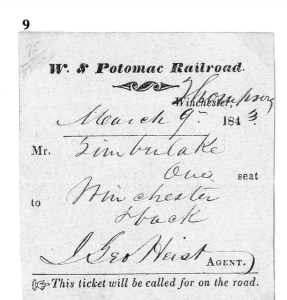

W. & Potomac Railroad.

Winchester,

March 9ᵗʰ 184 3

Mr. Trimbulake

One seat

to Winchester
& back

J. Geo Heist AGENT.

☞ This ticket will be called for on the road.

10

M Balt. & Ohio R.R. Main Stem. P

From _____ to
GREEN SPRING RUN.

☞ It is included in the Contract between the Company and the Passenger who holds this ticket, that he shall show the same to the Conductor, as often as requested, and surrender it on demand; also, that he shall not ride or stand on any Baggage or Freight Car, or on the Platform of any Car, or expose any part of his person outside of the Car; and that he shall be entitled to the transportation of Eighty Pounds of Baggage free, (no article being considered Baggage except Wearing Apparel,) when the same shall be given to the Baggage Master, to be checked or marked in accordance with the rules of the Company; that the Company shall not be liable for the loss or detention of Baggage, unless it has been properly checked or marked, and in no case for an amount exceeding $100, unless by special agreement.

☞ GOOD FOR THIS DAY ONLY.

_____ 185_

F _____ Agt. W

11

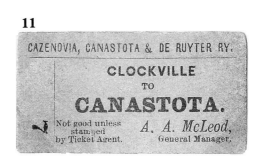

CAZENOVIA, CANASTOTA & DE RUYTER RY.

CLOCKVILLE
TO
CANASTOTA.

Not good unless stamped by Ticket Agent.

A. A. McLeod,
General Manager.

12

DELAWARE & HUDSON CANAL Co.
NORTHERN RAIL ROAD DEPT.

WEST TROY
TO
TROY

Not good unless stamped by Ticket Agent.

20187

NO STOP-OVER GIVEN HEREON

B 10 D. McKendrick G.T.A.

13

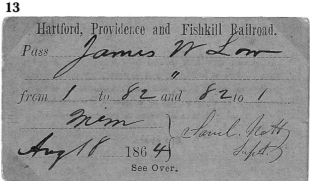

Hartford, Providence and Fishkill Railroad.

Pass James W Low
"
from 1 to 82 and 82 to 1
Mem
Aug 18 186 4 Saml. Rott Supt.

See Over.

14

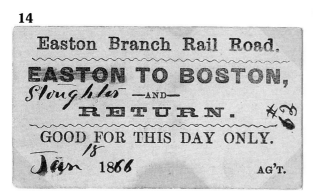

Easton Branch Rail Road.

EASTON TO BOSTON,
Sloughter —AND—
RETURN. #2

GOOD FOR THIS DAY ONLY.

Jan 18 1866 AG'T.

15

NEW YORK & HARLEM RAILROAD.

West Mount Vernon
TO
WHITE PLAINS.

☞ Good this Day Only.

7115

W. Van Arsdale

Very early practice in America and the rise of the large card in competition with Edmondson.

16

N.Y. Prov & Boston R.R.

KINGSTON
TO
WESTERLY.

29797

GOOD FOR THIS DAY ONLY.

F. B. Noyes
G.T.A

customer and proceeded to introduce his ideas throughout their railway system. In May 1840, the world's first adhesive postage stamps were put on sale in Britain. Thus two of the world's most striking and hugely successful international throw-aways were conceived within three years.

The comprehensiveness of Edmondson's service is not always appreciated; before long he was supplying dating presses, nippers for ticket inspectors and storage cases for tickets. He died in June 1851, just before his 59th birthday. In less than 14 years he had revolutionised the entire process of fare collection and established a system that has already endured for a century and a half. His son, John Beeby Edmondson, managed the business until he died in 1887.

The name Edmondson is arguably the most over-exercised word in ticket collecting circles. Within a very few years his ticketing concept reached much of Europe — France 1841, Switzerland 1850, Netherlands 1857[3] — and during the second half of the 19th century spread to every major railway-operating country. One factor in this was the amount of British capital invested in the building of railways in various parts of the world. The British expertise that accompanied this capital included Edmondson's methods. Yet in Japan, the Philippines, Central Africa and, conspicuously, North America, Edmondson products met considerable local competition, particularly from paper tickets bound into pads or books. These proved remarkably versatile in their application and remain the standard method in many places today. The paper and larger card ticket in its many guises has been favoured throughout North America. **Items 10** to **16** are examples of the wide range of early United States practice in the period of John Edmondson's stewardship in Europe and provide a useful comparison with developments in Britain. They are all from the period 1850 to 1887. Perhaps the most noticeable feature is the lack of a printed serial number in three cases. The already established Americanism 'Good for . . .' is well represented and shows clearly on the 1850s specimen.

The Edmondson system was soon copied by other firms, not always under licence from the inventor. Sometimes the railways themselves printed under licence in return for royalties on a route mileage basis. From the late 1840s these competitors employed equipment sold by the firm effectively in direct competition with its own establishment, although the family enjoyed a near-monopoly during perhaps its first 15 years in business. The happy result of this period of licence and piracy was that the Edmondson card, sometimes bearing and sometimes without a printer's imprint, gained footholds in all of the railway continents and even today survives somewhere in each.

As indicated above, a number of railways, especially in North America and parts of Australia, never employed the Edmondson card at all. Even so, pockets of success remain in Australia, parts of Asia, South America and Africa. The Edmondson card passed its heyday before World War 1. Just when it was serving the railway industry best, its demise was signalled by the appearance of numerous alternatives. Not the least of these was an increasing assortment of issuing machines, some of which actually contrived to manufacture a self-printed cut card ticket by the pressing of a button or the insertion of a coin by intending travellers. Such a signal was the introduction of machines by the Paris Metro when it opened in 1900. In Britain the pre-printed card ticket was challenged in 1911 by the arrival of a German Regina at Birmingham. This had served well in Cologne for several years. **17** is an example of an output from the model installed at Birmingham — not the very earliest, but a 1913 issue of a design second in its range. Similarly, in the United States, well organised

town and interurban railways from as early as 1865 retained thin paper forms and later a range of portable validating devices which would not have accepted the small, more rigid European card called 'Edmondson'. Many of the North American city forms required a vast amount of printed matter often including value scales, calendar panels and extensive conditions of issue, all doubled or trebled into duplex or triplex folded designs.

The popularity of the Edmondson card is due in no small measure to its shape and size: 57×31mm. In the booking office it is stored in tubes and handled with devices many of which were products of Thomas Edmondson's firm. When it is passed from booking clerk to passenger and passenger to ticket inspector, it is just large enough for each to handle with finger and thumb at the same moment. When one finds its way (or escapes!) into a private collection, it is small enough to be mounted in a postage stamp album or similar binder, about 15 to the average page, often by means of photocorners rather than the flimsy stamp hinge (see Chapter 15).

One thinks of Edmondson tickets as CARDS of the uniform size quoted. However, Thomas Edmondson and his successors manufactured some non-standard products, generally to suit the individual requirements of their customers. The firm's central works in Manchester ceased 120 years of trading in 1960, by which time the term 'Edmondson' in a ticketing context had long ceased to indicate exclusively the family of Thomas and his son John. It had come to signify the size and shape of a card ticket, regardless of where in the world or by whom it was made. The term often encompassed tickets which the purist would prefer to label quasi-Edmondson. Examples include the much thinner cards still being used for many local trips in North America. In fact, these are generally attributed either to a printer named Hill or to the influence of the émigré George Bailey, whose contribution is considered in the next paragraph. This thin version was also tried in Austria and Switzerland but did not last as a separate cut card. It also appeared in Ceylon (Sri Lanka) in 1940 and lasted several years. It was exceptionally widespread in Japan, parts of China and Korea. These oriental versions were of Edmondson length and thickness but only 25mm wide. The standard Edmondson size never reached North American railways in any strength, but it was not totally excluded from that continent. Edmondson-made tickets were taken to the United States by travellers and returning businessmen. They served to encourage local thinking that the ticketing methods of Britain might usefully be imported and tested on the railroads. In 1854 the Baltimore & Ohio and Boston & Worcester Railroads purchased their ticket supplies direct from John Edmondson. Other early users are recorded in **Items 18** to **20** issued in the period 1867 to 1889.

Early in 1855 George Bailey, then working in Canada, came to New York State in company with his colleague Julius Movious. The two partnered a William Barr of the Dunkirk & Erie Railway and together they set up a printing business — some reports say they first used presses obtained from Manchester — and almost immediately purchased the North American rights to all of the British patents concerned in this story. The business opened in Buffalo later the same year. Not surprisingly, Bailey's first customer was the Boston & Worcester who would not now need to wait the eight weeks for ships to make the trip from England. The Pennsylvania Railroad followed shortly afterwards by placing orders with Bailey. Soon he was supplying tickets of the Edmondson size to the Chicago Burlington & Quincy, Illinois Central and Philadelphia Wilmington & Baltimore Railroads. The competition of a George Hill and others who introduced a somewhat thinner and often slightly larger card ticket soon took

17

Gt. Western Ry.   Gt. Western Ry,
Birmingham S.H.   Birmingham S.H.
★1   TO
Acocks Green & S. Yardley
4d. THIRD CLASS 4d.
Issued subject to the conditions and
regulations set out in the Company's
Time Tab es, Bills and Notices.
Acocks G. & Y'dley. Acocks G. & S.Y'dley

18

New York & New England R.R.
Good only for passage on trains which
stop regularly at the Stations named.
WILLIMANTIC
TO
PUTNAM.

19

Syracuse, Chenango & N. Y. R. R.
SYRACUSE
CAZENOVIA.
A.C.Beldon Man'r

21

I. N. W. R.
FIRST CLASS
INNISKEEN
TO
DUNDALK
Edmondson, Printer-Dame-st, Dublin

23

SOUTHERN & E.L.RYS.   E.L.& SOUTHERN RYS.
WORKMAN'S TICKET   WORKMAN'S TICKET
HONOR OAK P'K   **SURREY DOCKS**
TO   TO
SURREY DOCKS   **HONOR OAK PARK**
Via New Cross Gate.   Via New Cross Gate
4½d. THIRD CLASS   THIRD CLASS 4½d
FARE   FARE
NOT TRANSFERABLE.   NOT TRANS ABLE
Available on the DAY Available only by the
of issue ONLY.   Special Cheap Train for
See conditions on back. the Working Classes

20

Ft. Wayne, J'n & Sag.
Railroad.
Mosherville
TO
Wilson's.
278

24

G. E. R
Buckhurst Hill
to
Fenchurch St
First Class
4600   4600

27

London Electric Ry,   Lon. Elec. Ry.
Available day of issue ONLY   Available...
W mbley (L.M.S.)   Golders Green (1) to
(1)   TO   WEMBLEY (LMS)
GOLDERS GREEN
Change at Euston   Including Entrance to
Not Transferable   BRITISH EMPIRE
B.E.E. 1/6 Day V lid   EXHIBITION
3rd.Cl.Fare 1/4½   1/6
(See Back)   3rd.Cl.Fare 1/4½
(See Back)

29

Romney Hythe & Dymchurch Rly
DYMCHURCH (Marshlands) to
NEW ROMNEY
(Passenger Ticket Only)
SINGLE FARE 5d
See Cond ...ns on back.

22

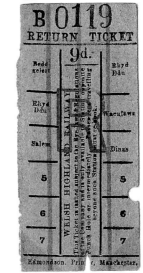

B 0119
RETURN TICKET
9d.
WELSH HIGHLAND RAILWAY
Edmondson. Prin... Manchester.

28

N. L. R.
CAMDEN TOWN to
HAMPSTEAD HEATH
d. Third Class (Parly 1¼d.
Issued subject to the Company's
Published Regulations.   8,10
Hampstead H'th   Hampstead H'th
5046

31

WOOLW...H Dockyard
TO
CHARLTON
PARLY THIRD.
Charlton   Charlton
4342

32

S. B. C. R.   S. B. C. R.
FARNBOROUGH   **COVE WOOD**
GREEN   TO
TO   **FARNBOROUGH**
COVE WOOD   **GREEN**
Child Return Fare 6d   Child Return Fare 6d
PULLMAN or EXPRESS   PULLMAN or EXPRESS
Issued subject to the Com-   Issued subject to the Com-
pany's Rules & Regulations.   pany's Rules & Regulations.
Availab ...y of issue only.   Available day of issue only.
Bell ...   Bell Punch Co., London.
...London.
0115   0115

33

West London Extension Ry.
This ticket is issued subject to the
Bye-Laws Conditions and Regulations of the
West London Extension Railway Co.
CHELSEA TO
WEST BROMPTON
(E)
Third]   9(S)   [Class
WEST BROMPTON   FARE -/1
2629

**Acceptance of Edmondson
products in America, Ireland,
London and the Southeast.**

25

G. N. R.
OMNIBUS TICKET
RETURN
Issued at
Southampton
King's Cross
TO
WATERLOO L.&S.W.
For one journey only
by G. N. R. Omnibus.
G. N. R.
OMNIBUS TICKET
Issued at
Southampton
Waterloo L.& S.W.
TO
KING'S CROSS
For one journey only
by G. N. R. Omnibus.
189

26

0495
L. B. & S. C. RY.
SPECIAL
19th DECEMBER 1899
LONDON
TO
ANY STATION
FREE] Third Class.
[SEE BACK.
L. B. & S. C. RY.
SPECIAL
19th DECEMBER 1899
Any Station
TO
LONDON
FREE] Third Class
0495

30

309
S. E. & C. RYS
EXCESS FARE
1s. 3d. Paid at
CHARING CROSS
Over Distance to
...
No. ...
[Class
309

from Bailey his monopoly — he had in any case been charging heavily[4] for his products. Bailey's business declined sharply and in 1882 he returned to England and died the following year in York.

In 1860 the Baltimore & Ohio Railroad became the first to use a machine-numbered coupon-strip ticket for inter-company fares. This was prepared for traffic through to the Camden & Amboy, New Jersey, Philadelphia, Wilmington & Baltimore and Washington Branch Railroads, a conglomeration of titling which, in British practice, would almost certainly have been distilled into a simple regional title. Along with the increasingly popular 'thin' Edmondson probably started by Hill, such tickets combined to further reduce the incidence of the Edmondson card — a pity, because by now the railroads of America were well on their way west; Chicago was already supplying the many new lines to its west, and northwards into Canada. A contemporary American newspaper[5] wrote: 'Now that civilisation has got safely over the Mississippi by steam, we see no reason why we may not live to see her take a *first class ticket* in a lightning train for the shores of the Pacific'.

Sufficient specimens of the standard size survive to record its continuance in Canada and the United States,and from about 1885 in Mexico also, all alongside the preferred Bailey-type — so-called because, although as mentioned, it was more likely that Hill first introduced the competition with Bailey, the American industry had already attached Bailey's name to its ticketing practices, just as Thomas Edmondson's name now firmly belonged to the railway tickets of Europe and other parts. It is likely that Bailey marketed Edmondson cards under his own brand name in the period leading up to competition by Hill and others. Nevertheless, Bailey's name did not last industry-wide as did that of Edmondson.

It is believed[6] the 'slim' Japanese tickets were home-grown from their very first railway days in 1872. Certainly this was probable on the Imperial, later Government (now National) Railways. Only a few companies were to adopt the true standard size and then always using a locally produced type of board quite unlike the thick, absorbent but rigid material seen elsewhere. To this day Chile is a user of another major variant upon this size theme. The commonest small card ticket there is the standard 57×31mm but of very much thicker material and made with a coarser centre-ply of low durability. As long after invention of the system as 1846, cards were in use in Britain with sub-standard sizes only mimicking the now well-established dimensions. See for example the North British Railway tickets in Chapter 3.

There were Edmondson premises in Manchester, London, Glasgow and Dublin. 21 is a Dublin works print of a standard CARD dated 1872 and 22 a Manchester works print (also later, 591) of a soft pasteboard probably of 1935-36 vintage. The former was designed to be stamped in a conventional dating press (of Thomas Edmondson's pattern) at the station of issue, while the latter would be validated by a hand-punch on the vehicle during actual travel, and usually not given any kind of date. This 'soft' product was more familiar on town tramways (see Chapter 5) and a host of non-transport services, but it also served well on some heavier railways. Both tickets bear the Edmondson firm's imprint.

Well before his death in 1887, John Edmondson claimed to have supplied tickets to 'nearly every railway company in the British Isles'. At least 30 of the 40 or more companies were Edmondson customers three years after the family opened in Manchester. There were 80 companies operating by 1847 and 350 by the year 1885. Janice Anderson and Edmund Swinglehurst[7] make the very fair assessment that 'the complexity of the numbers of companies in Britain issuing their own tickets is

a source of continued interest to the ephemerist who specialises in tickets'.

We demonstrate the widespread and rapid acceptance of the system throughout the British Isles with the following illustrations of 69 pre-1939 Edmondson-style tickets. They are not intended to indicate the date of adoption by the railway concerned.

London and the Southeast
23 dates from 1924 and is of the East London and Southern Railways but still using the style of the former LBSC. 24 was sold in 1867 by the Great Eastern at a station now on London Underground's Central Line; the back reads 'Not Available by Express Train'. 25 was issued in 1903 at the port of Southampton, probably to a passenger disembarking from an ocean liner. It was valid on the horse-drawn omnibuses plying between Waterloo and King's Cross stations. It would have virtually ensured that the passenger used one of the railway-owned 'buses and also created goodwill by obviating the need for the passenger to rebook in London (See also 260).

26 is a special excursion of the LBSC in 1899. Similar tickets of varying dates are frequently found in collections. 27 is from the Hampstead Line part of the London Electric Railway in connection with the Wembley Exhibition of 1924/5. 28 is a parliamentary single of 1894 from the North London Railway. 29 is an early (1928) ticket of the Romney, Hythe and Dymchurch Railway. 30 seems to have been presented in 1901 to a First Class passenger of the SEC who arrived at Charing Cross without a proper ticket. 31 is from the South Eastern in 1883. Many companies did not include their name on the face of their early tickets although some had a monogram on the back. 32 came from the narrow-gauge Surrey Border & Camberley Railway in 1938. 33 represents the West London Extension Railway (See Chapter Five) and dates from 1901.

The Isle of Man and Jersey
34 is a Go-As-You-Please ticket of 1938 from the Isle of Man Railway. It would have been valid on two days selected by the passenger. 35 is a Militia Ticket of the Jersey Eastern Railway, probably of 1907, and 36 is from the Jersey Railways & Tramways in 1902. The reader will note the prominent letter 'T' which was a station destination code adopted about 1885, in this case indicating First Tower. Other letters in the code were A, B, C, D, F, H, L, M, P, R and W.

The South and Southwest
Two tickets from the Isle of Wight are 37 from the Freshwater, Yarmouth & Newport Railway about 1900 and 38 sold on the Isle of Wight Railway in 1921. Just across the Solent, 39 was used just five days after the opening of the Lee-on-the-Solent Railway in 1894. This company leased its lines to the South Western Railway in 1906 and the route was closed to passengers in 1931. 40 took a day excursionist the full length of the Liskeard & Looe Railway in 1908, the same year as the holder of 41 travelled on the Plymouth, Devonport and South Western Junction Railway. Returning briefly to the Isle of Wight, we note from 42 that a subscriber took the tram to Ryde Pier Head in the late summer of 1876. 43 is a ticket from the Weston, Clevedon and Portishead (Light) Railway in 1938; further tickets of this line are shown in Chapter 10.

Scotland
44 is from the Dundee & Arbroath Joint Railway in 1904. 45 is a child's ticket of the Glasgow & South Western in 1896; the

34

ISLE OF MAN RAILWAY Co. 1938
TWO 5/- GO-AS-YOU
DAYS PLEASE
Issued in accordance with general regulations
Not transferable. Must be given up on expiry.
Available 3rd. Class between ALL STATIONS
on any 2 days (need not be consecutive) within
7 days from date of issue.

| Sun | Mon | Tue | Wed | Thu | Fri | Sat |

3363

35

Jersey Eastern Ry. Co.
(Limited.)
MILITIA
Grouville
TO 2
ST. HELIER
Second Class
Available for
day of issue only
and not transferable

Jersey Eastern Ry. Co.
(Limited.)
MILITIA
St. Helier
TO
GROUVILLE
Second Class
Available for
day of issue only
and not transferable

7446 7446

36

THE JERSEY RAILWAYS & TRAMWAYS
(LIMITED.)
Issued subject to the Company's Bye-laws
MILLBROOK
TO
FIRST TOWER
Second Class Single 1d.
AVAILABLE FOR DAY OF ISSUE ONLY

1362

37

Freshwater Yarmouth & Newport Ry.
FRESHWATER
Series 1) TO
COWES
Change at Newport
THIRD CLASS FARE 1/2
Not transferable. Issued subject to the Regulations
& Conditions stated in the Company's Time Tables.

6665

38

REVISED FARE
Isle of Wight Ry.
Available day of issue only.
SANDOWN
Series 3) TO
ST. HELENS
Via Brading
3rd. Class (Parly) Actual Fare 6d
Not Transferable. Issued subject to the
Co's Bye Laws & Published Regulations

5519 5519

39

LEE-ON-THE-SOLENT RAILWAY.
FORT BROCKHURST
to
LEE-ON-THE-SOLENT
THIRD CLASS, FARE 3d
See Notice at back

672

40

L. & L. Rly.
DAY EXCURSION
RETURN
Liskeard
TO
LOOE
Third Class 1/-
Not Transferable.
Issued subject to
Conditions published
at the Stations.

L. & L. Rly.
DAY EXCURSION
RETURN
Looe
TO
LISKEARD
Third Class 1/-
Not Transferable.
Issued subject to
Conditions published
at the Stations.

5086 5086

41

P. D. & S. W. J. R.
GUNNISLAKE
TO
CALLINGTON ROAD

| CALLINGTON ROAD | THIRD Fare 6d | CALLINGTON ROAD |

0415 0415

42

Ryde Pier Railway.
Toll Gates to Pier Head
SERIES 3.
Subscribers Tram Ticket
SECOND CLASS
Not Transferable. Issued subject to the Company's Bye Laws & Published Regulations.

9339

43

W. C. & P. L. RLY.
PRIVILEGE
CLEVEDON
to
PORTISHEAD
Available on day of issue only
SECOND CLASS

W. C. & P. L. RLY.
TICKET.
PORTISHEAD
to
CLEVEDON
Fare 3d.
SECOND CLASS.

1316 1316

44

Dundee & Arbroath Joint Ry.
Third Class. Fare 3d
Dundee East
TO
WEST-FERRY
1
West Ferry

8685

45

G. & S. W. Ry. Issued subject to
the Conditions in their Time Tables.
CHILD'S TICKET.
THIRD CLASS
Troon to
PRESTWICK (G. & S. W.)
Fare—1½d.

520

46

G. N. of S. Ry. Issued subject to the
regulations in the Co's Time Tables.
Kittybrewster
TO
SCHOOLHILL
THIRD CLASS.
1. 6 Schoolhill 1 Fare 1d.

2B40

47

I. & P. JN. RY.
DUNKELD to ELGIN
Parliamentary.
This Ticket is issued subject to the
regulations in the Co's Time-Tables.

174

48

N. B. R.
T A Y P O R T
Tayport TO Tayport
D U N D E E
Tay Bridge Tay Bridge
6d 3rd CLASS 3rd 6d
Issued subject to the Bye-Laws and Regulations
of the N.B.R. Co. and to the Conditions stated in
their Public Time Tables. NOT TRANSFERABLE

8540 8540

**Edmondson in the outer islands, in the South, the Southwest
and Scotland; on a tramway, narrow gauge and main line
railways.**

49

Ambleside FURNESS RAILWAY Ambleside
WINDERMERE LAKE

EXCESS TICKET, 6d.

This Ticket entitles holder of THIRD
CLASS TICKET to travel FIRST between
the same points on WINDERMERE LAKE
subject to the conditions on which the
THIRD CLASS TICKET was issued.
It must be produced on demand and
given up when finally leaving the STEAMER
See Notice on Back.

AP.15 03

50

GARSTANG & KNOT END RAILWAY.

GARSTANG
TO
PILLING
Fare 6d.

Issued subject to conditions stated
in Co's Time Bills & Notices.

THIRD | 2 Pilling. | CLASS

1897

51

Gt.C.R. Ticket for an Article UNDER 2 CWTS
Accompanying the Passenger and conveyed at
Mileage Scale at PASSENGER'S RISK

FAIRFIELD for Droylsden
To

On   Ry.
Description of article
to be inserted by
Booking Clerk.

CARRIAGE PAID......s....d
This Ticket must be given up on arrival SEE BACK

1986

52

Great Western Railway
ROCK LANE
TO
HOOTON
SECOND CLASS

NO 4 63   921

53

LANCASHIRE & YORKSHIRE RAILWAY.
Issued subject to the regulations and conditions in
the Co's Time Tables, Books, Bills & Notices.
Available on day of issue only.

SECOND CLASS
HASLINGDEN
TO
ACCRINGTON

218 Accrington   Fare 4d.

30 SP 99   5898

54

MINIATURE RAILWAYS OF GREAT BRITAIN, Ld.
Available at Time of Issue only.

GIPSYVILLE
&
BLACKPOOL

This Ticket is issued on the understanding
that the Company is not liable for any accident
which may occur to the passenger whilst on the
Company's premises or trains.

FARE   -   -   ADULT 2d
Williamson, Ticket Printer, Ashton

4854

55

N.S.R. SECOND CLASS.

CONSALL To
FROGHALL

AVAILABLE FOR ONE JOURNEY ON DAY OF ISSUE ONLY

Turn over   Froghall 91   Fare 3d.

22 NO.11   028

56

N.W.&L. Ry.C.
Issued subject to the printed conditions
and regulations of the Company
Available on date of issue only.

NESTON & PARKGATE To
LIVERPOOL (Landing Stage)
Via Seacombe

THIRD CLASS.

Neston&P.   Neston&P.
Liverpool L Stage   Liverpool L Stage
F 11½d.

4 MR 97   2450

57

Issued by the S & N W Co.   Issued by the S & N W Co.
subject to the conditions   subject to the conditions
in their Time Tables.   in their Time Tables.
Not Transferable.   Not Transferable.

First   Class.   First   Class.
Kinnerley   Hanwood
To   To
HANWOOD   KINNERLEY

KINNERLEY

39   39

58

CAMBRIAN RAILWAYS
Issued subject to the Conditions
stated in the Co's Time Tables.

PORTMADOC (Down) To
AFON WEN

THIRD CLASS PARLY   FARE -/8

Portmadoc (Dn)   Portmadoc (Dn)
Afon Wen   Afon Wen

AU 13 15   3736

59

CARDIFF RAILWAY,
ONE DOG (Accompanied by Passenger)
(Value not exceeding £2)

WHITCHURCH
TO

CARRIAGE PAID   s   3

This Ticket is available for a Single journey only
and must be given up at Destination Station.

See conditions on back

388

60

CORRIS RAILWAY. This Ticket is issued
subject to the Regulations & Conditions
stated in the Company's Time Tables Posters
& Excursion Notices.

FIRST CLASS FARE 7d.

MACHYNLLETH
TO
CORRIS

349

61

D R & C Ry
Issued subject to the con-
ditions in the Time Tables of the respective
Co's over whose lines this ticket is available.

PARLIAMENTARY
CORWEN To
RUTHIN

10 JU 71   4574

The standard card served well in the Midlands, Northwest and Wales.

62

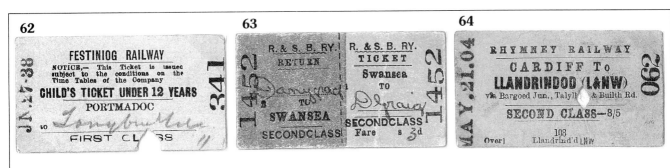

FESTINIOG RAILWAY
NOTICE.— This Ticket is issued
subject to the conditions on the
Time Tables of the Company
CHILD'S TICKET UNDER 12 YEARS
PORTMADOC
to *Tonybwllen*
FIRST CLASS

63

R. & S. B. RY. | R. & S. B. RY.
RETURN | **TICKET**
Damaged | Swansea
TO | TO
SWANSEA | *Dyraig*
SECONDCLASS | SECONDCLASS
| Fare s 3d

64

MAY.21.04
RHYMNEY RAILWAY
CARDIFF To
LLANDRINDOD (L&NW)
via Bargoed Jun., Talyll & Builth Rd.
SECOND CLASS—8/5
108
Over] Llandrind'd LNW

65

JAN.20.04
T. V. R.
CARDIFF (Riverside)
TO
GRANGETOWN
Early Third Class 1d.
This ticket is issued subject to the
Company's Bye-Laws & conditions
stated on Time Bills.

66

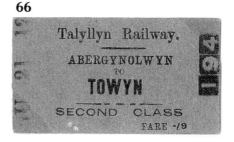

Talyllyn Railway.
ABERGYNOLWYN
TO
TOWYN
SECOND CLASS
FARE -/9

67

VALE OF RHEIDOL RLY. | VALE OF RHEIDOL RLY
This Ticket is issued sub- | This Ticket is issued sub-
ject to the Bye-Laws and | ject to the Bye-Laws and
Regulations of the com- | Regulations of the com-
pany and to the conditions | pany and to the conditions
stated in their time tables | stated in their Time Tables
Available for return on |
day of issue only, |
CapelBangor | Aberystwyth
TO | TO
ABERYSTWYTH | **CAPEL BANGOR**
RETURN | FORWARD
CHILD | CHILD
THIRD CLASS | THIRD CLASS
FARE 0s5d |

68

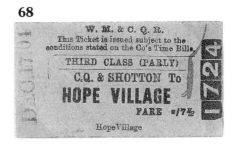

DEC.10.01
W. M. & C. Q. R.
This Ticket is issued subject to the
conditions stated on the Co's Time Bills.
THIRD CLASS (PARLY)
C.Q. & SHOTTON To
HOPE VILLAGE
FARE =/7½
HopeVillage

More of Wales, with narrow gauge and main line
representation. Yorkshire, the Northeast and East Anglia all
success stories for the Edmondson card.

69

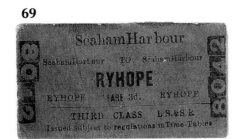

SeahamHarbour
Seaham Harbour TO Seaham Harbour
RYHOPE
RYHOPE FARE 3d. RYHOPE
THIRD CLASS L.S.&S.K.
Issued subject to regulations in Time Tables

70

JAN 13.6
YORK
to
POCKLINGTON
First Class
This ticket is issued subject to the regu-
lations and conditions named in the Co's
time tables and bills for the present month.

71

West Riding Railway.
Series A   Series A
SANDAL to
SANDAL   SANDAL
DEWSBURY (G.N.)
DEWSBURY (G.N.) DEWSBURY (G.N.)
By G. N. Train
Fare 7d.   Third Class   Fare 7d.
SEE CONDITIONS ON BACK.

72

945
Norfolk & Suffolk Joint Rys. Com.
Not transferable.
OVERSTRAND to
OVERSTRAND   OVERSTRAND
MUNDESLEY-ON-SEA
Mundesley-on-Sea   Mundesley-on-Sea
FARE 5d THIRD CLASS FARE 5d
SEE CONDITIONS ON BACK.

73

Southwold Ry. | Southwold Ry.
PRIVILEGE TICKET | **PRIVILEGE TICKET**
Issued subject | Issued subject
to Regulations in the | to Regulations in the
Companys Time Tables | Companys Time Tables
Southwold |
TO | TO
| **SOUTHWOLD**
Third Class | Third Class
Actual Fare | Actual Fare

74

JUY.28.77
THETFORD & WATTON RY
BARNHAM
TO
THETFORD BRIDGE
THIRD CLASS.

horizontal lines are red. **46** came from the Great North of Scotland Railway in 1904. **47** is an Inverness & Perth Junction Railway print; the company became part of the Highland Railway in 1865 but this ticket was sold 28 years later in 1893. **48** is a neat North British Railway ticket of 1907.

The Midlands and the North West

49 is an excess ticket of the Furness Railway permitting first class travel on Lake Windermere in 1903; it is yellow and white with horizontal red lines. **50** was sold on the Garstang & Knot End Railway, probably in 1902. **51** is an article ticket of the Great Central Railway of 1914. The GW single (**52**) is dated 1863. **53** reminds us that second class still existed on the Lancashire & Yorkshire Railway in 1899. **54** was sold by the Miniature Railways of Great Britain around 1912. This company operated both in Blackpool and in Sutton Park, near Sutton Coldfield. The name Gipsyville is believed to refer to the gipsy encampment on the sand dunes beyond the end of Blackpool's pleasure beach in the period before 1920. The same company's track at Sutton Park was one of the few public park railways which 'went somewhere'. It served Wyndley (also seen on tickets as Windley), where a café and other attractions were to be found. **55** is a North Staffordshire specimen of 1911, **56** from the North Wales & Liverpool Railway Committee of 1897 and **57** a specimen from the Shrewsbury & North Wales Railway produced about 1865.

Wales

58 came from the Cambrian Railways in 1915. **59** is a ticket of the Cardiff Railway, sold in 1935, twelve years after Grouping. **60** is a 1913 representative of the narrow gauge Corris Railway, sadly no longer with us. Other small Welsh railways are the Denbigh Ruthin & Corwen (1871 **61**), the Festiniog (1938 **62**), the Rhondda & Swansea Bay (1913 **63**), The Rhymney (1904 **64**), The Taff Vale (1904 **65**), the Talyllyn (1912 **66**), the Vale of Rheidol (1913 **67**) and the Wrexham Mold & Connah's Quay (1904 **68**). The Vale of Rheidol ticket represents the original company of 1902 before its amalgamation with the Cambrian. The title has been retained by the Cambrian, Great Western and British Railways, all of whom recognised the tourist value of this picturesque narrow gauge route into the mountains east of Aberystwyth.

Yorkshire and the Northeast

69 came from the Londonderry Seaham & Sunderland Railway about 1888. Londonderry is a small village in North Yorkshire.

Ryhope was later renamed Ryhope East and a further ticket bearing its name is illustrated in **536**. **70**, a 1866 specimen from the North Eastern Railway was one of a small group of similar vintage found in a 'junk shop' in Philadelphia, United States of America. Was it taken there by the original collector? The almost forgotten West Riding and Grimsby Railway is represented by **71**, dated 1908.

East Anglia

72 is a 1907 issue of the Norfolk & Suffolk Joint Railways, **73** from the Southwold Railway in 1929 and **74** from the short-lived Thetford & Watton Railway whose 14km of track enjoyed 10 years of independence from 1869 until absorbed by the Great Eastern in 1879.

Ireland

This island is represented by seventeen tickets.
Ballycastle Railway 1901 (**75**).
Belfast & County Down Railway 1936 (**76**).
Belfast & Northern Counties Railway 1905 (**77**).
Cork Bandon & South Coast Railway 1902 (**78**).
Cork & Macroom Direct Railway 1902 (**79**).
Dublin & Kingstown Railway 1862 (**80**).
    The first public passenger-carrying railway in Ireland, opened 17 December 1834. Leased to the Dublin Wicklow & Wexford Railway in 1856.
Dublin & South Eastern Railway 1920 (**81**).
Dublin Wicklow & Wexford Railway 1904 (**82**).
Dundalk & Enniskillen Railway 1865 (**83**).
    The return half of a standard vertical excursion ticket.
Dundalk Newry & Greenore Railway 1931 (**84**).
Great Northern Railway of Ireland 1935 (**85**).
Great Southern Railways 1937 (**86**).
Sligo Leitrim & Northern Counties Railway 1922 (**87**).
Strabane & Letterkenny Railway 1910 (**88**).
Tralee & Dingle Light Railway 1898 (**89**).
Waterford & Tramore Railway 1909 (**90**).
West Clare Railway 1902 (**91**).

75 — Ballyc... Railway. BALLYMONEY TO DERVOCK FIRST CLASS. For conditions of issue see Time Tables — 1444

76 — B. C. D. RY. CHILD'S TICKET John White Memorial Jun. S.S. Excursion. BELFAST to COMBER AND BACK SATURDAY, 13th JUNE, 1936. THIRD CLASS For Conditions of issue see Time Tables — Advertisements and back of this Ticket — 032

77 — B. & N. C. Ry. BELFAST (Y.R.) TO EDINBORO' (Cal..) Via Larne, Stranraer, Dumfries & Lockerbie. 1st Class Saloon 1st Class Bft. to Edin'o' Bft. to Edinboro' Via Locker FARE 22/6 (See Back) — 813

78 — C. B. & S. C. Rly. Special Excursion Second Class Fare- 2s.0d. Cork to COURTMACSHERRY AND RETURN Issued on Conditions mentioned on back hereof Available for day of issue only C'mas No 55 — 405

79 — C. & M. D. R. Third Class Fare- 4d. Available for the day of issue only. This Ticket is issued subject to the Co's Bye-Laws & Regulations. CORK To BALLINCOLLIG — 2011

80 — SUBSCRIBER'S TICKET. KINGSTOWN TO BLACKROCK FIRST CLASS — 191

81 — D & S E R LEOPARDSTOWN RACES 6th, MARCH 1920 FIRST or SECOND CLASS Not available by Members Train Subject to the Co's Bye-Laws & Regulations HARCOURT St. TO FOXROCK AND BACK NOT TRANSFERABLE Fare 3s, 0d — 160

82 — K D. W. & W. R. Second Class Fare 4d Available for the day of issue only. KILLINEY & BALLYBRACK TO KINGSTOWN 8...stown — 6237

83 — 90 D & S E R EXCURSION DUBLIN TO INNISKEEN First Class Not Transferable

84 — Dundalk Newry & Greenore Ry Issued subject to the conditions & regulations in the Cos Time Tables Books Bills & Notices BELLURGAN TO DUNDALK (QUAY STREET) THIRD CLASS 66...S) FARE -/7 DUNDA... T — 4208

85 — G. N. R. Ireland) Issued subject to the conditions and regulations in the Company's Time Tables Books, Bills and Notices. Not Transferable Bus Exchange Ticket THIRD CLASS LURGAN to (BusE) — 821

86 — G. S. Rlys. EXTENSION TICKET Issued in Exchange for Return Portion of T...No. Available up to Amount of EXTENSION 4 CLASS Not Transferable DUBLIN (Kingsbridge) To Via For Conditions of issue see back — 3236

87 — S. L. & N. C. R. SECOND CLASS. Fare - ...s. DROMAHAIR TO SLIGO — 1346

88 — S & L. R. SP'L EXCURSION I, N, Foresters Excursion THIRD CLASS 24th JULY 1910. Available for Day of issue only. STRABANE To LETTERKENNY & BACK LetterkennySp¹ — 211

89 — TRALEE & DINGLE LIGHT RAILWAY. Third Class Fare- 1s, 0d DINGLE To ANNASCAUL Annascaul — 3971

90 — W. & T. R. EVENING SPECIAL RETURN TICKET First Class Fare- 1s.0d. NOT TRANSFERABLE Available on day of issue only. WATERFORD TO TRAMORE — 1385

91 — West Clare Railway Third Class Fare- 5d. Available for the day of issue only. Subject to the Co's Bye-Laws & Regulations KILKEE TO MOYASTA Moyasta — 4075

**Acceptance of the familiar Edmondson card in Ireland from
Ballycastle in the Northeast to Dingle in the far Southwest.**

CHAPTER 2

Mechanised Tickets

We have seen that in the years immediately following its creation the Edmondson card was regarded almost universally as the complete solution to the ticketing problems of the age. Few operators looked for an alternative. Now, 150 years later, it is being replaced in all parts of the world by machines that collect fares, emit tickets and even open barriers for the passenger. Portable mechanical devices appear in the hands of travelling train staff on both main and branch lines. Yet the very variety of machines currently in use demonstrates that none is as universally acceptable to the present age as the Edmondson card was to contemporaries of its inventor.

The strength of Edmondson's system and the reason for its rapid acceptance lay not only in the ease of accounting but also in the fact that passengers could be booked in the minimum amount of staff time. Even where the standard size of card was not adopted, the principle of selling the passenger a tiny document proclaiming his right to travel has never been replaced. Current technology has merely provided ways of making machines create the document, performing part of the work of the booking clerk, the accountant, the ticket designer and the printer.

As long ago as 1907 and as far away as Cologne, the **Regina** machine was enabling the clerk to print and issue a detailed card ticket while the passenger stood before him. Suitably improved, this appeared at Birmingham Snow Hill station in 1911 with apparent success (see **17** Chapter 1). More recently **National Cash Register (NCR)** models, although doing little to speed the issue of tickets, have kept a running total of the value of sales to give the clerk a balance at the end of his shift of work.

Considerably more drastic is the machine that takes the traveller's money and issues his ticket, needing only to be emptied of money and restocked with card once or twice daily. Such machines appeared on the Central London Railway experimentally in 1904 and spread to other lines soon after World War 1, becoming part of the London scene.

For expensive equipment to be cost-effective it must displace staff. There has to be someone on duty at all but the smallest station during the day to deal with enquiries and unusual bookings, collect excess fares and inhibit vandalism and fraud. If one person can do all these things and have time to sell tickets as well, there is little point in installing a machine. Hence until the late 1980s one usually found machines appearing at the busier stations.

In very general terms, ticket machines fall into two groups:
1 Those which require the insertion of an external ticket (normally bearing a certain amount of printing) which is then validated, endorsed or simply examined.
2 Those which create a valid ticket from cut or continuous stationery held within the device.

The simplest and earliest examples of the first group must be the much-loved punch-type tickets, which appeared increasingly from 1878. They were, of course, pieces of printed card inserted into the jaws of a simple hole-punching device. The illustration (**112**) shows a ticket of early type from Kingston-upon-Hull; it was in fact produced by the Edmondson Company!

From the early years of this century there developed a movement away from the traditional systems of fare collection and ticketing in many parts of the world. A great variety of novel portable mechanical devices appeared in North American cities and also throughout Central America although they themselves are now being replaced by sophisticated electronic equipment. Some merely perforated the card or cut a single hole at a particular place in it: others clipped out a substantial triangular or rectangular portion. A parallel in Britain was the **Willebrew** system which cut away a long panel in such a manner that both the piece retained by the machine and that handed to the passenger indicated the amount of the fare. Although generally associated with bus operation, it was in service with minor railways in the UK (**162**).

Nowadays the ticket often performs a further function in that it is used by the passenger to open the entry or exit barrier. Inserted in a slot, it is examined by an electronic scanner and if valid will permit one person to pass. Normally it is returned to the passenger on entry to 'paid' areas of the system and retained on completion of the final permitted journey. As indicated above,

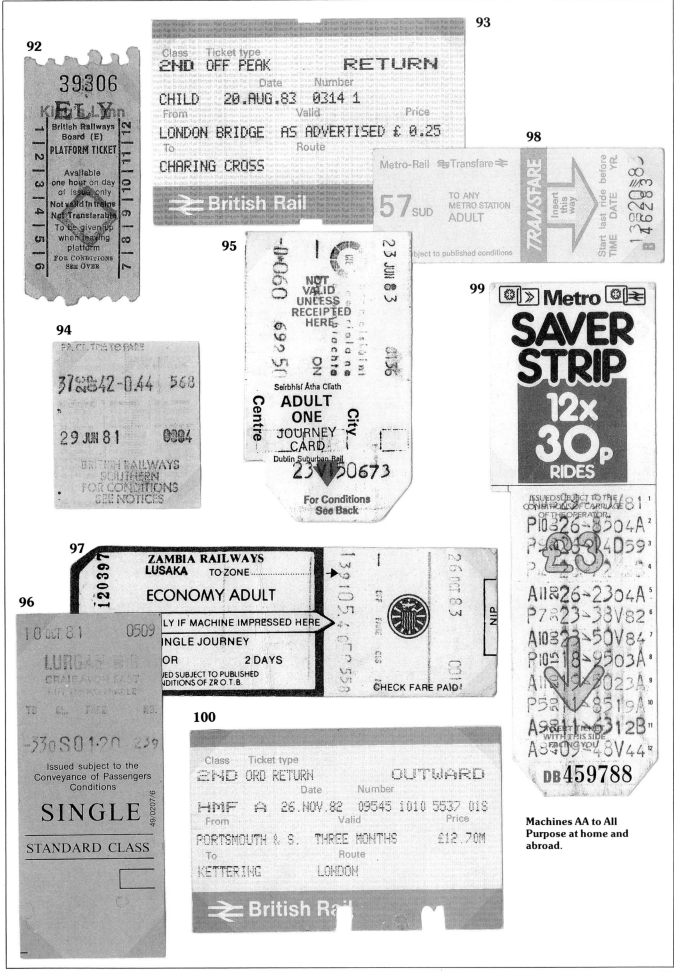

92

39306

ELY

British Railways
Board (E)

PLATFORM TICKET

Available
one hour on day
of issue only

Not valid in trains

Not Transferable

To be given up
when leaving
platform

FOR CONDITIONS
SEE OVER

1 2 3 4 5 6   21 11 01 9 8 7

93

Class	Ticket type	
2ND OFF PEAK		RETURN
	Date	Number
CHILD	20.AUG.83	0314 1
From	Valid	Price
LONDON BRIDGE	AS ADVERTISED	£ 0.25
To	Route	
CHARING CROSS		

≷ **British Rail**

98

Metro-Rail ≷≷ Transfare ≷

57 SUD   TO ANY
METRO STATION
ADULT

TRANSFARE

Insert
this
way

Start last ride before
TIME DATE YR.

B 13208

subject to published conditions

94

PR.CL TPE TE BABE

37 42-0.44 568

29 JUN 81   0004

BRITISH RAILWAYS
SOUTHERN
FOR CONDITIONS
SEE NOTICES

95

0060 692 50

NOT
VALID
UNLESS
RECEIPTED
HERE

ON

23 JUN 83   0135

Seirbhísí Átha Cliath

**ADULT
ONE**

JOURNEY
CARD

Dublin Suburban Rail

23 VI 50673

Centre   City

**For Conditions
See Back**

99

Metro

**SAVER
STRIP**

**12x
30p**
RIDES

ISSUED SUBJECT TO THE
CONDITIONS OF CARRIAGE
OF THE OPERATOR.	81 1
P10326-8904A	2
P 23 4D59	3
£3	4
A11826-2304A	5
P7323-38V82	6
A10822-50V84	7
P10518-9503A	8
A11 023A	9
P5 8519A	10
A9811 312B	11
A3409-48V44	12

INSERT TICKET
WITH THIS SIDE
FACING YOU

DB459788

**Machines AA to All
Purpose at home and
abroad.**

97

120397

ZAMBIA RAILWAYS
LUSAKA   TO ZONE.........

ECONOMY ADULT

LY IF MACHINE IMPRESSED HERE

INGLE JOURNEY

OR   2 DAYS

UED SUBJECT TO PUBLISHED
NDITIONS OF ZR O.T.B.

1391054 558

26 OCT 83

NIP

CHECK FARE PAID

96

10 OCT 81   0509

LURGAN

CRAIGAVON EAST

NOT TRANSFERABLE

TO CL TYPE RO.

-230 S 01.20 239

Issued subject to the
Conveyance of Passengers
Conditions

SINGLE

STANDARD CLASS

49/0207/6

100

Class	Ticket type	
2ND ORD RETURN		OUTWARD
	Date	Number
HMF	26.NOV.82	09545 1010 5537 019
From	Valid	Price
PORTSMOUTH & S.	THREE MONTHS	£12.70M
To	Route	
KETTERING	LONDON	

≷ **British Rail**

21

more sophisticated equipment is already in use. Prime examples are Hong Kong, the USA and Canada.[8]

Occasionally a system that has proved popular with operators has also produced a range of attractive or interesting tickets. The **Setright Speed** has been adopted by operators as far apart as Britain and Australia. This was a partly-printed narrow roll ticket bearing the name of the operator and endorsed with data such as the fare, serial and machine number at the time of issue.

More widespread is the **Ultimate**. It is always uniform in size and substance but may come in single form as from the Connel Ferry Viaduct or double as from Old Shoreham Bridge (**155**). The very similar **Ultimatic** rail travel ticket (which does not come in the smaller form) has the layout of the normal Edmondson Single or Return. The uniformity of both these products lends them very well to orderly mounting in albums.

However, it must be mentioned that some brands of machine-issued ticket are unattractive, uninformative both to passenger and collector, badly printed and sometimes barely distinguishable from a supermarket receipt. The latter description applies to specimens seen from **Chubb** machines used by London Underground Ltd and somewhat surprisingly, the Seaton Tramway in Devon. It may even be questionable whether some of the poorly printed specimens can sufficiently draw the passenger's attention to any conditions applicable to the contract of travel (see Chapter 14).

The attention of the present writers has been drawn to 90 different branded inventions, each with a distinctive ticket output. There is every reason to suppose that there are at least as many more. A comprehensive survey of machine-issued tickets would fill many volumes. However, the enthusiast ought to be conversant with the name and the general appearance of tickets emanating from the more popular machines and systems, if only to be able to understand the import of any offers of tickets that may be received.

Any attempt to categorise machine-issued tickets is complicated by the widespread similarity of successful systems once rival companies' products. The name Edmondson was only briefly confined to tickets produced by the original family of that name; soon all tickets of its dimensions were so called, regardless of printer. On the other hand, as we have just seen, the Edmondson Company was selling tickets we describe as 'punch-type'.

Just as one uses the proprietary noun 'Biro' to describe almost any ball-point pen, so ticket enthusiasts sometimes use names such as 'Edmondson', 'Bell Punch' and 'Ultimate' (and more recently emerged, almost worldwide — 'Cubic') to describe a system by the appearance of its ticket output rather than the identity of its manufacturer.

A well known product may be available under one brand name in one country and another elsewhere. Furthermore the actual ticket, especially where it has been partly pre-printed, may have been manufactured by a commercial group other than that which makes or markets the equipment that uses it. Manufacturers must adapt machines to meet customers' local needs and the resultant tickets may be unfamiliar elsewhere. The two **Bellgraphic** examples (**116** and **117**) effectively demonstrate this phenomenon, as do **580** and **585** (Chapter 11) under the Bell Punch Company imprint. Limitations of space preclude the illustration of many tickets and it is impracticable to show examples of every ticket variety that may have been created by any one brand or model.

The novice collector may be confused by the five types of ticket issuing system introduced experimentally by British Rail earlier this decade. These are the APTIS, INTIS, PORTIS, SSTIS, all of which are operated by the booking clerk or conductor-guard, and the more recent SPOTIS. This last-named is an automatic machine which goes into action upon the insertion of money by the customer. It is considerably more sophisticated than its counterpart on London Underground. It offers a menu of stations and categories, which are selected by pressing one of over 30 buttons, accepts five types of coin and gives change. An illustration of its tickets is given below.

Of the machines operated by railway staff, the INTIS and SSTIS require the insertion of a part-printed card bearing among other things the name of the destination station. These cards are stored in trays and time is expended as the clerk locates the one required, pulls it out and feeds it into the machine. The PORTIS and APTIS already contain the stationery and so print all the requisite information at the time of issue. The PORTIS is intended for use by conductor-guards. It is expected that APTIS will gradually supersede other booking office systems.

Modifications are constantly being made to these systems no less than to others, and indeed, as we write changes are expected in the layout of these tickets. Nevertheless, the novice may distinguish various ticket products in the following way. PORTIS is on thin paper, vertically printed and perforated top and bottom. Tickets from the other systems are of cheque card size on thin card. INTIS have square corners and the destination station is pre-printed or hand-written. SSTIS, at first similar with rounded corners, was later modified with squared corners. APTIS, printed black and SPOTIS normally printed blue, are almost indistinguishable; in each case the names of both issuing and destination station are printed by the machine. APTIS does, however, additionally print its machine number and a station audit code after the ticket serial number. SPOTIS tickets (listed below as **Agiticket** and **Autelca** models) have a rectangular cut-out centrally at their top and bottom edges.

The distillation below gives basic name or model, mention of at least one undertaking putting it to use currently or in the past and at least one illustration of its product. For the purpose of comparison, some examples of overseas users are also given. The reader will appreciate that many machines are versatile enough to produce tickets of very different size and appearance, their size often determined by the amount of printed text or endorsement required. The difference between vertical or 'portrait' and horizontal or 'landscape' arrangement of the printing, the thickness of board and the use of bright printing inks also contribute to the notion of a different type of ticket and may falsely suggest a different brand of machine. It is hoped that the illustrations will assist recognition of specimens which may come into an enthusiast's possession or conversation, at least in the earlier years.

AA (Associated Automation)
British Railways Board (E) (**92**)
In the King's Lynn specimen illustrated, the named station has been overstamped (Ely) by hand.

Agiticket (one of the 'SPOTIS' group)
British Railways Board (**93**)

Almex A
British Railways Board (E) and (S) (**94**)
Northern Ireland Railways

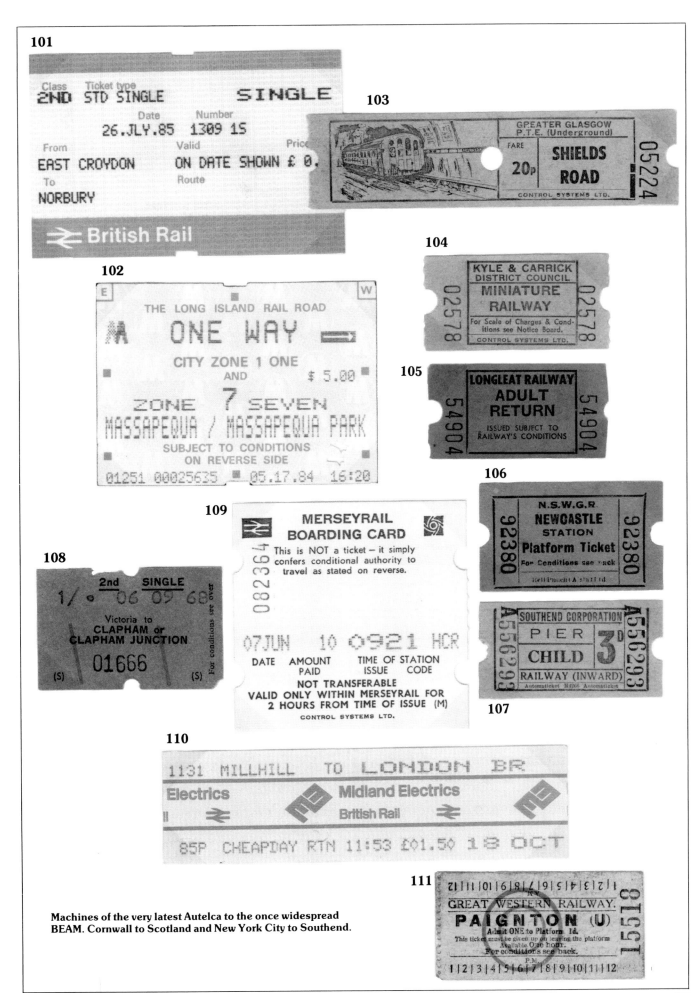

101

Class | Ticket type
2ND STD SINGLE | **SINGLE**
Date | Number
26.JLY.85 | 1309 15
From | Valid | Price
EAST CROYDON | ON DATE SHOWN £ 0.
To | Route
NORBURY

🚉 **British Rail**

103

GREATER GLASGOW
P.T.E. (Underground)
FARE
20p **SHIELDS ROAD**
05224
CONTROL SYSTEMS LTD.

104

KYLE & CARRICK DISTRICT COUNCIL
MINIATURE RAILWAY
For Scale of Charges & Conditions see Notice Board.
CONTROL SYSTEMS LTD.
02578 02578

102

E | W
THE LONG ISLAND RAIL ROAD
ONE WAY
CITY ZONE 1 ONE
AND $ 5.00
ZONE **7** SEVEN
MASSAPEQUA / MASSAPEQUA PARK
SUBJECT TO CONDITIONS
ON REVERSE SIDE
01251 00025635 05.17.84 16:20

105

LONGLEAT RAILWAY
ADULT RETURN
ISSUED SUBJECT TO RAILWAY'S CONDITIONS
54904 54904

106

N.S.W.G.R.
NEWCASTLE STATION
Platform Ticket
For Conditions see back
92380 92380

109

🚉 **MERSEYRAIL BOARDING CARD**
082364
This is NOT a ticket – it simply confers conditional authority to travel as stated on reverse.
07JUN 10 0921 HCR
DATE | AMOUNT PAID | TIME OF ISSUE | STATION CODE
NOT TRANSFERABLE
VALID ONLY WITHIN MERSEYRAIL FOR
2 HOURS FROM TIME OF ISSUE (M)
CONTROL SYSTEMS LTD.

108

2nd | SINGLE
1/ 06 09 68
Victoria to
CLAPHAM or CLAPHAM JUNCTION
01666
(S) (S)

107

SOUTHEND CORPORATION
PIER
CHILD 3ᴰ
RAILWAY (INWARD)
Automaticket H4266 Automaticket
A556293 A556293

110

1131 MILLHILL TO LONDON BR
Electrics | **M[2] Midland Electrics** | M[2]
II 🚉 | British Rail 🚉
85P CHEAPDAY RTN 11:53 £01.50 18 OCT

111

1|2|3|4|5|6|7|8|9|10|11|12
GREAT WESTERN RAILWAY.
PAIGNTON (U)
Admit ONE to Platform 1d.
This ticket must be given up on leaving the platform
Available One hour.
For conditions see back.
P.M.
1|2|3|4|5|6|7|8|9|10|11|12
15518

Machines of the very latest Autelca to the once widespread
BEAM. Cornwall to Scotland and New York City to Southend.

23

Insert Almex A
David MacBrayne Limited Steamers (Western Isles)
Irish Transport Company (Coras Iompair Eireann) (**95**)
The latter item, in addition to showing the 'square' Almex A
validation, is also overstamped at the foot by an Almex M
canceller.
Northern Ireland Railways (**96**)
Zambia Railways (**97**)

Almex M
Irish Transport Company (CIE. See previous entry)
Tyne & Wear Passenger Transport Executive (**98**)
West Yorkshire Passenger Transport Executive & BRB (**99**)
On the latter validation is red at railway stations and blue on
buses.

APTIS (All-Purpose Ticket Issuing System)
British Railways Board (S) (**100**)

Autelca (In Britain this is another of the 'SPOTIS' group)
British Railways Board (S) (**101**)
Note the Regional Letter 'S' after the Machine Number.
Long Island Rail Road, New York (**102**)

Automaticket
British Railways Board (H)
Greater Glasgow PTE (Underground) (**103**)
Kyle & Carrick District Council Miniature Railway (**104**)
Longleat Railway (**105**)
New South Wales Government Railways (**106**)
Southend Corporation Pier Railway (**107**)

Autoslot 3
British Railways Board (S) (**108**)

Autoslot 8
British Railways Board (M) (**109**)

Autoslot 10
British Railways Board (**110**)

BEAM (British Electric Automatic Machines)
British Transport Commission (M)
Great Western Railway (**111**)

Bell Punch
Among the simplest of validating devices — the use of a plier, and
later a patent punch to create a single hole in the body of the
ticket while sounding a bell to indicate the action.
Bermuda Railway Company
Hull City Tramways (**112**)
Liverpool Corporation Tramways
London & North Eastern Railway
Nigerian Railway (**113**)
Welsh Highland Railway

Bell Punch Printix
London Passenger Transport Board (**114**)

Bell Punch 'SP' ('Self-Printing')
London Passenger Transport Board (**115**)

Bellgraphic
London & North Eastern Railway
Malayan Railway (**116**, printed in Britain)
Southern Railway (**117**)

Brecknell Munro & Rogers
Festival of Britain (**118**)
London Passenger Transport Board

CGA (Compagnie Générale de'Automatismes)
London Transport Executive (II)
London Underground Ltd (**119**)

Crouzet
Greater Glasgow Passenger Transport Executive
Tyne & Wear Passenger Transport Executive (**120**)
*City services in Caracas, Lille, Lyons, Marseilles, Mexico, Paris
and Rio de Janeiro*
Strathclyde Passenger Transport Executive

Flexiprinter
British Railways Board (W) (**121**)

FUMP (Four Unit Multiple Printer)
London Transport Executive (II), (**122**)
London Underground Ltd

Gibson
British Transport Commission (E) (**123**)
London Transport Executive (I)
Woburn Park Railway

Handiprinter
British Transport Commission (E) (**124**)
British Railways Board (M)

Hugin
British Railways Board (E) & (M) (**125**)

INTIS (Intermediate Ticket Issuing System)
British Railways Board (H) (**126**) *and (S)* (**127**)

Landis & Gyr Rapidprinter
London Transport Executive (II), (**128**)

Landis & Gyr Sodeco
British Railways Board (S) (**129**)

Multiprinter
British Railways Board (W) (**130**)
British Transport Commission (E)
London & North Eastern Railway

NCR 21
British Railways Board (S) (**131**)
(See entry for 1970 in Chapter 16)

NCR 24
British Railways Board (S) (**132**)

NCR C51
London Transport Board (**133**)

112

B 9824
Hull City Tramways.
HESSLE R'D ROUTE.
2
FARE 1D.
BETWEEN
ST. JOHN STREET
AND
DAIRYCOATES.
This Ticket is available
on this Car only, and must
be given to the Inspector
on request.
Edmondson, Printer M'chester

113

A 0033
2 1D
2½
NIGERIAN RAILWAY
KURU—JOS SERVICE
UP
KURU
DORAWA
BUKURU
GADA
ZARIA MAGANDA
MEKIRI
JOS
DOWN
Bell Punch Co., London, Eng.
A
0033

114

23. MAY 34
1
LONDON PASSENGER
TRANSPORT BOARD.
PICCADILLY C.
TO
REGENTS PARK.
CHARING CROSS.
HOLBORN.
HYDE PARK CORNER.
AL DWYCH.
STRAND.
TOTTENHAM CT. RD.
BOND STREET.
TEMPLE.
WESTMINSTER.
or intermediately
PICCADILLY C.
47610

115

-5 MAY. 37
LONDON PASSENGER
TRANSPORT BOARD
PADDINGTON
3D
3D
52497

116

MALAYAN RAILWAY

CENTS	CENTS		11081
2D	10¢	26½	
FROM	TO	DATE	

NOT TRANSFERABLE. ISSUED SUBJECT TO RULES AND
REGULATIONS OF MALAYAN RAILWAY. [M. R. 1947]

117

SOUTHERN RAILWAY
NOT TRANSFERABLE
B 00811
Issued subject to the Bye-laws,
Regulations, Notices and Conditions
published in the Company's Bills
and Notices.
SURBITON   -1.NOV 1946
To
Via
CLASS   DES-
3   CRIPTION
£   S.   D.
OUTWARD
JOURNEY   16 1
BELL PUNCH COMPANY, LONDON.   A BELLGRAPHIC TICKET

118

FESTIVAL OF BRITAIN
SOUVENIR TICKET
Coin used was Tested, Change given
& this Ticket, Printed, Numbered, Dated
& Cut from a roll of plain paper in
less than One Second by a B. M. & R.
TICKET & CHANGE MACHINE
MANUFACTURERS
BRECKNELL, MUNRO & ROGERS LTD. BRISTOL 5.

119

634301 LONDON TRANSPORT 002946
PLATFORM ONLY
14 SE 84   FARE
FROM LIVERPOOL STREET 20P

120

29 NSH   20P   18 APR 83
119627   ADULT   12H59 · 229

123

s	d
00	01½

B. T. C. (E)
SHEFFIELD VICTORIA
M C No. 1
PASSENGER
LIFT

DATE	TICKET No.
SE20	6 4 6 8

121

2nd CHEAP DAY   BRB
Valid as advertised   (W)
Available from
Weston Super Mare
AND BACK   *1.25 *1.25
MYSTERY TOUR   G H F
Coach No   Seat No
enquire Ticket
NOT TRANS

Handwritten, hand-punched,
pre-printed, magnetic and
carbonised — for trams, lifts
and railway trains on surface
and underground lines — all
machine-issued.

122

LONDON TRANSPORT   MV4D
DATE   PRICE
040029 180C   40 R 80
RETURN   PENCE
TO VICTORIA (V)

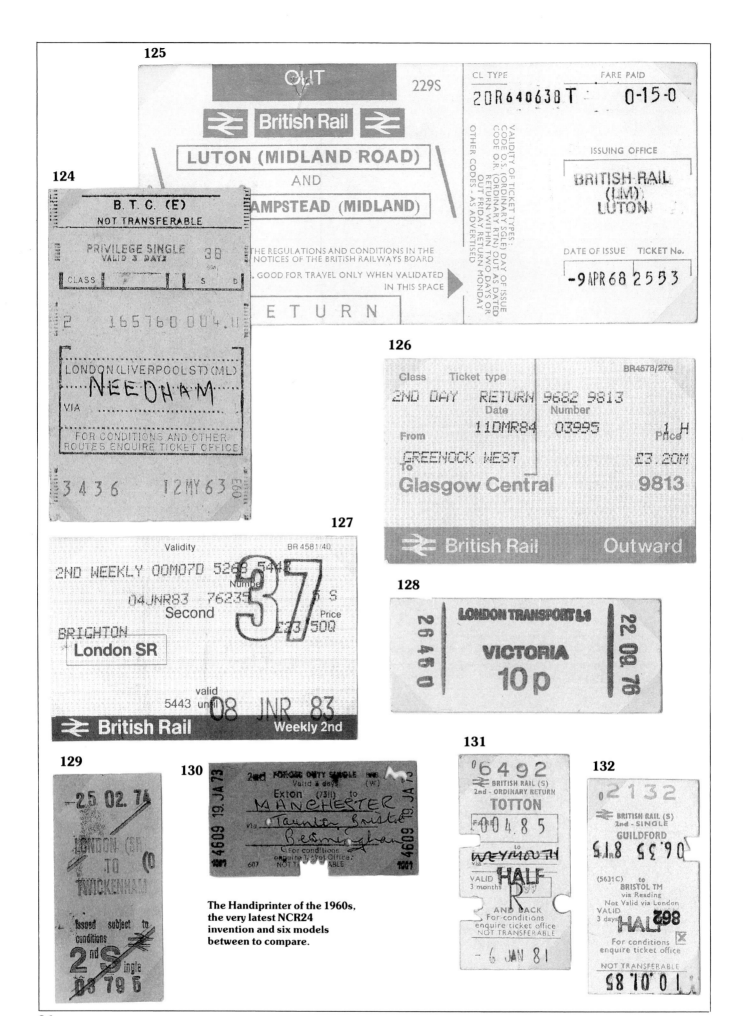

125

OUT 229S

≥ **British Rail** ≥

LUTON (MIDLAND ROAD)

AND

...AMPSTEAD (MIDLAND)

...THE REGULATIONS AND CONDITIONS IN THE
NOTICES OF THE BRITISH RAILWAYS BOARD

...GOOD FOR TRAVEL ONLY WHEN VALIDATED
IN THIS SPACE

R E T U R N

CL TYPE	FARE PAID
20R640638T	0-15-0

VALIDITY OF TICKET TYPES:
CODE O.S. (ORDINARY SGLE) DAY OF ISSUE
CODE O.R. (ORDINARY RTN) OUT AS DATED
RETURN WITHIN TWO DAYS OR
OUT FRIDAY RETURN MONDAY
OTHER CODES - AS ADVERTISED

ISSUING OFFICE

BRITISH RAIL
(LM)
LUTON

DATE OF ISSUE   TICKET No.

-9 APR 68   2553

124

B.T.C. (E)
NOT TRANSFERABLE

PRIVILEGE SINGLE   3B
VALID 3 DAYS

CLASS   S   D

2   165760 004.11

LONDON (LIVERPOOL ST) (ML)
NEEDHAM

VIA ....

FOR CONDITIONS AND OTHER
ROUTES ENQUIRE TICKET OFFICE

3 4 3 6   12 MY 63   E60

126

Class	Ticket type		BR4578/276
2ND DAY	RETURN	9682 9813	
	Date	Number	
	11DMR84	03995	1.H
From			Price
GREENOCK WEST			£3.20M
To			
Glasgow Central			9813

≥ **British Rail**   Outward

127

Validity   BR 4581/40

2ND WEEKLY 00M07D 5266 544E
Number
04JNR83 76235   **37** S
Second   Price
                        £23.500

BRIGHTON
London SR

valid
5443 until 08 JNR 83

≥ **British Rail**   Weekly 2nd

128

26460   LONDON TRANSPORT L1   22.09.76

VICTORIA
10p

129

-25.02.74

LONDON (SR)
TO
TWICKENHAM

issued subject to
conditions
2nd   Single
08 79 6

130

19.JA.73   2nd   FORCES DUTY SINGLE   73   19.JA.73

Exton (73II) to
MANCHESTER
via Taunton Bristol
Birmingham

For conditions
enquire Ticket Office
NOT TRANSFERABLE

4609   607   4609
1081   1081

The Handiprinter of the 1960s,
the very latest NCR24
invention and six models
between to compare.

131

0 6492
≥ BRITISH RAIL (S)
2nd - ORDINARY RETURN
TOTTON
Fare 004.85
WEYMOUTH
VALID
3 months   HALF
R
AND BACK
For conditions
enquire ticket office
NOT TRANSFERABLE

- 6 JAN 81

132

0 2132
≥ BRITISH RAIL (S)
2nd - SINGLE
GUILDFORD
06.55 8I5

(5631C)   to
BRISTOL TM
via Reading
Not Valid via London
VALID
3 days   HALF 862
For conditions
enquire ticket office

X

NOT TRANSFERABLE

T 10.01.85

NCR Pinpoint
British Railways Board (**134**)

Omniprinter
British Railways Board (S) (**135**)
Romney Hythe & Dymchurch Railway

PORTIS (Portable Ticket Issuing System)
British Railways Board (W) (**136**)
137 is a Training Ticket for a new type of PORTIS machine which was being developed in 1985/86.

Regina
Great Central Railway (I)[9]
Great Western Railway (**17**)

Revenue Control
British Railways Board (H) (**138**)

Rolltic
London Electric Railway
London Passenger Transport Board (**139**)

Setright Keyspeed
British Railways Board (H) (**140**)

Insert Setright Keyspeed
British Railways Board (H) (**141**)

Setright Multifare
London Transport Board (**142**)

Setright Multiset
British Railways Board (M) (**143**)

Setright Speed
Keighley & Worth Valley Light Railway (**144**)
Llandudno & Colwyn Bay Electric Railway (**145**)
Ravenglass & Eskdale Railway
Western Australian Government Railways (**146**)

Insert Setright Speed
London Midland & Scottish Railway
BRB/Western Scottish Motor Transport Company (**147**)

SPOTIS (Simplified Passenger Operated Ticket Issuing System)
Illustrated above under **AGITICKET** and **AUTELCA**

SSTIS (Small Stations Ticket Issuing System)
British Railways Board (H) (**148**)
Readers will note that the Return Ticket illustrated is a 'dummy' printed during a staff training session. Single Tickets differ from Returns in that the name of the destination station on the left-hand side is replaced by a line of dashes.

THORN EMI 1010
London Transport Executive (II), (**149**)

TICFAK 4000-8
West Miidlands Passenger Transport Executive (**150**)

TIM (Ticket Issuing Machines Ltd)
British Railways Board (M) (**151**)
Christchurch Quay Miniature Railway (**152**)
Keighley & Worth Valley Light Railway
London Electric Railway (**153**)
The Pullman Car Company
Swansea & Mumbles Railway

Ultimate
Brighton Corporation Transport Volks Railway (**154**)
British Railways Board (S)
British Transport Commission (H) & (S) (**155**)

Ultimatic[10]
British Transport Commission (E) (**156**)
London Transport Executive (I) (**157**)

Universal
British Railways Board (**158**)

Westinghouse Cubic
London Transport Executive (II) (**159**)

Westinghouse Multifare
London Transport Executive (II) (**160**)

Westinghouse Rapidprinter
British Transport Commission (E) (**161**)

Willebrew
Narrow Gauge Railways Limited (**162**)
Sligo Leitrim & Northern Counties Railway

133

0. - 1.6 JUN - 8

SINGLE FARE PAID | DATE

FROM
HAMMERSMITH
D1

LONDON TRANSPORT
4 94806

134

RAIL

Class	Ticket type
2ND	ORD SINGLE

	Date	Number
CHILD	08.MCH.85	02626

From
EUSTON

To
WATFORD JUNCTION   0801

1444

Route
01 M

Valid   Price
ON DATE SHOWN   £ 1.10X

➤◄ British Rail

135

For conditions enquire issuing officer   BRB(S)
NOT TRANSFERABLE
Validity from date of issue (see code below)
A & E—3 days, B—3 months, C & D—1 day, F—1 month
G, H & J—as advertised,   *—3 days (rebook single)

TYPE A—Ord. Single D—Cheap Off Peak G—Monthly Return
      B—Ord. Return   E—Priv. Single   H—Weekend Return
      C—Cheap Day   F—Priv. Return   J—Platform/Car Park
      *—Rebook (single)

FARE | TYPE | TO | CL | FROM | CH

00.06 J 40240

STATION CODE			
00London (SR)	76Eastleigh	49Littl'ton	40Sandown
47Bamham	85Fareham	34Petersf'ld	39Shanklin
48Bognor R.	31Fratton	33Ports. Hbr.	79South'pton
80Bournem'th	20Gatwick A.	84Ports. SS...	64Surbiton
41Brading	83Guildford	36Reading	52Sutton
24Brighton	37Haslemere	43Ryde Esp'de	50Wimbledon
46Chichester	45Havant	44Ryde Pr.Hd.	74Winchester
38Cosham	51Horsham	42Ryde S.J.Rd.	65Woking
32E. Croydon	35Liss	82Salisbury	53Worthing

29SE02 3196

136

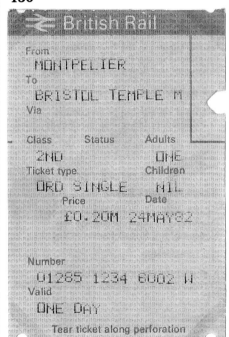

➤◄ British Rail

From
MONTPELIER
To
BRISTOL TEMPLE M
Via

Class	Status	Adults
2ND		ONE
Ticket type		Children
ORD SINGLE		NIL
Price		Date
£0.20M		24MAY82

Number
01285 1234 6002 W
Valid
ONE DAY

Tear ticket along perforation

137

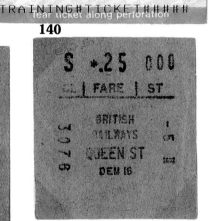

□ THORN EMI
Electronics

From
FITZWILLIAM#*####SGL
To
HEALING#*######## ➤◄
Route
#####################
Class   Adults
2ND############ONE##
Ticket Type   Children
STD#SINGLE#####NIL##
     Price   Date
#£333.35M#04.FBY.85#
Number
###6691###10#E#08.15
Valid
##771##8583628300000

TRAINING#TICKET#####
Tear ticket along perforation

141

➤◄   ➤◄

2ND DAY RETURN   0

GLASGOW
QUEEN ST.
TO ANY ONE STATION
AND BACK
AT THE RETURN FARE
SHOWN BELOW

FOR CONDITIONS SEE OVER

R

R *.23 000

CL | FARE | ST

BRITISH
RAILWAYS
QUEEN ST
8R01

138

SORD.   2
060671
➤ British Rail
Paisley St.James
Glasgow Central

THIS SIDE UP
Valid as advertised

AD £ -.-
39094

139

1 04452
LONDON PASSENGER
TRANSPORT BOARD
ELEPH. & CAS.
TO
LONDON BRIDGE.
OVAL.
WATERLOO.

Issued subject to the Bye-laws, Regulations and advertised Conditions of the Board

3rd Class   Available day of issue only

or intermediately
(1) S
ELEPH. & CAS.
1 04452

140

S *.25 000

CL | FARE | ST

3078

BRITISH
RAILWAYS
QUEEN ST
DEM 16

Innovation and obsolescence, ribbon machines and a personal
credit card device all feature here.

142

LONDON TRANSPORT

EUSTON -1|0-

S.M.F.

JA 14 7957

143

2nd. SINGLE
CALEDONIAN
ROAD
Valid day of issue only
(M)   See over

8639

147

A00111

SINGLE

SPATESTON –
JOHNSTONE STN.
and
GLASGOW
CENTRAL

By Interlink Bus
and Train

Not Transferable
For conditions
see over

Interlink

B.R./W.S.M.T.

018 24

144

Keighley & Worth Valley
Light Railway Limited

Keighley
Light R

1 2 05 17 2

Issued subject to the Co's Regulations
be produced or given up on demand

Issued subject
Must be produ

146

T. RAILWAYS   W.A. GOVT. RAILW

20 53 130

BLE. To be shown
vailable for travel as
icated.

NOT TRANSFERABLE. To be s
on demand. Available for tra
indicated.

145

BAY ELEC. R   LWYN BAY ELEC. RLY. LTD.   LLAN & COLWYN BAY ELEC. RLY. LTD.   LLAN & COLWYN BAY ELEC. RLY.

1 05 9 45   1 05 9 44

LLAN & COLWYN BAY ELEC. RLY. LTD.

148

Date	Tkt type	Class	Payment	
21AUG79	DY RTN	2ND	1H	.44M
9999	9961	ADLT	00041	ADLT
To			From	
TRAINING			TRAINING	
From	9961		To	9961
Argyle Street			Argyle Street	

British Rail   Outward

149

LONDON TRANSPORT   X21   008254

VICTORIA <D>

£0.40   01.JUN.85

150

Travel Ticket 2nd Class

2218

| DATE | TIME | FARE | ORIGIN. | TICKET TYPE |

5SE240947 065M1A3

MARSTON GREEN TO BIRMINGHAM NEW STREET

British Rail/West Midlands P.T.E.
See terms and conditions on reverse.

TICFAK 4000-8 from ALMEX SYSTEMS Ltd.   (4353)

151

MANSFIELD

BRITISH RLYS. (M.)

0083

COND. NO.

2

NO. OF
PKGES

DATE

25AP70

LEDGER
ACCOUNT

Ten tickets spanning 40 years, displaying manual insert cards
and the latest oxide magnetic encoded creation, with the
ubiquitous Setright Speed narrow strip.

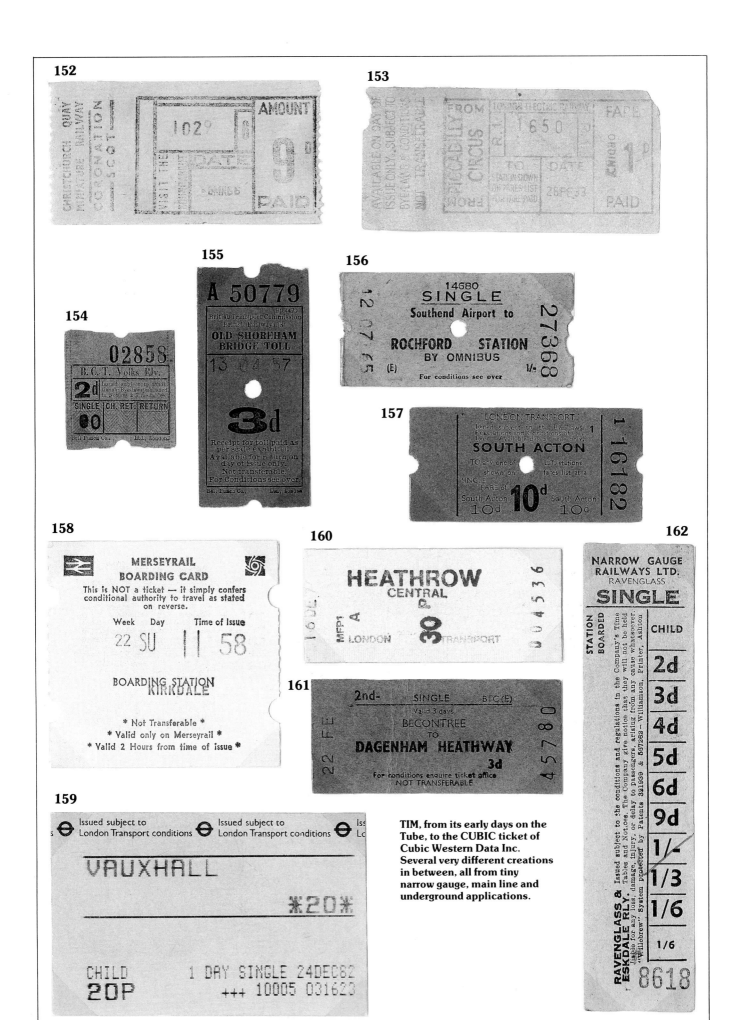

152
CHRISTCHURCH QUAY MINIATURE RAILWAY
CORONATION SCOT
VISIT THE
102°
AMOUNT
9 d
DATE
PAID

153
FROM PICCADILLY CIRCUS
LONDON ELECTRIC RAILWAY
1650
FARE ORDINARY 1 d
TO
DATE 26FE53
PAID
AVAILABLE ON DAY OF ISSUE ONLY SUBJECT TO BYE LAWS & CONDITIONS

154
02858
B.C.T. Volks Rly.
2d
SINGLE | CH. RET. | RETURN
00
Bell Punch Co. Ltd., London.

155
A 50779
BP4475
British Transport Commission
British Railways (S)
OLD SHOREHAM BRIDGE TOLL
13 04 57
3d
Receipt for toll paid as per scale exhibited.
Available for return on day of issue only.
Not transferable.
For Conditions see over.
Bell Punch Co. Ltd., London

156
14680
SINGLE
Southend Airport to
ROCHFORD STATION
BY OMNIBUS
(E)
For conditions see over
12 07 65
27368
1/-

157
LONDON TRANSPORT
Issued subject to the Bye-laws, Regulations and Conditions of L.T. Exec. Available day of issue only.
SOUTH ACTON
TO any one of the L.T. stations shown on fares list at a
SINGLE FARE of
South Acton 10d **10d** South Acton 10d
1
16182

158
MERSEYRAIL
BOARDING CARD
This is NOT a ticket — it simply confers conditional authority to travel as stated on reverse.
Week | Day | Time of Issue
22 | SU | 11 58
BOARDING STATION
KIRKDALE
* Not Transferable *
* Valid only on Merseyrail *
* Valid 2 Hours from time of issue *

159
Issued subject to London Transport conditions (×3)
VAUXHALL
20
CHILD
20P
1 DAY SINGLE 24DEC82
+++ 10005 031620

160
HEATHROW CENTRAL
MFP1 A
LONDON
30
TRANSPORT
965400
1695

161
2nd- SINGLE BTC (E)
Valid 3 days
BECONTREE
TO
DAGENHAM HEATHWAY
3d
For conditions enquire ticket office
NOT TRANSFERABLE
22 FE
45780

162
NARROW GAUGE RAILWAYS LTD.
RAVENGLASS
SINGLE
STATION BOARDED

	CHILD
	2d
	3d
	4d
	5d
	6d
	9d
	1/-
	1/3
	1/6
	1/6

RAVENGLASS & ESKDALE RLY.
Issued subject to to the conditions and regulations in the Company's Time Tables and Notices. The Company give notice that they will not be held liable for any loss, damage, injury, or delay to passengers, arising from any cause whatsoever.
Patents 321939 & 597262 — Williamson, Printer, Ashton.
"Willebrew" System protected by Patents
8618

TIM, from its early days on the Tube, to the CUBIC ticket of Cubic Western Data Inc. Several very different creations in between, all from tiny narrow gauge, main line and underground applications.

CHAPTER 3

1840s-1980s — The Then and Now Class

Most tickets collectors acquire represent actual travel; the movement of passengers from Point A to Point B, occasionally using other modes of transport or via a distant Point C. The accommodation of people travelling to and from their places of employment, to centres of education or simply to a spot in the sun for a pleasant sojourn, has traditionally been available in varying degree of comfort. In Britain, the descriptions became more or less standardised by the mid-19th century with the general use of First, Second, Third and Parliamentary Classes. Probably the Edmondson Company played no small part in this process as details of the accommodation offered by various companies and the terms used to describe them would come with orders for tickets and there would be considerable feedback of information to other customers in catalogues and less formally in conversation. Similarly, travellers would compare one company's service with another. The need for a widely accepted terminology became apparent. Outside Britain, standardisation was less conspicuous due in no small measure to differences in language, in culture and in climate. Dictated by respective national languages and local practices, by political and social doctrine and straightforward commercial considerations, varying standards of comfort or class of travel are expressed in a multitude of ways and usually indicated on the tickets sold. Close examination reveals some surprising differences of practice between companies, not always reconcilable one with another.

The best known early British railway, the Stockton & Darlington, joined the North Eastern Railway in 1863. At different times during its 38 years, the company issued a range of paper and large card tickets, to which the Edmondson card was added in 1844. Included among these were five separately specified classes — Inside, Outside, First, Second and Third Class. Some of these were sub-divided as for instance Outside First Class and Slow Train Second Class. Illustrated is a First Class ticket from the period commencing 1841 (**163**).

Inside and Outside designations were merely two basic choices; a numerical terminology would be less restricted and easily comprehended by the masses now beginning to take to travel in a way that had hitherto been denied to them. Britain's railways were influenced in these matters by stage coach practice which in some measure continued to be operated by the young railways. Indeed, during the earliest years of the Stockton & Darlington, passenger traffic was in the hands of stage coach proprietors who paid a fee for their use of the track. The Durham & Sunderland Railway in February 1840 introduced a combined coach-rail service to Stockton, charging 5/- Inside and 4/- on the slatted roof — Outside. The norm was for passengers to ride Inside in relative comfort or Outside with little or no protection from the elements. The North British Railway (**180**) shows how the passenger travelled Third Class by railway and Outside Class on his connecting stage coach, while a more affluent fellow traveller rode First Class and Inside (**164**). As an aside to this, one of the Authors recalls riding (over 100 years later!) ramshackle buses plying between Cairo and Suez along sand-swept apologies for trunk roads. Passengers travelled inside if they had paid a standard fare or clung (literally) outside for whatever 'arrangement' they could make with the conductor at the time. 'Outside' in that service included the nicety of laying flat on the roof. One wonders whether any similar system survives today in some less-developed territories.

As the stage coach influence faded, the choice for a passenger became that of a roof over him and possibly a seat under, or the total lack of such luxury. Tickets made this clear in a variety of ways.

In the early days of railways, no class guaranteed the standard managed on stage coaches. The railway vehicle might simply be a 'cage on wheels' — this is, a roof over, but no seats, no glass and just metal grilles for walls. It was by taking Inside First Class that one might ensure a fair degree of comfort. Some open-top four-wheelers were about as grand as a mineral wagon and offered standing room only. In fact, the Great Western Railway actually utilised a number of its mineral wagons, crudely adapting them as additional passenger vehicles to meet the extra traffic generated by the Great Exhibition of 1851. The stage coach had at least offered its outside passengers a bench seat in front, on the roof or to the rear. The London & Greenwich Railway, which had been offering an Imperial Class for 1/- for a journey of some 6km

163

Fighting Cocks
TO
Darlington.

No.   First Class,   0^s   8^d

day of   184

Please to hold this Ticket till called for.

164

NORTH BRITISH RAILWAY

EDINBURGH TO NEWCASTLE

FIRST CLASS & INSIDE

165

L. & N. W. R. Special. Available for **three days** Return as per Bill. **RUTHIN** (Circular Tour) TO **WARRINGTON** (Bank Quay) via Corwen, and Rhyl. Covered Carriage *over*

RUTHIN

L. & N. W. R. Special. **WARRINGTON** (Bank Quay) TO **RUTHIN** (Circular Tour) via Rhyl, and Corwen. Covered Carriage *over*

57

166

007

G.N.R. Excursion Return only on December 15, 1865. **King's Cross** to **YORK** Covered Carriage *See notice at back*

167

L. C. & D. R. **HANDEL FESTIVAL** JUNE 11th, 14th, 16th, & 18th, 1877. LONDON To C. PALACE (High Level) (Only available for the contingent satisfied by the CRYSTAL PALACE Company to be Members of the County Festival Choir) Covered Carriage. **Not First Class.**

2760

171

168

GLASGOW To **HELENSBURGH** PARL'Y—Open Carriage.

5354

169

Great Western Railway CARDIFF TO **SHIELDS** Via Newport, Wor'ster, & Midland Railway. **PARLIAMENTARY** (3rd) CLASS [Over

104

170

Via Hexham and Granton. **Sunderland** TO DUNDEE Gov. Ticket   N. E. R. This ticket is issued subject to the regulations and conditions stated in the Co's. time tables and bills for the present month.

310

Extremes — First Class Inside, or the rigours of 'Open Carriage'.

Midland & Glasgow & South Western Rlys

SEASON   ①   TICKET.
J^T T-9388.   FIRST CLASS. £43 13 0

DEC. 1, 1916, to MAY 31, 1917.

ALLOW

MR. G. H. BULLIMORE,
Department of Ministry of Munitions of War, Westminster, S.W.

TO TRAVEL BETWEEN

ST. PANCRAS AND CARLISLE
(via Loughboro', Alfreton, Sheffield, Darfield, Keighley and Settle);
AND

TRENT AND NOTTINGHAM.
Available also to and from Kettering and Nottingham (via Manton), and Nottingham and Trowell (via Radford), for through journeys only.
NOT AVAILABLE via DERBY.

Available also to and from Euston and Carlisle (via Shilton, Armitage, Whitmore, Hartford, Golborne, Coppull and Main Line) for through journeys only.

CARLISLE AND GLASGOW
(via Dalry and Barrhead).

This ticket is not transferable, and if transferred, or used by any one other than the person named on it, will be forfeited. It is issued on the terms that it shall be given up immediately on expiration, and that the holder shall be subject to the same Rules and Regulations as other passengers, as well as to the special conditions contained in the form of application for the ticket. The ordinary fare to be paid if the ticket is not produced when required.

Entd.....   GENERAL MANAGER, MIDLAND RAILWAY.

Entd.....   GENERAL MANAGER, G. AND S. W. RAILWAY.

FORFEITED IF TRANSFERRED.

and Open Class for half that sum, introduced its Third Class in 1839 with standing room only. (Incidentally, the public were permitted on payment of one penny to enter L&G land beside the track and then 'promenade' along the route. Surely this must represent an all-time low in the provision of facilities for early 19th century travellers?) In another example, there was a vehicle with a rounded roof which confined any passengers riding near the walls to a stoop, with no windows and no proper ventilation or lighting after dark. In 1845, when required to raise the standard of comfort by ensuring proper windows, the London & South Western Railway fitted glass to apertures in the roof of some Third Class vehicles — the relevant Regulations had failed to arrange that windows would be in the vertical plane enabling a view of the countryside.

'Covered Carriage' class ensured a roof protected from the weather and usually rudimentary seating gave a degree of support. **165** tells of a circular tour of north Wales that could be spread over three days and could take the traveller over tracks of the London & North Western and Great Western Railways long since closed. The ticket does not bear a date and was probably never actually sold. One would suspect that only a small number of such tickets were supplied to the station at Warrington. **166** is the return half of an Excursion from York to London by the Great Northern Railway 10 days before Christmas 1865, while **167** records special arrangements by the London Chatham & Dover Railway to enable members of the Handel Festival Choir to travel to Crystal Palace on four festival days in June 1897. It is interesting that the company was continuing to use the expression 'Covered Carriage' as late as this.[11] This outward half is overprinted 'CHOIR' but the high serial number would suggest the facility may have been available to a wider public. The West Midland, Great Western and Manchester & Milford Railways were three companies who used another and somewhat sinister term — 'Closed Carriage' — roughly equated with Inside Class.

In contrast, there was 'Open Carriage' (Outside) (**168**) in which standards varied enormously. Frequently the description meant literally nothing between scalp and sky. These severely austere classes were used for many of the earliest excursions offered in the country. Fortunately, such primitive amenities were not destined to become anyone's national standard. Outside and Inside soon engendered an intermediate grading and thus established the more readily understood First, Second and Third Classes and in some instances a class expressed numerically as Fourth. First, Second and Third were routinely available classes in 1835-6, well before there were lengthy main line railways. When the Grand Junction Railway opened on 4 July 1837, its classes of travel, if not its tickets, were more or less free of coaching influences. The company offered First Class and Second Class, both with seats and roof, and each was separately available as an outside facility. Another company, the Leeds & Selby Railway, introduced its First and Second Class early in 1835 and its Third Class in May 1837.

Inside and Outside were not generally known on railways which opened after the influence of the stage coaches had waned. The term 'Fourth Class' was never commonplace in Britain (but it survived in several overseas territories until the 1980s). The Manchester & Milford and Midland Counties (later Midland) Railways issued such tickets, as did Scotland's Edinburgh & Glasgow and North British Railways. The Great Northern Railway introduced Fourth Class in 1848 and even as late as 1853 it was provided on the Eastern Counties and Norfolk Railways (later amalgamated). About the same time the Great Western Railway seems to have carefully avoided specific mention of Fourth in its offer of an Open Excursion Coach for a fare somewhat cheaper

than Third Class. Fourth Class was mostly charged at 'one penny per mile'. The Manchester & Leeds Railway in its 1846 fare table advertised the '61 miles' (98km) Manchester to Leeds at 5/1d (about 25p today) whereas the appropriate First, Second and Third Class fares were 13/-, 10/- and 7/- respectively. Whether it was to discourage use of the penny fare over the shorter distances or for some other operational reason is not really our present concern, but it is interesting to note that in one fare table it was only at 22 miles (35km) that Fourth became cheaper than Third. Certainly in the early 1840s railway companies deliberately discouraged the use of the lower rates, preferring to bolster revenues from First Class travel. The Sheffield, Ashton-under-Lyne & Manchester Railway quoted fares for '1st, 2nd, 3rd and Cheap'. The last named again equalled 'one penny per mile' and was therefore effectively an alternative term.

No fifth grade of travel has been identified although this could well describe the level of comfort obtained by passengers who elect to travel in goods trains and on locomotive footplates. When the Great Western Railway opened its first line in 1838 the contractors authorised to carry freight were also empowered to take 'LOWER' passengers 'with the goods'. What class of travel was this? From Scotland's Highland Railway came paper forms for 'Passenger by Goods Train' to permit travel where the ordinary passenger stock was not in service. There were also Drovers' Tickets for those travelling home after delivering their charges. Frequently these fellows used little more than a fifth grade, especially when herded in with their charges on an outward trip to market.

In the Glasgow Dumbarton & Helensburgh item (**168**) it is seen how the words 'Open Carriage' are prefixed with the true class distinction — 'Parliamentary' as abbreviated. A further example is shown here from the Great Western Railway in the year 1880 (**169**). This ticket incidentally, was one of a number that literally fell off the back of a waste-paper lorry in January 1961 as it crossed Waterloo Bridge in London. It landed at the feet of its present owner while the rest were blown into the River Thames.

From November 1844, railways in Britain and Ireland were bound by Act of Parliament to provide some sort of service at 'one penny a mile'. Where the Third Class fare was in excess of this, there had to be an inferior class. Occasionally this was called Fourth or else Government Class (**170**) but more often it was styled 'Parliamentary'. A lengthy journey using Parliamentary Class, because of the way the very cheap trains were timed and detrainment ensured, could easily entail a series of overnight stops. For example: a 'Parly' trip from Dover to Torquay could quite normally be spread over four days; SE Dover to London on the first day, GW to Bristol on the second; Bristol & Exeter Railway as far as Exeter on the third day and, on the final day a South Devon train down the line to Torquay. This was typical for long journeys until the 1850s and 1860s when Third Class fares began to be reduced. Stocks of Parliamentary Class tickets remained at stations with few bookings for many years, in some cases into the approach to Nationalisation.

Nevertheless, few Parliamentary Class tickets were seen after World War 1 but one collector, the late Peter Embley, told the story of an elderly stationmaster in the Scottish Highlands who was convinced that such tickets could be sold only to Members of Parliament. As a result he retained a stock well into the late 1950s, standing firm against explanations, blandishments and entreaties of near-frantic collectors who sensed that they were so near to and yet so far from the ticket scoop of a lifetime.

The same Act required Third Class to include sheltered and seated accommodation. Nevertheless, the Glasgow Paisley & Greenock Railway as late as May 1846 continued to advertise

172

137
Bristol & Exeter
RETURN.
Not Available by
EXPRESS.
Bristol
2 TO
WESTON S-M.
First Class.

173

South Western Ry.
From SOUTHAMPTON
Best Cabin on board Steamer

No of Ry. Ticket
held by Passenger
This ticket must be shewn
whenever required & given up
on landing at HAVRE   (W)
069

174

0121   S. E. R. See Back.
Available Date of issue ONLY.
RED HILL to
BETCHWORTH
9d.   First.   9d.
B'worth   B'worth   0121

175

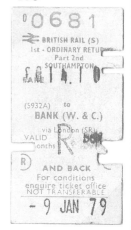

0 0681
BRITISH RAIL (S)
1st - ORDINARY RETURN
Part 2nd
SOUTHAMPTON
FARE £14.70
(5932A)   to
BANK (W. & C.)
via London (SR)
VALID
months   R
AND BACK
For conditions
enquire ticket office
NOT TRANSFERABLE
- 9 JAN 79

177

M. S. J. & A. R.
Manchester (Oxford Road) TO
ALTRINCHAM
By Cheshire Midland Trains Only
CHILD
FIRST CLASS EXPRESS
This ticket is issued subject to the
Company's regulations and to the
conditions in their Time Tables.

178

(No. 1)   (No. 1)
2nd - SINGLE   SINGLE - 2nd
(1st IN SHIP)   (1st IN SHIP)
215   Paddington to   215
Paddington   Paddington
TRALEE   TRALEE
TRALEE
Via Fishg'd H Rosslare Fermoy & Mallow
For alternative routes see book of routes
(W) 122/2 Fare 122/2 (W)
F   For Conditions For Conditions F
see over   see over

176

0003
L. & S.W.R.
Sir Ross Smith's Party
WEYBRIDGE
TO
WATERLOO
FIRST   CLASS
April 12th 1922
FOR CONDITIONS
SEE BACK.
- - - - - - - - - -
L. & S.W.R.
Sir Ross Smith's Party
WATERLOO
TO
WEYBRIDGE
FIRST   CLASS
April 12th 1922
0003

179

C.I.E. SECOND CLASS
7th MAR. 1965   Reduced Fare Ticket   RAIL
SCHOOLS G.A.A.   0208
CHILD
INIS Go
clu... meala ..ais
ENNIS To
CLONMEL & BACK
VALID DAY OF ISSUE ONLY
FOR CONDITIONS SEE BACK

180

NORTH BRITISH RAILWAY
No 480
EDINBURGH to NEWCASTLE
THIRD CLASS & OUTSIDE

181

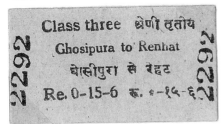

FLORIDA EAST COAST RAILWAY CO.
W. R. Kenan, Jr. and S. M. Loftin, Receivers
JACKSONVILLE (Depot) to
MIAMI   1240
Good for One Passage in COACH and limited to 30 days
in addition to date of sale. Maximum Baggage liability $100.00.
Subject to tariff regulations.
AC
0
366   General Passenger Agent

182

Sydney & Louisburg Railway
SECOND CLASS
09752
SYDNEY
— TO —
NEW WATERFORD
Good for one passage. Not transferable.

183

0041
SOUTHERN RAILWAY.
RACES
Available as advertised.
Epsom, Epsom Downs or
Tattenham Corner TO
(33) LONDON
Fare 7/6 No particular class
of carriage guaranteed.
FOR CONDITIONS
SEE BACK
SOUTHERN RAILWAY.
RACES
Available as advertised.
(33) London to (33)
EPSOM DOWNS or
TATTENHAM CORNER
Fare 7/6 No particular class
of carriage guaranteed.
0041

184

Class three श्रेणी तृतीय
2292   Ghosipura to Renhat   2292
घोसीपुरा से रेहट
Re. 0-15-6 रु. ०-१५-६

185

9507
S.E.&C.R. (SEE BACK)
WORKMAN
Available Day of Issue
ONLY. Not transferable.
Plumstead or
Woolwich Arsenal to
C... CHARING CROSS
S.137) Third Class 4 d.
S.E.&C.R. (SEE BACK)
Cannon Street to
WOOLWICH ARSENAL or
PLUMSTEAD
4 d. Third Class
Available only on the
day issued and by the
Special Cheap Train for
the Working Class. S.137
9507

186

For Laboring Men
GOOD FOR ONE FARE
Between the hours of
6.30 and 7.30 a.m., 12 and
1, 5 and 6 p.m.

Ride in 'Best Cabin' or an
Express Train, or partake the
economy of 'No particular
class'.

'Third Class without Seats' and 'Third Class with Seats' at a typical tariff of 1/- and 1/6d respectively.

As Britain's railways became a more or less comprehensive network and the lines of other countries continued to develop, so the class of travel gravitated to a simplified First, Second and Third. Third Class travel accounted for a full 70% of all railway bookings in Britain in the 1870s and reached 85% by the 1920s. Put another way: just before World War 2 economists were asking if there was propriety in allocating a quarter of a train's weight for a third of its running cost merely to attract two or three travellers in every hundred. All this goes some way to explaining why collectors today find early tickets for Second and First Class less abundant. Further explanation lies in the fact that a number of lines never offered Second Class at all. The Great North of Scotland Railway, when it opened in September 1854, provided only First and Third Class. The original Second Class in Britain progressively declined. The Aberdeen Railway discontinued Second Class late in 1855, perhaps preparatory to forthcoming amalgamation less than a year away. The class suffered a further severe setback on 1 January 1875 when the now mighty Midland discontinued it. The Midland decision affected its joint service with the Glasgow & South Western Railway, known as the Anglo-Scottish Run, reducing the choice of class to First and Third. The illustrated First Class Season Ticket (**171**) has suffered considerable damage but remains an interesting souvenir of World War 1. For the modest fare of £43 13s 0d (£43.65) an official of the then Ministry of Munitions was able to travel between London and Glasgow and also to Nottingham, over a period of six months.

Strangely, Second Class travel clung on almost until World War 2 on the London & North Eastern Railway's North London suburban lines. The casual passenger had the choice of First, Second or Third but Season Tickets were restricted to First and Second.

Enhancing the standards of First Class travel, some early companies would provide at appropriate cost the additional facility of a fast train. 'EXPRESS' became a separate class and some companies issued an Express Ticket (**177**) while others furnished the passenger with both an ordinary travel ticket and a supplementary 'add-on' one to permit entry to the faster train. This practice reached its peak in the early 1860s. The Bristol & Exeter Railway retained the enhanced class, with its separate tickets, into the 1870s (**172**), the GW till 1882, and as late as 1885 the LBSC were issuing Excess Fare cards for the difference between First Ordinary and First Express. It was still evident though not clearly stated in 'Boat Train' tickets of the Southern Railway as late as 1939. Much more recently, the British Railways Board have issued tickets which may be deemed an extension of First Class. These entitle exclusive occupancy for specialised purposes, as may be for a Military Courier travelling in circumstances of high security, or a Naval Policeman requiring secure and private quarters. Also in this rather-better-than-First range there was the London & South Western Railway's issues (**173**) which proclaimed 'Best Cabin on board Steamer'. These were available on the company's Southampton-Le Havre service. A currently available better-than-First foreign ticket variety is to be found on the Chicago & North Western company's lines where a ticket for 'Parlor 553' (and there were some '555') denoting exclusive use of a parlour car by members who have previously paid an annual surcharge of, it is said, $1,000, akin to a chartered coach or private club car in some other areas.

A small selection of classes is illustrated here to further demonstrate this aspect of ticket collecting.

First — South Eastern Railway 1900 (**174**).

1st/Part 2nd — British Railways Board (S) 1979 (**175**). No First Class was available on the final leg of this journey, from Waterloo to Bank.

First Class — London & South Western Railway 1922 (**176**). This ticket is the saddest of all. Sir Ross Smith was an Australian flying ace of the First World War. He received five awards for gallantry from King George V and a further one from the King of Hedjaz. After the war, he captained a crew of three to make the first flight from England to Australia, leaving Hounslow on 12 November 1919 and reaching Darwin on 10 December. April 1922 found him at Brooklands, by then aged 30, preparing to make the first flight round the world. The Vickers Company supplied him with a Vimy amphibian plane. On 12 April, a party of interested VIPs travelled down to Weybridge to inspect the plane and as we see from the ticket, the London & South Western Railway marked the occasion by allowing them a special party rate. The following day he flew the plane for the first time. It spun out of control, crashed, and he and his one passenger were killed. The euphoria of the previous day was destroyed in moments. **176** remained for one of that party a tragic souvenir of the last day of hopes and dreams of a brave gentleman who lost his life as he prepared to push the frontier of human achievement a little further.

First Class Express — Manchester South Junction & Altrincham Railway c1865 (**177**). The Cheshire Midland company referred to in this ticket was taken into the Cheshire Lines Committee system in 1865.

2nd/1st in Ship — British Transport Commission (W) c1950 (**178**). Hardened travellers are aware that the cheaper classes of travel by ship tend to be more rigorous than the 2nd or 3rd Class by rail. Hence many who would not contemplate First Class travel by rail are prepared to indulge in that luxury on the water.

Second Class — Irish Transport Company (CIE). Ireland 1965 (**179**).

Third Class & Outside — North British Railway 1846[12] (**180**). The stated journey of this ticket included over 96km between Berwick and Newcastle by stage coach. This service ceased when the railway link was completed in 1847. The procedure at this time was to enter each passenger's ticket details and serial number on a way-bill. An identical ticket numbered 445 was so entered for travel on 20 September that year. The size of this card is slightly smaller than the soon-to-be completely adopted size. Its opposite edges are not parallel — due to hand cutting from larger boards — suggesting Edmondson's newly devised 'guillotine machine' was not received by the printer concerned, Gellatly of Edinburgh.

First, Lower, Lower Ordinary, Mail, Inter(mediate), Ordy, and Upper are some of the distinctive classes encountered abroad and all freely to be found on tickets for the collector. Japan today offers what is literally headed 'De Luxe Romance Car Ticket' and of course no collector will be surprised to find tickets for Air Conditioned Class. The North American railways (railroads) are the home of First Class and Coach Class (**181**) and only rarely expressed the degree of comfort by ordinal numbers such as Second and Third. **182** shows a modern Second Class from Canada. The Newfoundland Railway and America's New York & Pennsylvania Railroad were two users of the term 'Third Class' in days gone by. Many lines in the western United States offered a Tourist Class — of a standard between First and Coach — more familiar on routes reaching the scenic National Parks and generally using obsolete First Class stock fitted with additional compartments. First Class on the country's major railways traditionally meant the standard adult fare while the lesser class was not normally specified in ticket text. One American correspondent described Second Class as being 'valid only in inferior vehicle', but did not say how this inferiority was judged or marketed.

The former Southern Railway of England, on tickets for travel to Epsom Races (**183**), actually specified the negative, with the words 'No particular class of carriage guaranteed', and what may be unique or at least peculiar to India appears on **184** from the Scindie State Railways, the words 'Class three' (sic).

This story should not pass without quoting from tickets of the pre-Grouping South Eastern & Chatham Railway, whose Workman Tickets stated 'Third Class' but qualified this still further with the words 'Special Cheap Train for the Working Class' (**185**), surely a delight for the social historian. Somewhat more evocative is the gem in **186** from Canada's Moncton Tramways where we find 'For laboring Men'.

In an authenticated incident in 1938, at Southfields station (then Southern Railway property), a Workman's Ticket was refused to a passenger by its booking clerk 'Because you are wearing a stiff collar and tie'. It was not simply a matter of travelling so as to arrive before eight in the morning.

CHAPTER 4

Season Tickets

In the summer of 1935, a 14-year-old lad spent a week in Margate. Too old for sandcastles yet too young to sit around with his parents, he decided to spend almost all his holiday money on a Weekly Holiday Season. On Monday morning he found his way to the now defunct Margate East station, made his purchase and caught the 10.06 to Canterbury. On Tuesday, he again arrived in time for the 10.06. As he reached for his ticket the stationmaster greeted him with a 'Good Morning'. On Wednesday he returned the greeting and kept his ticket in his pocket.

Without realising it, he was following a time-honoured pattern. The early Victorian Season Ticket holder would have been astonished if not outraged by a demand to see his document of title. Anyway, it was far more likely to be in his desk than his pocket. It was part of a railwayman's job to know his regular travellers. Even in the early years of the British Transport Commission, if the traveller were old enough and tolerably well dressed, he could usually get through both entry and exit barriers at any City terminus on the strength of an authoritative bark of 'Season'.

The ticket itself reflected the importance of the customer. More often than not described as a 'Contract Ticket' (although as we shall see in Chapter 14 *any* railway ticket represents a Contract) a typical example would consist of a printed form on which the dates of validity, the journey, the fare and name and address of holder were written in ink. The whole would be pasted on to a leather backing about 100mm by 80mm bearing the company's name or crest and would fold neatly to protect the written matter (**187**). Although, with few exceptions, this style of ticket disappeared from the railways of the UK before the Grouping of 1923, it lingered on in an unexpected place.

Cosens & Co Ltd began to run their Buff Funnel Steamships out of various South Coast resorts between from Weymouth and Poole to the Isle of Wight in 1852. They provided free passes for their shareholders and sold Weekly or other short period Season Tickets at least from 1913, pasting the pass or ticket on an imitation linen backing (**188**). These tickets continued in use at least until 1966.

The early Season Ticket holder would certainly travel First Class. Few Second or Third Seasons were seen before this century. Indeed on the London suburban lines of the LNER, where all three classes survived almost until World War 2, only First and Second Class Seasons could be obtained, even during the 1930s.

A little should be said about the pricing of the Season Ticket. Needless to say, the cost must reflect the convenience to the company of not having to sell a ticket each day at the busy period, the value of having a 'captive' customer once the ticket has been bought and the advantage of receiving payment well before the service is to be rendered. On the other side, the customer needs an inducement before parting with a substantial sum of money, so often at an inconvenient time such as immediately after Christmas or summer holiday.

Pricing policy has of course varied from company to company and from time to time. One would expect the discount on an Annual Ticket in particular to be greater at a time of high interest rates, but the recent tendency of firms in the larger towns to provide employees with interest-free loans repayable by monthly deductions from salary has played its part in keeping discounts low.

The saving on the purchase of a Season Ticket rather than a separate ticket each day increases with the length of the journey. At one time, it was assumed that the short-distance traveller might travel home to lunch and thus make four journeys a day (see under Erith in Chapter 5). For this reason, on a journey of almost 5km, the Weekly Season Ticket was more expensive than 10 or even 12 Singles. Nowadays, the price of a Weekly Season for between 5 and 14km is approximately that of eight or nine Singles, while at 96km it is little over four. The Monthly Ticket (which may last anything between 28 and 31 days according to the month of purchase) is priced at slightly less than four Weeklies while the Annual Ticket costs about 10 times that of the Monthly.

Various groups of customers have enjoyed reduced rates for Season Ticket travel. The well known 'Red Line' facility of the Southern Railway was an inducement to London workers to live on the South Coast. Quarterly (or longer) Tickets available only at the home station or stations and the London termini were sold at a

187

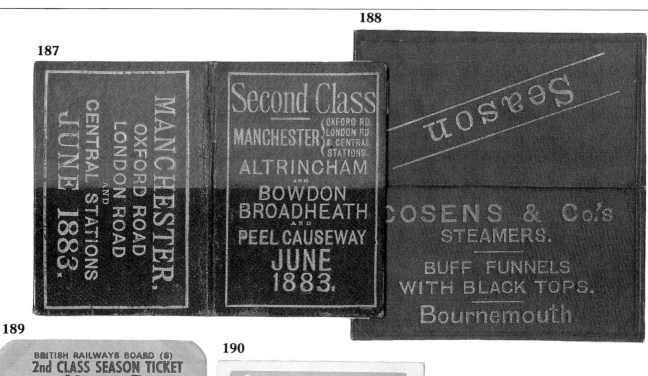

MANCHESTER.
OXFORD ROAD
LONDON ROAD
AND
CENTRAL STATIONS
JUNE 1883.

Second Class
MANCHESTER {OXFORD RD. LONDON RD. & CENTRAL STATIONS.
ALTRINCHAM
AND
BOWDON
BROADHEATH
AND
PEEL CAUSEWAY
JUNE 1883.

188

Season

COSENS & Co's
STEAMERS.

BUFF FUNNELS
WITH BLACK TOPS.
Bournemouth

189

BRITISH RAILWAYS BOARD (S)
2nd CLASS SEASON TICKET
Valid for 02 M 25 Days Until
OPERA
BETWEEN NEWHAVEN TOWN or
NEWHAVEN HARBOUR
AND LEWES J
½ RATE
VIA
(5331-A)
Nᵒ 1746
This ticket is NOT
TRANSFERABLE
and must be given
up on expiry
FOR CONDITIONS ENQUIRE AT TICKET OFFICE
16 JAN 74 Date Issued

190

British Rail
Newhaven Town and
Harbour
Valid until 02 JLY 76
Lewes
SCHOLAR
Nᵒ 0093
2 Month
Days
Date issued S.O. (533
26 APR 76
see over

192

BRITISH RLYS. (W)
WEEKLY SEASON
No. 2888
36
EXPIRES
BRITISH RLYS. (W)
THIRD CLASS
HALF RATE 7/2
Rate
27 NOV 1954
BETWEEN
SMALL HEATH & SPARKBROOK &
LEAMINGTON SPA
TO BE GIVEN UP IMMEDIATELY ON EXPIRY

191

THIRD CLASS. BRITISH TRANSPORT COMMISSION (S)
79
WEEKLY SEASON
TICKET
FOR CONDITIONS
SEE BACK
Nᵒ 0786
J
BETWEEN SLADE GREEN
AND CHARING CROSS, CANNON STREET,
WATERLOO (E), LONDON BRIDGE, HOLBORN VIADUCT,
BLACKFRIARS or ELEPHANT & CASTLE
Via Barnehurst and St. Johns or Erith and Catford or Nunhead.
Available at Intermediate Stations via Greenwich only.
UNTIL ⅔ Rate £ - . 12 . 0

**Early gold-blocked leather, followed by colour-printed linen
and plain cards — for all seasons.**

193

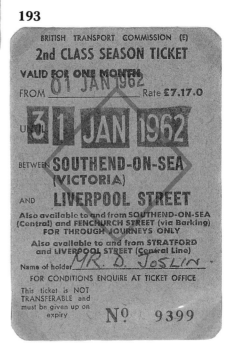

BRITISH TRANSPORT COMMISSION (E)
2nd CLASS SEASON TICKET
VALID FOR ONE MONTH
FROM 01 JAN 1962 Rate £7.17.0
UNTIL 31 JAN 1962
BETWEEN SOUTHEND-ON-SEA
(VICTORIA)
AND LIVERPOOL STREET
Also available to and from SOUTHEND-ON-SEA
(Central) and FENCHURCH STREET (via Barking)
FOR THROUGH JOURNEYS ONLY
Also available to and from STRATFORD
and LIVERPOOL STREET (Central Line)
Name of holder MR D. JOSLIN.
FOR CONDITIONS ENQUIRE AT TICKET OFFICE
This ticket is NOT
TRANSFERABLE and
must be given up on
expiry
Nᵒ 9399

194

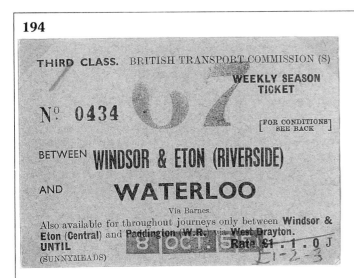

THIRD CLASS. BRITISH TRANSPORT COMMISSION (S)

07

WEEKLY SEASON TICKET

Nº 0434

[FOR CONDITIONS SEE BACK]

BETWEEN **WINDSOR & ETON (RIVERSIDE)**

AND **WATERLOO**

Via Barnes.

Also available for throughout journeys only between Windsor & Eton (Central) and Paddington (W.R.) via West Drayton.

UNTIL **8 OCT 5** Rate £1.1.0 J

(SUNNYMEADS) £1-2-3

195

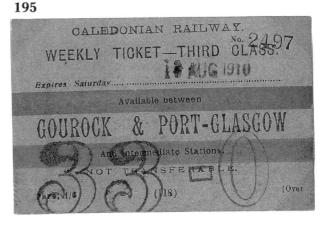

CALEDONIAN RAILWAY.

WEEKLY TICKET—THIRD CLASS. No. 2497

18 AUG 1910

Expires Saturday......

Available between

GOUROCK & PORT-GLASGOW

330

And Intermediate Stations.

NOT TRANSFERABLE.

Fare 1/6 (F18) [Over

196

BRITISH RAILWAYS BOARD (S) 2ND CLASS

OFF-PEAK WEEKLY SEASON TICKET

VALID UNTIL

04 JLY 70

BETWEEN **PLUMSTEAD**

AND **LONDON (S.R.)**

£001.3.0 RATE

530 (5178)

This Ticket is NOT TRANSFERABLE and must be given up on expiry

Nº 2372

FOR CONDITIONS ENQUIRE AT TICKET OFFICE

29 JUN 70 Date Issued

197

British Rail

Robertsbridge **2**

Valid until **03 JLY 83**

London Transport Travelcard

ZONE **1** CENTRAL

£029.00 Price

Via London (SR)

7 **2nd**

Nº 0000 s

Date issued S.O. (5226 A

7 Day **27 JUN 83** see over

198

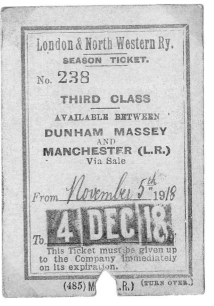

London & North Western Ry.

SEASON TICKET.

No. 238

THIRD CLASS

AVAILABLE BETWEEN

DUNHAM MASSEY

AND

MANCHESTER (L.R.)

Via Sale

From *November 5th* 19/8

4 DEC 18

To

This Ticket must be given up to the Company immediately on its expiration.

(485) M .R.) (TURN OVER.)

200

L M S THIRD CLASS WEEKLY SEASON

For Conditions see Back Rate 6·10½

Available between

BROOKLANDS & KNOTT MILL & D.

UNTIL

21 JUN 52

Sign Here in full

199

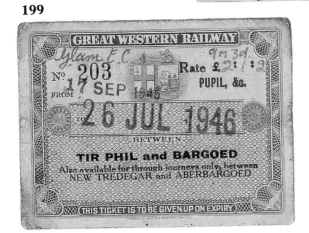

GREAT WESTERN RAILWAY

Ylam F.C.

Nº 203 17 Rate £2·1·2

FROM **17 SEP 1945** PUPIL, &c.

TO **26 JUL 1946**

BETWEEN

TIR PHIL and BARGOED

Also available for through journeys only, between NEW TREDEGAR and ABERBARGOED

THIS TICKET IS TO BE GIVEN UP ON EXPIRY

THOMAS DE LA RUE & COMPANY LIMITED

The precision of the Great Western to the austere prints of the British Transport Commission. Scotland, England and Wales shown by eight Seasons.

201

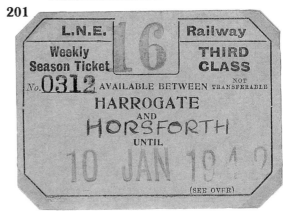

L.N.E. **16** Railway

Weekly Season Ticket THIRD CLASS

Nº 0312 AVAILABLE BETWEEN NOT TRANSFERABLE

HARROGATE

AND

HORSFORTH

UNTIL

10 JAN 194

(SEE OVER)

discount of about 17%. They carried a red stripe from top right-hand corner to the bottom left. During the 1930s the cost of a Quarterly Season from stations in the Brighton area to London was under £10. By 1947 it had advanced to £15 7s 0d but remained at this figure for several years. The advantage to the Southern was that their main lines could be used mornings and evenings by commuters travelling in the opposite direction to the day tripper. Only at midday on a Saturday did both groups metaphorically collide. The British Transport Commission and British Railways Board continued the facility until 1964 and even then allowed existing holders to renew their tickets for a year or so longer. A recent perquisite of the Season Ticket holder is the entitlement to the Railcard described in Chapter 8.

Juniors under 18 years of age have enjoyed reduced Season Ticket rates from British Rail. As a general rule all schoolchildren under 16 years of age are entitled to half-rate tickets. Young persons up to the age of 18 if still at school or working and earning less than a specified amount may travel at ⅔-rate. Where the child is attending a Local Authority school, the Authority usually meets the cost of the ticket. **189** and **190** were held by the same young lady; she was attending a private school in 1974 and a County Council school in 1976! **191** is a Weekly Ticket at the ⅔-rate. Note the printed 'J'. Printed tickets bearing a '2nd Class SCHOLAR SEASON TICKET' heading have also been seen. **192** is an example of a half-rate Weekly Ticket.

Besides the rubber-stamped 'W' to indicate that the ticket has been sold to a lady (can we hope to copy the Australians with a 'L' one day?), Season Tickets are particularly prone to coloured overprints — usually red. A large 'C' on the Eastern Section of the Southern Region would indicate that the London terminus is Cannon Street; while on the Western Section it would tell the ticket examiner that the passenger is entitled to travel on the Waterloo & City Line (better known to its regulars as 'The Drain'). Other Southern Region overprints (not illustrated) include 'CX' for Charing Cross, 'W' for Waterloo and 'B' for London Bridge (a legacy from SEC days).

Some other overprints are less obvious. Where a ticket was also valid on London Transport (now London Underground Limited) it would often be printed with a red or green diamond (**193**) although the Eastern Region sometimes favoured diagonal lines, a device also used to indicate a Privilege Season Ticket.

194 is interesting as a hybrid of the intermediate and non-intermediate stations types. Issued at the now unstaffed Sunnymeads station, it was available at all stations on the Southern Region line from Windsor & Eton (Riverside) to Waterloo and also for throughout journeys only on Windsor's Western Region line to Paddington. Careful inspection of **191** will indicate that while the passenger from Slade Green could use any of the three Dartford Loop routes to London, she was restricted to the intermediate stations on the Greenwich line only.

195 is a Weekly Ticket of the Caledonian Railway sold in the high summer of 1910, while **196** represents a short-lived experiment on Southern Region in Weekly Tickets valid at off-peak times only. **197** was valid in the London Transport Central Zone 1; it will be noted that the device of the red diamond has been abandoned.

198 is a Monthly Season for an 18km journey and cost just £1 1s 9d (£1.09). The holder may not have used it every day; the Armistice ending World War 1 came six days after the ticket commenced. The GW's high standard of printing extended to their Season Tickets. **199** was for a 'Pupil, &c'; on the back the booking clerk has written the words 'Not available during School Holidays'. The fare of £2 1s 2d (£2.06) seems to have been paid

by the Glamorganshire County Council. **200** and **201** represent the standard LMS and LNER Weekly Season formats respectively. **202** is a pre-standard Southern Railway Quarterly Season of 1927. The holder, Mr Frederick H. Smith, was a well known ticket enthusiast. When he died in 1957 most of his collection of 140,000 railway and roadway tickets were distributed among his fellow members of the then Ticket & Fare Collection Society.

This chapter commenced with a mention of Holiday Seasons. One feature of these tickets is that they could always be purchased at any time in the week and then ran for seven days — a facility only extended to ordinary Weeklies during the 1980s. The general rule was for somewhat detailed information to be printed on the front and a map of the area of validity to fill the back. **203** shows that the LMS were using the term 'Contract' as late as 1939. **204** shows the back of a GW Holiday Season sold on 13 August 1936 at Torre. Since Nationalisation, Holiday Season Tickets have tended to carry a list of stations on the boundaries of the area rather than a map.

A mere £9 in the summer of 1957 purchased a weekly 'Freedom of the Line' Season Ticket valid throughout the London Midland Region of BR. The child's version cost half this, but only a flat £4 if for travel with an adult on each journey.

Exciting facilities were offered to Mancunians in Whit-Week of 1950 by the Town Holiday Runabout ticket. From three stations in the southern suburbs, one could travel at will over a period of five days to and from Southport, Blackpool, Morecambe, Fleetwood and even the Lake District for just £1 7s 6d (£1.37) (**205**). The serial number 001 would suggest that few holidaymakers took up the offer.

The most consistent feature of London Transport Seasons is their size, which varies little from 74mm×51mm, making them slightly smaller than the modern credit card. The Board's name has never appeared on the front of the ticket but the conditions on the back were headed 'London Transport (Railways)' until about 1950 when the brackets were dropped. Despite the abolition of First Class travel on 1 February 1940, they continued to describe themselves as '3rd' and '2nd' until the advent of the Travelcard in 1983. First Class Seasons are rarely seen.

Until the changes of colour and format in 1977, the colours of ordinary adult Third and later Second Class tickets were purple on green card for periods of a quarter or longer, black on green for a month or over, while Weekly Tickets were black on purple. Tickets issued to ladies carried a diagonal stripe (**206**). Tickets for young persons were variously brown (if at ⅔-rate — any period), red (if at ½-rate — any period) and purple on yellow (term tickets for a schoolchild) although at least one blank orange ½-rate ticket has been seen.

The changes of 1977 were absolute. The format changed from landscape (horizontal) to portrait (vertical), the security background was altered from tiny print under the date of expiry only to an overall design, the requirement that a Weekly Ticket be signed was omitted and the LT logo appeared for the first time (**207**). Weekly Tickets remained black on a slightly paler purple card and those for longer periods were at first black on pale green but from about 1982 the Annual Ticket became black on a yellow and pink plastic laminated card. In 1983, all these types were superseded by the Travelcard.

London Transport suddenly became a political issue in 1981 and its story has been excellently recounted by Paul Garbutt[13] where the ticket enthusiast may learn the background to the changes of the 1980s. The Travelcard was introduced on 22 May 1983 and is valid on both train and omnibus. It is rather like a

202

SOUTHERN RAILWAY.
THIRD CLASS SEASON TICKET
No. 8772
ISSUED SUBJECT TO CONDITIONS ON OTHER SIDE.
Available from _____ 19
Pass
Until **9 JUL 1927**
CROYDON (EAST or WEST) &
LONDON (LONDON BRIDGE VICTORIA
CANNON ST. CHARING CROSS)
NOT available at South Croydon.
THREE MO

203

E.R.O. 43964/9.
LONDON MIDLAND AND SCOTTISH
RAILWAY COMPANY.
Holiday Contract Ticket.
NOT TRANSFERABLE.
THIRD CLASS. Tour No. **6**
No. 109 Rate 10s. 6d. N
When signed by Holder this Ticket is
available between the Stations shown on
the other side by the routes indicated.
Valid until **18 JUN 39**
(3246)
Issued subject to the Conditions and Regulations
in the Co.'s Time Tables, Books, Bills and
Notices and in the Railway Co.'s Book of
Regulations relating to Traffic by Passenger Train
or other similar service.
O. GLYNNE ROBERTS,
Secretary,
EUSTON STATION.
Signature
of Holder
State Mr., Mrs., or Miss.
Date valid
from
This Ticket must be given up to the Company
NOT V.

204

205

British Railways (M) FOR
CONDITIONS SEE BACK
THIRD CLASS
TOWN HOLIDAY
RUNABOUT TICKET
Valid between
EAST DIDSBURY BURNAGE
& MAULDETH RD
and
CONISTON WINDERMERE T.
or LAKESIDE (W) MORECAMBE
FLEETWOOD BLACKPOOL
SOUTHPORT (C.ST)
and intermediate stations
and between
AMBLESIDE BOWNESS
and LAKE SIDE on the
WINDERMERE LAKE
STEAMERS
From 29th MAY
to 2nd JUNE 1950

206

2nd CLASS QUARTERLY SEASON TICKET BETWEEN
BALHAM and BOROUGH
UNTIL **2 APR 73**
DIRECT
Mrs. J. M. CURSON
Holder's Name
FOR CON

207

2nd class weekly
£7.60
see over
Hounslow Central
Heathrow Central
69
Route Direct
Expires Saturday **21 MAY 1983**

208

Travelcard LONDON TRANSPORT
ZONES
1 2 3a
CENTRAL INNER OUTER
Expires **10 JUN 84**
See over
Valid only when
shown with
Photocard No.
L 6322
£7.40 North Ealing
Weekly ⊖ 03999

209

Travelcard LONDON TRANSPORT
ALL ZONES
and London Transport Buses
outside Greater London
Expires
See over
CHILD Photocard
not required
£3.20
CHILD
Weekly ⊖ 010938

210

Travelcard LONDON TRANSPORT
ZONE **3b** Ⓦ
OUTER
Expires **19 JUN 84**
See over
Valid only with
Photocard No.
L 1316
£2.80 Hounslow Central
Weekly ⊖ 02751

The familiar Edmondson size with the latest weekly cards from
London conclude a display of 24 Seasons.

Holiday Season in that it gives the holder freedom to travel in a specified area.

Two years earlier London Transport had introduced the 'City Zone' and 'West End Zone' with flat rate rail travel within each. These were now combined into Central Zone 1 (comprising more or less the Inner Circle and the lines within it), Inner Zone 2 (including such places as East Putney, Clapham North, Manor House, Willesden Green and North Acton) and Outer Zones 3a (including Wimbledon, East Ham, Bounds Green and Neasden), 3b (Richmond, Morden, Upney, Southgate, Greenford and Hounslow Central) and 3c (the rest of the Greater London Council area). It should perhaps be said that Zones 2 and 3 had existed for bus travel since 1981.

For rail but not for bus travel, the area was otherwise divided into four sectors — North, South, East and West. One could purchase a Travelcard for any zone or any number of adjacent zones (**208** and **209**) but unless the card included Zone 1, rail travel was limited to one sector only. Thus all such suburban cards carried the letter 'N', 'S', 'E' or 'W' and for example the scope for rail travel of the holder of a 3bW card (**210**) would be severely restricted in rail travel to two short stretches of the Piccadilly Line and one of the Central but would be able to hop on a bus not only in the Western sector but in such exotic places as Morden, Leytonstone and Mill Hill. Travelcards from stations outside GLC territory specified the area of such rail travel in addition to the other information. The sector restrictions were waived on 6 January 1985.

Changes made during 1985 have included the enlargement of the Travelcard to about 83mm×57mm and the introduction of the Capitalcard. Costing about 15% more than the corresponding Travelcard, this can also be used on British Rail lines within the appropriate zone. The face carries both the London and BR logos but otherwise has every appearance of a BR Season.

Two other major changes of the early 1980s affected both British Rail and London Transport. Firstly, we have seen the Weekly Season replaced by the Seven Day Ticket. Whereas the Weekly invariably ran from Sunday to Saturday, the Seven Day can commence on any day of the week. Secondly, there has come the requirement that Season Ticket holders carry a numbered photocard (issued free at booking offices on presentation of a passport-style photograph) and the photocard number is written on each Season issued to that person. Both photocard and Season Ticket must be carried by the passenger. Introduced by London Transport, it was adopted by British Rail on 1 January 1985 for holders of Monthly or longer period tickets and to Seven Day Ticket holders from 1 September 1985.

June 1986 saw the advent of the One Day Capitalcard issued from British Rail stations outside the London Transport Area. They permit travel into London, almost complete freedom of all rail and bus services within the area and travel home. These also have the general appearance of a BR Season.

CHAPTER 5

The London Scene —
A Specialised Collection

After a while, the ticket enthusiast may decide to concentrate his attention on a particular area, often but not invariably his own locality. London is a likely choice, not necessarily for reasons of sentiment or local loyalty.

Alone in Britain the Capital has maintained its rail system largely intact. Since World War 2 its inadequate road system and lack of parking facilities have combined with a tradition of distancing one's residence from place of work to support sufficient commuter traffic to keep railways alive and stations staffed. The tradition is not new; by 1690 a commuters' stage coach was running on weekday mornings from Clapham to the City, over 6km distant, and returning each evening. The effect of well over a century of intensive passenger traffic has been to provide good supplies of tickets from most periods. By reason of their very numbers, they remain comparatively easy to obtain at reasonable prices.

For some collectors the first problem is to define London. Until the middle of the last century the name signified The Square Mile (2½sq km) of the City of London, lying on the north bank of the Thames but controlling a tiny area on the south. City and suburbs together came to be known as The 'Metropolis'. In 1855, Parliament set up the Metropolitan Board of Works and gave it an area composed of parts of Kent, Middlesex and Surrey. In 1889, the County of London was created with an almost identical area. Its shape was more or less oval with a perimeter 4-11km from the City and roughly coincided with the limit of the built-up area. It now totalled 303sq km (117sq miles).

As parts of adjoining counties came to be urbanised, the expression Greater London was coined. In the meantime the Metropolitan Police Area expanded and by 1900 covered almost 1,560sq km (600sq miles). Even greater was the London Transport Area created in 1933, stretching in the southwest as far as Horsham, 58km from London by road. In 1965, the Greater London Council commenced to administer an area of just over 1,550sq km, smaller than that of the Metropolitan Police who by then were responsible for at least another 260sq km. The words 'Greater London' were thus given a meaning as had been Metropolis over 100 years before. In 1970 the London Transport Area was reduced to coincide with that of the GLC.

A problem not confined to London is the difficulty of drawing a clear distinction between railways and tramways. Many early tramway undertakings described themselves as light railways while conventional railways have been known to collect fares on the train and to take up passengers other than at formal stations. Many rail ticket enthusiasts have found themselves led across this bridge into the world of tram tickets. The London area was served by many tramway companies and we propose to mention some of these.

The tramway era coincided with that of **Bell Punch** style tickets. The most informative group of tickets was the Fare Board type which set out the two limits of each permitted journey opposite each other; the conductor clipped the fare stage at which the passenger boarded and the passenger could travel as far as the stage named immediately opposite the punch hole. Thus it is always possible to tell from the ticket the direction in which the passenger was travelling. The Named Fare Stage ticket mentioned the various stages once only and the ticket was clipped at the stage to which the passenger could travel. There is no indication of the direction in which the car was travelling although if the journey ended near a terminus an intelligent guess can often be made. Tickets of either of these groups are often described as 'geographical'. In another group only the number of the fare stage is given and without an extensive background knowledge of the undertaking no detail of the journey can be deduced.

Transport historians tell us that many stretches of track started life as the offspring of an independent company, sometimes sponsored by local businessmen whose main concern was to acquire a line that would carry their goods. At other times an existing company was simply looking for profitable traffic. Usually the line would enjoy a period of nominal independence, even if run from the outset by a local main line company or group. During these early years its title may or may not have appeared on tickets. With jointly-run railways a heading bearing the name of a joint committee or management board might persist for many years. Additionally, there were cases of these 'joint' tickets themselves being jointly-titled with other railways and tramways. Such tickets are much sought-after by collectors. In recent years rare titles have fetched prohibitive prices at auction although it is fair to say that specimens from the London area are not among the most expensive.

The paragraphs that follow arrange a number of companies into a convenient alphabetical order. Together these could form the basis of a recommended 'London Collection', and no doubt readers will enjoy the challenge of adding further titles from the past and the ever changing present. A moderately determined collector who joins one or more of the various enthusiasts' societies and maintains a correspondence with fellow members should have little difficulty in obtaining representative tickets from 60% or 70% of such companies within four or five years.

We have striven to avoid turning this book into another transport history but some explanation must be given of the origin of the 'UndergrounD' heading. Each of the lines forming London's underground network began as an independent venture and the earliest tickets simply bore the name of the company. In July 1910 three companies — the Bakerloo, the Hampstead and the Piccadilly — combined under the title 'London Electric Railway' and this name soon found its way to the tickets. At about the same time, a larger but looser grouping more in the nature of a management committee was being brought together under the general supervision of Albert Stanley (later Lord Ashfield), and secured Parliamentary approval in 1915.

Despite its title UndergrounD, this group included not only the London Electric, the Central London, the City & South London and the District Railways (not the Metropolitan) but also the London General Omnibus Company and a number of tramway undertakings. Needless to say, the tickets of the bus and tramway concerns did not bear the new title but it began to appear on railway tickets in 1911.

Alexandra Park Electric Railway

Alexandra Park (containing Alexandra Palace) and Crystal Palace have much in common. Both were laid out in countryside in mid-19th century and became the two playgrounds of Victorian and Edwardian London, one to the north of the Metropolis and the other to the south. Crystal Palace saw Britain's first electric tramway in 1881, demonstrated for six months but no tickets have been seen. The Palace briefly saw electric traction again in 1911 at the time of the Festival of Empire (qv).

Alexandra Park hosted London's first tramway to take current from a cable. A short pleasure line was opened in May 1898 on a somewhat experimental basis and seems to have run until about September the following year. The only ticket seen is a blue roll type of simplistic design, cancelled in a bell-punch.

Baker Street & Waterloo Railway

An underground railway opened on 10 March 1906 from Baker Street to Kennington Road and soon extended to connect with the City & South London Railway at Elephant & Castle. Kennington Road was renamed Westminster Bridge Road and later became Lambeth North. The London *Evening News* coined the name 'Bakerloo' and this stuck. Tickets with the 'BStW' heading were used until 1910 when the railway amalgamated with the Piccadilly and the Hampstead lines to form the London Electric Railway. Although this led to a more or less standard ticket format, ticket colours remained diverse, the Bakerloo retaining blue and the Piccadilly and Hampstead their yellow and lilac colours respectively.

There were a number of through bookings to or via other railways with text suitably indicating the systems concerned (**211**). Those to stations on the City & South London Railway via Elephant & Castle were generally on white board with pink coloured bands and those to London & South Western stations via Waterloo were the LSW standard Third Class pink with two vertical black bars.

Barking Town Urban District Council Light Railways

This council operated tramways from December 1903 until 16 February 1929. Some short-lived joint arrangements existed with East Ham, West Ham and London County Council services, each with special ticket issues. Tickets generally were by J. R. Williams, and Glasgow Numerical Printing Company.

Belle Steamers

Worked a steamboat service from London Bridge to various East Coast points, including Clacton and Yarmouth. Return Tickets sometimes included a railway travel option. **212** shows a Midland Railway joint issue for the St Pancras-Ramsgate return trip using Third Class, and Fore Cabin on the boat.

Bexley (Urban District) Council Tramways

This system was principally a single long route from Bexleyheath via Welling to Plumstead. Tickets, printed by the Punch & Ticket Company, were issued up to August 1917 when the adjoining Dartford Light Railways became associated and the operating title changed to suit.

Bexley Council Tramways and Dartford Light Railways

The Bexley Council took over the running of the Dartford service as an emergency measure in 1917 (see Dartford entry) and the arrangement was formalised in 1921 by the creation of a joint Management Committee. The lines became part of the London Transport network in 1933.

British Rail(ways)

This is a wide-ranging label used to denote Britain's nationalised main network. Its exact constitution has changed a number of times giving rise to marked changes in tickets. The historical position has evolved as follows:

1 British Transport Commission 1 January 1948, operating through a series of Executives, of which The Railway Executive and London Transport Executive (I) were responsible for railways. In this book we have treated these Executives as separate entities, principally because their tickets have frequently been uniquely titled or identified in conditions of issue.

2 Abolition of all the Executives except that for London, 1 September 1953, and henceforth direct operation by the Commission, still on a regional basis with identifiers remaining as E(Eastern), M(London Midland), S(Southern) and W(Western). Other regions had no lines in London.

3 Abolition of the Commission 1 January 1963 and a new British Railways Board in charge. The Board retained the regional letter patterns and, with modifications, does so today. At the same date London Transport Executive became London Transport Board removing the last vestige of the Nationalisation Executives.

Central London Railway

This was the nucleus of the present far-flung Central Line of London's Tubes. The line was opened to the public in 1900 from Bank to Shepherd's Bush with a flat fare of 2d which lasted for

211

Baker Street & Waterloo Ry.
Oxford Circus TO ...
Fare

212

162
(London Agent)
Midland Railway & Belle Steamers
Available for one journey only during the Season.
RAMSGATE to LONDON (ST PANCRAS)
Fore Cabin & 3rd Cl.
(SEE BACK)
Midland Railway & Belle Steamers.
Available on day of issue only.
London (St. Pancras) to RAMSGATE
3rd. Cl. & Fore Cabin.
FARE 6s. 0d. (See back)
London Agent 162

213

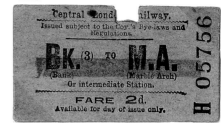

Central London Railway.
Issued subject to the Coy.'s Bye-laws and Regulations.
BK. (3) TO M.A.
(Bank) (Marble Arch)
Or intermediate Station.
FARE 2d.
Available for day of issue only.
H 05756

214

Central London Railway.
Issued subject to the Coy.'s Bye-laws and Regulations.
Wood Lane (1) TO BK.
(Shep. Bush) (Bank)
Or Intermediate Station.
FARE 3d.
Available for day of issue only.
A 54456

215

Central London Railway.
PRIVILEGE TICKET
Available for SEVEN DAYS including day of issue. Not Transferable.
Notting Hill Gate (1) to
ANY STATION ON District Railway
(BOW ROAD to HIGH ST. PUTNEY BDGE, EALING, HOUNSLOW or SOUTH HARROW)
London Electric Railway.
City & S. Lond. Rly. Cent. Lond. Rly.
3rd. Class FARE 1½d.
P 439 1-439

216

Central London & Baker Street & Waterloo Rlys.
SHEPHERDS BUSH (5) 14
WOOD LANE TO
ELEPHANT & CASTLE OR
15 WATERLOO 17
Or Intermediate Station
CHANGE AT OXFORD CIRCUS STATION
S.A. FARE 4d.
Available for day of issue only.
[See over]
7659 7659

217

C. L. R.
L.E.R. & L.G.O.C.
B Available day of issue only
Highgate TO
MUSWELL HILL (Broadway)
3rd. Class Fare 6d.
To be cancelled on 'BUS
Oxford Cir. (1)
20637

218

Charing Cross, Euston & Hampstead Rly.
CHALK FARM
TO (No. 1) 62
CHARING CROSS OR
50 COLDERS GREEN 66
(or any intermediate Station.)
FARE 2d. [SEE OVER.
4112 6

219

UNDERGROUND
Charing Cross, Euston & Hampstead Rly.
Issued subject to the Coy's Byelaws, Regulations and advertised conditions.
Available on day of issue only.
TOTTENHAM COURT ROAD
No. 1 TO
SOUTH KENTISH TOWN
or HIGHGATE
FARE 2d. or intermediately
9066 9066 108 108

220

City & South London Ry.
Issued subject to the Co's Regulations.
Available on day of issue only
ANGEL TO
WOOD LANE S.1
Change at Moorgate Via Bishop's Road
1st. Class on Met. Ry.
FARE 6d.
300 300

221

City & South Lond. Ry.
CHEAP DAY (SUNDAY)
Moorgate
Oxford Circus
Tottenham C't Rd
or intermediately
(1) TO
BALHAM
Not Transferable.
THIRD CLASS
(SEE BACK)
000 1

222

C. & S. L. R.
Issued subject to the Co's Regulations
R.E.C. VISIT TO S.3.
KING WILLIAM STREET
Platform Ticket 1d.
016 016

223

UNDERGROUND
CITY & SOUTH LONDON RAILWAY
11
Mr C. Herz
is entitled to travel between
BANK and CLAPHAM ROAD
AVAILABLE UNTIL
30 NOV. 13
NOT TRANSFERABLE
RATE £0 8s. 0d.
CANCELLED AT A.T. 13
SEASON TICKET.
NO. 321
THIS TICKET IS TO BE GIVEN UP ON EXPIRY.

224

C. & S.L. C.C.E. & H. Rys.
Ren. on day or day of Sat'rday, issue of or Issued subject to the Co's' Regulations.
Not Transferable.
Highgate S.1. TO
LONDON B'ge Subway
Change at Euston
Fare 8d.
4 4

225

C. & S.L. G.N. & C. & G.N. Rys.
Available only on day of issue.
See Conditions on back.
ELEPHANT & CASTLE
TO S.1
EAST FINCHLEY
Via Moorgate Subway & Finsbury Park
Fare THIRD CLASS Fare 7d.
734 734

226

C. & S. L. R. & L. B. & C. Rys.
Available on the Date of issue ONLY.
SEE CONDITIONS ON BACK
KING'S CROSS TO
FOREST HILL f.h.
Via London Bridge & Subway.
7½d. THIRD CLASS. 7½d.
0047 0047

London, showing underground and surface lines, buses and boats, all evidently happy with the standard card ticket.

about seven years, giving the affectionate nickname The 'Tuppenny Tube'. **213** and **214** are Singles, each with the company's typical 'lettered stations', and **215** a through Privilege Single mentioning two other local railways. **216** shows a Bakerloo Line (grey) specimen and **217** the portion of a Central London, London Electric and London General Omnibus Company joint-issue 'To be cancelled on the BUS'. Note the perforation created by a special punch supplied to the bus conductor. Other joint headings refer to Overground Limited and London United Tramways.

Charing Cross Euston & Hampstead Railway

This is now part of the Northern Line. When opened in June 1907, it comprised a line from Charing Cross (the present Embankment) to Golders Green and a branch from Camden Town to Highgate (the present Archway). Travel was free on the first day and attracted an estimated 140,000 passengers.

At first the railway used buff coloured station-to-station Edmondson cards. It shortly changed to all-white tickets with code numbers suffixed to the station names (**218**). The numbers were dropped after a few years. **219** is a later issue with the UndergrounD logo.

City & South London Railway

Opened 18 December 1890 to become the first of London's electric Tube Railways. The line today forms part of the Northern Line. The original line ran from King William Street to Stockwell but was later extended to Clapham Common and, in 1926, achieved Morden. At its other end it reached Euston. The earlier King William Street terminus was abandoned and tickets to or from that station are somewhat rare.

In the early days fares were collected at the entry turnstiles, with no receipt given. The first tickets were probably fourpenny returns sold at the same turnstiles. Earlier tickets did not indicate a class but the words '3rd Class' began to appear from about 1914. There were a number of through bookings to other lines and generally both company titles were printed on the ticket. **220** represents an interesting through journey to the Metropolitan station at Wood Lane with First Class travel on the latter company's tracks.

221 is the return half of a Sunday Cheap Day ticket of the early 1930s and is coloured blue-white-pink. **222** was not printed by the company; it is a souvenir of the Railway Enthusiasts' Club visit in 1957 to the long closed King William Street station. **223** is a white Season Ticket of 1913. The next four tickets all involve other companies. **224** is the return half of a journey over the rails of the then Charing Cross, Euston & Hampstead Railway. **225** represents a single trip on Christmas Day 1907 from Elephant & Castle to East Finchley, changing at Moorgate to the Great Northern & City Railway and again at Finsbury Park to take a Great Northern Railway steam train to East Finchley. Today, this journey can be made without change via Euston and Camden Town. **226** appears to have been a London Brighton & South Coast printing and as such a departure from the common practice that tickets be printed by their issuing company.

227 dates from June 1929. We have mentioned that the LGOC was part of the UndergrounD group. This facilitated the provision of through bookings by rail and bus. Here is the bus portion of a journey from Moorgate to Raynes Park in the heart of Southern Railway territory. The bus conductor would cancel the ticket with a special punch and hand it back to the passenger. Hence these 'bus halves' are seen more frequently than their railway portions.

Croydon Corporation Tramways

The Corporation entered the tramways field at the turn of the century when it took over the horse-drawn trams of the Croydon Tramways Company, leased the tracks to the British Electric Traction Company for a while and finally began operation themselves in June 1906. They provided a variety of tickets, including the 'Norwood' prints with their 1d cedar and 2d blue.

Interest mainly centres on the through services to London in co-operation with London County Council. Until 1926, both networks had tracks to the county boundary at Norbury and passengers had to change cars. In that year the final $1\frac{1}{2}$m of connecting rails were laid and both Croydon and London cars ran on the 16-18 Route. The significance of the two numbers was that few trams reversed on the busy Victoria Embankment: most crossed into North London by either Westminster or Blackfriars Bridge and returned south by the other. Route 16 from Purley and Croydon ran over Westminster Bridge and back across Blackfriars while the 18 took the opposite route. Croydon and London cars each carried their own tickets. **228** is a Croydon print by the Bell Punch Company of about 1926/7.

229 is a Bell Punch item bearing the titles of both Croydon and the South Metropolitan Tramways & Lighting Company printed for a journey between the Gloster Public House (well within the Croydon County Borough area) and Penge which then lay in Kent. Only the back of the final Croydon ticket (**230**) is shown; its interest lies in the advert for the South Eastern & Chatham Railway (which had a share in East Croydon station). The offer includes a day trip to Boulogne for 10/- (50p)!

Croydon & Norwood Tramways Company

A horse tramway which lasted from August 1883 until late in 1888, supplying its passengers with punch-type tickets printed by Whiting. It is believed (but unverified) that cancellation was by tearing away the ticket corners rather than punching!

Croydon & Oxted Line

Both the LBSC and the SE ran trains over the line from Selsdon Road station (renamed Selsdon in 1935 and closed in 1983) to a junction just beyond Hurst Green where the LBSC trains continued their way south. Those of the South Eastern joined the main line to Dover. The two companies shared the printing of the tickets and each included a 'Croydon and Oxted Line' or similar subtitle. **231** and **232** are both LBSC printings, the first being a buff and red First Return of 1901 and the other a blue and red Second Return of 1900.

Croydon Tramways Company

This company ran horse trams from 1879 until taken over by the Croydon Corporation in 1900. Earliest tickets were oversize cards of very simple design; Whiting prints followed. All CTC tickets seen have liberal punchmarks and snips perhaps indicating extensive attention by inspectors.

Dartford Light Railways

Tramways in the guise of 'Light Railways', operated on a main line from the Bexley boundary to Horns Cross, with a branch to Wilmington. In 1917 Dartford lost its entire fleet of cars in a disastrous fire. Working was taken over by Bexley Council in August 1917. Tickets are not common. One pattern seen is a white Bell Punch 1d geographical stating 'J. G. White & Co Ltd' as lessees.

227

B City & S. L. Ry & L. G. O. C
Available day of issue only.
South Wimbledon
TO
RAYNES PARK
OXFORD AVENUE
(Via Merton Park)
3rd Class Fare 6d.
Moorgate (1)

228

Cg 5700
D 3
16-18

Parker / Embankment
Royal Oak / Savoy St. Strand
Red Deer / Westminster Bridge road Short Route
Swan Croydon
Greyhound Croydon / Gt. Charlotte Street York Road or Christ Church Short Route
West Croydon Station / Elephant & Castle or Fitzalan St. Short Route
Mersey Road / Kennington Gate
Thornton Heath Pond
Warwick Road / Angel Road
Tylecroft Road / Brixton Stn. (Stockwell road or Acre Lane)
Norbury (Station or Hermitage Bdge) / Water Lane
Greyhound La Streatham / New Park Road
Streatham (or St. Leonard's Church) / Telford Avenue

Bell Punch Company, Uxbridge.

229

Nc 4300

CROYDON CORPORATION TRAMWAYS AND THE SOUTH MET. ELECTRIC TRAMS & LIGHTING Co., LTD.
Fare   G. & P.   Fare
3d Through Ticket 3d
Available only on Car on which over the lines of the Croydon Corporation Tramways and the South Metropolitan Electric Tramways in the section punched. Must be shown or given up on demand. Issued subject to Bye-laws.

| Gloster and Penge | Penge and Gloster |

Bell Punch Company

230

S. E. & C. RAILWAY.
From EAST CROYDON STATION.
Cheap Excursion Facilities during the Summer Season to the South-East Coast.

| RETURN FARES | Half-Day 2/6 | Long Period 8 or 15 Days 7/3 | Whole Day 3/- | Monthly 10/- |

Sunday Excursion to Boulogne 10/- June to Sept.
'Phone or Call:
112a, GEORGE ST., CROYDON (Tel. 405)
FRANCIS H DENT, General Manager.

231

0231
L. B. & S. C. RY.
Croydon & Oxted Line
This half available for 8 Days including Date of issue and return.
See conditions at bar
VICTORIA TO
OXTED
First Cl. 5s. 10d

232

1455
L. B. & S. C. RY.
Croydon & Oxted Line
Wednesday Cheap Ticket.
Available on the Date of issue ONLY. SEE BACK
LONDON [London Bridge or Victoria] (*)
OXTED
SECOND CL. 3s. 0d.

233

1122
DISTRICT RAILWAY
Available for day of issue only.
VICTORIA (D.R.)
TO
ROYAL OAK
Series 2
VIA SOUTH KENSINGTON & ADDISON ROAD
6d SECOND CLASS 6d
Not available Via High St. (Kensington)
ROYAL OAK
1122

234

4434
DISTRICT RAILWAY.
Available on day of issue only.
Westminster
TO
MARK LANE
ORDINARY CAR (3rd Class) FARE 2d
4434

235

1970
DISTRICT RAILWAY
Available for day of issue only.
HIGH STREET (Kensington)
TO
VICTORIA (D.R.)
Series 1
VIA SLOANE SQUARE
4d FIRST CLASS 4d
1970

236

0000
District & G. E. Rys.
Tourist Ticket.
[Lowestoft]
For conditions see back
WEST KENSINGTON
TO
LOWESTOFT
Via Mansion House [Dist] & Liverpool St [G.E.] Stations.
[W Kensington] THIRD
0000

237

6530
DISTRICT & G. N. & B. RLYS
Available on day of issue only.
Hammersmith
TO
BARONS COURT
ORDINARY CAR (3rd Class) FARE 1d
6530

238

THIRD CLASS   via Oxford Circus   ONE MONTH
UNDERGROUND District and London Electric Railways.
AVAILABLE BETWEEN
St. James Park AND Notting Hill Gate
Via CHARING CROSS AND L. E. RAILWAY
UNTIL 12 JUL 1918
SUBJECT TO CONDITIONS SHOWN ON OTHER SIDE HEREOF.
RATE £ : 13 : 2
EC 4
No

239

966
DISTRICT RLY & L. G. O. C.
Available day of issue only.
Hammersmith
TO
BARNES
Red Lion or Sun Inn
3rd Class Fare 5
To be cancelled on 'B'
Charing Cross (1)

240

3064
DISTRICT RLY & LONDON United Tramways
Charing Cross
to TURNHAM GN.
3rd Class on District Ry
Single Fare 3d
To be given up at
HAMMERSMITH ST.
3064

241

3 277
D. 5
MONUMENT
TO (2)
BOW ROAD. (Via Mark L. & Mile End)
VICTORIA. (Via Temple)
FARRINGDON STREET. (Via Mark Lane)
ANGEL OLD STREET. (Via Mark Lane & change Moorgate)
SHOREDITCH (E.L.) (Via Mark Lane & change Whitechapel)
ROTHERHITHE. (Via Mark Lane & change St. Mary's or W'chapel)
or intermediately
MONUMENT (2)
5
D. 5 CLASS Available day of issue only.
3 277
District & Met. Rys.
Issued subject to the Coy, Byelaws, Regulations & advertised Conditions.

242

5916
EAST LONDON RAILWAY
Joint Committee.
WAPPING to
DEPTFORD ROAD
1d Third Class 1d
Issued subject to Regulations in respective Companies' Time Tables.
Deptford Rd.   Deptford Rd.
55916

243

3087
EAST LONDON RY.
JOINT COMMITTEE
SHADWELL
3rd Cl   (1)
2d to
SURREY DOCKS
SHOREDITCH
ALDGATE EAST (direct)
BOW ROAD (change Whitechapel or St. Mary's)
or intermediately
Issued subject to Bye-Laws, Regulations and advertised Conditions of the Committee. Available day of issue only.
2d (1)
SHADWELL
3087

244

8040
East London & Metropolitan Rys.
Available on the DATE of issue ONLY.
This Ticket is issued subject to the Regulations & Conditions stated in the Company's Time Tables & Bills.
NEW CROSS
Series 20   [Series 20
TO
LIVERPOOL STREET [MET]
VIA ALDGATE EAST.
3d. THIRD CLASS. 3d.
8040

More underground and main lines, to which are added tramways and buses. Examples of the Scheme Ticket and the better known punch-type so often found with an imprint of the Bell Punch Company.

245

E.L. & L.B. & S.C. RYS
H.D.M.P. 18th Aug 87
WHITECHAPEL ETC.
to BRIGHTON
SHOREHAM &
WORTHING
THIRD CLASS
[SEE BACK]
0614

246

EXCURSION TO RYE HOUSE AND GARDENS
BY THE
EASTERN COUNTIES RAILWAY,
On MONDAY, 16th of JULY, 1855.

TICKETS, THERE AND BACK, 2s. 6d. EACH,
INCLUDING ADMISSION TO THE BALL ROOM.
A Quadrille Band and Masters of the Ceremonies are engaged.

1559 Special Trains will leave the Bishopsgate Station, Shoreditch,
at a quarter before and at 10 o'clock in the Morning—
returning from Rye House at half-past 8 in the Evening.

247

SEE BACK.
Return Fare 2d
(See Back)
Wg 4981
Market Place
Bexley Heath and
Carlton Road
Barnehurst
Bridge and
Top of Pier Road
Northumberland
Heath and
Ballast Wharf
Carlton Road
and
Mayfield Road
Top of Pier Road
and Belvedere
Station
Ballast Wharf
and
Railway Farm
Mayfield Road
and
Abbey Wood

248

FESTIVAL
PLEASURE PARK
EMETT RAILWAY
1/-
SINGLE
156220

249

GREAT CENTRAL RAILWAY
Issued subject to the Regulations and Conditions in
the Company's Time Tables Books Bills and Notices
ON DATE OF ISSUE ONLY
LONDON (Marylebone)
TO
HIGH WYCOMBE
FIRST CLASS
London M   4/-   London M
High Wycombe   High Wycombe
30 JA 07   0711

250

GREAT CENTRAL RAILWAY.
ON DATE OF ISSUE ONLY.
LONDON (Marylebone)
TO
HUDDERSFIELD
via Penistone
THIRD CLASS
CHILD.
SEE CONDITIONS ON BACK. FARE 7/7
24 AP 08   340

251

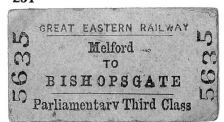

GREAT EASTERN RAILWAY
Melford
TO
BISHOPSGATE
Parliamentary Third Class
5635   5635

252

G.E.R.   G.E.R.
Half-Day Excursion
RETURN TICKET.
LIVERPOOL St [EM]   LIVERPOOL St [EM]
TO
CLACTON-on-SEA & Back
For return Train see Excursion Bill.
Clacton   THIRD CLASS   Clacton.
FOR CONDITIONS SEE BACK.
4703   4703

253

G.E.R.   G.E.R.
Issued subject to Regu-   Issued subject to Regu-
lations in Co's Time Tables   lations in Co's Time Tables
CLAPTON   LIVERPOOL St
TO   TO
LIVERPOOL St   CLAPTON
Available only on the   Available only on the
WEDNESDAY   WEDNESDAY
in the week ending   in the week ending
JUNE 20th 1908   JUNE 20th 1908
THIRD   THIRD
Not Transferable.   Not Transferable.
0453   0453

The art of the
typographer combines
with inventiveness of the
draughtsman.

254

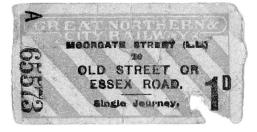

GREAT NORTHERN &
CITY RAILWAY
MOORGATE STREET (L.L.)
TO
OLD STREET OR
ESSEX ROAD.
Single Journey.
1D
A 6573

255

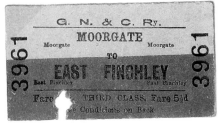

G. N. & C. Ry.
MOORGATE
Moorgate   Moorgate
TO
EAST FINCHLEY
East Finchley   East Finchley
Fare   THIRD CLASS, Fare 5½d
See Conditions on Back
3961   3961

256

G.N. & C. RLY
Workman's Ticket
MOORGATE
TO
FINSBURY PK. (L.L)
Available for RETURN
JOURNEY on day of
issue only.
Return Fare - 2d
SEE OVER
56649

District Railway

The Metropolitan District Railway opened the day before Christmas 1868, with its title popularly shortened to District Railway. This form appeared, variously further abbreviated, on most tickets. Throughout its history, the company worked closely with the Metropolitan Railway. The full title was mostly confined to Season Tickets, many large paper tickets and, when part of a joint title with the London United Tramways, as space occasionally permitted. In Edmondson cards there was invariably some form of abbreviation.

233 is an 1899 Second Class Single, blue with the red Circle Line overprint (cf 339 of the London Tilbury & Southend). **234** is a green Third Single of c1900. **235** comes from 1906, First Class, buff with the red Inner Circle overprint and the letter 'V' as a quick destination identifier.

Six tickets display a selection of joint titles. **236** was for a 1906 trip out of London as far as Lowestoft on the Great Eastern Railway. Note that the original white and red ticket was issued by the GE's Lowestoft station and therefore this homeward portion was the righthand coupon. **237** is joint with the Piccadilly company, plain deep green and dated 1910. **238** is a white and green London Electric joint issue Season Ticket from the summer of 1918. **239** is a bright red 'bus half-Edmondson joint with the LGOC issued c1920. **240**, another half-Edmondson this one green, is dated 1902 and joint with LUT. It represents the rail part of the journey and unlike the tram part, should have been surrendered at Hammersmith. The sixth ticket here is **241**, white, joint with the Met and a full Scheme Ticket print for First Class.

East Ham Urban District Council Tramways

Opened in June 1901, it was one of the very earliest London area municipal lines. Some through routes ran across West Ham and the adjoining LCC system. Tickets were by the Bell Punch, and later the Punch & Ticket Companies, and included both named and numbered stage types.

East London Railway

Marc Brunel (1769-1849) completed the first tunnel under the River Thames in 1843. It was the end of a 40-year saga. Robert Vazie had published a plan for such a tunnel in 1802, Parliamentary powers were obtained in 1805 and three years later Richard Trevithick drove 350m before the river broke in. Brunel commenced work in 1824 but chronic lack of funds and repeated deaths among the workforce caused it to take a further 19 years. It catered for pedestrians only and in the event few cared to use it.

In 1865 the East London Railway Company was incorporated to build a double track through the tunnel and trains began to run from Wapping (**242**) on the north bank to New Cross (now New Cross Gate) on the south on 7 December 1869. Over the next 10 years various minor extensions and spurs were built, the most important being an extension northwards to Shoreditch (**243**) where it could connect with the Great Eastern main line into Liverpool Street.

It thus became one of the few routes connecting North and South London and was first served by LBSC trains from Croydon. SE trains followed in 1880 but the Metropolitan and District Railways were also interested and commenced a service in 1884. The GE joined the struggle for passengers in 1886. The line was electrified in 1913 and trains were henceforth provided only by the Metropolitan. London Transport took over in 1933.

Such a history has ensured a wealth of variety to delight the ticket enthusiast. Earlier tickets are likely to be headed 'East London Railway' with 'Company' only mentioned in the conditions of issue, while later ones refer to the 'Joint Committee'.

Through bookings to Southern Railway points, though normally headed with an East London title were likely to be of any style from 'pure' LT to 'straight' SR in appearance. A few surprising hybrid designs have also appeared from time to time.

Jointly-headed specimens include those of LBSC-style from New Cross to Metropolitan stations (**244**), and the more distant bookings such as **245** through to Brighton, Shoreham or Worthing, in Sussex. The former is clearly from the Joint Committee era, while the latter, dated 1887, bears a good deal of Company legacy (See also **23**).

Eastern Counties Railway

This was an 1862 constituent of the Great Eastern Railway. A 'blank-to-blank' Monthly Pass dated 1859 has been seen. It is large, blue in colour and completed for journeys between London and Stratford. Here we show a very early Excursion Ticket (**246**) of 1855, in which the text tells its own tale. Note the lingering practice of a handwritten serial number '1559'.

Erith Urban District Council Tramways

This isolated system started carrying fare-paying passengers in 1905. Its principal route ran from Abbey Wood to Northumberland Heath and Bexleyheath. Erith tickets seem to have been exclusively by the Punch & Ticket Company. One unique practice was the selling of *two* Workman Tickets in the morning hours (except Saturdays) to each passenger who required to travel home in his lunchbreak at Workman rates. One was for immediate use on the outward trip and the other, identical but punched in a special panel, for use on the midday journey (**247**). Elsewhere, this would almost certainly have been met by a ticket for FOUR journeys or a so-called 'Double Return'.

Festival of Empire All-Red Line

Here was a purely temporary electric railway installed in the grounds of Crystal Palace in 1911. The Festival's 'All-Red Line' ran between the pavilions of the various participating countries and these gave their names to its seven stopping places. A 6d ticket from Canada Station on a large green roll by Williamson was typical.

Festival Pleasure Park — Emett Railway

The 1951 Festival of Britain was conceived as an invigorating tonic for the people after their recent wartime austerity and as a centennial commemorating Prince Albert's Great Exhibition of 1851. (Officialdom may consider these aims transposed!). There was an entirely 'serious' group of exhibitions on the South Bank site near Waterloo Bridge and other, some would say frivolous, facilities in Battersea Park, up river. Of these latter, was this Emett Railway, which, in spite of its humorous-associations, was physically a genuine railway. Leaflets advertised the line as the 'Far Tottering & Oyster Creek Line'.

Tickets were at first untitled **Automatickets** (also see Chapter 2), but after the exhibition closed, the railway survived as a small business until 1954, using titled tickets as illustrated by **248**. This 1/- blue matched a 6d yellow sold to children.

General Steam Navigation Company

A company in business from 1824 to 1963 with services between London Bridge and Kent and Essex resorts with some cruises to nearby Continental ports. It was a cheap but slow form of transport (in 1938 a day trip to Ramsgate permitted 25min ashore) and ships returned to London late at night. Some excursions gave the passenger the option of disembarking at Tilbury and completing the journey by rail and this was reflected in the wording of several of the tickets.

Gravesend Ferry

A ferry over the River Thames from Tilbury and owned originally by the London Tilbury & Southend Railway. Tickets of c1911 were Edmondsons in LTS-style, but titled with just the above two words. These were in unusual colours, examples being Tilbury-Gravesend pale blue and pale pink, Gravesend-Tilbury yellow and bright blue. Workman Returns were green and grey respectively.

After the Grouping of 1923 there were ordinary green LMS prints, though often with the legend 'Ferry Ticket'. When Nationalisation came along, BR (Eastern Region) tickets were issued from Tilbury, but Gravesend, being south of the river came under The Railway Executive's Southern Region.

Gravesend & Northfleet Electric Tramways

This line failed by less than 4km to connect with the Dartford system at Horns Cross. Closure came in February 1929 so that the company did not need to be considered in the LPTB amalgamations of 1933. Tickets were typical Bell Punch products, earlier geographicals eventually gave way to numbered stage types. An unusual ¾d adult fare geographical stage print is known. Other tickets included large weekly cards printed by Auto-Tickets Limited.

Great Central Railway

The former Manchester Sheffield & Lincolnshire Railway took the above name in August 1897. The company was grouped into the London & North Eastern Railway in 1923, but upon Nationalisation in 1948 there were difficulties in deciding its destiny. Portions have at different times gone to the Eastern, London Midland and Western Regions of British Rail, while the Met & GC (see Chapter 12) went to the London Transport Executive almost outright.

Great Central stations in pre-Grouping days had their own fairly distinctive style of tickets and adopted the LNER standards after Grouping. Two Marylebone issues are illustrated: **249** is a 1907 local London First Class Single, and **250**, a more distant Third Single for a child the following year. Colourings respectively are plain white, and green with a white panel (the child fare designation).

Great Eastern Railway

The Great Eastern was a major pre-Grouping railway company running into London's Liverpool Street and Fenchurch Street termini. It became part of the LNER in 1923.

Tickets were a little exceptional in that originally separate colours were used for the Up and Down directions — eg Third Class green Up and buff Down. Another departure from normal British practice was that the homeward or return portion of a two-coupon card ticket was printed on the right. From about 1914 onwards colours were gradually standardised in favour of those formerly for Down journeys, the return coupons moved over to the left, and instead of being of a distinctive colour took a black diagonal line or stripe. The few exceptions included bookings via the Woolwich Ferry which had three vertical black lines and tickets to St Pancras carrying a horizontal red band.

Here the illustrations are of an 1872 Parliamentary Third (**251**) for a journey into London; and two 1908 tickets, namely **252** an Excursion one-coupon return to Clacton-on-Sea, and **253** from Clapton available on the Wednesday of the week ending 20 June 1908. The latter would be one of a batch of six tickets sold together on the Monday morning of that week.

Great Northern & City Railway

This company opened between Finsbury Park and Moorgate in 1904, and was purchased by the Metropolitan Railway in June 1913. London Passenger Transport Board took control in 1933.

The railway had differential fares from the start. Nevertheless, there was a 2d 'all-the-way' roll ticket very similar to some from the Central London and Bakerloo companies. Other soft roll types included various 1d issues with a background of oblique coloured stripes (**254**) and Returns double in size (with a curious American flavour). Edmondsons were adopted later, some with numerical and colour codes for their stations of origin, destination, or both. When the Met took control they introduced their own familiar styles and First Class facilities. Edmondson cards are represented here by **255** from Moorgate, and **256**, a 1919 Workman's Ticket for a trip between the two termini.

Great Northern Piccadilly & Brompton Railway

This railway (the present Piccadilly Line) opened from Finsbury Park to Hammersmith 15 December 1906, partly in the Tube and partly open to the sky. Four years later the company was renamed London Electric Railway and took in the Bakerloo and Hampstead railways (qv).

Edmondson tickets and differential fares were applied from the start. A code of 13 varieties identified the destination. Where the colour had to be repeated, the sequence was retained but an overprinted red band was added (**257**). **258** was issued for a through trip on to the London United Tramways just a few months after the railway opened. Note the joint heading on a card which states 'To be exchanged on the tramcar' and which had three blue lines (representing three stages on the tram from Hammersmith) overprinted on a plain green coupon, the railway half of which was red. The third illustration shows one of the final patterns, a yellow ticket (**259**) with stations stated in full (the earlier white ones indicated stations by initials only), and the familiar UndergrounD logo in black. This style continued some while into the days of the London Electric title.

Great Northern Railway

The main line northwards from King's Cross. Opened in March 1848 and grouped into the London & North Eastern Railway in 1923.

For a very long time the company's Third Class tickets were an unusually dark blue, with the child's fare version overprinted by a red line (also an unusual feature). The company's London lines provided a good many peculiarities for the ticket hobbyist. Certain issues between GN and Metropolitan Railway points were headed 'G.N.R.', with no mention of the Met and in normal GN styles and colouring, but with three vertical red lines added. A nicety was the use on some tickets of the legend 'The Great Northern Railway Company's King's Cross Station', a somewhat long-winded but evidently then fashionable way of avoiding confusion with the smaller company's station. Further specialities were cards through to the Great Northern & City Railway coloured green and buff and frequently given the destination suffix '(Tube Station)'. A red star overprinted on some blue Third Class cards for through Tube bookings was another exceptional feature which continued some time into Grouping days. Some Return Tickets with a half-fare snip panel carried a station-of-origin code number, a practice adopted by the later LNER company. This would perhaps be

257

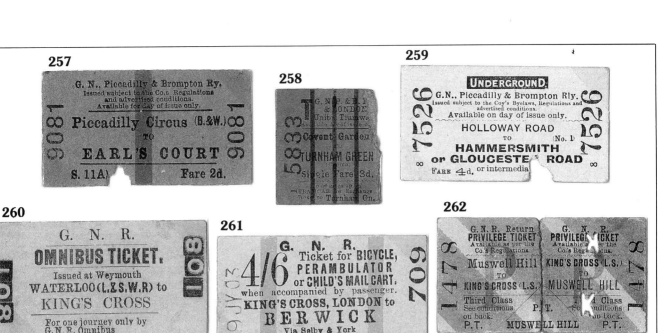

G. N., Piccadilly & Brompton Ry.
Issued subject to the Co.s Regulations
and advertised conditions.
Available for day of issue only.

Piccadilly Circus (B.&W.)
TO
EARL'S COURT
S. 11A)   Fare 2d.
9081   9081

258

G. N. P. & B. & LONDON
United Tramwa
Covent Garden
TURNHAM GREEN
Single Fare 3d.
TRAMCAR or Exchange
Ticke to Turnham Gn.
5833

259

UNDERGROUND
G. N., Piccadilly & Brompton Rly.
Issued subject to the Coy's Byelaws, Regulations and
advertised conditions.
Available on day of issue only.
HOLLOWAY ROAD
TO
HAMMERSMITH (No. 1)
or GLOUCESTER ROAD
FARE 4d.   or intermedia
7526   7526

260

G. N. R.
OMNIBUS TICKET.
Issued at Weymouth
WATERLOO (L.&S.W.R) to
KING'S CROSS
For one journey only by
G. N. R. Omnibus
1108

261

G. N. R.
4/6   Ticket for BICYCLE,
PERAMBULATOR
or CHILD'S MAIL CART,
when accompanied by passenger.
KING'S CROSS, LONDON to
BERWICK
Via Selby & York
SEE CONDITIONS ON BACK.
29 JY 03   709

262

G. N. R. Return
PRIVILEGE TICKET
Available as per the
Co's Regulations.
Muswell Hill
TO
KING'S CROSS (L.S.)
Third Class
See conditions
on back.
P.T.   P.T.
MUSWELL HILL

G. N. R.
PRIVILEGE TICKET
Available as per the
Co's Regulations.
KING'S CROSS (L.S.)
TO
MUSWELL HILL
Third Class
See conditions
on back.
P.T.
1478   1478

263

G. N. R. Return
Available day of issue only
For one journey only,
CITY ALBION
ATHLETIC CLUB.
Winchmore Hill
MOORGATE ST.
(L. W. A?)
Third Class
See conditions
on back.   386
WINGHM   C.A.
8723

264

KING'S CROSS
7
AND
GORDON HILL
AVAILABLE UNTIL
31 JULY 1914
HOLDER OF TICKET
Mr. Sommerfeld
THIRD CLASS   THIRD CLASS

265

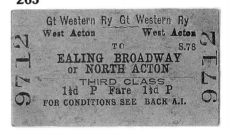

Gt Western Ry   Gt Western Ry
West Acton   West Acton
TO   S.78
EALING BROADWAY
or NORTH ACTON
THIRD CLASS
1½d P Fare 1½d P
FOR CONDITIONS SEE BACK A.I.
9712   9712

266

Gt. Western Ry.
ROYAL OAK TO   S.30
NORTH EALING
NORTHFIELDS
(Change Hammersmith)
CLAPHAM SOUTH
(Change Padd'n or Baker St
& Waterloo or
Elephant& Castle)
HENDON CENTRAL
(Change Euston Sq.
& via Warren St.)
EAST FINCHLEY
CRANLEY GARDENS
Change Euston Sq. & via
Warren St. or Ch'ge Kings X)
TURNPIKE LANE
(Change Kings X)
SHOREDITCH
ROTHERHITHE
BOW ROAD
(Direct via Aldgate East)
or INTERMEDIATELY
3rd Cls. FARE 8d C
FOR CONDITIONS SEE BACK
5111   5111

267

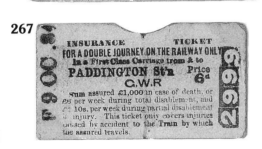

INSURANCE   TICKET
FOR A DOUBLE JOURNEY ON THE RAILWAY ONLY
In a First Class Carriage from & to
PADDINGTON St'n   Price
G.W.R   6d
Sum assured £1,000 in case of death, or
£6 per week during total disablement, and
£3 10s. per week during partial disablement
by injury. This ticket only covers injuries
caused by accident to the Train by which
the assured travels.
F900.8?   2999

268

Gt. Western Ry.
CHEAP TICKET
WEEK END
For day and by train
Shown on Bills & Notices
MARLOW
TO
Paddington (1)
Via Maidenhead
Second Class 4/9
WL   SEE BACK

Gt. Western Ry.
CHEAP TICKET
WEEK END
For day and by train
Paddington (1)
TO
MARLOW
Via Maidenhead
Second Class 4/9
WL   SEE BACK
4693   4693

269

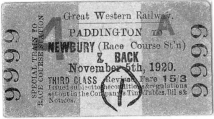

Great Western Railway.
PADDINGTON TO
NEWBURY (Race Course St'n)
& BACK
November 5th, 1920.
THIRD CLASS   Revised Fare 15/3
Issued subject to the conditions & regulations
set out in the Company's Time Tables, Bil s &
Notices.
SPECIAL TRAIN TO RACE COURSE STATION
9999   9999

270

Gt. Western Ry.   Western Ry.
ROYAL OAK   ROYAL OAK
TO   (S. 4)
NOTTING HILL   (& LADBROKE GROVE)
2d   SECOND CLASS   2d
Issued subject to the conditions & regu-
lations set out in the Company's Time
Tables Books & Bills.   (U)
NOTTING HILL & L.G   NOTTING HILL & L.G
4005

271

B 00492
S.6
GREAT WESTERN RAILWAY
Issued at North Acton
Receipt for
EXCESS FARE
WORKMAN
3d
WOOD LANE (C.L.)
TO
NORTH ACTON
AND BACK

272

G.W.R. Cheap Return
For day of issue by
trains as advertised
Charing Cross
(Change Tottenham Ct Rd
or Oxford Circus.)
or INTERMEDIATELY
Via East Acton to
EALING Broadway
3rd. Class S.35
Available for Return to
Ealing Broadway (Dist)
FOR CONDITIONS

G.W.R Cheap Ticket
For day of issue by
trains as advertised
Ealing Broadway
Via East Acton to
CHARING CROSS
(Change Oxford Circus
or Tottenham Ct Rd)
or INTERMEDIATELY
3rd. Class S.35
SEE BACK   W. H
885   885

Still in London — on buses,
main line and underground
rails — collecting cheap,
weekly, excess, privilege and
ordinary fares.

273

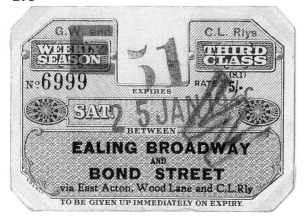

274

275

276

277

282

278

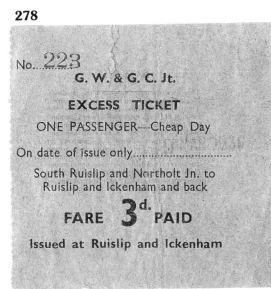

279

280

281

283

285

284

The 'banknote-style' of the
Great Western Season to the
somewhat complex half-penny
geographical punch-type.
Simplicity in 1864, Cheap
Fares in 1897 and overstamped
'W(oman)' in the 1930s.

expected to start at the number 1 for King's Cross but in fact it took the number 4 allowing, we surmise, for points between that station and Moorgate on the Metropolitan line.

260, a fine yellow 1903 card was issued 'down south' at Weymouth for use on a horse-bus plying between the arrival station Waterloo and second departure point at King's Cross (see also notes given for **25** in Chapter 1). **261**, also dated 1903 permitted a Bicycle, Perambulator or Child's Mailcart to be carried all the way to Berwick for 4/6d (23p today). **262** is a Privilege Ticket of 1905 — blue with white diagonal stripes and red overprinted letter 'P'. **263** suggests that in 1906 members of the City Albion Athletic Club enjoyed a special rate to and from Winchmore Hill. Colouring is white with a large green central spot (think of a medicine ball!), while **264** is a fine bright yellow Season Ticket from July 1914.

Great Western Railway

Many people think of the GW in London simply as Paddington station with two main routes leading one to the northwest and the other to the southwest. In fact it owned or shared ownership of many tracks and stations served by the Metropolitan, West London, West London Extension and Central London Railways, and as landlord often printed and dictated the format of the tickets they sold.

During the first years after opening, Metropolitan Railway stations sold GW-style tickets, although during the days when tickets for journeys over part of the Inner Circle carried either an 'O' (Clockwise — Outer) or 'I' (Anti-clockwise — Inner) overprint, the appropriate designation appeared on the otherwise pure GW-style ticket. Some bookings from GW-owned stations to UndergrounD destinations carried a black skeleton overprint on the left, eg CH for Hampstead, BW for Bakerloo and PB for the Piccadilly lines.

Passengers travelling from stations on the Central Line between Shepherd's Bush and Ealing Broadway received conventional GW tickets (like **265** sold as late as 25 January 1947) but with the extension of the Scheme Ticket by the LPTB in the 1930s, the GW produced many in similar style (**266** carries the normal GW conditions on its reverse side). One concession to London Transport was the printing of Privilege Tickets to LT stations in contemporary green and purple colours.

Alone among the Big Four, the GW retained the corporate name it had enjoyed before Grouping. There was thus an unbroken life for the company's title for 113 years between its incorporation in 1835 and absorption in 1948. It had no need to print new tickets in 1923 and waited until about 1934, when it rather casually altered the colour of its Third Class from buff to green (formerly used for Parliamentary Class). It is probably fair to say that the standard of printing achieved by the Great Western for its tickets has never been surpassed and perhaps not even elsewhere achieved. In addition to the quality there was also a wide variety of categories and colours. Sadly, only a tiny selection can be reproduced here.

267, of 1889, is a yellow Insurance Ticket giving £6 per week to its First Class holder in case of total disablement. The rather quaint wording explains that the cover is only for an accident to the train! **268** would have taken its holder for a weekend in 1902 for just 4/9d (24p). The enthusiast does well to suspect that any pre-dated Excursion Ticket with a number ending with three or four nines is either a printer's proof or a copy sent to station staff for information. However, **269** at least tells us that any racegoer of 1920 could have travelled on Guy Fawkes Day to Newbury on presentation of a similar blue and white ticket; **270** is a Second

Class ticket between two stations on the Paddington to Hammersmith line.

271 is an unusual wartime Workman's Excess Fare, pre-printed with both the return fare and the journey. **272** is another wartime issue whose purchaser back in 1941 was entitled to travel from Ealing Broadway to Charing Cross over the Central Line route with a change at either Oxford Circus or Tottenham Court Road. He could have gone direct on a District Line train and one wonders whether he was tempted to cheat!

The Great Western entered into arrangements for joint working in London with at least six companies, producing more interesting tickets. **273** carries the initials of both the GW and Central London companies. It was in fact valid only over the GW-owned line to Shepherd's Bush and CL track from there to Bank. This item demonstrates the artistic safety background designed for the company by Messrs de la Rue in the early 1930s. After 1933, the heading on these tickets was changed to reflect the new LPTB joint-owners.

As joint lessee of the West London Railway (also see separate entry) with the London & North Western (LMS from 1923) and one-third owner of the West London Extension Railway (also later), the GW produced tickets for sale at the various stations. **274** represents a somewhat roundabout journey from Chelsea on the Extension Railway to Farringdon Street on the Metropolitan in 1867 by Parliamentary Class.

Arrangements were made with the Great Central for joint ownership of tracks northwest of Northolt and this produced not only GW printings (**275**) but also Great Central (**276**) and then LNER printings (**277**). **278** is an interesting Excess Return issued at Ruislip barrier to a passenger from the presumably sometimes unstaffed South Ruislip.

The association with the Metropolitan Railway has already been noted. It was particularly important in the case of the Paddington to Hammersmith Line. Opened in 1863, it was served only by Great Western trains for the first three years and then the Met took over. The tickets were generally headed 'GW & M Rys' (**279**) or later with the word 'Joint' added (**280**); **279** was sold in 1867 and is interesting as being from a West London station to one in which the Met was interested; **280** is a white 1900 issue demonstrating the 'I' and 'O' used for Circle Lines.

Harrow Road & Paddington Tramways Company

Opened in 1888, this was a horse tramway sold to the Metropolitan Electric Tramways in 1902. The new owners abandoned part and electrified the rest. Tickets inspected include several with distinct North Metropolitan appearance — particularly a 2d blue by Bell Punch.

Herne Bay Steamboat Company

Like many other steamer companies formerly operating on the Thames, this one issued through tickets via Tilbury Pier to the former London Tilbury & Southend Railway.

Highgate & Hampstead Cable Tramways Ltd

A 1.067m gauge line of almost 2km length up Highgate Hill opened on 27 May 1884. The line closed following a serious accident in December 1892. Tickets were by Whiting. The ones seen are 1d white for one stage up or all the way down, and 2d purple (**281**) for all the way up.

Ilford Urban District Council Tramways

Opened in March 1903. Tickets were mostly, perhaps even exclusively geographicals by Punch & Ticket Company and Bell

286

Insurance Ticket
FOR A DOUBLE JOURNEY ON THE RAILWAY ONLY
IN A PASSENGER CARRIAGE FROM & TO
London Bridge St'n Price 2d.
(ML) LB&SCR
Sum assured £200 in case of death, or
£1 5s. per week during total disablement,
and 6s. 3d. per week during partial disablement by injury. This Ticket only covers
injuries caused by accident to the Train
by which the Assured travels. (See Over)

5364

287

0370

L. B. & S. C. RY.
TICKET FOR BICYCLE.
When accompanied by passenger.
EAST CROYDON TO
Victoria.V.
RATE 6d.
This ticket must be given up on arrival.
FOR CONDITIONS SEE BACK

0370

288

1901

L. B. & S. C. Rwy.
LONDON SUNDAY SCHOOL.
22nd JUNE 1904.
KENSINGTON TO
C. PALACE & BACK
INCLUDING ADMISSION
THIRD CLASS. ADULT or CHILD
[SEE BACK

1901

289

0053

L. B. & S. C. RY. | L. B. & S. C. RY.
Issued subject to condi- | Issued subject to condi-
tions in Co's Time Tables | tions in Co's Time Tables
LONDON B'DGE | TULSE HILL
TO | TO
TULSE HILL | LONDON BRIDGE
Available on the | Available on the
SATURDAY | SATURDAY
in the week ending | in the week ending
JULY 31st 1909. | JULY 31st 1909.
THIRD CLASS. | THIRD CLASS.

0053

290

0182

L. B. & S. C. RY.
Excursion, EXCESS TICKET.
Available on the Date of issue ONLY.
SEE CONDITIONS AT BACK.
ARUNDEL TO
LONDON [LONDON BRIDGE or VICTORIA.]
1s 0d. THIRD CLASS. 1s. 0d.
Available on SUNDAY or MONDAY.

0182

291

7565

L. B. & S. C. & D. Rys.
Available for day issue
or following or if
issued on Saturday to
following Monday
Hammersmith D R
2) U TO S.1
NEW CROSS
Via West Kensington
Temple & St. Mary's
Third Class 1.0
Not available Via
High St. (Kensington)

292

3533

L. C. & D. R.
HERNE HILL
TO
KING'S ✠
Metropolitan Co's Station
Third Class 7d.
(SEE OTHER SIDE) KING'S X (Met)

3533

293

6237

L. C. & D. R.
ONE SHILLING DAY.
Including Admission
C. Palace (High)
(S. 47.) T.
VICTORIA
Third Class
1s 6d
Available to return by
the Brighton Co's line

294

2778

L. C. & D. R.
RETURN
Ludgate Hill
(S. 83) TO
BRIXTON
Third Class.
6d
See Other Side.

8778

L. C. & D. R.
Brixton
TO (S. 83)
LUDGATE HILL
Third Class.
6d
Available on the
day of issue only.

295

2G

L C & D. R.
RETURN.
BROMLEY
(S.1.) TO
KING'S ✠ G.N.R.
First Class.
over

297

Lh 7715
UP | DOWN
D. 1
Cambridge | Blooms-
Heath | bury
Station | to
to | Shoreditch
Goswell | Church
Road |
46-B
L.C.C. Trams. Ticket available only on
Car on which issued, subject to the Council's
bye-laws.
Shoreditch | Goswell
Church | Road
to | to
Blooms- | Cambridge
bury | Heath
Station

296

Ht 0538
L.C.C. TRAMWAYS
PUPIL or GUIDE
TWO-JOURNEY TICKET
Available for each
Journey on one car only
within the County of
London.
Issued subject to
Council's bye-laws.
14
To be examined, can-
celled on each car
boarded and handed
back to passenger.
2ND JOURNEY-CANCEL HERE

298

9043
D. 2
Blackfr's Bg.
or Westminstr
Bg. or Water-
loo Station to
New Cross G.
Bermondsey
New Road to
Blackfth Rd.
Blackfr's Bg.
or Westminstr
Bg or Water-
loo Stn to Old
K. Rd. Stables
Canal Bridge
Greenwich
Terminus
Waterloo Sta
to Rye Lane
Stables.
Asylum Rd.
Old K. Rd. to
Cmberwll Grn
LUGGAGE
2222222222222
LONDON COUNTY COUNCIL TRAMS. Ticket available only on Car on which issued.
Blackfriars Bg.
or Waterloo
Station or
Westminster
Bridge or
Blackfth Bg
New Cross G.
to New road
Blackheath
New road
Hunsrth Rd
Stables
Old Kent Rd
Greenwich
Terminus to
Canal Bridge
Greenwich
Terminus to
Waterloo Sta
Rye Lane
Stables to
Old Kent Rd
Cmberwll Grn
to Asylum
Rd, unt
LUGGAGE

299

TL 3381
DOWN | UP
D. 1/2
Waterloo | John
Bridge | Carpenter St
York | Waterloo
Road | Bridge
| Blackfriars
Elephant | Southwark
and Castle | Bridge
9-d | Waterloo
| Station
Fitzalan | York
Street | Road
New | Elephant
Street | and Castle
| Fitzalan
Kennington | Street
Gate | New Street
Dorset | Kennington
Road | Gate
Swan, | Dorset
Stockwell | Road
Clapham | Swan,
Road Stn. | Stockwell
Plough, | Clapham
Clapham | Road Stn
Nightingale | Plough,
Lane | Clapham
Balham | Nightingale
Station | Lane
Tooting | Balham
Bec Road | Station
Tooting | Tooting
Broadway | Bec Road
L.C.C. Trams. Ticket available only on Car on which issued, subject to the Council's bye-laws

300

Io 1653
26 E L.C.C. TRAMWAYS
6d Ret. 56 58 60
62 84
For Return Journey only
Change at Brixton Station
Forest Hill Station
Change at Elephant
Tower Bridge and Dulwich
Library or Peckham Rye
Waterloo Sta and Lordship
Lane Stn. or Peckham Rye
Change at Camberwell Grn.
London Terminus and Dulwich
Library or Stuart Rd
York Rd. Gt Charlotte Street,
St. Geo's Ch. or Regency St.
and Lordship Lane Station
Fitzalan St. Elephant or Vaux-
hall Sn. & Forest Hill Sn.
Camberwell Gate or Kennington
Gate and Cranston Rd.
Change at Greenwich Ch.
Tower Bridge & Blackwall
Tunnel or Obelisk; Lewisham
Tooley St. & Blackheath Rd.
or Blackwall Lane
Dulwich Laby. or | Grove Pk. Stn.
Stuart Rd | Backwall Tnl &
and London Termn | Forest Hill Station
Lordship La. Stn | Southover or King
and York Road | William St. &
or Regency Street | Lordship Lane Stn.
Forest Hill Stn & | Glenbow Road or
Vauxhall Station | Blackh'th Rd
or Elephant | & Dulwich Library
Cranston Rd and | Beckenham Lane
Kenington Ch | or Lewisham
or Camberwell Gte | Obelisk and
Tyrle Vale and | Whateley Road
Camberwell Gn |
St. Laurence Ch. | Bellingham Rd or
Catford & Dan- | Lewisham Liby
mark Hill Sn | & E. Dulwich Stn
Transfers issued UP

Insurance, Saturday, Excess
Fares, Choir, Pupils and
complex geographicals all have
their part to play.

Punch. They included a 1d Workman Return. An interesting side-collection may be made up of the self-advertisements and slogans found on the reverse of many Ilford specimens. Examples include 'Your tram receipts pave your streets' and 'Your trams are not on the rates — do your bit to keep them off'.

Lea Bridge (Leyton & Walthamstow) Tramways Company

Opened in May 1883 with horse-drawn trams. Tickets seem to have been headed without the Leyton and Walthamstow element of the corporate title. There were geographical tickets from the Bell Punch Company and a variety of transfer-type forms on issue right up to purchase by the LCC in July 1908.

Leyton District Council Tramways

This system was opened in December 1906 and included some through trams into the County of London in the area of Moorgate, Aldgate and West Ham. The LCC took full control in July 1921. One ticket is shown (**282**).

London Brighton & South Coast Railway

The LBSC started life simply as the London & Brighton Railway back in 1840 and produced a variety of tickets for the London area. The South London Line from London Bridge to Victoria by way of Peckham, Brixton and Clapham was electrified in 1909 and about this time its tickets began to carry a 'SLL' sub-heading and a bright red stripe. The LBSC had the peculiarity of providing deep red coloured Ordering Tickets (often described elsewhere as 'Reminder Tickets' and, uniquely in Australia as 'Alarm Cards'), inserted towards the end of a ticket run or series so as to appear prominently at the time a reminder to reorder was most needed. The print on the face of these tickets would be the same as the ticket to be ordered but their function was spelt out on the back. The Southern Railway followed this practice for a while from 1923.

Of the tickets illustrated, **283** is a First Class Return in white which also included admission to Crystal Palace in 1867. Presumably the Crystal Palace Company had to rely on the LBSC to tell them how many tickets were sold and how much of the proceeds was due to them. **284** is a blue Second Class Single from 1864. **285** was sold in 1897 and appears to have been a Special Cheap Ticket to enable the holder to visit Belmont Asylum (later Belmont Mental Hospital). This ticket is on white card while the stripes and diagonal markings are red.

286 is another of those obsolete Insurance Tickets. The one we saw for a Great Western journey (**267**) cost 6d and assured a First Class traveller of £6 a week during total disablement but this costs 2d and provides only £1 5s 0d (£1.25) for its Third Class holder! The Bicycle Ticket (**287**), seems a little expensive at 6d for 19km back in 1904 but in yellow colour with overprinted red lines gave its holder some artistry to gaze at during the twenty minute journey.

Again with West London association is **288** for a member of a Sunday School party en route for Crystal Palace back in 1904. It is white with a central red band and could have been used either by an adult or a child. **289** is a pre-dated Workman's Ticket of 1909 on green card with overprint in red. It was the practice of some companies to sell these tickets in a batch of six at the beginning of the week; perhaps the purchaser of this card was given the day off! **290** is pink with a red diagonal band. It would seem to represent the conversion of a Day Excursion to a Week End Ticket.

Jointly-headed tickets of this company, in terms of the lines and arrangements they represent, are extraordinarily interesting to collect. Here reproduced is **291**, initial-headed for both the Brighton company and the District Railway. This item is a grey card and the portion shown is overprinted with the familiar Inner Circle device.

London Camberwell & Dulwich Tramways Company

A somewhat obscure tramway company operating between Queen's Road Peckham and East Dulwich from 1884 until 1904. Tickets are scarce.

London Chatham & Dover Railway

Opened as the East Kent Railway in February 1858, and changed to this title in August the following year. The company set up a common Management Committee with the South Eastern Railway in 1899 and tickets of both companies were soon headed SEC. Both companies merged into the Southern Railway 1 January 1923.

The original, and independently worked, railway is represented here by four illustrations: **292**, a fine Third Class Single shows that rather refined Maltese Cross in the expression of King's Cross (Met) station and nicely refers to it as the Metropolitan Railway's property. **293** is another item affording admission to Crystal Palace as well as travel thereto; colouring of this 1899 ticket is white with green stripes. **294** is an ordinary buff and green Return Ticket of 1900 to the now defunct Ludgate Hill. **295**, again with that King's Cross embellishment, but now rather older, is dated 1866. It is a plain white ticket. The return coupon only is shown.

London County Council Tramways

The LCC came into existence under a local government reorganisation of April 1889. The Council set about acquiring tramways as soon as it was administratively able. There were acquisitions in North London by 1896. One sizeable early takeover was that of the London Tramways Company south of the Thames in January 1899.

The Council acquired an important ticket printing works at Effra Road, Brixton, where almost all of its ticket needs were met. Some stock was supplied by the Bell Punch Company for the lines in North London (until c1911), but generally the LCC did not 'buy-in'. The Effra Road prints, at least in their later years, were consistently white-centres with coloured edges. They characteristically carried coloured overprints of one sort or another and most were given geographical stages with or without added stage numbers. Certainly it was difficult to observe any real standardisation of size and overall appearance. Effra Road tickets were generally printed for individual routes or groups of routes and in this and other ways took on a fairly distinctive image. Not surprisingly, the earliest patterns show strong influence of design from the constituent London tramways in the south, and of North Metropolitan tramways in the north.

A group of five tickets is shown to display route numbers, low (½d) fares, printed categories and geographical stages, overprints, and five different finished sizes, all in soft pasteboard material. See **296** to **300**.

The LCC evidently did not favour the joint titling of tickets. Even though there were numerous through routes to and from other systems and much overlapping of services, few joint-titles appeared commencing with the LCC element. One example worth a mention would be that of LCC & Metropolitan Electric Tramways. For this, Returns with the quite normal (Effra) styling but headed 'LCC & MET' were issued. This referred in its conditions to 'Council's & Company's bye-laws' — an uncommon item for collectors to search out.

London Deptford & Greenwich Tramways Company

Opened in 1880 as the London & Deptford Tramways, this was a horse-tram service. The LCC took over in 1904. Tickets were by Whiting and had unusual numeric-geographic stages printed in a wide variety of colours.

London Electric Railway

Formed of the Bakerloo, Hampstead and Piccadilly companies in 1910 (each entered separately). There were no immediate physical junctions between the tracks of these constituents. The routes simply met at interchange stations and lines crossed at different levels below ground.

Ticketing practice retained the colours used by the former companies for a majority of the issues under London Electric rule. Through bookings created some exceptions — eg former Hampstead company to District Railway points were green with two white bars, while the same bookings from former Piccadilly stations were green with three blue lines overlaid (**301**). Scheme Tickets came into use on the Hampstead and Piccadilly sections about 1922.

Two other tickets are illustrated. **302**, a blue Single through to the Met with mention of the Central London (The 'N' overprint was an indicator that holders were to change at Notting Hill Gate. When this ticket was issued it would have been necessary to literally leave the premises and walk across the road to join the second train), and **303**, a buff Single via the City & South London and, dated 1916, now with the UndergrounD logo at the head.

A large number of jointly-titled tickets survive. Examples include: the LE with Central London and City & South London Railways, and with several 'bus operators, including London General (**304**) and Overground Limited (**305**). The Overground bus company had started its activities as the 'Dangerfield OVERGROUND Service' before becoming a Limited Company and changing to the simplified title. It was taken into the LPTB in 1933. Others named the Metropolitan Electric, and LCC Tramways. Tenacious searching and collecting will reveal further examples.

London General Omnibus Company

This old-established, originally French-controlled company, provided many through tickets to tramways and underground railways in the London Area. The early French title was the 'Compagnie Générale des Omnibus de Londres'. LGOC was London's principal bus operator through till the 1933 reorganisation.

Some early through bookings were to the Central London Railway, the Lea Bridge and South Metropolitan tramways. Transfers to and from the Croydon Corporation lines and the services of London United were other items for the collector. A number of LGOC arrangements with London operators are illustrated under respective companies' entries. See for example: **217, 227, 304** and **305**.

London & Greenwich Railway

This railway opened in 1836 as the first steam-operated line into London. Interestingly, the company was not removed from the *Stock Exchange Register* until 1924. It had been finally (in legal terms) absorbed into the Southern Railway at the Grouping of 1923. The company is well known to collectors for its rather impressive metal tokens, which served as re-usable tickets.

London & India Dock Company

Since 1908, a constituent of the Port of London Authority. Tickets were similar to those known later with the PLA's heading. A Workman's Ticket for the Third Class journey from Royal Albert Dock to Custom House in 1904 cost 1d; its colouring was very strong bright-orange.

London Midland & Scottish Railway

The LMS was the largest of Britain's Big Four railways formed by the 1923 Grouping and competed with the GW to be the most prolific issuer of unusual tickets. It acquired three London termini, the major ones at Euston (from the LNW) and St Pancras (formerly Midland) with the mainly suburban Broad Street (North London Railway) and a substantial interest in Fenchurch Street (the terminus of the London Tilbury & Southend Railway). The LTS joined what geographically seems an unusual fold with its acquisition by the Midland a decade before. Standardisation of ticket styles was only gradual and the 1920s and even 1930s produced hybrid designs containing features of both the constituent companies. Nowhere was this LMS feature more noticeable than on the former Southend lines.

306 was issued in 1924 and retains the Midland design apart from the new owner's heading. **307** and **308** are from waterway and roadway 1930s excursions where there were other attractions. **309** is a standard First Class Weekly Season for use on the former North London Railway's tracks. This mentions on the reverse that it is not valid unless signed by its holder. It was not so signed yet presumably was honoured — a phenomenon the world over.

310 is a fascinating Day Excursion to Dublin's Westland Row from East Ham. There was once a spur from East Ham to Woodgrange Park and it would appear from the ticket that the excursionist was expected to take a circuitous trip round North London to St Pancras and then make his own way to Euston. By the time he had clambered on to the Holyhead train at Euston, he would have felt that the major part of the journey was over. Sadly the ticket does not tell us how much the trip would have cost him or how long he would have spent in Dublin's Fair City.

311 was printed in 1949, during the honeymoon period after Nationalisation when the old company titles were still heading some tickets.

The LMS was party to a number of joint working arrangements with other companies but mainly well outside the Metropolis. We mention three that produced tickets of interest to the London enthusiast:

1   An agreement with the District Railway led to the printing of tickets which offered the passenger the option of travel by a train of either company.

2   Through bookings from LMS stations to Tilbury and thence by vessels of the General Steam Navigation Company. These ranged from fairly ordinary Singles and Returns via Tilbury Pier and the Thames Estuary to a curious fully-printed 'Box Tricycle' ticket for a trip from Walthamstow to Margate. How sufficient demand for such as this could be created is possibly worth a debate. The writers recall the famous 'Stop Me and Buy One' ice-cream cart traders who worked the streets of London and other cities up and down Britain in the 1930s. Surely they would not have contemplated taking their tasties and cart that far for business?

3   A Joint Committee with the Great Western Railway was concerned with lines in several parts of the country but in

301

UNDERGROUND
London Electric Ry.
Issued subject to the Cos' Bye-laws, Regulations and advertised conditions.
Available day of issue only.
HOLBORN
TO   No.1
TURNHAM GREEN
Change at Hammersmith or South Kensington
3rd. Class on District
FARE d

302

London Elec Ry.
Issued subject to the Cos' Bye-laws, Regulations and advertised conditions.
Available day of issue only.
KNIGHTSBRIDGE
(1)   TO
WOOD LANE or QUEENS RD.
(Central London Rly.)
or intermediately
Via South Kensington or Gloucester Road & Notting Hill Gate
3rd. CLASS on METROPOLITAN RY.
FARE 3d

303

UNDERGROUND
London Electric Ry.
Issued subject to the Cos' Bye-laws, Regulations and advertised conditions.
Available day of issue only.
KENTISH TOWN
(1)   TO
LONDON BRIDGE
Via Euston & C. & S.L. Ry
FARE 3d.

304

London Electric Ry & London General Omnibus Company.
Available day of issue only
Strand
(1)   TO
HIGHGATE
3rd. CLASS (SINGLE)
This half is for Rail journey only
Muswell H. (B'way)
(SEE BACK)

305

B L.E.R. Lon.General & Overg'd O'busCos
Available day of issue only
Finsbury Park
or Manor House to
STAMFORD HILL
or Finsbury Park to
STOKE NEWINGTON STATION,
or HARRINGAY
(The Salisbury)
3rd. Class Fare 5d.
To be cancelled on 'Bus
& Aldwych (P)

306

30 JY 924 & S. 30 JY 924
This Ticket is issued subject to the Regulations & Conditions stated in the Co's Time Tables & Bills
AVAILABLE ON DAY OF ISSUE ONLY.
Woodgrange Park to
BARKING
THIRD CLASS.   1X(S)   FARE 1½d.
Barking

307

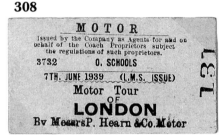

L. M. & S. R
FOR CONDITIONS SEE BACK (4105)
ADVERTISED DAY EXCURSION
SEPTEMBER 28th, 1935
Sail on River
THAMES
S A I L

308

M O T O R
Issued by the Company as Agents for and on behalf of the Coach Proprietors subject the regulations of such proprietors.
3732   O. SCHOOLS
7TH. JUNE 1939   (L.M.S. ISSUE)
Motor Tour
OF
LONDON
By Messrs P. Hearn & Co. Motor

309

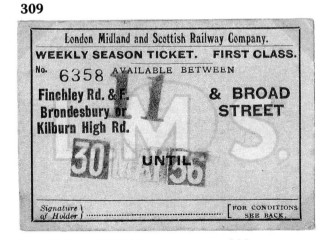

London Midland and Scottish Railway Company.
WEEKLY SEASON TICKET.   FIRST CLASS.
No. 6358 AVAILABLE BETWEEN
Finchley Rd. & F.
Brondesbury or
Kilburn High Rd.
& BROAD STREET
30   UNTIL
Signature of Holder
FOR CONDITIONS SEE BACK.

310

L.M.&S.R. FOR CONDITIONS SEE BACK
DAY EXCURSION
Return as per bill
3rd.Cl.Steamer&Rail
Dublin(W.Row)
TO
EAST HAM
Via Dun Laoghaire)
Kingstown Holyhead
Euston & St.Pancras
and Woodgrange Park
3282 (D)
DUBLIN W ROW

L. M. & S. R
DAY EXCURSION
3rd-Cl Rail&Steamer
East Ham
TO
DUBLIN (W.ROW)
Via Woodgrange Park
St. Pancras & Euston
and Holyhead & Kings town(Dun Laoghaire)

311

C342
L. M. & S. R.
For Conditions See Back
DAY EXCURSION
Valid as advertised
OUT 7th MAY 1949   RET 7th MAY 1949
HUDDERSFIELD   TO
WEMBLEY STADIUM STATION&BACK
Via MARYLEBONE
THIRD CLASS

313

L. N. E. R.
CHEAP DAY
WOOD GREEN
(Alexandra Park)
TO
FINSBURY PARK (1)
Available on day of issue only as per Bills
SECOND
For conditions see back
WOOD GR

312

L.M.&S.and G.W.J'ntRys.
Issued subject to the conditions & regulations in the Cos Time Tables Books Bills & Notices in the Railway Cos Book of regulations relating to traffic by Passenger Trains or other similar service WO
KENSINGTON ADDISON ROAD   TO
EARLS COURT
(R)
THIRD CLASS   11W(S)   FARE ½
EARLS COURT

Note Thames boats and riverside coaches as well as prewar suburban Second Class. Note through journeys on buses, and to Ireland via local and main line railways.

London only with the West London and West London Extension Railways (see GW above and WL below). Of interest here is **312**, a purely LMS printing from Kensington.

London & North Eastern Railway

This company's 1923 Grouping arrangements took in the Great Northern company's King's Cross station; and Fenchurch Street and Liverpool Street from the Great Eastern, while Marylebone was the contribution of the Great Central.

The gradual standardisation of LNER tickets will be considered in Chapter 12. Influence of the constituent Great Northern company on format was substantial although colours were changed. The blue of the GN Third Class gave way to LNER green and their pink Second Class reappeared in blue.

The prewar Second Class was retained on certain LNER suburban lines until the end of 1937 (**313**) and also in connection with particular Boat Trains for Continental connections. Scheme Tickets appeared on the LNER about 1939 but as might be expected, for journeys to London Transport stations only. Brief comparison of these with similar issues by the Southern and Great Western companies of the time, shows them to be quite good representations of the format mainly associated with London Transport. Some specimens seem to be LT-printed and therefore take on even more of a true London Scheme Ticket image. A unique LNER Shelter Ticket (**450**) which makes a grand addition to any London collection, is dealt with in some detail in Chapter 7.

Finally here, it is of interest to mention Dog Tickets from the last few years of the LNER system in London. A majority were LNER-printed and styled. A minority were quite clearly London Transport products, with an unmistakable LT appearance. Some even mentioned the safety of dogs on escalators — when presumably it was known that the holders (human and canine) would be riding LNER metals.

Illustrations for this company conclude with a group of eight tickets. **314** — issued in the September following the first year of Grouping still displays the style of the former Great Central Railway. **315** is a fine three-coupon Edmonson for a picturesque circular trip into Norfolk around 1937. Note the tiny centre coupon for use by Messrs Smiths Motor Boat. **316** also comes from the 1930s, in this case for booking a seat on the train named. **317** is a very clearly worded Platform Ticket of c1938. **318** was issued in 1932 for six days of travel (and the many punchmarks indicate that the holder got full value for money) overstamped with 'Week No 17'. **319** represents reserved accommodation on a ride to York in 1934. **320** was issued 18 months after the company lost its identity to British Railways while **321** survived a full five years after Nationalisation. If there were sufficient First Class bookings of this Sleeping Car journey in 1953, the very low serial number suggests the ticket is one from a reserve stock held during the interim of changeover to British Railways' ownership.

Jointly-titled tickets with the LNER mentioned are fairly numerous and quite varied in design. Season Tickets available via Marylebone *or* Paddington, when fully printed thus and for a journey to an underground station would usually show a title joint with the Great Western Railway and London Passenger Transport Board. Similarly, tickets via Marylebone and the Bakerloo would refer in the title to the London Electric. **322** illustrates one of the joint arrangements we have explained earlier; in this case with the LMS as a partner.

London & North Western Railway

This important main line company originated in 1846. With principal centres at Manchester, Liverpool, Birmingham and London, it became the major component of the LMS in 1923. It has left us a legacy of interesting London tickets. The company had run feeder bus services to connect with trains serving Watford, Harrow and Tring. Many of the tickets were Edmondsons headed 'L.N.W.R. Road Motor Car' (on at least one occasion 'Road' was erroneously printed as 'Rail'). The company also worked a bus service between Euston and Waterloo using flimsy square paper tickets.

323 and **324** demonstrate the unique dating system employed by the company and a number of others in an effort to inhibit ticket fraud. The order of the three elements (year, month and day) was interchanged annually. In the first three decades of the present century it was often difficult to decide[14] whether, say, '20 DC 15' was sold on 20 December 1915 or 15 December 1920. **323** is clearly an 1899 transaction by which on payment of 1½d the holder of a Season Ticket from Broad Street was permitted to travel home from Euston. **324** is a Second Class Single in the opposite direction, 9 April 1896.

325 records an experiment in dating by perforation (a method used elsewhere to good effect — notably Northern Ireland, Austria and Lithuania). **326** is the '(Going)' (ie Outward) half of a Return to Ballybay — transport between the Dublin termini not included.

London Passenger Transport Board

The huge London organisation installed in July 1933. The Board took over all underground railways, all tramways and most of the buses in the then area of Greater London. This was not Nationalisation but rule by an independent statutory body. The Board lost its identity to the first London Transport Executive in 1948, which was Nationalisation. The ticketing scene was most complex, considering all the modes of transport involved (let us not forget the Thames) and the expanse of the area, plus a multiplicity of through bookings and jointly-administered trips. Here therefore it is essential to be uncommonly brief.

London Regional Transport

LRT was created by an Act of Parliament effective from June 1984. It took control of London's bus services and underground railways formerly operated by London Transport Executive (II). Early in 1985 the railways were placed in the care of a wholly-owned subsidiary company named London Underground Limited (qv).

Certain rail travel tickets are known with the LRT title in the period between inception of LRT and the commencement of LUL in 1985: eg Special Rail Tour tickets of September 1984 and Travelcards dated early in 1985, the latter valid on buses as well as underground trains.

London Southern Tramways Company

Another of London's fascinating former horse-tramways. Opened in 1883, this line operated between Vauxhall, Camberwell, Brixton and Norwood and was taken over by the LCC in 1906. The company at one time had ideas of building a light railway out as far as Farnborough (Kent). Tickets of the London Southern were fully-geographical and printed first by Whiting, then the Bell Punch Company.

London & South Western Railway

Opened as the London & Southampton Railway in 1838 terminating at Nine Elms station, but later extended to its rightful place at Waterloo. London operations included the Waterloo &

314

L. N. E. Ry.
NOT TRANSFERABLE,
and subject to the regulations and conditions in
the Company's Time Tables, Books, Bills & Notices.
ON DATE OF ISSUE ONLY

MARYLEBONE
TO
GERRARDS CROSS
THIRD CLASS   Fare 2s. 2d.
Marylebone   Marylebone
GerrardsCross   GerrardsCross

315

0004

L. N. E. R.
CIRCULAR TRIP
Wroxham
(A 918) TO
LIVERPOOL ST
BY RAIL
including
Pullman
Supplement.
THIRD

G. Smith & Sons
BOAT TRIP
(A 918) on
NORFOLK
BROADS
By
Messrs Smiths
Motor Boat.
Available on day of issue.
For conditions see back

L. N. E. R.
CIRCULAR TRIP
LIVERPOOL ST
(A 918) TO
WROXHAM
BY RAIL
including
Pullman
Supplement.
THIRD

0004

316

L. N. E. R.
WEST RIDING LIMITED
CAR   SEAT NO
From KING'S CROSS (A747)
Available for one journey only when
accompanied by a THIRD CLASS
Rail Ticket.
SUPPLEMENT FARE 2s. 6d.

0044

317

L.N.E.R.
PLATFORM.   ADMIT ONE
KING'S CROSS
This ticket is issued on condition that
the Company will not be liable
to the holder for any injury
or loss, personal or otherwise,
however caused.   (H)
1 D.
c   73375

318

29 APL 32

L. N. E. R.
WEEKLY TICKET.   2nd Class.
For conditions see back.   Price 4s. 10d.
ST JAMES ST
(No. 2)
TO
LIVERPOOL ST
and back.
Mon Tue Wed Thu Fri Sat

2670

319

L. N. E. R.
RESERVED ACCOMMODATION
IN EXCURSION TRAINS.
KING'S CROSS (S.M.) to
YORK
AND RETURN.
ON DATE SHEWN ON BACK HEREOF.
This ticket is not valid except on production
of a passenger ticket covering the journey and
must be shewn and given up when required.
FEE 6d.

223

320

L. N. E. R.
CAMPING PARTY
JUVENILE
UNDER 16 YEARS
Liverpool St
(M)
TO
DOVERCOURT BAY
Available on day of
issue only.
THIRD
For conditions see back

3740

321

L. N. E. R.   6 45
SLEEPING CAR TICKET.

KING'S CROSS LONDON (A 855) to
Berwick or any Station North thereof

Charge 36s. 0d.

The holder of this Ticket must also have
a First Class Railway Ticket.   This Ticket
must be shewn and given up when required.

0041

322

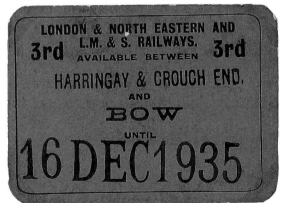

LONDON & NORTH EASTERN AND
L.M. & S. RAILWAYS.
3rd   AVAILABLE BETWEEN   3rd

HARRINGAY & CROUCH END,
AND
BOW
UNTIL
16 DEC 1935

326

RAILWAY (GOING)
Conveyance between the
Termini Dublin not include
SecondClass EXPRESS
London Eu n WO
To HOLYHEAD
via Stafford & Crewe
& from KINGSTOWN
BALLYBAY
via Dandalk
head BY   over

323

06.SE.90.

LONDON & NORTH WESTERN RAILWAY
EXCESS FARE
on Willesden & Broad St. Season ticket returning from Euston Available on day of issue only

Euston (E.N.) to
CHALK FARM (L.&N.W.)
Third]   FARE -/1½   Class
This Ticket must be produced with the Season
Ticket to the Ticket Examiner and Collector
and is to be surrendered to the latter

212

324

96 AP

London & North Western Ry.
Issued subject to the conditions & regulations in
the Co's Time Tables Books Bills & Notices & unless
stated therein to be as NOT available by Irish Mail.

WILLESDEN (No. 3.) TO
EUSTON
Second] 21 (NO.3)(S.) [Class
EUSTON   FARE -/6

1632

325

Issued by the L. & N.W.R.Co., subject
to the Company's regulations, and to the
conditions in their Time Tables.
THIRD CLASS
London Euston E.O To F
Harrow
1, E.O Harrow

1657

327

APR 13 76

L. & S. R.
TULSE HILL
(a. 2)
TO
HERNE HILL
THIRD CLASS PARLIAMENTARY
(See Back)
(Herne Hill)   (Herne Hill)

4238

A named train and a trip on The
Broads, or express and
sleeping car rides, all with the
Edmondson card ticket. Note
the much-clipped card for
weekly travel where, curiously,
only one journey per day is
recorded.

City Railway (see separate entry) and numerous suburban lines. The company's title was often abbreviated on Return Tickets to 'South Western Railway'.

The company was a little unconventional with its use of Pink (usually denoting Second Class) for its Third Class (**327**) tickets. Another innovation, introduced in 1881 and again in 1917, was the apparent economy measure of two tickets printed side-by-side on one standard Edmondson card and severed at the time of sale to passengers (see notes entered for the Southern Railway).

Tickets through to the Piccadilly underground via the District Line had an overprint of three blue lines, and Workman Returns via the District carried an overprinted letter 'D'. Through bookings to South Eastern Railway stations via Waterloo were green (the SE colour), while those to Cannon Street were marked with a 'C'. A further specialty was the series for trips to Bisley Camp. These were without mention of a class and had the choice sub-title 'Bisley Tramway'. Local Waterloo & City tickets of the LSW were punch-type (**407**) fares being collected on the trains. LSW Second Class was gradually phased out from 1916-17 and some tickets contained such wording as '3rd Class only if 2nd Class is not provided'.

Return Tickets were generally in a vertical format with their upper coupon being the return portion. Examples of these are: **328**, a deep blue card for a family journeying in 1870; **329**, buff and green for an Early Daily Workman travelling on a District train over LSW metals in 1909; **330**, a green card used by a Territorial (soldier) returning by District train to Richmond during 1914; and **331**, a somewhat mysterious unissued white Return of c1910 for First Class travel to Bayswater on the Inner Circle line. Was the passenger expected to go via Richmond and Gunnersbury?

The remaining illustrations for this company are: **332**, a fine early, but undated Second Class local Single coloured deep blue for the same Bayswater journey; **333**, a 1915 Season Ticket endorsed 'Pupil' and on very heavy pink (Third Class) board, with a shining gilt-edge presumably held by an Emanuel Scholar; **334**, a flimsy buff coloured Excess Fare form by Waterlow & Sons, undated and, quaintly worded 'Not to be travelled upon'.

Not many jointly-titled tickets included the LSW. **335** is the return half for a trip to Earlsfield from LBSC territory at Victoria. The style is clearly LBSC. It will be noted the LSW is mentioned first, being the railway on which the (homeward) journey commenced, whereas, on the outward half of this ticket the LBSC was so honoured.

London Street Tramways Company

This title covered a small group of horse-trams beginning their activities in November 1871 and worked in the area of Holborn, Clerkenwell and Hampstead Heath. The North Metropolitan Tramways acquired the company in 1897.

Earliest tickets were flimsy white papers about 75mm square torn out of perforated books supplied by the printers, J. W. Morgan & Co. In due course Whiting-printed punch-types came along but in an unusual size, almost square, measuring 40mm to almost 50mm. A conventional punch-type of 1883 or later is shown as **336**.

London Tilbury & Southend Railway

Promoted by the Eastern Counties and London & Blackwall Railway companies, the LTS commenced operations in 1854. It had no London terminus but was permitted to run into Fenchurch Street under the auspices of its Eastern Counties parentage. It became a section of the Midland Railway in 1912 and thus went to the LMS at the 1923 Grouping.

Tickets tended to be of different colours for Up and Down journeys. After 1912 the Midland used their own title, with the LTS mentioned as a section (**363**). However, LMS tickets of 1923 and later contained many indications of a LTS origin. **337** seems to be a District printing with the WC monogram a code for Whitechapel (the route would have been mainly over the Whitechapel & Bow Railway) (qv). **338** in pink and white offered a longish weekend in Southend. Most such tickets required the holder to return by Monday. It was sold in 1906 as was **339**, a Single to a Circle Line station and so carrying the 'O' overprint. The recipient of **340** seems to have been a Southend resident who tarried so long in London that his Weekend Return was no longer valid. **341** reminds us that in 1910 one could travel on the Romford to Upminster spur by First Class carriage.

London Tramways Company

South London's largest horse-trams operator, the company was acquired by London County Council in 1899 (Notices were served on some councils as early as 1891). The oldest tickets seen have their serial *numbers* overprinted in a distinctive colour. These were followed by similar punch-types on which only the serial *letters* were overprinted. Reproduced is one pink punch-type (**342**) with its 'Zr' overprinted in bright blue. The reverse of this ticket, incidentally, offers a rather poignant comment that the people were then buying too many foreign matches, thus damaging the inland industry and creating 'Unemployed in East London'.

London Transport

This title is to be expected on tickets after 1 July 1933. It occurs freely as a common abbreviation for any of the first five authorities listed here:

1 London Passenger Transport Board 1933-1947.
2 London Transport Executive(I). An Executive Committee of the British Transport Commission 1948-1962.
3 London Transport Board 1963-1969.
4 London Transport Executive(II). A division of the Greater London Council 1970-1984.
5 London Regional Transport 1984-.
6 London Underground Limited 1985-.

It should be particularly emphasised here that successive London administrations have been extremely helpful to enthusiasts in making available supplies of obsolete passenger tickets. This policy has sustained the hobby among collectors the world over in a way that would not otherwise have been possible. See individual entries for further detail.

London Transport Board

Functioned from January 1963 until the end of December 1969. Tramways, so much a feature previous to the LT Executive, had gone by 1952 so that with this authority we are concerned with heavy railways and the underground lines, but not much else.

From about 1964 there were various experiments with automatic electronic barriers using magnetic-encoded tickets (Chapter 2). Most of these were yellow. Exceptions were some Season Tickets (brownish) and a few Off Peak Tickets (pink). **Rapidprinter** machines produced a series of red or black coded tickets and very similar cards fully pre-printed, were issued from Richmond for LT trains operating on the Southern Region. Acton Town had some special shiny-surfaced cards a little larger than Edmondsons, with three rows of magnetic bars on the reverse. Yellow Season Tickets with two rows of coding bars along one

328

FAMILY TICKET.
WATERLOO
(...1) TO (2.M)
INSTOW
SECOND CLASS
(See Back)

329

L.& S.W.R. 3rd Class
Early Daily Workman
before 7.a.m. Fare 2d
SOUTHFIELDS
S.3 TO
PUTNEY BRIDGE
& HURLINGHAM
District Railway

330

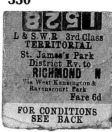

L.& S.W.R. 3rd Class
TERRITORIAL
St. James's Park
District Ry. to
RICHMOND N
Via West Kensington &
Ravenscourt Park
Fare 6d
FOR CONDITIONS
SEE BACK

331

BAYSWATER
(S.1) TO Fare 3
KINGSTON
(Via West Kensington
& Shaftesbury Road)
FIRST CLASS
THIS COMPANY WILL
NOT BE LIABLE FOR
(See over)
KINGSTON
(S.1) TO
BAYSWATER
(Via Shaftesbury Road
& West Kensington)
FIRST CLASS
THIS COMPANY WILL
NOT BE LIABLE FOR
(See over)

332

L.& S.W.R.
Fare 1/7
KINGSTON TO
BAYSWATER
(Via Shaftesbury Road and West
Kensington)
SECOND CLASS
(Bayswater) (Bayswater)
THIS COMPANY WILL NOT BE LIABLE FOR
(S.1) (See over)
CANCELLED

333

LONDON & SOUTH WESTERN RAILWAY.
Pupil
No. 134 Available from 26 Apl 1915
Issued subject to Conditions on other side.
NAME OF HOLDER Master E.L. Littlewove
THIRD CLASS SEASON TICKET.
ASHTEAD & Clapham Jt
25 JUL 15
To expire
Rate £ 1·39

334

London & South Western Railway.
(401A)
No. 3. 4256
EXCESS FARE PAID
AT
Wimbledon North.
9D.
NOT TO BE TRAVELLED UPON.
The Passenger is requested to see that this
Ticket is torn from the Book on payment,
and to destroy it on leaving the Company's
premises.
Waterlow & Sons Ltd., Printers, London Wall, London

335

0376
L.& S.W. & L.B.& S.C. RYS.
This half available for 2
DAYS including Date of
issue and return.
EARLSFIELD TO
VICTORIA
Via Clapham Junction
SECOND CL. 1s.0d.
Passengers must chas

336

En 9302
LONDON STREET TRAMS
COMPANY.
Holloway Road
and
Copenhagen St.
Roman Road,
("Peacock Arms")
and
King's Cross.
Copenhagen St.
and
Clerkenwell Rd.
FARE 1d TO OR FROM
Issued subject to the Compy's
Bye-Laws and Regulations.

A hefty Season Ticket with its
polished edges alongside
equally effective paper and
pasteboard patterns.

337

L.T. & S. & DISTRICT RYS.
Available for day of issue only
BOW ROAD
B TO Series 12
WHITECHAPEL
1d THIRD CLASS 1d
5261 5261

338

L.T. & S. RY. | L.T. & S. RY.
Week-End Ticket. | Fench' St
Southend | For conditions see back
For conditions see back | hereof.]
hereof.] | Southend
Fenchurch St | TO
[7] TO | Fenchurch St
SOUTHEND | Available on any day [train
Fench' St | service permitting] up to
| & including the Tuesday
| following date of issue.
| Southend
THIRD | THIRD
0454 0454

339

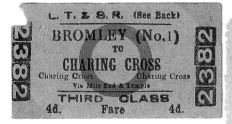

L.T. & S.R. (See Back)
BROMLEY (No.1)
TO
CHARING CROSS
Charing Cross Charing Cross
Via Mile End & Temple
THIRD CLASS
4d. Fare 4d.
2382 2382

340

LONDON, TILBURY & SOUTHEND RAILWAY.
No. 3756/178 Westcliff Station, Jan 26 190 7
Train 3 Class Passenger,
From Fench St To Westcliff
Why collected Excess fare paid £ : 3 : 6
Collector EH Gt Return

341

L. T. & S. R. (See Back)
ROMFORD (No.1)
TO
UPMINSTER
Upminster   Upminster
FIRST CLASS
4d.   Fare   4d.

342

7506
Blackfriars or Westminster Bridge and New Cross Gte
Bermondsey New Road and Blckheath-rd
Canal Bridge and Greenwich.
St. George's Church and Rye Lane Stables
THE LONDON TRAMWAYS CO., LTD. FARE
Issued subject to the Company's Rules and Regulations.
TO OR FROM
LUGGAGE
2d.
222222222222222

343

7 I 8 I 9 I 10 I 11 I 12
LONDON UNDERGROUND
PLATFORM TICKET
Valid one hour on day of issue only
For access to
WEST HAMPSTEAD
Not valid for travel
(TOLL)   20p
NOT TRANSFERABLE
1 I 2 I 3 I 4 I 5 I 6
-1DEC85
1293

344

Ka 0007
Down   Shepherd's Bush   Fare 1D
Hammersmith Broadway
Richmond Bridge
Young's Corner
Turnham Green Church
Kew Bridge
Half Acre, Brentford
Busch Corner
Fire Station (Isleworth)
Twickenham (London Road)
Twickenham (Junction of Stanley and Hampton Roads)
Park Road (Hampton Hill)
Garrick's Villa
Teddington Ch. (Broad Street)
St. Alban's Ch. (Teddington)
Kingston Bridge
Hampton Court Palace
LONDON UNITED TRAMWAYS, LIMITED.
Passengers must not break their journey.
This Ticket must be punched in the Section to which the Passenger is entitled to travel.
Up
Issued subject to Co's. Bye-laws.

345

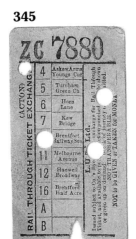
ZC 7880
4 Askew Arms Youngs Cur
5 Turnham Green Ch
6 Horn Lane
7 Kew Bridge
11 Brentford Railway Stn
12 Melbourne Avenue
16 Hanwell Broadway
A Brentford Half Acre
B
RAIL THROUGH TICKET EXCHANGE (ACTON)
L.U. Ltd.
NOT TRANSFERABLE

346

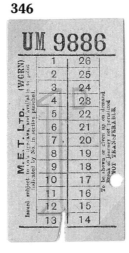
UM 9886
1	26
2	25
3	24
4	28
5	22
6	21
7	20
8	19
9	18
10	17
11	16
12	15
13	14
M.E.T. Ltd. (WGRN)
NOT TRANSFERABLE

347

Metropolitan Railway
NOT TRANSFERABLE
Available on day of issue only
Swiss Cottage
Series 6, M   TO   V
Baker Street
FARE 1½d   THIRD CLASS   1½d
650   650

348

282
Metropolitan Ry.
INTERCHANGE PRIV'GE T'KT
Available for One Month
Neasden
TO   8.1
MOORGATE ST.
Via
1st Class Fare
Metropolitan Ry.
INTERCHANGE PRIV'GE T'KT
Available for Seven days
Moorgate St.
1 W   TO   8.1
Neasden
Via
1st Class Fare   SEE BACK
282

349

METROPOLITAN RAILWAY.
No. 2867   Rate £ - : 2 : 9
Mr. L. L. Alcock
Is entitled to travel between
LIVERPOOL STREET
AND
FARRINGDON ST.
VIA
MOORGATE STREET
Available from 1. 11. 13 to
31 JAN 1914
THIRD CLASS   SEASON TICKET
THIS TICKET IS TO BE GIVEN UP ON EXPIRY.
SwB

350

Metropolitan Railway.
Available on day of issue only.
Swiss Cottage
TO
WEST HAMPSTEAD
THIRD CLASS FARE 1½.
67 9148   67 9148

351

6734
Metropolitan Ry.
Baker Street
2 (S.1) TO (A
PORTLAND ROAD
Second Class 3d.

352

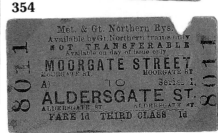
Metropolitan Railway
NOT TRANSFERABLE
Available on day of issue only.
ALDGATE EAST
0   (Series 1)   TO
BAKER STREET
INCLUDING ADMISSION TO
MADAME TUSSAUD'S EXHIBITION
VIA KING'S CROSS
T.E.   SECOND CLASS FARE 1/4   ADULT
025   025

353

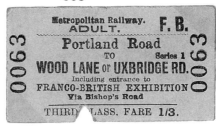
Metropolitan Railway.   F.B.
ADULT.
Portland Road
TO
WOOD LANE or UXBRIDGE RD.
Including entrance to
FRANCO-BRITISH EXHIBITION
Via Bishop's Road
THIRD CLASS. FARE 1/3.
0063   0063

354

Met. & Gt. Northern Rys.
Available by Gt. Northern trains only
NOT TRANSFERABLE
Available on day of issue only
MOORGATE STREET
MOORGATE ST.   MOORGATE ST
A)   TO   Series 1.
ALDERSGATE ST.
ALDERSGATE ST   ALDERSGATE ST.
FARE 1d   THIRD CLASS   1d
8011   8011

Two London exhibitions visited by the railway tripper and tickets for the London tramway rider, all with one of the Capital's very latest Platform cards.

edge of the reverse side appeared at one or two stations. These and others characterise the wide range of specimens to be found.

Certain stations were given cash-register machines which stamped the fare paid on to pre-printed 'universal' Station-of-Origin vertical format tickets. In 1968 most Station-of-Origin Singles and Returns were altered to an austere design showing little more than serial number, station and fare. This pattern of changes and variations continued, usually under the guise of 'modernisation'.

In the last year of the Board (1969) former LTS stations which their trains had been using, were transferred outright by British Rail. This led to some curious hybrid ticket prints from the line to Upminster.

London Transport Executive (I)

This first LT Executive was a part of the British Transport Commission's empire. The word Executive appeared in ticket conditions. On many (though not all) Scheme Tickets, earlier Board prints had been worded to the right but now, for the Executive began to show non-scheme printing on the left. Joint lines in the area were transferred to the LTE outright thus eventually simplifying the tickets concerned. Steam-hauled trains ceased to be used on LTE lines (For Chesham branch, see **736**) in September 1960 and special Souvenir Tickets were produced stating this by an overprint in red inks.

An intriguing range of cards that collectors may encounter, is printed for use from the 'station' at 'Stopatum'. Beware! These were dummies used in a fully-equipped booking office, holding **Rapidprinter** machines, at a staff training centre (**148**, **462** and **463** are related collectibles).

On the tramways there were 'Last Tram Week' tickets of several face values issued on the then remaining Embankment, Woolwich and Abbey Wood routes. Look out too, for a large white card ticket dated 5 October 1955 which admitted guest passengers to Baker Street station for a renaming ceremony giving new postwar nameplates to the locomotive *Sherlock Holmes*.

London Transport Executive (II)

Effective 1970, the word Executive replaced the word Board in conditions of issue. Decimal currency was only a year away in Britain. The Executive therefore was already issuing increasing numbers of dual-currency tickets. Issues with £sd fares were immediately distinguishable from the previous Board ones, even where there were no conditions of issue. Dual-currency tickets with an LTE mention must therefore not be from the first LTE defunct in 1962.

Familiar £sd fares were deleted progressively after February 1971 leaving the decimal versions we know today. Automatic barrier schemes were extended, but not for exit barriers at that time. Oxide-backed tickets which these schemes employed were even seen in an Edmondson weight which soon proved unsuitable for the gate equipment. Magnetic-encoded Season Tickets were discontinued. Conditions of issue had been removed from most station tickets in 1968.

London Underground Limited

This is the present operator of London's Tube Railways, which was effective from May 1985 as a subsidiary of London Regional Transport. As we write, tickets are beginning to circulate among collectors — those so far seen are without the 'Ltd' suffix (**343**).

London United Tramways Ltd

This tramway system opened in 1901, forming the first electric STREET railway in the London Area (The Alexandra Park installation had been on private land). The system went to London Passenger Transport Board in 1933, although some sections had earlier been purchased by London County Council.

LUT tickets were by Bell Punch and, at first, geographicals (**344**, coloured buff). Later more use of numerical stage panels was made. **345** shows one such ticket for 'Rail Through Ticket Exchange'. This latter form, in a salmon coloured pasteboard. Many issuing machines were in use from c1931. There are many LUT tickets jointly-titled with other authorities. Four of the more easily acquired items were joint with the Central London, District, London Electric, and Piccadilly companies.

Metropolitan Electric Tramways Ltd

Opened in 1904 and transferred to the LPTB in July 1933. In its later years the company experimented with various ticket machines, such as TIM which had tickets with the complicated heading 'MET, LUT & SMT Cos' reflecting the group to which the MET belonged, and making the machines available to be switched between them. The ticket shown (**346**), is a 1d white numerical stage punch-type of the late 1920s. One or two joint issues are known apart from the above. There were through tickets to Tube lines via Golders Green with the LE named.

Metropolitan Railway

The world's first city public underground railway. The line opened in 1863 and from that time, until its incorporation into the LPTB in 1933, produced a range of tickets almost as profuse and quite as individually interesting as any comparable main line company in the country. This line, perhaps with its associate the District, could well support a collection-within-a-collection for any enthusiast.

Earliest tickets were plain white for First Class and green for Third. Second Class tickets were certainly blue by 1868 and probably earlier. Later the colours were First lilac/grey, Second blue, Third buff, in each case carrying the Circle overprints whenever applicable. Over many years the company printed its station names with a curious mock-antique mixed typeface (**347**), creating a useful anti-fraud device. This may be recognised by its very tall initial letters and, strangely, very small upper case letters worked in wherever the character would otherwise have a descender. The whole affair was reminiscent of LBSC practices, but with less refinement. Another virtually all-Met practice was to place a tiny numeral 1 or 2 conveniently in the text of Return Tickets, denoting respectively the outward and homeward coupons (See **348** and **351**). The exact value of this feature remains a mystery to the writers, since the figures were too small to be instantly identified at barriers.

Six further Metropolitan tickets are reproduced. **349** is a white Third Class Season from 1914; **350** is a bright green Third Single dated 1908; **351** is a blue Second Class Return from 1868 (the lower or outward coupon would have been buff coloured). The final two tickets are related to exhibitions in London. **352** was for travel to and admission at Madame Tussaud's in 1904; colours are blue (Second Class) with red overprints. Lastly, **353** is a plain buff (Third) Single for the Franco-British Exhibition of 1908 at the newly built White City.

A variety of jointly headed issues may be found by the collector. Five examples are shown here: **354** naming the Great Northern Railway and available only by their trains, blue and dated 1901; **355** joint with the Great Western, a typical 1930s buff blank card made out for the trip to Oxford. **356** includes the LCD heading on a plain green card from 1908. **357** includes the District associate, grey, with red Inner Circle overprint and black monogram. Date is

355

16 APL 34

Metropolitan & G. W. Ry·s
PRIVILEGE TICKET
Available for One Week
Hammersmith
TO
OXFORD. GW.
Via
THIRD CLASS
SEE CONDI··S ON BACK
1894

356

8114

MET. & L. C. & D. R.
MOORGATE STREET
MOORGATE ST. (S. 20) MOORGATE ST
SNOW HILL
THIRD CLASS
1d.   1d.
Available on the day of issue only.
See other side.
SNOW HILL   SNOW HILL
8114

357

4379

Metropolitan & District Ry·s
Available for day of issue only.
MONUMENT
K   TO   (Series 35
ALDGATE EAST
VIA MARK LANE
1d THIRD CLASS 1d
4379

358

6394

Met. & Midland Rys.
Available by Midland trains only.
NOT TRANSFERABLE
Available on day of issue only
ALDERSGATE STREET
ALDERSGATE ST.   ALDERSGATE ST.
Z   TO   Series 8
KING'S CROSS
KING'S CROSS   KING'S CROSS
FARE 1d THIRD CLASS 1d
6394

359

1904, APR 2
9879
M.R. Available for RETURN
on the day of issue or following
day or from a Saturday to the
following Monday night.
King's Cross to
KENTISH TOWN
THIRD CLASS
(See back)
M.R. Available on
day of issue only.
Kentish Town to
KING'S CROSS
THIRD CLASS
(Fare 5d)
9879

360

253
Midland Railway
Moorgate Street
To
··NTISH·TOWN
·latform)
Second Class
(over)

361

MIDLAND RAILWAY.
ONE BICYCLE
ACCOMPANIED BY PASSENGER.
Issued at St. Albans
with bicycle ticket No.
EXTRA (INSURANCE) CHARGE ONE PENNY.
To be surrendered with the bicycle ticket.
SEE CONDITION ON BACK.
388

362

MIDLAND RAILWAY This Ticket is issued
subject to the Regulations & Conditions stated in
the Company's Time Tables & Bills.
FIRST CLASS.   FIRST CLASS.
AVAILABLE ON DAY OF ISSUE ONLY.
(H.L.) **KING'S CROSS** to (H.L.)
LEYTON
FARE 10d   FARE 10d
King's ✠ Leyton   King's ✠ Leyton
561

363

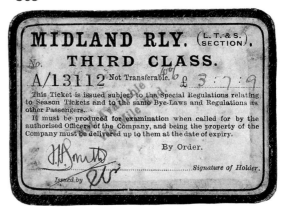

MIDLAND RLY. (L. T. & S.
                    SECTION).
THIRD CLASS.
No.
A/13112 Not Transferable. £ 3 : 7 : 9
This Ticket is issued subject to the Special Regulations relating
to Season Tickets and to the same Bye-Laws and Regulations as
other Passengers.
It must be produced for examination when called for by the
authorised Officers of the Company, and being the property of the
Company must be delivered up to them at the date of expiry.
By Order.
_____ Signature of Holder.
Issued by

364

B 0742
MIDLAND RAILWAY.
EXCESS **Receipt for** FARE
1d
PAID AT
KENTISH TOWN

365

2939
Millwall Docks Co.
Fare 3d.
Millwall Jn
Issued subject
to Regulations in the
Company's Time Tables
Millwall Docks
TO
MILLWALL JUN
Millwall Dks
THIRD
2939

Mock leather on the Midland
and monograms on the
Metropolitan, with pedal cycles
and extra penny charges form
an intricate collection of
tickets.

366

5292
First Class.
BLACKWALL
RAILWAY
TO
BOW
Not available beyond
BOW. Fare
Issued subject to the
Company's Published
Regulations.

367

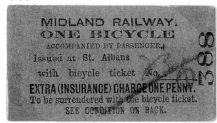

25
First Class.
SHADWELL
or **STEPNEY**
TO
SHOREDITCH
Not available at Bow,
or Broad Street.
Not transferable.
Issued subject to the
Company's Published
Regulations.

368

9758
N.L.R. Return   N.L.R.
FINSBURY P'K   **DALSTON JUNCTION**
TO   R   TO   R
DALSTON JUNCTION   **FINSBURY P'K**
VIA CANONBURY   VIA CANONBURY
3rd. Class 5d   3rd. Class 5d
Not transferable.
Issued subject to the   Issued subject to the
Company's Published   Company's Published
Regulations.   Regulations.
DALSTON JUNC
FINSBURY PARK
9758

1903. Finally **358**, a green card dated 1901, is headed 'Midland Railway' and is available only by their trains.

Midland Railway

This great British railway was formed in May 1844 and thus, before its inclusion in the Grouping of 1923, which placed it with the LMS company, it had time to produce a great range of tickets. It indeed did do this. The early prints were First — yellow, Third — originally yellowish which changed to grey, but green for children, and Second — blue (abandoned in 1875). A characteristic Midland practice was to use negative (or cameo) serial number numerals at one end (usually the lower on Returns — see **359**) of Edmondsons and conventional, positive numerals at the other. This device was also carried on for a short while on some transitional tickets of the LMS. For certain bookings in areas obviously influenced by the Metropolitan Railway, there were cards with a very-Midland design but in Met colours. White soft roll-type bus tickets for Midland-operated services between St Pancras, Victoria and Waterloo (probably also Charing Cross) with the company's heading are also to be collected. **360** is a bright yellow Return from 1870; **361** is a plain blue, c1910 Insurance Ticket for a bicycle. **362** is a First Class Single on white card. **363**, a fine 1913 Season Ticket, is white on a green linen-finished backing, valid over the entire LTS system. Finally **364**, is a thin white pasteboard pad-ticket for Excess Fares c1920.

Millwall Docks Company

Tickets of this company were printed by the Great Eastern Railway, who also worked passenger services over the Millwall Lines. This substantial influence may be seen in **365**, a green card from 1909.

New Palace Steamers Ltd

Another former River Thames operator with through bookings via Tilbury Pier and the London Tilbury & Southend Railway.

North London Railway

Opened in 1850 and always under LNW influence as regards its tickets, and especially so after 1909. Chalk Farm was its main junction with that company. In 1922, the year before Britain's Grouping upheaval, the company was completely absorbed into the LNW. Almost immediately there were LNW tickets from NL stations.

For many years after 1865/6 tickets had numerical overprints denoting the destination, including some stations on neighbouring lines. Examples were Broad Street code 1 and Richmond code 29. Subsequent modifications to the plan necessitated the introduction of 'A' suffixes. For example, South Acton was 24A (See **371**) and South Bromley 14A. There was also a directional colour scheme, with carefully devised mixed-directional colours where the train-routes so dictated.

366 from 1867 rather nicely refers to the early neighbour London & Blackwall Railway on its white and brown striped card. Also from 1867 is **367**, white with a purple stripe. **368** shows the code '4' (for Dalston) on a green and buff Return of 1899, and the same code appears on **369** of 1901, a yellow and red card Single. **370** was sold in 1905, is green, and now without a code.

North London Tramways Company

Originally (c1882) part of an earlier North London Suburban Trams Company, this company operated between Finsbury Park, Wood Green and Ponders End. Operation was taken over by the North Metropolitan Tramways in 1891. A variety of geographical tickets running as high as 5d in face value are known. Also known are tickets with a corner torn away (see note under Croydon & Norwood).

North Metropolitan Tramways Company

A sizeable horse-tramway system which later became the northern routes of the London County Council system. Its first section was opened at Whitechapel in 1870. Routes each had a range of geographical tickets, some patterns included numerals printed alongside the stage name.

North & South Western Junction Railway

Opened in August 1853. Jointly owned by the LNW, North London and Midland Railways. The LNW influence was greatest through its North London association. Tickets were exactly like those of the North London company. One specimen (**371**) is shown here with the '24A' overprint for South Acton, matching the code used by the NL. This card is green and dated 1899.

Port of London Authority

The Authority acquired railways from various formerly independent dock companies. Some had passenger train services and their own headed tickets. One such service ran from Custom House over the Royal Albert Dock Line. The PLA also ran several river cruise trips for which titled tickets were issued.

One somewhat battered PLA Workman Ticket is illustrated as **372**. This is a plain buff card dated 1935. **373** is a white First Class Single of 1922 from Royal Albert Dock at 1/5½d (7p); **374**, which was never issued but seems an earlier print, required a payment of 4/6d (22½p) for a similar journey by Special Boat Train.

Pullman Car Company

Pullman travel is normally thought of as being a fairly long-distance affair and therefore might not be expected to enter into this chapter. However, Pullman cars travelled from many London termini. **375**, a white card, was issued in 1954, the year in which the British Transport Commission purchased the Pullman company.

Railodok Electric Cars

Not a railway, but a train of battery-electric road-cars moving around the grounds of the Wembley Exhibition of 1924. The name and its on-ticket description is so capable of misleading that it seems prudent to include a brief entry for purposes of elimination. One Bell Punch product is shown as **376**.

Railway Clearing House

Like the foregoing, this was not a railway or tramway. The RCH was set up in 1842 to regulate inter-company accounting. Although not formally wound up until 1963, its effectiveness waned in 1923 when so many of its members were 'lost' to the Big Four. Nationalisation in 1948 all but killed off its usefulness. For the hobbyist, the RCH is an important entity. There were interesting free passes, generally concerned with travel on Clearing House business. Many of these were headed for the company over whose tracks the journey was to be made, but as the issuing body, the RCH would usually be the first mentioned. (See **702** in Chapter Sixteen.)

South Eastern & Chatham & Dover Railways

In 1899 two companies, the SE and LCD came under a single Management Committee and at first used this always-plural form of title. **377** — an ordinary Third Class Single on a buff coloured

369
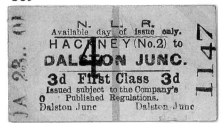

N. L. R.
Available day of issue only.
HACKNEY (No.2) to
DALSTON JUNC.
3d First Class 3d
Issued subject to the Company's
Published Regulations.
Dalston Junc   Dalston Junc
1147

370

N. L. R.
BROAD STREET to
HARRINGAY
VIA CANONBURY
Third Class 3d
Issued subject to the Company's
Published Regulations.
BROAD STREET
HARRINGAY
6699

371
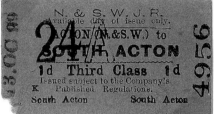

N. & S. W. J. R.
Available day of issue only.
ACTON (N.&S.W.) to
SOUTH ACTON
1d Third Class 1d
Issued subject to the Company's
K   Published Regulations.
South Acton   South Acton
4956

372
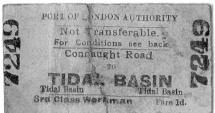

PORT OF LONDON AUTHORITY
Not Transferable.
For Conditions see back
Connaught Road
TO
TIDAL BASIN
Tidal Basin   Tidal Basin
3rd Class Workman   Fare 1d.
7249

373

PORT OF LONDON AUTHORITY.
Not Transferable and issued subject
to the conditions of the Bye-Laws
and Regulations of the Port of London
Authority.
E Royal Albert Dock E
TO
FENCHURCH STREET
Fenchurch Street   Fenchurch Street
FIRST CLASS   Revised Fare 1/5½
5450

374

PORT of LONDON AUTHORITY.
1st. SINGLE   1st. SINGLE
ROYAL ALBERT DOCK
R. A. DOCK   R. A. DOCK
LIVERPOOL St.   TO   LIVERPOOL St.
LIVERPOOL STREET
(BY SPECIAL BOAT TRAIN)
4/6   FARE   4/6
For conditions see over. For conditions see over.
9886

375

PULLMAN CAR COMPANY LIMITED
Cooks 1193 Agency
CAR B SEAT NO. 13
From   KING'S CROSS
TO   DARLINGTON
Available for one journey only when
accompanied by a FIRST CLASS
Railway Ticket. PRICE 11s.0a.B
FOR CONDITIONS SEE BACK
0297

376

Pb 6862
A
B
C
RAILODOK ELECTRIC CARS
WEMBLEY EXHIBITION 1924
THIS TICKET TO BE SHOWN ON DEMAND.
OUTWARD JOURNEY   HOMEWARD JOURNEY
B
A
Bell Punch Co., Uxbridge 7-24

377

S. E. & C. & D. RYS.
ELEPHANT & CASTLE
ELEPHANT & C   ELEPHANT & C
TO
GOWER STREET
Via Snow Hill Change at Aldersgate Street
THIRD   CLASS
4d.   4d.
Available on the day of issue only
See Other Side
GOWER STREET   GOWER STREET
5199

378

S. E. & C. RY.
TICKET FOR ONE BICYCLE PERAMBULATOR
OR CHILDREN'S MAIL CART.
Accompanied & at OWNERS RISK
CANNON STREET to
any Station on the S. E. Ry.
not exceeding 50 miles.
Rate 1 0d.   See Back
2877

379

5653
S. E. & C. R.
Available for 2 DAYS
including Date of issue
and return (See Back
Cannon Street to
BLACKHEATH
First. 1/8
S. E. & C. R.
This half available on
the Date of issue ONLY
Blackheath to
CANNON STREET
1/8 First.
5653

380

S. E. & C. & E. . S. (See back
Available day of issue ONLY
2] HITHER GREEN to
HITHER GREEN   HITHER GREEN
WAPPING
CHANGE AT NEW CROSS
4d   Third   4d
Wapping   Wapping
1072   10X2

381

S. E. & C. & G. W. RYS.
Available Day of issue
ONLY. (See Back
Red Hill to
OXFORD
Via Reading
11/8 Second
065

Special boat trains and prams,
battery-electric cars and main
line Pullmans are represented
here.

card — dates from about 1900. About 1901, tickets headed SEC began to appear (see below).

South Eastern & Chatham Railway

As mentioned above, the SEC heading appeared around 1901. The jointly-managed companies issued some intriguing tickets, including many varieties jointly-titled. Seven specimens are shown, with six of them marking different company arrangements. **378** enabled a bicycle or child's vehicle to travel from Cannon Street in 1901 and was coloured green and buff. **379** is also from 1901, but coloured plain buff with a red overprint identifying the destination. The first of the joint issues is **380**, a deep green card of 1909 — mentioning the East London Railway. Joint with the Great Western, **381** is the outward half of a Return to Oxford in 1905. The LBSC assisted in the transportation of military personnel travelling to Epsom on buff card ticket No 535 (**382**) in 1906. **383** is a green Single also of 1906 including the initials of the London & South Western company. The final item, a green Single of 1906 (**384**), refers to the Metropolitan Railway.

South Eastern Metropolitan Tramways Company

Opened in 1890. A London horse-tram system which operated from Catford to Greenwich and later became part of the LCC system in 1902. Tickets were geographicals by the Whiting company and some other numerical stage types are of unidentified source.

South Eastern Railway

This was the senior partner in the 'SE & CD' arrangements dealt with above. The company ran its first trains in 1842. Its London termini were Cannon Street, Charing Cross and London Bridge, with some services out of Victoria from where there were parallel services with the Brighton company as far as Redhill and inter-available tickets which variously mentioned one or both companies at different times. The railway used a series of special ticket overprints in the London Area. Three of these were an X for Charing Cross, W for Waterloo and C for Cannon Street (**379**).

Three tickets are shown for the SE: **385**, a white Single dated 1898; **386**, a Bicycle Ticket, green and white and dated 1898; and, the earliest one, **387**, a green Third Return coupon from 1871. The four jointly-titled items represent arrangement with three other railway companies: **388**, with the Great Northern Railway, green and dated 1890; **389** and **390** the Brighton company, both white with red over-markings; and finally **391**, the Met, a buff card with the familiar red Inner Circle marking.

South London Tramways Company

Opened in 1881 and operated in the area of Southwark Bridge, Clapham, Battersea and Wandsworth before being purchased by the LCC in 1902. Early tickets were oversized punch-types, including some that were almost square. Later true Bell Punch and Whiting products were issued. Numbered-stage tickets are known, but here we show one geographical — **392**.

South Metropolitan Electric Tramways & Lighting Company

Opened in 1906. The company issued punch-type tickets with its own title and also a variety of jointly-titled patterns with Croydon Corporation.

South Metropolitan Electric Tramways Ltd

This was the successor of the foregoing company in 1913, taken over by the LPTB in 1933. Like its earlier body, the company issued tickets jointly with Croydon, and some mentioning the LGOC are known. **393** shows a typical numbered-stage ticket. Its colour is somewhere between buff and orange: appropriately it carries an advertisement for a famous brand of pale ale on the back.

Southern Railway

As regards levels of passenger services, nationally this was the smallest of the 'Big Four' companies formed by the 1923 Grouping, but the largest within the London area. Generally it can be described as having absorbed railways south of the Thames, notably the London & South Western, the Brighton company and the South Eastern & Chatham group.

Tickets were eventually standardised in a style not unlike that of the LSW, although the pink colouring of the Third Class gave way to green. Many of the earlier ticket prints were in the constituent companies' styles (note **394** ex-LSW although not over a former LSW line and **395** an ex-Brighton company style) with only the heading changed. Note in **395** the unusual use of the definite article 'The'. The Southern was the only one of the Big Four issuing standardised vertical Return Tickets (**396**); no doubt this was a legacy from the main pre-Grouping constituents, all of which had also used this type.

Second Class survived on the Southern for some local routes around Chatham for about nine months but by 1924 was restricted to Boat Trains. Tickets for the Boat Train services included a supplementary charge, denoted by a thin red line across the card (**397**, complying with European convention).

In the Richmond and Wimbledon areas there were vertical Scheme Tickets used for through bookings to underground lines, all printed by the Southern in carefully matching standards. Also from Richmond came a few Cheap Day tickets for underground journeys, on blue board instead of the standard colour — buff in 1934, when green was gradually introduced. Rail Motor tickets were generally by Bell Punch but with an unusual stage-punching arrangement in vertical format.

From as early as 1854 there had been special workings of funeral trains from near Waterloo (using a private platform approached from Westminster Bridge Road) to the Necropolis station at Brookwood where a large private cemetery exists. First and Third Class Mourners' Tickets were issued in a style generally like the standard Special Arrangement tickets in which the Southern were specialists.

The letters C, W etc which the earlier South Eastern company had used to identify different central London stations were continued for a while after Grouping on certain Workman Tickets. Later there was a temporary and not-too-successful switch to numerals — 1 for London Bridge, 2 for Cannon Street and 3 for Waterloo. Just as many years later there were numerous errors with printed dual-currency fares, so these codes produced a variety of mistakes.

On Season Tickets there were similar codes — B for London Bridge, C for Cannon Street and CX for Charing Cross. This scheme lasted into the 1970s. Another overprint on Seasons (which survived into the 1980s) was a diamond denoting a through ticket to London Transport.

During the Wembley Exhibition of 1924-5 through Cheap Day tickets existed from various Southern stations via Charing Cross. These tickets were almost all of Metropolitan Railway style (and probably their prints).

Workman Tickets to underground lines all seem to have carried a 'DW' overprint (**398**) instead of the normal simple 'W'. This probably reflected differing regulations applicable on the Tubes.

382

S.E.& C.& L.B.&.S.C.RYS.
Soldier on Furlough or
Seaman on Leave
in uniform.
Available day of issue only
hatham (M.L.) to
EPSOM
VIA VICTORIA
3/0 Third Class
535

383

6008 6008
S.E.&C & L.&.S.W.RYS.
Available Day of issue ONLY. (See back
LOUGHBORO JUNCTION to
LOUGHBORO' JUNC. LOUGHBORO' JUNC
TULSE HILL
TULSE HILL TULSE HILL
Via Herne Hill
1½d Third 1½d

384

336 336
S.E.& C.& MET.RYS. SEE BACK
Available Day of issue ONLY.
New Cross (S. E. & C.) to
RICHMOND
Via Aldgate East, King's Cross, Bishop's Road
and Hammersmith.
10d Third Class 10d

385

4942 4942
S. E. R.
BETCHWORTH to
CHARING CROSS
4/0 First. 4/0
Children over 3 and under 12 years
half fares. under 3 years free.
Charing X Charing X

386

8017 8017
SOUTH EASTERN RAILWAY.
TICKET FOR ONE BICYCLE PERAMBULATOR
OR CHILDREN'S MAIL CART.
Conveyed at OWNERS RISK
CHARING CROSS to
Station
Rate 1s 0d See back

387

MR 8171
Blackheath
TO
LONDON BRIDGE
Third Class.
See Back.

388

4629 4629
SOUTH EASTERN & GREAT NORTHERN RYS
London Bridge to
STROUD GREEN
5d. Third 5d.
Children over 3 and under 12 years
half fares. under 3 years free
back

389

1614
Tunb. Wells to
C] LONDON
S First 13
This Ticket is available by
an S.E. or L.B.&.S.C. train
of the same class to any Sta
tion on either company in
London

390

0605
FRIDAY TO TUESDAY
Tunb'ge Wells to
C] LONDON
S First S.6
If used for any other Station
than those named the ticket
will be forfeited and the full
fare charged. [See Back

391

8606 8606
S.E.& MET RYS 1see back
Available Date of issue ONLY
S.5 NEW CROSS [S.E] to
BISHOPSGATE
B'gate B.gate
Via East London Line or Via Blackfriars
Junction or Via Cannon St. & Mark Lane
3½d. Third. 3½d.

392

Me 2049
UP DOWN
East Hill & Queen's Rd. | Hop Exchange & Vauxhall.
Falcon & Wandsworth Road station | Obelisk & Wandsworth Road Station
Ascension Church & Devonshire Road. | Westminster Bridge & Wandsworth Road Station
Queen's Rd. & Vauxhall. | Vauxhall & Queen's Rd.
Wandsworth Road Stn. & Westminster Bridge. | Devonshire Road & Ascension Church.
Wandsworth Road Station & Obelisk. | Wandsworth Road Station & Falcon.
Vauxhall & Hop Exchange. | Queen's Rd. & East Hill
1 D.
South London Tramways Company
Issued subject to Company's Bye-Laws.

393

TT 8782
1	12
2	11
3	10
4	9
5	8
6	7
S.M.T. LTD.
Issued subject to Co's Bye-laws and available
to point indicated by No. in Section, mach d.
NOT TRANSFERABLE.
To be shown or Given up on the off Break
of journey if demanded.

394

000 000
SOUTHERN RAILWAY.
This ticket is issued subject to the By-laws
Regulations and Conditions stated in the
Company's Time Tables Bills and Notices
Available on DAY of issue ONLY.
(S.3) GIPSY HILL to (S.3)
Gipsy Hill Gipsy Hill
Balham Balham
BALHAM
THIRD CLASS THIRD CLASS
Fare 4½d. Fare 4½d.

395

0970 0970
THE SOUTHERN RAILWAY COMPANY.
Available on the DATE of issue ONLY
ThisTicket is issued subject to the Regulations
& Conditions stated in the Company's Time
Tables & Bills
CLAPHAM JUNCTION
Series I.] TO [Series I.
CHELSEA & FULHAM
THIRD CLASS.
3d. Fare. 3d.

396

0466
SOUTHERN RAILWAY.
Issued subject to the Bye-laws,
Regulations & Conditions in the
Company's Bills and Notices.
Monthly as advertised.
Bude to
WATERLOO
Via Halwill & Okehampton
First Class. Fare 99/10
NOT TRANSFERABLE.
SOUTHERN RAILWAY.
MONTHLY RETURN.
Waterloo
Bude
Waterloo to
BUDE
Via Okehampton & Halwill
First Class. Fare 99/5 10
0466

397

0000 0000
SOUTHERN RAILWAY.
SPECIAL HALF-FARE TICKET
Available for One Week including day of issue and
expiry. Issued subject to the Conditions (a) on the
Half-Fare Ticket Order and (b) on back hereof.
BOAT EXPRESS
Folkestone Harbour to
Folkestone Har. Folkestone Har.
Victoria Victoria
VICTORIA
(Issued at Boulogne)
FIRST CLASS FIRST CLASS

The pram ticket here is similar
to *378* but for a 'blank' station.
394 was the first of its series to
be sold while *397* was sold in
France.

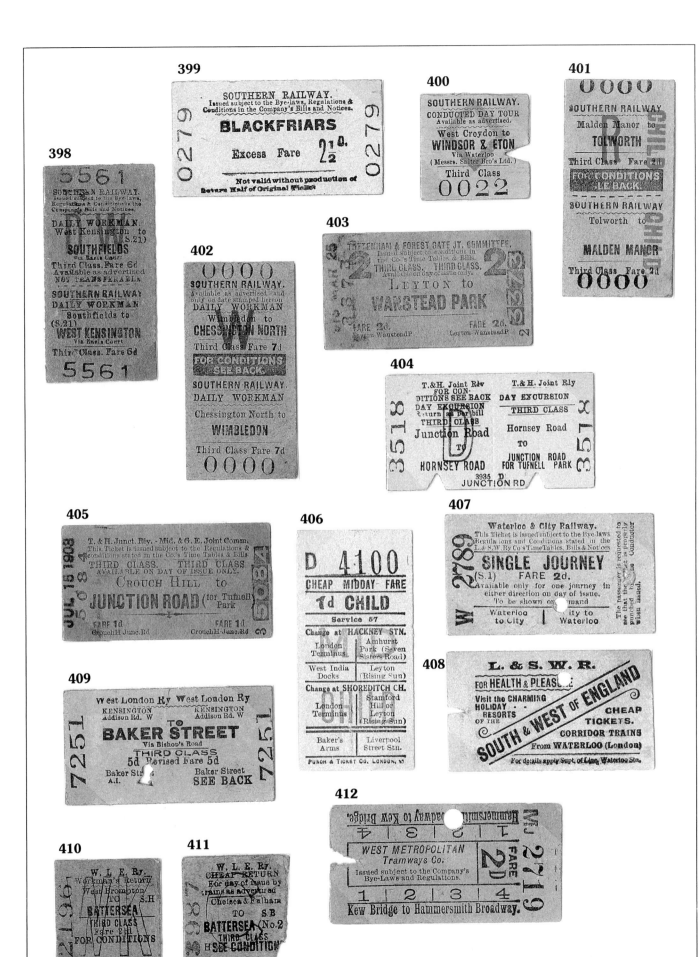

398

5561

SOUTHERN RAILWAY.
Issued subject to the Bye-laws,
Regulations & Conditions in the
Company's Bills and Notices.

DAILY WORKMAN.
West Kensington to
(S.21)
SOUTHFIELDS
via Earls Court
Third Class. Fare 6d
Available as advertised
NOT TRANSFERABLE

SOUTHERN RAILWAY
DAILY WORKMAN
Southfields to
(S.21)
WEST KENSINGTON
Via Earls Court
Third Class. Fare 6d

5561

399

0279

SOUTHERN RAILWAY.
Issued subject to the Bye-laws, Regulations &
Conditions in the Company's Bills and Notices.

BLACKFRIARS

Excess Fare 2½ᴰ.

Not valid without production of
Return Half of Original Ticket

0279

400

SOUTHERN RAILWAY.
CONDUCTED DAY TOUR
Available as advertised.
West Croydon to
WINDSOR & ETON
Via Waterloo
(Messrs. Salter Bro's Ltd.)
Third Class
0022

401

0000

SOUTHERN RAILWAY
Malden Manor to
TOLWORTH
Third Class   Fare 2d
FOR CONDITIONS
SEE BACK
SOUTHERN RAILWAY
Tolworth to
MALDEN MANOR
Third Class   Fare 2d
0000

CHILD   CHILD

402

0000

SOUTHERN RAILWAY.
Available as advertised and
only on date stamped hereon
DAILY WORKMAN
Wimbledon to
CHESSINGTON NORTH
Third Class Fare 7d
FOR CONDITIONS
SEE BACK
SOUTHERN RAILWAY.
DAILY WORKMAN
Chessington North to
WIMBLEDON
Third Class Fare 7d
0000

403

TOTTENHAM & FOREST GATE JT. COMMITTEE.
Issued subject to conditions in
the Co.'s Time Tables & Bills.
THIRD CLASS.   THIRD CLASS.
Available on day of issue only.
LEYTON to
WANSTEAD PARK
FARE 2d.   FARE 2d.
n. WansteadP   Leyton-WansteadP

2   2

404

3518

T.&H. Joint Rly   T.&H. Joint Rly
FOR CON-   DAY EXCURSION
DITIONS SEE BACK
DAY EXCURSION   THIRD CLASS
Return as per bill
THIRD CLASS   Hornsey Road
Junction Road   TO
TO   JUNCTION ROAD
HORNSEY ROAD   FOR TUFNELL PARK
3935   D
JUNCTION RD.

3518

405

5004

T.&H. Junct. Rly. - Mid. & G.E. Joint Comm.
This Ticket is issued subject to the Regulations &
conditions stated in the Co.'s Time Tables & Bills
THIRD CLASS.   THIRD CLASS.
AVAILABLE ON DAY OF ISSUE ONLY.
CROUCH HILL to
JUNCTION ROAD (for Tufnell
Park)
FARE 1d.   FARE 1d.
CrouchH Junc.Rd   CrouchH Junc.Rd

JUL 15 1903

406

D   4100
CHEAP MIDDAY FARE
1d CHILD
Service 57
Change at HACKNEY STN.
London	Amhurst
Terminus	Park (Seven
	Sisters Road)
West India	Leyton
Docks	(Rising Sun)
Change at SHOREDITCH CH.
London	Stamford
Terminus	Hill or
	Leyton
	(Rising Sun)
Baker's	Liverpool
Arms	Street Stn.
PUNCH & TICKET CO. LONDON. W

407

2786

Waterloo & City Railway.
This Ticket is issued subject to the Bye-laws,
Regulations and Conditions stated in the
L. & S.W. Ry Co's Time Tables, Bills & Notices
SINGLE JOURNEY
(S.1)   FARE 2d.
Available only for one journey in
either direction on day of issue.
To be shown on demand
Waterloo | City to
to City | Waterloo

The passenger is requested to
see that the ticket is properly
punched by the Conductor
when issued.

W

408

L. & S. W. R.
FOR HEALTH & PLEASURE
Visit the CHARMING
HOLIDAY
RESORTS
OF THE
SOUTH & WEST OF **ENGLAND**
CHEAP
TICKETS.
CORRIDOR TRAINS
From WATERLOO (London)
For details apply Supt. of Line, Waterloo Stn.

409

7251

West London Ry   West London Ry
KENSINGTON   KENSINGTON
Addison Rd. W   Addison Rd. W
TO
BAKER STREET
Via Bishop's Road
THIRD CLASS
5d Revised Fare 5d
Baker Street   Baker Street
A.I.   SEE BACK

7251

410

2196

W. L. E. Ry.
Workman's Return
West Brompton
TO   S.H
BATTERSEA
THIRD CLASS
Fare 2d
FOR CONDITIONS

411

7887

W. L. E. Ry.
CHEAP RETURN
For day of issue by
trains as advertised
Chelsea & Fulham
TO   S.B
BATTERSEA No.2
THIRD CLASS
H SEE CONDITIONS

412

Hammersmith Broadway to Kew Bridge.

1 3 4
WEST METROPOLITAN
Tramways Co.
Issued subject to the Company's
Bye-Laws and Regulations.
| 1 | 2 | 3 | 4 |
Kew Bridge to Hammersmith Broadway.

FARE
2D

2719

The London & South Western proudly advertising corridor
trains and the authors displaying two 'first issues'.

In the 1930s some Southern local Singles appeared in a strange 'two-at-view' format, always believed to have been a drastic economy measure (See **436** in the next Chapter). Examples the writers have seen came from stations on the former LSW (mostly Putney area), repeating two brief experiments by that company. As with many other specimens, the first patterns were pink which later gave way to green. The Southern revived this measure during the 1939-45 war, and curiously, confined it to the same stations.[15]

Four further Southern Railway tickets are shown. **399** is an Edmondson Excess Fare card coloured green and issued as late as 1960. The next SR item is half of a slightly unusual Return (**400**) for a Conducted Tour including use of a Salter Brothers' steamer and railway Third Class.

The Southern constructed two new suburban branches: the St Helier line and that to Chessington. The latter was intended to continue to Leatherhead where it would have rejoined the main network. In fact it reached Maldon Manor and Tolworth in time to open on 29 May 1938 and achieved Chessington North and South on 28 May 1939. World War 2 intervened to halt progress and the project was never completed. **401** and **402** are the first Return Tickets sold at Maldon Manor and at Chessington North. Today they are of interest as typical SR prints of those years.

Tottenham & Forest Gate Joint Committee

The line served between the two places named and was owned by the Midland and London Tilbury & Southend Railways jointly. When the Midland acquired the Tilbury company in 1912, the Committee became a wholly-owned Midland property. A Midland-printed ticket of the line is shown as **403**. The date appears to be 1913.

Tottenham & Hampstead Joint Railway

Later version of the entry below, and, due to the Grouping of 1923, was jointly-owned by the LMS and LNE Railways. Its title disappeared altogether with Nationalisation in 1948. **404** is probably from 1937. It is on buff card, unissued, and of clear LMS influence.

Tottenham & Hampstead Junction Railway

A line opened in 1868 and linking South Tottenham with Gospel Oak and jointly-owned by the Midland and Great Eastern Railways (**405**), whose names sometimes appeared after the title. Following the Grouping, the line became known as the Tottenham & Hampstead Joint Railway (above).

Walthamstow Council Light Railways

There were electric lines opened in 1905, mostly in Walthamstow itself. Tickets were chiefly by the Punch & Ticket Company with a few early ones by Bell Punch. Scarce Whiting, Auto-Tickets and Colleys issues are also known. A Punch & Ticket pattern is shown here for a child's Cheap Mid-Day Fare across LCC tracks into London (**406**).

Waterloo & City Railway

This was the Capital's second Tube Line. It was opened in 1898 but never formed an integral part of the Underground or its groupings. The London & South Western Railway were the first owners, followed in turn by the Southern Railway and the British Transport Commission. Fares were at first collected at turnstiles in cash and later on the trains in exchange for punch-type tickets. There were also some passenger-operated ticket machines and, from about 1940, conventional booking offices dealt with most

fares. A typical LSW buff Single is shown (**407**). Also reproduced is the reverse (**408**) side of a later LSW Single, depicting one of that company's self-advertisements, which so often make pleasant reading.

West Ham Corporation Tramways

Tickets were originally (1904) by Glasgow Numerical Printing Company, and later the Punch & Ticket Company. All were geographicals at first but soon became less-descriptive numerical-stage prints. Several tickets titled jointly with the East Ham tramways are also known. See litigation notes in Chapter 14.

West London and West London Extension Railways

We have already noted these two railways in connection with the Great Western and elsewhere. The West London Railway was the first to be opened in 1844, running from Willesden to Kensington; the Extension Railway followed in 1863 continuing the route to Battersea, with spurs permitting through working to Clapham Junction and to Victoria. The West London was leased jointly by the GW and LNW, two companies who took a third share each in the Extension and the LBSC and LSW taking a sixth only. The intermediate stations were St Quinton Park, Uxbridge Road, Kensington itself (called at different times Addison Road and Olympia), West Brompton, Chelsea and Fulham and finally Battersea. It has remained an important link between North and South London but apart from a few trains running non-stop from Clapham Junction to Kensington, there have been no passenger services serving stations on the line since 1940 (in fact Battersea was destroyed by bombing in the winter of 1940/41).

Here we illustrate a ticket bearing the West London Railway heading (**409**). Clearly a GW production, it is buff and dated 1921. The two Extension Railway tickets are also GW prints and date from 1939. **410** is grey and **411** is the contemporary green. **33** is a LNW printing in pale green.

West Metropolitan Tramways Company

This title lasted from early in 1882 until taken over by the LUT in 1894. The tramway was horse-operated in the area of Shepherd's Bush, Acton, Hammersmith and Kew Bridge. Tickets seen have been 1d white, 2d blue (**412**) and 3d green, all in this 'nice old style'.

Westerham Valley Railway

An abortive attempt at preserving a section of former British Railways line in Kent. The railway never actually opened, but managed an exhibition on the local station. For that it issued souvenir Platform Tickets on yellow card.

Whitechapel & Bow Railway

A 1902 company owned by the District and LTS railway companies, which became part of London Transport Executive in 1948. The two tickets shown are: **413**, a 1948 Soldiers Furlough return, and **414**, a typical Scheme Ticket from 1946. Colours are buff and green respectively.

Woodside & South Croydon Joint Line

This was a property of the SE and LBSC railways, opened in 1885. Tickets of both these partners are known with the title showing under that of the issuing railway and in their own styles for each, the last being SEC-style at the 1917 closure. The one ticket here (**415**) sets out the initials of the South Eastern & Chatham Railway on a green Return coupon dated 1908.

413

3rd Cl W&BR
SOLDIERS FURLOUGH
SPECIAL TICKET
Issued subject to the Bye-
Laws, Regulations & Condi-
tions of the Railways and
to the Special Conditions
relating to Cheap Tickets.
Available day of issue only.

Mile End
To
Any Station on back
Not transferable

414

1591
W & BR
BOW ROAD
to Ealing
Broadway
(Dist or GW)
(via Ealing Com
or Wood Lane)
Alexandra Pal.
Northfields
North Ealing
Southgate
Burnt Oak
Neasden
or intermediately
BOW ROAD
1591

415

2496
S.E. & C.R.
Woodside & South Croydon
Joint Line.
Available Day of issue or
following Day (SeeBack)
Selsdon Rd to
WOODSIDE
Third 5d

After touring the City (above), tickets for the longer-distance traveller. Still displaying the widespread use of the Edmondson card, with a much larger form for reserving space in the Smoking car.

416

G.C. Ry.
P. T.
Available for One Week
NOTTINGHAM(Victoria) to
LONDON(MARYLEBONE)
THIRD CLASS
L.P.T
LondonM
SEE BACK
Fare 2s 7d
LondonM.

417

MIDLAND RAILWAY.
FIRST CLASS.
Aviemore
TO
LONDON (KINGS CROSS)
Via Dunfield, Forthbridge, Berwick, York, &
(Over.) London K.C.V.D.
93
Fare
77/8

418

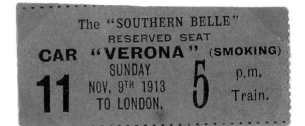

The "SOUTHERN BELLE"
RESERVED SEAT
CAR "VERONA" (SMOKING)
SUNDAY
11
NOV. 9TH 1913
TO LONDON.
5
p.m.
Train.

419

0169
L.N.E.R.
CONTINENTAL SERIES.
KING'S CROSS
TO
BRADFORD
Via Carcroft
Available for 33 Days
FIRST
For conditions
see back
KING'S
L.N.E.R.
CONTINENTAL SERIES.
BRADFORD
TO
KING'S CROSS
Via Carcroft
C.
S.
215
FIRST
For conditions
see back
CROSS
0169

420

G45
L. & N. W. R.
SPECIAL.
L. D. EXCURSION
Return as per bill
LONDON (EUSTON)
TO
RED ROCK
Covered Carriage
over
EUSTON
L. & N. W. R.
SPECIAL.
L. D. EXCURSION
as per bill.
Red Rock
TO
LONDON (EUSTON)
Covered Carriage
over
G45

421

19-DE-01
N.S.R. THIRD CLASS.
STOKE-ON-TRENT To
LONDON (EUSTON)
Via Colwich or Norton Bridge.
AVAILABLE FOR ONE JOURNEY ON DAY OF ISSUE ONLY
Turn over
FIELD
1035
Fare 6/1

422

2152
P. P. & W. Joint Rys.
Available for one journey only to be completed within Four days of issue.
NEWTON STEWART TO
LONDON (EUSTON)
VIA ANNAN CARLISLE & L. & N. W. Ry.
Third]
a/c)
[Class
TURN OVER)
EUS
FARE 27/6
2152

423

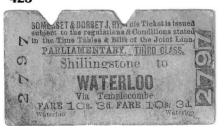

2797
SOMERSET & DORSET J. Ry. This Ticket is issued
subject to the regulations & Conditions stated
in the Time Tables & Bills of the Joint Line
PARLIAMENTARY. THIRD CLASS.
Shillingstone to
WATERLOO
Via Templecombe
FARE 1s. 3d. FARE 1s. 3d.
Waterloo
Waterloo
2797

424

0689
SOUTHERN RAILWAY.
Available to return by any
train at or after 6.0. a.m.
SUNDAY or by any train on
ON DAY.
BRIGHTON TO
VICTORIA
1st Class. Fare 14/0
For conditions see b

425

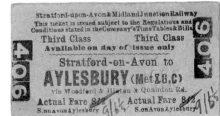

406
Stratford-upon-Avon & Midland Junction Railway
This ticket is issued subject to the Regulations and
Conditions stated in the Company's Time Tables & Bills
Third Class
Third Class
Available on day of issue only
Stratford-on-Avon to
AYLESBURY (Met&G.C)
via Woodford & Hinton & Quainton Rd.
Actual Fare 8/0
S. on Avon Aylesbury
Actual Fare 8/0
S. on Avon Aylesbury
406

Tickets for Travel to London

An interesting *finale* to a London Collection is a selection of tickets for journeying to that city. A third of a century ago, families still travelled together by rail and as a crowded train arrived at a London terminus with fathers holding the tickets while laden with suitcases, the children mixing with friends made on the train, examination and collection at the barrier was far from an exact science! Many tickets remained in a waistcoat pocket, to become at first a souvenir and later a prized collector's item, an item of historic ephemera preserved for all time.

In those days, stations stocked a wide variety of tickets to their London terminus and in the decade after Nationalisation, the Regional Audit Offices were generous to *bona fide* collectors with donations of unsold obsolete specimens. For these two reasons, there are within the hobby reasonable numbers of sometimes unusual pre-1939 tickets to London. Ten have been selected at random.

416 is a Great Central issue of 1907. The First Class Single (**417**) from the Highland Railway's Aviemore was used in 1906. The unnumbered **418** guaranteed a seat in a smoking compartment on the 'Southern Belle' from Brighton in 1913. Had **419** ever been sold, it would have brought someone by First Class carriage from Bradford; the heading 'Continental Series' and the strange period of availability combine to suggest that it represented the first stage of a foreign holiday.

Red Rock, the starting point of the unsold Special Long Date Excursion by one of the LNW's covered carriages (**420**), is a suburb of Wigan. The date of printing of the ticket is uncertain but the station closed early in 1949. **421** is a Third Class Single from the North Staffordshire Railway's Stoke-on-Trent for the reasonable price even in 1901 of 6/1d (30½p). The limitation 'Available for one journey on day of issue only' was normal NS wording. **422** came from the Portpatrick & Wigtownshire Joint Railways about 1900.

423 brought someone up from North Dorset in the late 1890s; they would have changed on to the LSW at Templecombe. The printing is Midland — one of the Somerset & Dorset's masters. **424** brought a Weekender back home from Brighton in the days of the steam-hauled 'Southern Belle' while **425** was intended to take a customer of the Stratford-upon-Avon & Midland Junction Railway along now lifted tracks to Aylesbury around 1925.

Reproduced in many books are GW buff Third Class Singles from Plymouth to Paddington ending with the words 'Issued on Board White Star Line SS Titanic'. Of course these never reached the ill-fated vessel and were not sold. They remain gruesome reminders of a tragic event.

CHAPTER 6

The Severed-Half Ticket

Be it half of a large paper ticket or of a popular Edmondson card, the severed-half is the Cinderella of the hobby. Its many critics point out that the roughly-torn edge gives it an untidy appearance and also that its print is small and cramped. Some would emphasise that 'the other half is missing'. Its few champions plead that the most interesting and unusual offers made by railway companies are their return trips and details of such journeys and the company's stipulations are to be found in that tiny print. A point less often made is that in pre-Grouping days, Return Tickets were often printed in bright colours in order to attract the instant attention of barrier staff required to monitor the varied tickets coming into their hands. The half-Edmondson is likely to offer any collector more than half of the average interest to be derived from a whole ticket.

The offer of a cheap return fare is almost invariably an attempt to attract the person who would not otherwise use the railway. Restrictions must be imposed not only to keep the ticket holder away from the busy peak hour services but also to ensure that the facility cannot be conveniently used by the regular traveller or the annual holidaymaker. Otherwise revenue would be not gained but lost. Strict conditions as to the times of travel and the amount of luggage permitted (generally hand luggage only on the outward journey and a limited weight on the return) are included in the terms of the travel contract. Nowadays, these are rarely specified on the ticket which simply carries a phrase such as 'Available as Advertised' but in yesteryear some at least were printed on the ticket. They tended to be set out on the return half rather than the outward, presumably to ensure the traveller was appraised of the limitations throughout both journeys.

Occasionally the half-Edmondson ticket is all that can be found to represent its particular company (**441**), station or booking office practice. In the absence of the much-maligned half, great slices of railway history might be omitted from a collection. Colours and styles, serial numbers and security background patterns can all be studied from the half-ticket.

The two-coupon return ticket all but vanished from the British scene in 1970 (see Chapter 16) but there remain plenty in circulation among collectors. Do not despise half-tickets! Enjoy

them for the visual appeal of their often bright colours as well as their archival aspect.

Twenty-four fairly typical specimens are illustrated on Page 74.

First row

Three tickets (**426-428**) of the London Brighton & South Coast Railway, selected as much for their variety of printed device as for their individual category and journey detail. The fourth ticket (**429**) was purchased in 1881 at Looe in Cornwall. It is mainly yellow in colour. The Workman's Tickets are on white card with red overprints. The square overprint was normally the return portion while the large red spot signified the outward half. The Commercial Traveller's ticket was for use 'Monday to Friday' in 1907.

Second row

Three tickets of the London & South Western Railway and one (**433**) from the London Tilbury & Southend Railway. The diagonal cross was a routine convention for marking return coupons, red, green and blue were the principal colours for this. The LTS used an equally distinctive single vertical red band. The right hand ticket with a similar band (**432**) was for a trip by steamer along the coast of Normandy and, unlike the others in this group, is perforated on two sides and taken from a larger card.

Third row

434 and **435** — the Special Shopping Tickets — were the brain child of the British Transport Commission's Southern Region and lasted from October 1954 to 5 September 1963. Each was sold only on certain days in midweek after the morning rush hour and the holder had to be on the train for home by 4.30pm. They were on purple card with the 'S' overprint in red. Despite their short lifetime they spanned the transition from Third Class (**434**) to Second (**435**) and from named London Termini to the general 'London' version. **435** was sold on the last day of the facility. The other two tickets in the row are not portions of Return Tickets but individual Singles. In each case the idea of printing two tickets side

426

L. B. & S. C. RY.
Workman's Ticket.
VICTORIA
TO
HACKBRIDGE
6d. Third Cl.
NOT TRANSFERABLE.
Available on the Day
of issue ONLY.
See conditions on
0208

427

L. B. & S. C. RY.
WORKMAN'S TICKET
FOREST HILL
TO
WANDSW'TH COM.
THIRD CLASS. 8d.
REVISED FARE.
NOT TRANSFERABLE.
Available only by the
Special Cheap Train for
the Working Classes.
1610

428

0083
L. B. & S. C. Ry.
Commercial Traveller.
FRIDAY TO MONDAY.
LONDON B'DGE
TO
HAYWARDS H'TH
THIRD CL. 3s. ½d.
[SEE BACK

429

L. & Cdn. Ry.
RETURN.
MOORSWATER to
LOOE
Not Transferable
Third Class (S.)
Issued subject to
Conditions published
at Stations.
1623

430

6868
South Western Ry.
This Ticket is issued subject to
the Regulations & Conditions
stated in the Company's Time
Tables & Bills
ASCOT
TO S.1
BRACKNELL
2nd Class Fare 7d

431

6868
South Western Ry.
ONE DAY EX'N
This Ticket is issued subject to
the Regulations & Conditions
stated in the Company's Time
Tables & Bills
BERE ALSTON
TO S.3
PLYMOUTH FRIARY
3rd Class Fare

432

No 1059 (London, T.O.)
L. & S.W.R.
EXCURSION.
HAVRE
to
TROUVILLE.
(By Steamboat.)
First Class.

433

L. T. & S. R.
DAY EXCURSION
RETURN
Available day of issue only
Fenchurch St.
S.1. TO
SOUTHEND (No.1)
Third Class
Fare 2s. 9d.
SEE BACK
3672

434

3rd SPECIAL
SHOPPING
Return journey to
commence not later
than 4.30 p.m.
Victoria or Waterloo
TO
STAINES CTL.
(S)
For Conditions see over
2479

435

2nd - SPECIAL
SHOPPING
Not available for
use on trains leaving
after 4.30 p.m.
London
to
PURLEY (D.)
(S)
For conditions see o
8170

436

SOUTHERN RAILWAY.
This ticket is issued subject
to the Company's Bye-laws
Regulations & Conditions
in their Time Tables, Not-
ices & Book of Regulations
Available Day of Issue Only
Wimbledon
(S.23) to
CLAPHAM JCT.
Third Class Fare 5½d
1246

437

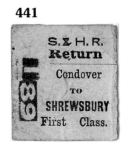

1st SINGLE LOR
For c'nditions see back
Herculaneum
to
BROCKLEBANK
or any inter. Station
Fare 9d.
1 S. 16
BROCKLEBANK
0423

438

HALF DAY
EXCURSION - 3rd
(S.T. D269)
Oakwood Tech Sch
Rotherham
(Central)
TO
WEMBLEY HILL
23rd April, 1955
(E)
For conditions see over
0400

439

2nd - ORDINARY
RETURN
Poole to
DORCHESTER SOUTH
by Rail or Hants
and Dorset Motor
Services or Southern
National Omnibus
(S) Fare 42p
(or conditions
over
B
0811

440

L. C. & D. R.
HALF-CROWN DAY
Including Admission
C. Palace (High Level)
TO
LORDSHIP LANE
First Class,
3s. 0
See other side.
028

441

S. & H. R.
Return
Condover
TO
SHREWSBURY
First Class.
189

442

Great Weste
EALIN
HAY
THIRD C
Issued subject to the
on the Co's. Time Bill
Hayes
4427

443

.563
Gt. Western Ry.
BEBINGTON
2 to 1s
CHESTER
Second Class

Much may be learned
from halves. All
imaginable overprints
and devices are in their
designs. *440* includes
admission, *444* a very
short-lived local venture
and *447* currency in
process of change.

444

3528
Brighton & Rottingdean Sea-
shore Electric Tramroad Co.
BRIGHTON
(Kemp Town)
and OVINGDEAN or
Rottingdean.

445

L. M. & S. R.
HALF DAY
Exc'n
Valid as advertised
3rd Cl. St'mr & Rail
Rowardennan
To
BALLOCH
Via Balloch Pier
For conditions
see back
090

446

T. V. R.
RETURN
RADYR
TO
CARDIFF (Queen St)
T.V.R.
Second Class
1/2
See Notice on back.
1769

447

ORDINARY
RETURN 2nd
Hurst Green
to
OXTED
Fare 1/2
For conditions
see over (S)
128624

448

D. & A. Jnt. Ry.
WEEK END TICKET.
Outward Half
THIRD CLASS.
rbroath
TO
JOHNSHAVEN
VIA L
n vL. (W.... VER.
744

449

Isle of Wight. Newport
Junc J. Railway
Newport
1 (S.1) TO
HORRINGFORD
Second Class
Not Transferable. Issued
subject to the Company
Bye Laws Published
Regulatio
1560

by side was tried as an economy measure. They were never popular with booking staff who had to sever them on issue and generally finished up with a number of unsold halves at the end of the shift. **436** is a typical Southern Railway issue of 1933 and **437** a 1943 specimen from the since-dismantled Liverpool Overhead Railway. The lessons of the first experiment had been forgotten at Waterloo by 1940. The system was adopted for a short while by the SR and LNER as a contribution to the war effort!

Fourth row
438 is for an Excursion from Rotherham's Oakwood Technical School to Wembley Hill. A large number of similar pre-printed outward halves for various school parties from South Yorkshire and adjoining counties have been seen and one wonders what happened to the ticket examination and collection at Wembley Hill on that day, to say nothing of any audit department control. **439** is another child's ticket, issued on 1 May 1975 and offering the holder a choice of travel by rail or by one of two bus companies.

440 from the London Chatham & Dover Railway recalls one of the popular Crystal Palace 'Half Crown Days' (12½p in today's currency). The next item is a rare yellow First Class return dated 1863 from the Shrewsbury & Hereford Railway (**441**).

Fifth row
442 and **443** are both from the Great Western Railway and illustrate distinctively different booking office procedures. **443** is blue-green and the top half of a vertically printed two-coupon card instrumental in returning a passenger to Chester in 1863. **442** is buff and actually a scissored piece cut from a horizontally printed one-coupon Single Ticket of 1881. While **443** is a Return Ticket in itself, **442** is a contrived half-fare Single. Presumably no Child Singles were in stock and so an ordinary adult Single was

bisected to create two tickets at half fare. The first of these would require the clerk to transfer the serial number by manuscript, leaving the machine numbered piece on hand for the next identical booking. Several such pairs of ticket portions sharing the same serial number but with different dates of issue have been observed. It has to be remarked that there would have been some risk attached to gripping a half-card while presenting it to the jaws of a ravenous (Edmondson) dating press!

444 comes from the Brighton & Rottingdean Seashore Electric Tramroad. This was the famous 'Daddy Long Legs', a unique installation operating on track laid below high water level along the seashore at Brighton, Sussex. Opened on 10 November 1896 and closed early in 1901 to make way for sea defence works, the line lasted a little over four years. Probably the only British shore-based railway vehicle to be treated as a marine vessel under the Board of Trade rules of the day, 'Daddy Long Legs' was required to carry lifebelts. This item is the outward half of an 1898 Return Ticket. **445** was someone's souvenir of a half-day cruise on Loch Lomond on 30 June 1951. Rowardennan is a hotel on the east bank of the Loch opposite Glen Douglas. The rail part of the excursion was minimal; the distance from Balloch Pier to Balloch is almost 1km. Perhaps the holder walked it and so retained the ticket.

Sixth row
446 is from Wales' Taff Vale Railway. **447** was printed immediately before the change to decimal currency in February 1971. It illustrates a typical dual-currency fare of 1s 2d or 6p. The two remaining tickets are from Scotland's Dundee & Arbroath Joint Railway and dated 1904 (**448**) together with an 1879 piece from the Isle of Wight (Newport Junction) Railway (**449**), which subsisted on the Isle of Wight from 1875 to 1887.

CHAPTER 7

Tickets on the Fringe

Previously it has been shown that Edmondson's invention spread across the British Isles. There was no reason why it should be limited to travel on rails or indeed to travel alone; the system was clearly valid for any transaction involving the receipt of money, the proof of which had to be in the form of a document which in its turn would be rapidly recognised by some other person.

On the very periphery of the interest of the transport ticket collector lie a number of receipts and even curios in the form of Edmondson cards. Some represent ancillary services provided by a railway company; others have no connection with travel but mimic its tickets and so strike the interest of some casual recipient. Some of both types are illustrated in this chapter.

Tickets to safety
During World War 2, although previously the intention was not to allow such use, public demand required that Underground stations of London Passenger Transport Board (LPTB) be available nightly as air raid shelters. It was generally thought that air raids would be short, violent affairs. When all-night raids started, people began to take bedding down with them and slept on the platforms and even in the passages. Some sort of order was created within a few days, when white lines were painted down each platform, one more or less in the centre and the other about 18in from the edge. Until 9pm the shelterers had to keep behind the first line but then could advance as far as the second. In practice, these rules were rarely observed. There was so little room left on platforms quite early in the evening that travel by Underground was to say the least dangerous. Of course, deaths by passengers falling under trains in this way were never announced for reasons of security.

Before very long, some local authorities provided wooden bunk beds placed hard against the walls furthest from the platform edge. These helped to confine shelterers to the area of greatest safety and keep them as far as possible away from *bona fide* travellers. Refreshment and other facilities were provided. A special refreshment train toured the system nightly after the normal timetable service had closed down. One problem was keeping children amused. After a short while, they took to making

train rides — as shelterers, they were already within the 'paid' zones and thus could ride and return without much ado — as a form of diversion and without regard to the nuisance derived from overcrowding of the trains. At this time (the Balham incident excepted), the Underground was the one safe way of getting around London. In the Balham incident a bomb severed the water main under Balham High Road and water flooded into the station and many were drowned. Seconds later an omnibus travelling in the blackout, fell into the bomb crater.

Regular users of these shelters below ground were issued with 'Seasons' headed with the name of the relevant Metropolitan Borough or other Local Authority. These tickets are considered as outside the scope of this essay, as they were neither railway nor railway-jointly-issued, despite being available upon railway property. They do however, make useful supporting pieces for the collector of war ephemera and helpful asides for the social historian.

Of direct interest here, yet considerably less well known, is the blue Edmondson card issued to casual users of the railway shelters. These were valid for one night and headed with a railway title 'London Passenger Transport Board' (as abbreviated) or in one case — 'London & North Eastern Railway' — always with the words '. . . in conjunction with The Local Authority'.

The LNER exception was Highgate station, opened on 19 January 1941. Until 1938 London Transport's Northern Line had ended at the present Archway station, then known as 'Highgate'. The tunnel had been extended nowthwards under the line of Archway Road to join the LNER's branch from Finsbury Park to Alexandra Palace, High Barnet and Edgware just north of that company's Highgate station. London Transport trains took over the running of the High Barnet service and the Edgware as far as Mill Hill East (the rest being eventually abandoned) while the LNER and its successor retained the Alexandra Palace service until closure in July 1954.

An interchange at the present Highgate station was urgently required but the gradient of Archway Road, which is almost as steep as the nearby Highgate Hill, made it impossible for the tube trains to surface at Highgate. Accordingly, a standard tube station

450

L.N.E.R in conjunction with
The LOCAL AUTHORITY

Admit one Person for Shelter
(if available) at

HIGHGATE Station

Persons permitted to use this
Station as, or as a means of access to, an
Air Raid Shelter do so at their own risk
in all respects,
FOR FURTHER CONDITIONS SEE BACK

897

451

11 JY 44 LONDON TRANSPORT in conjunction
with The LOCAL AUTHORITY

Admit one Person for Shelter
(if available) at

PICCADILLY CIRCUS Station

Persons permitted to use this
Station as, or as a means of access to, an
Air Raid Shelter do so at their own risk
in all respects,
FOR FURTHER CONDITIONS SEE BACK

065

452

I 000

3rd Cl LNER 1
C
10d HIGHGATE
to East Acton
(via Wood Lane)

Trinity Road
Enfield West
Putney Bridge
Chiswick Park
Surrey Docks
or intermediately

HIGHGATE

000

453

3rd Cl LT
SOLDIERS FURLOUGH SPECIAL TICKET
Issued subject to the Bye-Laws, Regulations
and Conditions of the Board and to the Special
Conditions relating to Cheap Tickets.
Available day of issue only.

UXBRIDGE to

Any ONE station on back
or intermediately
Transferable

247 56

454

3rd Cl LT 2
SERVICES
LEAVE TICKET.
Issued subject to the
Bye-Laws, Regulations
and Conditions of the
Board and to the Special
Conditions relating to
Cheap Tickets. Available
for 3 Months including
day of issue and return.

Any station on back

to CHARING CROSS
NOT TRANSFERABLE

3rd Cl LT 2
SERVICES
LEAVE TICKET.
Issued subject to the
Bye-Laws, Regulations
and Conditions of the
Board and to the Special
Conditions relating to
Cheap Tickets. Available
day of issue only.

Charing Cross
To
Any station on back
NOT TRANSFERABLE

25898

455

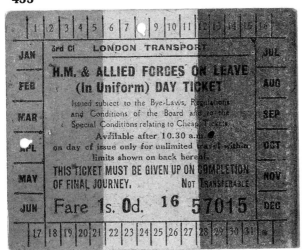

| 1 | 2 | 3 | 4 | 5 | 6 | 7 | | 9 | 10 | 11 | 12 | 13 | 14 | 15 | 16 |

JAN 3rd Cl LONDON TRANSPORT JUL

FEB **H.M. & ALLIED FORCES ON LEAVE** AUG

(In Uniform) DAY TICKET

MAR Issued subject to the Bye-Laws, Regulations SEP
and Conditions of the Board and to the
Special Conditions relating to Cheap Tickets.

APL Available after 10.30 a.m. OCT
on day of issue only for unlimited travel within
limits shown on back hereof.

MAY THIS TICKET MUST BE GIVEN UP ON COMPLETION NOV
OF FINAL JOURNEY. Not Transferable

JUN Fare 1s. 0d. 16 57015 DEC

| 17 | 18 | 19 | 20 | 21 | 22 | 23 | 24 | 25 | 26 | 27 | 28 | 29 | 30 | 31 | * |

456

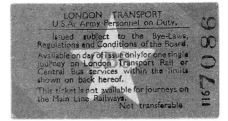

LONDON TRANSPORT
U.S.A. Army Personnel on Duty.

Issued subject to the Bye-Laws,
Regulations and Conditions of the Board.

Available on day of issue only for one single
journey on London Transport Rail or
Central Bus services within the limits
shown on back hereof.

This ticket is not available for journeys on
the Main Line Railways.
Not transferable

1167086

458

B.R.E. CHIEF ACCOUNTANT,
REVENUE OFFICE
COVERING TICKET

3113

SHEFF. MID. To ST. PANCRAS
Description 2ND ORD RETURN
Nos. out of order 26/2008 - 26/2201 inc.
for Chief Accountant
26.11. 1969
See over

3113

457

PHILADELPHIA TRANSPORTATION COMPANY

AIR RAID EMERGENCY TICKET
Issued in Event of Air Raid Warning

This Ticket will Permit Passenger to Re-board STREET CAR, TRACK-
LESS TROLLEY (or Bus Routes 23-A, 55, 73, 83) or Re-enter SUBWAY-
ELEVATED STATION Immediately Following All-Clear Signal.

A MISDEMEANOR
The sale, barter, or transfer of this ticket
or its presentation for passage by anyone other
than the person to whom issued, constitutes a
misdemeanor under the laws of the State of
Pennsylvania, punishable by fine or imprison-
ment or both.
Act approved June 13, 1911. P. L. 903.

Conductor, Operator or Cashier
will issue this ticket, in accordance
with current regulations, as passengers leave vehicle or station.

ISSUED GOING

N E S W

459

British Railways Board
CREDIT CARD
Class & Description
2 S C D
From FRESHFIELD
To BOOTLE
Nos. 4750 - 4813 inc.
Insert in bundle/tube &
shew as non-issued when
numbers reached. And
card sent with RETURN
to AUDIT in support of
entry.
Ref. PC1/5
Date 2 -10. 64
for REV ACCOUNTANT
29242

460

SOUTHERN RY.
Available for 3 Days including day of issue
This ticket is issued subject to the Bye-Laws,
Regulations and Conditions in the
Company's Time Tables, Bills and Notices

REVISED FARE REVISED
WORTHING
TO
YORK
Via London, Kings Cross & L.N.E.R.
30/5 THIRD CL. Fare 30/5

0025

321 8

Wartime London with Allied
Forces travel on duty and on
leave. Five of America's
eastern cities issued tickets
designed to cope with air raids
that thankfully never came.

was built under the existing LNER station but the latter company remained the freeholders. The LNER heading thus appeared on the Shelter Ticket (**450**) as on Northern Line travel tickets. **451** represents the pure-LPTB type. **452** is a 'first day' travel issue of 19 January 1941. Supporting the reminiscences of these belligerent times are: Soldiers Furlough Special single journey ticket, typical of its time — the early 1940s (**453**). Services Leave Ticket for one local return journey (**454**). Day Ticket in patriotically coloured panels of red, white and blue, and printed for 'unlimited travel' within a specified zone by His Majesty's and Allied Forces. The main sale centre was a special booth in Trafalgar Square. A leave pass had to be produced by the purchaser. This was a type of London ticket so widely used in those days that it is conceivable our more senior readers may recognise it and recall personal circumstances of its use (**455**). USA Army Personnel on Duty ticket, in this case (**456**) for members of the Army's Central Base Sector ('CBS').

Before leaving Tickets to Safety, an American example deserves mention. Although there was no truly belligerent raid over America's eastern seaboard during World War 2, a number of authorities prepared and issued to staff packs of Air Raid Emergency Tickets (**457**, Philadelphia) or Blackout Emergency Tickets (eg Baltimore) to be given to passengers in the event of a raid. These were valid on local railway lines as well as buses, without distinction, as all the five cities concerned operated both modes.

There was one true emergency over New York in the period (plus several practice drills). It proved to be a false alarm occasioned by failure of the coastal observation stations to positively identify one aeroplane as a friend, early one morning about 1944. The plane was therefore properly classified as a foe for about 5min, long enough to awaken residents with wailing sirens which screamed at 4am. This was authenticated by a resident of the time (who was also a ticket collector) who reports 'The all-clear sounded so rapidly afterwards that I doubt there was time to issue any tickets to late-night riders. Tickets *were* of course used during the practice drills'.

No underground shelter tickets came from American cities in the way they did from wartime London. Very few eastern and western cities possessed an underground system in the 1940s and those that did exist were too close to the surface to be considered a protection.

Ancillary services

Covering Ticket (**458**). This category was issued to stations by audit department staff to cover agreed faults and discrepancies. When the inserted serial number was reached in sales, the ticket would be withdrawn and returned to audit offices with the relevant report.

Credit Cards (**459**) performed a similar function. This particular item was issued to credit the absence of 63 tickets. Such a quantity accounted for in this way could mean 63 tickets were spoiled in the course of manufacture and not passed for delivery to the station concerned, or possibly a local mishap which rendered them unsaleable.

Reminder Tickets. In Britain this function was met with a ticket which was printed identical to those reminded of but produced on a distinctively different board (usually red). **460** is typical of former South of England practice, headed Southern Railway but with clear transitional influences of the earlier London Brighton & South Coast Railway. In a later method the Southern Railway

used a ticket which exactly duplicated one of the saleable specimens, including use of the same board, but which was overstamped with the words 'Reminder. Not to be issued'. Nevertheless, some were issued and indeed one of the writers was sold one such card for its printed fare at a station in Sussex early in 1950!

Cross-hatch Ticket (**461**) is not a printed category, nor possibly official jargon, but one coined for the purpose of this explanation. It derives from the blue (sometimes green or brown) cross-hatching applied to make the card significantly different from all other railway tickets likely to be in any way associated. Such cards were sent to audit departments by printers, accompanying each completed printing order. The mock serial number was the reference to be used when ordering further supplies. Each cross-hatch specimen was then securely filed by audit staff and amended from time to time to take account of changing station names, regulations, fares, etc.

Training staff in ticketing procedures has necessitated some highly unusual ticket specimens. These are, however, modified sufficiently to avoid their later misuse. In **462** note the contrived destination 'BBBB' and its zero-fare. **463** displays a positive fare for a totally improbable journey from an Oak to a Beech (also see PORTIS and SSTIS in Chapter 2).

Car Parking and Cycle Storage. Before World War 2, the gratuitous use of the station yard by the motorist who continued his journey by train was regarded as part of the business of attracting customers and charging for the service was scarcely considered. The earliest Car Park Ticket the present writers are able to produce is **464** from the busy town of Shrewsbury of 16 December 1941. Although carrying a GW&LMS Joint heading, the conditions on the back that purport to absolve the company from any liability specify only the GW company.

The charge of one shilling (5p) was the norm in pre-nationalisation days although the LMS generally charged 6d (2½p). **465** was issued on 7 October 1947 while on 29 April 1950 in early BTC days the former SR station at Herne Bay was demanding a shilling (**466**).

In the grim wartime days of November 1943, one could leave a bicycle on the premises of the Manchester South Junction & Altrincham Railway's Dane Road station over a period of seven days for sevenpence (**467**). The holder of a LMS pre-1939 Holiday Contract Tour Ticket could share his holiday with his cycle on payment of 5/3d (26p) (**468**).

469 is a British Railways ticket in pre-standard SR style. Betchworth station has been unstaffed for almost a quarter of a century but someone was on duty on Boxing Day 1957 to receive one shilling for the services of the car park. Three months earlier the same motorcar had enjoyed the right to park for a whole week at nearby Belmont for three shillings (15p), again receiving a pre-standard ticket (**470**). **471** was printed in the Decimal Currency age — the charge at Warrington (Bank Quay) was 13p. The charge at Oxshott on 5 March 1976 was 17p (**472**) while by August 1980, the fee at Inverkeithing had advanced to 35p (**473**). Nearby Rosyth Halt had been selling tickets marked 10p only 18 months before (**474**).

Motorcycle parking is usually cheaper. One such vehicle was left at Kingswood & Burgh Heath on Leap Year Day 1956 for just 6d (**475**) while on 22 June 1976 tickets printed for 9d (4p by then) were still being sold at Sittingbourne & Milton Regis (**476**).

The modern Period Parking ticket contains a stipulation that it

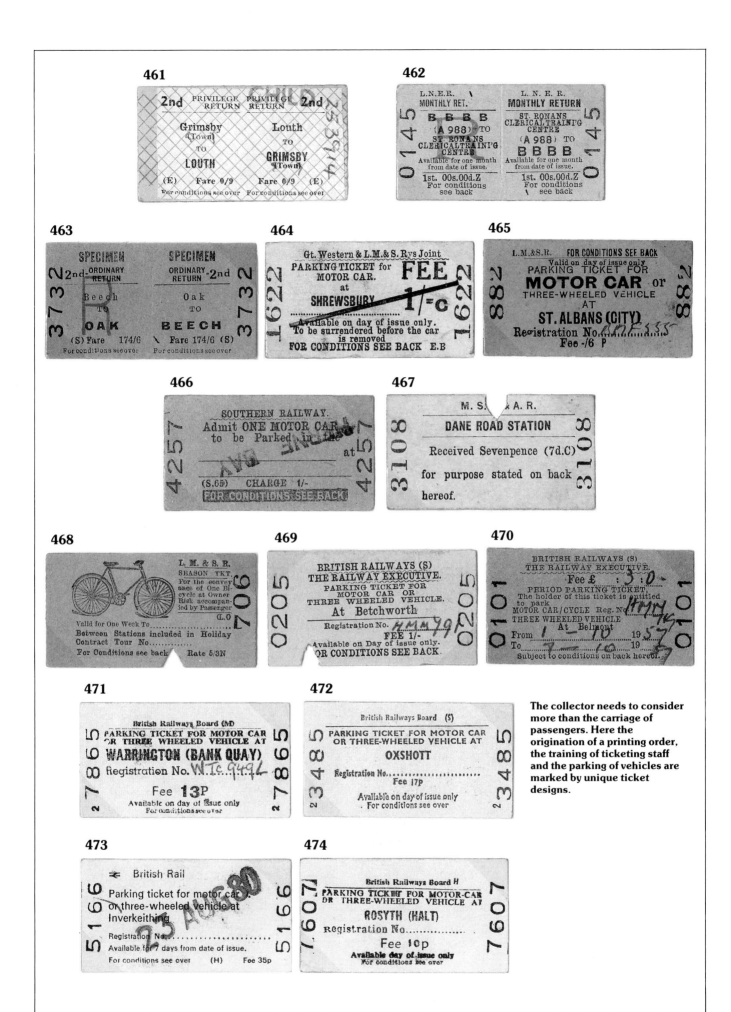

461

2nd PRIVILEGE RETURN — PRIVILEGE RETURN 2nd

Grimsby (Town) — Louth
TO — TO
LOUTH — GRIMSBY (Town)

(E) Fare 0/9 — Fare 0/9 (E)

For conditions see over — For conditions see over

462

L.N.E.R. MONTHLY RET. — L.N.E.R. MONTHLY RETURN

B B B B — ST. RONANS CLERICAL TRAIN'G CENTRE
(A 988) TO — (A 988) TO
ST. RONANS CLERICAL TRAINI'G CENTRE — B B B B

Available for one month from date of issue. — Available for one month from date of issue.

1st. 00s.00d.Z — 1st. 00s.00d.Z
For conditions see back — For conditions see back

0145 — 0145

463

SPECIMEN — SPECIMEN

2nd ORDINARY RETURN — ORDINARY RETURN 2nd

Beech — Oak
TO — TO
OAK — BEECH

(S) Fare 174/6 — Fare 174/6 (S)

For conditions see over — For conditions see over

3732 — 3732

464

Gt. Western & L.M.& S. Rys Joint
PARKING TICKET for
MOTOR CAR
at
SHREWSBURY

FEE 1/=c

Available on day of issue only.
To be surrendered before the car is removed
FOR CONDITIONS SEE BACK E.B

1622 — 1622

465

L.M.&S.R. FOR CONDITIONS SEE BACK
Valid on day of issue only
PARKING TICKET FOR
MOTOR CAR or
THREE-WHEELED VEHICLE
AT
ST. ALBANS (CITY)
Registration No.
Fee -/6 P

882 — 882

466

SOUTHERN RAILWAY.
Admit ONE MOTOR CAR
to be Parked in the
_____ at
(S.65) CHARGE 1/-
FOR CONDITIONS SEE BACK

4257 — 4257

467

M. S. & A. R.
DANE ROAD STATION
Received Sevenpence (7d.C)
for purpose stated on back
hereof.

3108 — 3108

468

L.M. & S.R.
SEASON TKT.
For the convey-
ance of One Bi-
cycle at Owner
Risk accompan-
ied by Passenger
C.O

Valid for One Week To............
Between Stations included in Holiday
Contract Tour No............
For Conditions see back   Rate 5/3N

706 — 706

469

BRITISH RAILWAYS (S)
THE RAILWAY EXECUTIVE.
PARKING TICKET FOR
MOTOR CAR OR
THREE WHEELED VEHICLE.
At Betchworth
Registration No. HMM79
FEE 1/-
Available on Day of issue only.
FOR CONDITIONS SEE BACK.

0205 — 0205

470

BRITISH RAILWAYS (S)
THE RAILWAY EXECUTIVE.
Fee £ : 3:0
PERIOD PARKING TICKET,
The holder of this ticket is entitled
to park
MOTOR CAR/CYCLE Reg. No. HMM76
THREE WHEELED VEHICLE
At Belmont
From 1 10 19 57
To 19
Subject to conditions on back hereof.

0101 — 0101

471

British Railways Board (M)
PARKING TICKET FOR MOTOR CAR
OR THREE WHEELED VEHICLE AT
WARRINGTON (BANK QUAY)
Registration No. WTc9492
Fee 13P
Available on day of issue only
For conditions see over

2 78865 — 2 78865

472

British Railways Board (S)
PARKING TICKET FOR MOTOR CAR
OR THREE-WHEELED VEHICLE AT
OXSHOTT
Registration No............
Fee 17P
Available on day of issue only
For conditions see over

2 3485 — 2 3485

473

British Rail
Parking ticket for motor car
or three-wheeled vehicle at
Inverkeithing
Registration No............
Available for 7 days from date of issue.
For conditions see over   (H)   Fee 35p

5166 — 5166

23 AUG 80

474

British Railways Board H
PARKING TICKET FOR MOTOR-CAR
OR THREE-WHEELED VEHICLE AT
ROSYTH (HALT)
Registration No............
Fee 10p
Available day of issue only
For conditions see over

7607 — 7607

The collector needs to consider
more than the carriage of
passengers. Here the
origination of a printing order,
the training of ticketing staff
and the parking of vehicles are
marked by unique ticket
designs.

475

BRITISH RAILWAYS (S)
THE RAILWAY EXECUTIVE.
PARKING TICKET FOR
MOTOR CYCLE
At Kingswood & Burgh Heath
Registration No.
FEE 6d.
Available on Day of issue only.
FOR CONDITIONS SEE BACK.
0053   0053

476

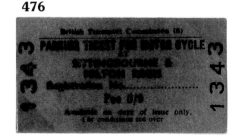

PARKING TICKET FOR MOTOR CYCLE
SITTINGBOURNE &
Available on day of issue only.
For conditions see over
1343   1343

477

BR3507/4
BRITISH RAILWAYS BOARD
PERIOD PARKING TICKET
The holder of this ticket is entitled to park
MOTOR   Reg
CAR/CYCLE No
at
C 76572 Until **05 NOV 75**
This ticket to be displayed
on car windscreen   NOT TRANSFERABLE

478

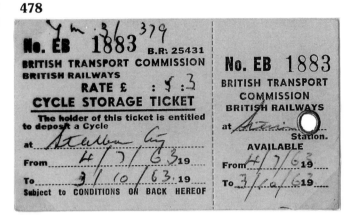

No. EB 1883   B.R: 25431
BRITISH TRANSPORT COMMISSION
BRITISH RAILWAYS
RATE £   : 5 : 3
CYCLE STORAGE TICKET
The holder of this ticket is entitled
to deposit a Cycle
at
From   4 / 7 / 63 .19
To   3 / 10 / 63 .19
Subject to CONDITIONS ON BACK HEREOF

No. EB 1883
BRITISH TRANSPORT
COMMISSION
BRITISH RAILWAYS
at   Station.
AVAILABLE
From   4 / 7 / 63 .19
To   3 / 10 / 63 .19

479

L. M. &   S. R.
HIGH TEA TICKET
IRLAM SCHOOL
VALID ONLY IN
THIRD CLASS DINING SALOON
on Special Excursion Train
from ST. PANCRAS
18th JUNE 1932   CLO Issue
This ticket must be given up to Dining
Attendant before High Tea is served
144

480

Great Northern Hotel, Rostrevor.
Two Day Hotel Coupon
Including Afternoon Tea and Dinner on day of
arrival: Breakfast, Luncheon, Afternoon Tea
and Dinner on the following day; Breakfast
on the third day; Bedroom for two nights, and
attendance.
For Conditions of issue See Hand Bills
........CLASS RAIL TICKET NO.........
NOT TRANSFERABLE   ISSUED AT
BELFAST
0522

481

CITY OF DUBLIN STEAM
PACKET COMPANY
Available for Seven Days from date of issue
DUBLIN (NORTH WALL)
TO
LEICESTER
Via Liverpool Central, Cheshire Lines & Chinley
Saloon & 3rd   Fare 20s 4d
See back
1000

482

FOR CONDITIONS SEE BACK OF TICKET
BRITISH & IRISH STEAM PACKET CO. LTD.
Available for 7 DAYS from date of issue.
DUBLIN (147)
TO
BIRMINGHAM(NEW ST.)
via B. & I. S. P. Co's Steamer Lime St. & L. M. & S. Rly.
THIRD   B'ham   Fare
STEAM   (147) D. 3. S   38/11 R
770
25 NO

483

FOR CONDITIONS SEE BACK OF TICKET
BRITISH & IRISH STEAM PACKET CO. LTD.
Available for 7 DAYS from date of issue.
Dublin North Wall (147)
TO
LONDON(Euston)
via B. & I. S. P. Co's Steamer to Liverpool
Lime St L. M. & S. Rly
SALOON &   Fare
THIRD CLASS   78/5
7500
21 NO

484

CÓRAS IOMPAIR ÉIREANN.
"S.S. Dun Aengus"
EVENING CRUISE
IN GALWAY BAY
ADULT FARE
6/-
For Conditions see back
2538
24 JL 58

485

3 9954
LONDON TRANSPORT I
Issued subject to the Bye
Laws Regulations & Con-
ditions of the Executive
Available on day of issue
only for passing through
from WARWICK RD. to
EARLS COURT RD. Exit
NOT AVAILABLE
BY TRAIN
RETURN TOLL 2d (A)
LONDON TRANSPORT I
Issued subject to the Bye
Laws Regulations & Con-
ditions of the Executive
Available on day of issue
only for passing through
EARLS COURT Station
to WARWICK RD. Exit
NOT AVAILABLE
BY TRAIN
RETURN TOLL 2d (A)
3 9954

More parking of vehicles, with
High Tea and Hotel services
added to rides by evening
pleasure boat account for
further collectibles.

486

MORECAMBE PIER & PAVILION
Company Limited.
PAVILION TICKET
4d
(NOT TRANSFERABLE)
This ticket must be retained to be
available as a pass out check
P.T.O.   Seats not guaranteed.

CHILD 60p

Central London Rover

See over

Date **06 MCH 82**

009176

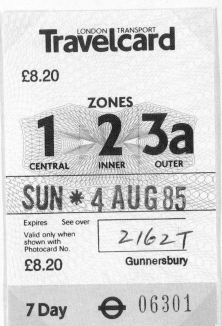

LONDON TRANSPORT
Travelcard

£8.20

ZONES

1 2 3a

CENTRAL · INNER · OUTER

SUN * 4 AUG 85

Expires   See over
Valid only when shown with Photocard No.

2162T

£8.20   Gunnersbury

7 Day   06301

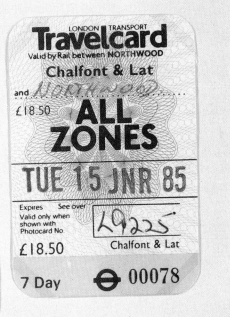

LONDON TRANSPORT
Travelcard

Valid by Rail between NORTHWOOD

Chalfont & Lat

and *Northwood*

£18.50   **ALL ZONES**

TUE 15 JNR 85

Expires   See over
Valid only when shown with Photocard No.

29225

£18.50   Chalfont & Lat

7 Day   00078

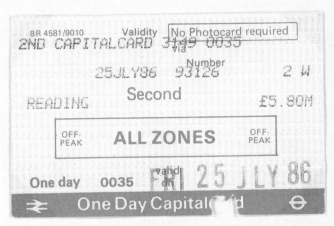

BR 4581/9010   Validity   No Photocard required

2ND CAPITALCARD 3149 0035   via

25JLY86   Number   2 W
93126

READING   Second   £5.80M

OFF PEAK   **ALL ZONES**   OFF PEAK

One day   0035   valid on   **FRI 25 JLY 86**

≷ **One Day Capitalcard** ⊖

Valid Off Peak as Advertised

Class   Ticket type   Price

2ND CAPITALCARD   £10·60X 03MCH87 3744

Valid on   Number

03 MCH 87   08100 592902

Between   Valid

SOUTHAMPTON PKWY & R 1 23C LONDON ONEDAY

Route/also available at

valid within R zone(s) indicated

≷ **One Day Capitalcard** ⊖

London Transport goes for colour but British Rail remains sober.

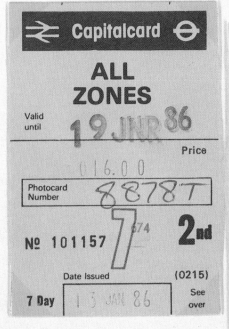

≷ **Capitalcard** ⊖

ALL ZONES

Valid until   **19 JNR 86**

Price
016.00

Photocard Number   8878T

No 101157   **7** 574   **2nd**

Date Issued   (0215)

7 Day   1 3 JAN 86   See over

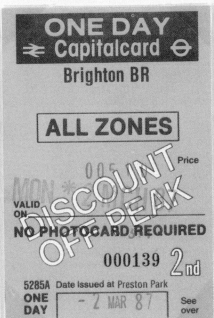

ONE DAY
≷ **Capitalcard** ⊖

Brighton BR

ALL ZONES

005   Price

MON *   DISCOUNT OFF PEAK

VALID ON
NO PHOTOCARD REQUIRED

000139   **2nd**

5285A   Date Issued at Preston Park

ONE DAY   - 2 MAR 87   See over

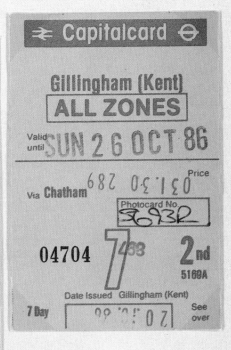

≷ **Capitalcard** ⊖

Gillingham (Kent)

ALL ZONES

Valid until   **SUN 26 OCT 86**

Price
Via Chatham   682 03.1.30 289

Photocard No.   3693R

04704   **7** 433   **2nd**

5169A

Date Issued   Gillingham (Kent)

7 Day   20.10.86   See over

487

BRITISH TRANSPORT COM. (M)
INTERNATIONAL RLY. CONGRESS
LONDON
Willesden Exhibition 26 to 29 May 1954
ADMIT ONE CHILD
WILLESDEN EXHIBITION
(21)
Charge 0/6
FOR CONDITIONS SEE OVER
1080

488

PRAM LABEL
—
MANORS
AND
WHITLEY BAY
P 3756/2

489

PACIFIC RAILWAY,
New York
TO
SAN FRANCISCO
via Niagara
Chicago, and
Salt Lake.
Issued subject to
conditions on back.
8670

490

7 8 9 10 11 12
British Transport Commission (N)
MONKWEARMOUTH
PLATFORM TICKET 1D.
Available One Hour on Day of Issue only
Not Valid in Trains. Not Transferable.
To be given up when leaving Platform.
FOR CONDITIONS SEE OVER
1 2 3 4 5 6
1823

491

EAST LANCASHIRE
LIGHT RAILWAY CO. LTD.
ADMIT ONE ADULT TO
BURY TRANSPORT MUSEUM
CHARGE AS ADVERTISED
VALID DATE OF ISSUE ONLY
Subject to the Company's conditions
5170

492

BRISTOL AND EXETER RAILWAY
GREAT WESTERN RAILWAY
BLEADON AND UPHILL
Owners of this Station, past and present
BRITISH RAILWAYS
Yieldingtree Railway Museum Trust
0029

493

Museum of British Transport
—
SOUVENIR TICKET
Clapham cl.
1d   See other side   1d
4411

494

Stockton & Darlington Railway
150th Anniversary 1825—1975
Admit Holder to Grandstand for
Steam Cavalcade from Shildon
on 31 August 1975
Price £3.00
6802

495

HEATON PARK TRAMWAY
AD 1596
10p
Manchester Transport Museum Society
CITY OF MANCHESTER
Issued subject to regulations.
Admission to DEPOT and MUSEUM
Williamson, Printer, Ashton

496

Michael Farr   1st class
Christmas Greetings
to Peter Wootton
via Seaford
With good wishes for 1983   (F)
453

497

Intimation to all Travellers!
OPENING OF NEW WAY.
Boldness to enter into
the
Holiest   By a NEW and
by the   Living Way
BLOOD OF JESUS   which He hath
consecrated for us.
Hebrews 10. 19.20.
Are You Saved by the Blood?
G.R.T. No. 5.   Pickering & Inglis, London and Glasgow

498

HOW DO THEY PUT MILK
IN COCOANUTS?
COME TO HAYFIELD

499

ADMISSION FREE.
Outward Half to   Return Half
King's Apartments,   Amazed at the work of this
Royal Pavilion, Brighton   wonderful Englishman,
to view   A Genius, the late
The Famous Richold   Richard Old,
Exhibition.   England's Greatest
The wonders of the world   Craftsman.
at a glance, including   You must see to believe.
Milan Cathedral, the   P.T.O.
£20,000 Model.

500

CHRISTMAS : EXCURSION
OUTWARD   RETURN
PERMIT   PERMIT
Bearer to   Bearer to
STAY OUT   RETURN
ALL NIGHT   HOME
on Xmas Eve   on Xmas Morn
This Ticket is Transferable
Issued subject to the usual Conditions
Williamson, Ticket Printer, Ashton-u-Lyne
3301   3301

501

Ffynnonllwynygog
(Discovered and recorded as famous as
early as 1696.)
OLD PUMP ROOM
LLANDRINDOD WELLS.
AVAILABLE FOR DAY OF ISSUE ONLY.
Not Transferable. 6d.
To be shown each time of entry.
001003   3799

Among tickets on the fringe, some of the above are at the very
periphery. Note *493* is an attempt to resemble early styles
while *494* marking 150 years makes no such attempt.

be displayed on the vehicle's windscreen (**477**) while the Period Cycle Storage Ticket is normally of two coupons, one to be held by the owner and the other tied to the cycle (**478**).

Hardly a travel ticket is **479**. It is clipped so presumably was instrumental in ensuring that a pupil of Irlam School received a suitable high tea on the long journey home from St Pancras on 18 June 1932. **480** offered something more substantial, two days board at the Great Northern Hotel at Rostrevor. The details are spelled out carefully — afternoon tea and dinner on the day of arrival, followed by breakfast, luncheon, afternoon tea and dinner on the following day and breakfast on the third day together with bedroom for two nights and attendance. However, this ticket was never issued!

Three single packet boat tickets from Dublin (North Wall) included rail travel on the British mainland. **481** took someone to Liverpool and on to Leicester in December 1905 for £1 0s 4d while **482** and **483** each travelled with someone in November 1949. Another railway-issued ticket is **484**, for an evening cruise, to allow the holder to watch the June sun go down on Galway Bay in 1956 for just six shillings (30p).

485 is familiar to most ticket enthusiasts. Earls Court District Line station has an exit at each end of the platforms, one leading to the mainly residential Warwick Road and the other to Earls Court Road with its shops and buses. Local residents found the station a most convenient way of getting from one road to the other and would purchase a penny Platform Ticket at one barrier and surrender it at the other. London Transport took a realistic view of the matter and in due course printed Return Tickets! **486** is an example of the Edmondson system in use by the proprietors of Morecambe Pier. The LMS dating code system was officially abandoned in 1948 yet **487** bears the date of issue on the back as '54 MY 29'.

Finally, **488** was intended to be attached to a pram carried in the guard's van on its way from Newcastle-upon-Tyne to the Northumbrian Coast. Colours varied according to the destination — this was blue, Monkseaton took red and Tynemouth and Cullercoats shared buff.

The spoof

At a cursory glance, **489** is an exciting item. Its design is clearly influenced by travel tickets of authentic railway issue (one might suspect the Lancashire & Yorkshire Railway style). Its 'journey' is quite the most scenic one could imagine, if not the most lengthy of the period it mimics in North America, say 1890-1910. For all this, the print is a British spoof advertising a theatrical production with an American flavour at local Assembly Rooms. Sadly the name of the town was not shown.

The trip from New York to San Francisco, at all times in its railway history, would have been documented by a lengthy strip of inter-company coupons. Moreover, there has certainly never been any railway working out of New York with 'Pacific' in its corporate title. World railway history is sprinkled with company titles which display their directors' aspirations of reaching far off cities and rivers. The New York, Westchester & Boston was a case in point. At home, the Manchester & Milford company had similar pretentions. But for any director to have thought in terms of a 'New York, Chicago & Pacific' would be somewhat fanciful. Nevertheless, a similarly far-reaching corporate plan has come to pass with the advent in 1971 of AMTRAK, explained in Chapter 16.

If the new collector has managed to avoid a mistaken view of the Training Tickets and the spoof half-ticket, he could nevertheless be deceived by **490**, unless and until he examines its reverse side. This Edmondson card is, on the face side shown, in every respect an ordinary Platform Ticket of the period up to 1957. It has however, been produced more recently, and thankfully, endorsed on its reverse side 'Reproduction by Tyne and Wear County Council Museums'.

There are spoof tickets used for admission to railway-orientated museums (**491**). Inside the museum the old-fashioned Platform Ticket machine will deliver for the visitor a souvenir (**492** and **493**) on receipt of the appropriate coin. The organisers of the festival centred around the 150th Anniversary of the Stockton & Darlington Railway printed Edmondson tickets for all sorts of purposes — providing entry to audio/visual displays, or admission to a grandstand (**494**), were two of many.

495 is a violet punch-type ticket permitting admission to Manchester Transport Museum and reminiscent of a tramway ticket of yesteryear. Rather different is **496**, a personal card by the well known ticket printer and collector Mr Michael Farr.

Advertisements

Many traders and commercial establishments, clubs and pressure groups and special interest organisations have from time to time found value in printing a resemblance of the passenger ticket as a means of advertising their facilities and opinions. Such creations of the advertiser's art take the form of large paper ephemera and small metal tokens, heavy card squares and modest booklet slips, but with predictable certainty they often copy the physical shape and size of the ubiquitous Edmondson card. Five examples are shown in which it will be noted there are religious, commercial and festive applications. All are tickets on the fringe (**497** to **501**).

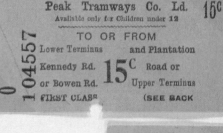

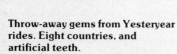

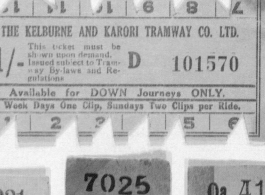

Throw-away gems from Yesteryear rides. Eight countries, and artificial teeth.

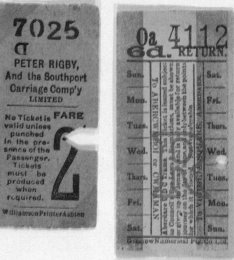

L.M.R.

LONGMOOR

OAKHANGER

ROYAL CORPS OF TRANSPORT
RAILWAY SOCIETY

VALID ONLY FOR 5th JULY, 1969

MEMBER'S TICKET

BLUE SALOON SPECIAL

B6 4333
ASHOVER LIGHT RAILWAY.
UP	5d	DOWN
	Single Journey	
Chesterfield Road		Hurst Lane
Holmgate		Woolley
Stretton		Fallgate
Hurst Lane		Ashover

Bell Punch Co., Uxbridge, 3-25

00721
S.E. & C.R.
Admit
ONE CAB
(On one occasion)
TO
CHARING X.
Station.
CHARGE 1d

This ticket must be shown when requested by the Station Officials.
Its acceptance is evidence that the holder agrees to comply with the Rules, Regulations and requirements of the Managing Committee.

McC. & Co. Ltd., London.

A 2647
W. Sx. R. (S. Ty.)
CHEAP DAY EXCURSION
CHILD Half Fare
CHICHESTER SIDLESHAM
HUNSTON SELSEY
Return Fare 4d Third Class

Torbay Steam Railway
ADULT RETURN
PAIGNTON TO GOODRINGTON SANDS
THIRD CLASS
ISSUED SUBJECT TO COMPANY'S CONDITIONS
08607

Torbay Steam Railway
ADULT RETURN
GOODRINGTON SANDS TO PAIGNTON
THIRD CLASS
08607

A. C. C. Ltd.
ASHINGTON LINTON
Child 2d.
0048

WIRRAL RY. VOLUNTEER RETURN HALF
This ticket is issued subject to the conditions stated on the Company's Time Bills. Available on day of issue only.
DAY OF ISSUE ONLY.
THIRD CLASS
Birkenhead Park TO HOYLAKE
343

WIRRAL RY. VOLUNTEER IN UNIFORM
This ticket is issued subject to the conditions stated on the Co.'s Time Bills. Available on day of issue only.
THIRD CLASS
Hoylake TO B'KENHEAD PARK
Fare 7d
343

L.N.E.R.
CHILD
THE "EASTERN BELLE" PULLMAN LTD.
Skegness (A918) TO LIVERPOOL ST
Available on day of issue only.
First Class Fare 6s 3d including Pullman supplement.
For conditions see back.
0015

L.N.E.R.
CHILD
THE "EASTERN BELLE" PULLMAN LTD.
LIVERPOOL ST (A918) TO SKEGNESS
Available on day of issue only.
First Class Fare 6s 3d including Pullman supplement.
For conditions see back.
0015

G. N. R. Excursion
Return either May 19 or 21, 1864
King's Cross to DONCASTER
First Class.
See notice at back.
006

GREAT WESTERN RAILWAY.
No. 137 Rate £ 11:6
M 'V Somerfield
Is entitled to travel by any of the Company's Trains which are available for ordinary Passengers
BETWEEN GREENFORD
AND Paddington
Via Perivale or West Ealing
FROM Nov 4 TO Dec 3 1912
inclusive.
SUBJECT TO THE CONDITIONS SHOWN ON OTHER SIDE.

Gt. North & Gt. Eastern Joint Ry.
HAXEY to YORK
Via Selby
Fare 3s.9d. Third Class
SEE CONDITIONS ON BACK.
1849

0018
London to GLEMSFORD
Second

MILK IS NATURE'S FINEST FOOD.
and more milk
PULL
PAT. No 262522

EASINGWOLD
EASINGWOLD RAILWAY.
Easingwold TO ALNE
Fare 4d.
SECOND CLASS
Issued subject to conditions in current time tables
9283

L.M. S.R.
Issued subject to the conditions & regulations in the Cos Time Tables Books Bills & Notices & in the Railway CosBook of regulations relating to traffic by Passenger Train or other similar service
WOLVERHAMPTON TO STOKE (LM&S)
Via Penkridge & Norton Bridge
THIRD CLASS 150(S) FARE 4/-
STOKE
NO 7364 2887

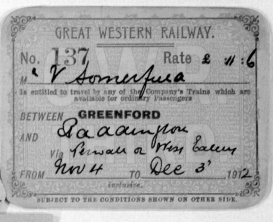

English miscellany with a journey to Belgium.

L&NWR Return Half
Available for Six Months from date of issue
Steerage & 3rd Class
Antwerp to Grimsby by M.S.&L.R.Co's Boat & from Grimsby TO EDGE HILL
141

L&NWR Outward Half
Available for One WEEK from date of issue
3rd Class & Steerage
Edge Hill To Grimsby via Lymm Sale Manchester Ll'd & from Grimsby TO ANTWERP
By M.S.&L.R Co's Boat

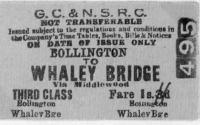

G. C. & N. S. R. C.
NOT TRANSFERABLE
Issued subject to the regulations and conditions in the Company's Time Tables, Books, Bills & Notices ON DATE OF ISSUE ONLY
BOLLINGTON TO WHALEY BRIDGE
Via Middlewood
THIRD CLASS Fare 1s.3d
Bollington WhaleyBge
495

FURNESS RAILWAY.
ONE DOG (ACCOMPANIED) BY PASSENGER
Liability Not Exceeding £2
FOXFIELD TO
CARRIAGE PAID
This Ticket must be given up on arrival.
TURN OVER.
AU 4 39

CHAPTER 8

Railcards and Flat Fare Tickets

The Senior Citizen Railcard made its appearance on 1 April 1975. For the sum of £4 (for a very short time VAT at 8% was added) a man of 65 years of age or lady admitting to 60 could purchase a card valid for a year and permitting Second Class single or return travel at half rate on Tuesdays, Wednesdays and Thursdays. The tickets used were normally ordinary 'CHILD' printings but as these were phased out, they were gradually replaced by 'HALF' tickets.

The idea was not entirely new. During the latter part of 1973 and throughout 1974, a number of selected stations in the Bournemouth area had sold special Senior Citizen Monthly return tickets at approximately single fare. The tickets were standard NCR 21 style on pale purple card headed '2nd CHEAP PERIOD (SENIOR CITIZEN)' (**502**).

From 1976 onwards the senior citizens were given a choice of two Railcards, one at £6 allowing the holder to buy ordinary Single and Return Tickets and most of the various Day Returns and one of £3 for Day Returns only. Since then the prices of the cards have drifted upwards but the distinction between the two has remained. They now also permit First Class travel. In the autumn of 1984 the minimum age for a man was reduced to 60.

The Family Railcard appeared in June 1979, following a pilot scheme lasting over three years which had permitted purchasers of Day Return Tickets at certain holiday periods to take children with them for a nominal sum (originally 25p) regardless of distance. It is available for Second Class travel only and permits one or two adults to travel half fare with up to four children at a nominal flat rate. The main condition is that there must be at least one child in the party. **503** indicates the type of ticket issued for a child, while the interest in **504** lies in its limitation to the Portsmouth to Ryde Ferry.

The Young Persons' Railcard is available only to persons under 24 years of age. It differs from the others in that outside July and August it sets minimum fares for weekday journeys commenced before 10am. It is also restricted to Second Class travel. Less commonly seen are Forces Railcards, which also enable the holder to take children at the flat rate, Disabled Persons' Railcards, which extend to the holder's escort, and a Railcard for the Annual Season Ticket holder. The last-named may take a child at the flat rate and also nominate any adult to share the facilities.

British Rail introduced a new fare structure on 13 May 1985. One result of this is that the saving on tickets other than Day Returns has been reduced to 34%. Of interest to the collector is the advent of otherwise standard Singles and Returns with the word 'DISCOUNT' added in tiny green print.

November Bonanza

In 1980, holders of Senior Citizen Railcards received a remarkable bonus from British Rail. It was an offer of a Return Ticket after 9.30am each Monday, Tuesday, Wednesday and Thursday in the month of November and the first part of December between any two stations on the system, including the Isle of Wight, for just £1. The tickets varied from station to station according to the issuing system in use, but the commonest was the upright Edmondson. **505** makes specific reference to the Sealink Services (then still owned by BR) to and from the island.

The reader will note that the NCR 51 (**506**) carried the name of the issuing station, but otherwise the tickets bore no obvious indication of either station of issue or intended destination. The tickets were treated by the more sophisticated traveller and apparently accepted by BR staff as giving the holders the freedom of the system for the remainder of the day. Indeed it is difficult to see what else they could do. The effect was to encourage the joyrider (as distinct from the person making a routine family visit) and presumably this was the very type of extra traffic BR had intended to attract.

While the Season Ticket holder grumbled at the lack of seating on his train, the senior citizen related travellers' tales of London to Perth and back in a day and of weekends spent with distant relatives by the simple expedient of purchasing a second ticket for the return journey. The purchaser of **507** boarded a train at an unstaffed station north of Norwich on 17 November 1980 and obtained it on the train. It is expressed to be 'valid for one single journey at fare shown' for no provision is normally made for Return Tickets on that line. Was this the reason why it was

502

°**0014**
2nd - CHEAP PERIOD
(SENIOR CITIZEN)
POKESDOWN
to   (S)
FARE 02.05
BRIGHTON
via Sway, Netley &
Havant
VALID
as advertised
R   O
AND BACK
For conditions
enquire ticket office
NOT TRANSFERABLE
1 6 AUG 73

503

24 **0062**
British Rail (S)
Flat Fare Ticket
(5344A) (Set 2)
FARE
£ 00.50
Valid only with and taking
the Conditions of A
Tickets issued to holder
of Family/Senior Citize
Railcards
and special
Railcard
Conditions.

For conditions
enquire ticket office
NOT TRANSFERABLE
0 SEP 79

504

3 **3411**
British Rail (S)
Flat Fare Ticket
(5344A) (Set 1)
FARE
£ 001.75
Valid only with and taking
the Conditions of Adult
Tickets issued to holders
of Family/Senior Citizen
Railcards
and special
Railcard
Conditions.
Portsmouth – Ryde Ferry
only.
For conditions
enquire ticket office
NOT TRANSFERABLE
8 SEP 19

505

42 **5165**
2nd ⇌ OFF PEAK
RETURN
Flat Fare Ticket
(5344A)
Fare 01.00
Valid only after 0930 hours
on date shown hereon, for
journeys by B.R. trains, by
persons presenting valid
Senior
Citizen
Railcards
Also available
on Sealink Ferry Services
to/from the Isle of Wight.
For conditions
enquire ticket office   (S)
NOT TRANSFERABLE
2 4 NOV 80

506

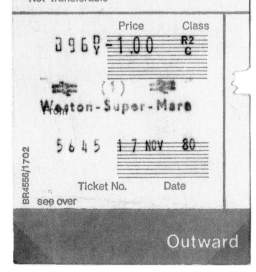

⇌ British Rail   Return
Inter-City   Off Peak
Return
Flat Fare Ticket
Valid only after 0930 hours on date
shown hereon, for journeys by B.R.
trains, by persons presenting valid
Senior Citizen Railcards. Also avail-
able on Sealink Ferry Services
to / from the Isle of Wight.

Issued subject to the Regulations and
Conditions in the Publications and Notices
of the British Railways Board.
Not transferable

	Price	Class
	0 9 6 D 1.00	R2
	Y	C

(1)
Weston-Super-Mare
5645 1 7 NOV 80

Ticket No.   Date
BR4556/1702
see over

Outward

507

1.00 495.00
17 NOV 80   0371
NORWICH
DIVISION BRB(E)
Valid for one single journey
at fare shown

508

EUSTON
TWING
TICKET OFFICE
12 NOV 1980
EUSTON
WIN

509

2nd. SAYER RETURN BRB
(M)
PR Valid out as dated
Return within one calendar month
02.MY.82 London (Euston)
Manchester Piccadilly
to
LONDON
(Euston)   11.00
For conditions
enquire Ticket Office
1184   NOT TRANSFERABLE
5357 MANCHESTER (Piccadilly) 02.MY.82

510

°**0037**
0
2nd ⇌ Special
Promotion
Return
LEWES
Fare
5329A
BR
Via
AND BACK
(R)
Valid as advertis
Issued subject to BRB
conditions of carriage
Not Transferable (S)
85

Note the Flat Fare collected by
issue of two very different size
forms. *504* was often displaced
by *506* from about 1966.

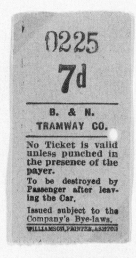
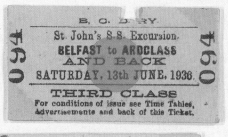

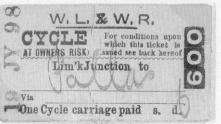

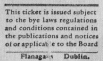

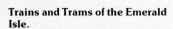

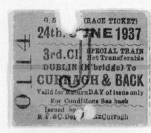

Trains and Trams of the Emerald Isle.

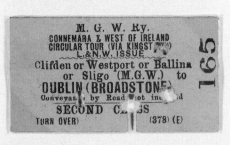

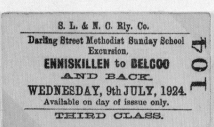

88

L. N. E. R.
GRANGE
TO
KEITH
3rd SPECIAL RETURN
(Valid 7 Days)
Date ....
Issued at Cairnie Junction
0312
For Conditions, see back
ADULT FARE 9d

G. N. of S. Ry.
Issued subject to the regu-
lations in the Co.'s Time
Tables.
THIRD CLASS
Aberdeen W
TO
CULTER
Fare 8d.
7162

2nd-EARLY MORN-ING RETURN | EARLY MORN-ING RETURN-2nd
D
Singer to (Q) DRUMCHAPEL | Drumchapel (Q) to SINGER
Fare -/6 | Fare -/6
For conditions see over | For conditions see over
9272 9272

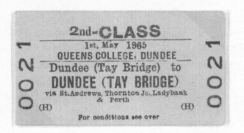

2nd-CLASS
1st. May 1965
QUEENS COLLEGE, DUNDEE
Dundee (Tay Bridge) to
DUNDEE (TAY BRIDGE)
via St.Andrews, Thornton Jc.,Ladybank
& Perth
(H)   (H)
For conditions see over
0021 0021

D. & B. JOINT LINE. | D. & B. JOINT LINE.
ISLAND of BUTE TOUR. | ISLAND of BUTE TOUR.
Valid during Season.
Rothesay TO RENTON | Renton TO ROTHESAY
via Kyles of Bute & Craigendoran | via Craigendoran
Cabin & Third Class. | Third Class & Cabin
Fare 3/11 | Fare 3/11
VALID IN NORTH BRITISH TRAINS ONLY. | VALID IN NORTH BRITISH TRAINS ONLY.
NotTransferable (Over.) | NotTransferable (Over)
1511 1511

HIGHLAND Ry.
Outward Half
Hopeman
TO
ELGIN
Fish Sellers Ticket
THIRD CLASS.
Fare 1/2
This Ticket is issued sub-
ject to the regulations in
the Co's Time Tables.
5696

Glasgow Fa
Glasgow
to
PERTH
1st Class.
Available
97

Glasgow Fa
Glasgow
to
PERTH
2nd Class.
Available
97

Glasgow Fa
Glasgow
to
PERTH
3rd Class.
Available

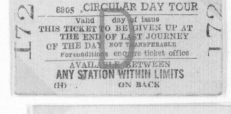

G. B. & K. J. RY.
THIRD CLASS.
POLLOKSHAWS
TO
STRATHBUNGO
4 Strathbungo Fare 1d.
4 AP. 84
41138

WHITE CORRIES LTD.
GLENCOE CHAIRLIFT
RETURN JOURNEY
R
3766

HALF RATE
2nd WEEKLY SEASON
(H) Rate 4/2
11
Available between
Bellshill &
GLASGOW (CENTRAL)
Until 24 Oct. 59.
For conditions see over
0079

B.R.B. 2nd-NORTHERN CITIES
8805 CIRCULAR DAY TOUR
Valid day of issue
THIS TICKET TO BE GIVEN UP AT
THE END OF LAST JOURNEY
OF THE DAY NOT TRANSFERABLE
For conditions enquire ticket office
AVAILABLE BETWEEN
ANY STATION WITHIN LIMITS
(H) ON BACK
L72 L72

(4565N) 1962
2nd-SINGLE
CANADIAN PACIFIC STEAMSHIP CO.
Greenock Princes Pier to
GLASGOW (CENTRAL)
By Special boat train
FARE (H)
For conditions see over
0000 0000

BRITISH RAILWAYS BOARD
FREEDOM OF SCOTLAND
GOLD TICKET
FOURTEEN DAYS UNLIMITED TRAVEL
between
ALL STATIONS ON BRITISH RAILWAYS
in
THE SCOTTISH REGION
also
Berwick and Carlisle
and
Stations Berwick to Kelso via Coldstream
and on
Clyde Coast and Loch Lomond
Steamer Services of the Caledonian
Steam Packet Company, Limited,
Kyle of Lochalsh/Kyleakin Ferry
Valid From   18 AUG 1965
To   31 AUG 1965

A record of 18 journeys North of the Border.

A 9959
FARE 3½D
LEVEN
GALLATOWNE
THE PEOPLE
Issued subject to the Bye-laws
Bell Punch Co., Uxbridge. 9449

No. 1) N. B. R.
Thurs. or SatAfternoon
Newcastleton
TO
CARLISLE
3rd CLASS 3rd
Valid on Day of issue only
Issued subject to the Bye-
Laws & Regulations of the
NBRCoto the conditions
stated in theirPublicTime
Tables. Not Transferable
1211

Set D
2nd-DAY
TOUR NO. 12
EASDALE
to
GLASGOW
(Queen Street)
by coach to OBAN
thence rail
Forconditionsseeov
17L

discarded on arrival in Sussex or did the holder intend to stay overnight?

508 is the reverse of a NCR 21 Flat Fare Ticket similar to **505**. It bears the Euston date stamp for 12 November 1980 and was used for a trip to Liverpool; the 'M' for London Midland Region is used on the face in place of the '(S)' of **505**. The holder of **506** from Weston-super-Mare seems to have used it for a single journey to Brighton. However, despite the exceptions we have illustrated, the majority of tickets were similar to either **505** or **508** and gave no indication to railway officials or anyone else where the holder had come from or where he was going. Even if it had been desirable to compel the traveller to nominate his destination at the outset, it was quite impracticable to print special tickets for every possible journey and the use of blanks to be completed in ink would have put an intolerable burden upon booking office staff.

The concession was repeated in the November of the following years. In 1984, the cost was increased to £2 and restrictions aimed at inhibiting the long-distance traveller were introduced. The pattern in 1985 was similar except that the card holder could obtain Saver Return Tickets at a discount. **509** is a machine-printed Saver Return from Manchester to London at the ordinary 1982 fare of £11 while in November 1985, the holder of **510** was able to travel from Lewes to London and on to Broad Green near Liverpool for £8. With the sale of Sealink, travel between Portsmouth and Ryde was no longer permitted but BR secured the agreement of the Red Funnel Line to take the globetrotters between Southampton and Cowes. In 1986, travel on the Red Funnel ferries attracted a surcharge of a further £2.

The May 1985 changes in fare structure did not affect cheap day return travel in the area southeast of a line from Weymouth by way of Banbury, Cambridge and Ipswich to Harwich but restricted it elsewhere to journeys of 80km (50 miles) or less. This has tended to confine the November peregrinations of the elderly enthusiast to the southeast but he may still be seen, probably wearing tweeds, carrying a packed lunch (for time is too precious to be spent in restaurants) consulting a large pocket watch at frequent intervals. He is always ready to chat on either of two topics: time-keeping in the 1930s and his own part in developing the railways of Britain: 'Of course, Gresley would never design a single bolt without having a chat with me first'!

Network SouthEast

The special status of the southeasterly corner of Britain was further enhanced on Saturday 21 June 1986 when the area (slightly extended to include King's Lynn) was formally dubbed Network SouthEast. On that day, a special £3 ticket of cheque card size gave the holder the freedom of the network and this was followed by a similar £4 day a few weeks later.

October saw the advent of the Network Card, granting the 34% discount on many journeys within the area to either holder or his or her nominee. They may take three adults with them at the same rate and four children at a flat rate of £1 apiece. From the enthusiast's point of view, this should lead to a considerable increase in the number of 'Discount' tickets sold, including from early 1987, the new variety of Discount Cheap Day Return. The children will presumably be issued with the ubiquitous and uninformative Flat Rate Ticket (**503** to **505**).

Postscript

At Christmas 1985, many Railcard holders received a charming greetings card from the Railcards Manager. It showed a winter scene of snow and ice. Only one object was in motion — an IC125 High Speed Train.

CHAPTER 9

Lost Railways of Brighton and County Durham

In Chapter 5 we noted that the railway network of the London area has not been greatly affected by closures. Elsewhere in Britain and Ireland the situation is very different. Any representative collection of the tickets of a particular locality must certainly include specimens from long lost stations and almost forgotten routes. Many such lines had a comparatively short history.

The current railway map of Britain looks very different from that of 1930. Yet if comparison is made with that of 1860 or 1870, the difference is far less marked. The routes with the highest potential traffic had been identified and built early in the Railway Age: those that came later were the marginal ones less able to survive competition. Brighton and the rural west of County Durham are very different areas in almost every way. Yet both demonstrate this tendency..

Take the map of Brighton in 1846, insert the spur from Preston Park to Hove, add the local stations of Aldrington, London Road and Moulsecoomb and you are looking at the map of 1986. The lines that came later were the ones that disappeared. Similarly, in County Durham the railways that climbed up into the Pennines were late-comers and barely survived until Nationalisation.

In the next few pages, we shall consider railways that appeared in these two districts late in the 19th century and for a while served the local folk as they went about on their daily occasions, to work, to market, to sightsee or to visit relatives and friends. We shall reproduce a few of the tickets they used.

The Kemp Town Branch

Of the Brighton lines to be considered, this was the first to be built and the last to be finally abandoned. Opened on 2 August 1869, it left the Brighton to Lewes line just beyond London Road station (built in 1877) and boasted an intermediate station at Lewes Road (**511**) and a short-lived halt at Hartington Road (1906 to 1911). It afforded the passenger a quite spectacular journey. The centre of Brighton lies at the junction of two valleys, one followed by the A23 road to London and the other by the A27 to Lewes. It crossed each in turn on high viaducts, twice granting scenic views across Brighton's roof tops before suddenly plunging into a tunnel to emerge at the Kemp Town terminus. However, railways do not survive on dramatic urban vistas alone. The sad fact is that on arrival at Kemp Town the passenger had travelled rather more than 4km and was now just 1½km from his point of departure.

The line was closed to passenger traffic after the last day of 1932 but remained open as a goods line (mainly coal and banana supplies) on the 'one engine in steam' basis until 26 June 1971. On that day a diesel unit provided a well-patronised hourly service at 25p adult return and 15p child in aid of the Southern Railwaymen's Homes.[16] Dismantling commenced the following week. **512** is a child return on blue card from Kemp Town and **513** an adult return on red card from Brighton. **514** is an LBSC Rail Motor issue of 7 November 1908 while **515** is the return portion of a Second Class Return from the intermediate station of Lewes Road of 23 March 1904.

The Line to the Devil's Dyke

Only for the first few months of its life did it seem that the Brighton & Dyke Railway would ever pay its way. The Devil's Dyke is a deep ravine in the South Downs about 8km northwest of Brighton. It is a beauty spot and enjoys extensive views to the north. It had already begun to develop as an excursionists' venue when the line was opened in 1887. By the turn of the century its diversions included a cableway across the ravine and a steep grade funicular to the foot of the Downs. The heyday had ended by the advent of World War 1 but it remained a beauty spot.

The railway did not reach the summit; it ended about 1km from the main viewpoint and even worse, a good 60 metres below. The motor coach took its passengers all the way. Apart from serving a golf course, it enjoyed no local traffic until 12 January 1934 when Rowan halt was opened to serve a new housing estate (**516**). Some commuter services were run but relief had come too late. It was closed on the night of 31 December 1938. **517** was issued at Hove on 19 July 1933 and is perhaps indicative of the level of traffic: West Brighton had been renamed 'Hove' on 1 July 1895. It will be noted that the title cites the 'B&D&LB&SC Rys'. The company was eventually absorbed by the Southern in 1923; **516** and **518** are last-day tickets of 31 December 1938.

DEMERARA RAILWAY
ONE BICYCLE
Accompanied by Passenger.
LEGUAN
TO
GEORGETOWN
(through)
3979

PORT SAINT-DENIS
RÉUNION 5
1re Classe 1/4 Tarif (1)
121

PARIS·MONTPARNASSE 5 B·CORRESPONDANCE
JERSEY (ST HELIER)
PAR ST MALO·ST SERVAN
DEMI PLACE | VALIDITÉ 7 JOURS | 2e CLASSE PRIX 0·00 R.8.38
0000 0000

C. K. & P. Ry.
KESWICK
TO
WORKINGTON (LNW)
Via Cockermouth
THIRD CLASS
Workington LNW FARE 1s.9d.
0494

V. T. G. R.
2nd Class—R.
TUNAPUNA
To S. JOS
FARE 07c.
Not transferable. Issued
0203

0426 PLATFORM TICKET
ASSUAN
5 MILL.

B.C. ELECTRIC RLY. CO. LTD.
VANCOUVER STREET RAILWAY SYSTEM
VANCOUVER
GOOD FOR ONE FARE
20639

MELBOURNE & H. BAY RAILWAY.
Melbourne & St. Kilda,
MONTHLY TICKET.
MAY, 1865.
First Class.
This Ticket is issued to and accepted by

Platform Ticket Charge
Shanghai N. 7¢.
Available for one hour on date of issue only.
This ticket does not entitle the holder to board any train.
Subject to the Bye-Laws & Rules of the Railway.
5567

GREAT WESTERN RAILWAY.
EMBARKING CHARGE
AT
BREST
ONE FRANC
Each person paying a toll is requested
to obtain a Ticket for the amount paid.
163

LOS ANGELES RAILWAY
OCT. 30 NOV. 5 1938 INCLUSIVE
ZONE 1
Pass must remain in possession of passenger during entire trip.
109355
Form WP1
$1.00 WEEKLY PASS
Beniamino Gigli in "Andrea Chenier"
LOS ANGELES SEASON
San Francisco Opera Company
Shrine Auditorium Nov. 5-12
Take "J" Car direct

WINNIPEG ELECTRIC COMPANY
TRANSFERABLE
SUBJECT TO CONDITIONS ON BACK
AND INSPECTION ON REQUEST
WEEKLY PERMIT 25¢
GOOD ONLY FOR WEEK ENDING
June 14
1947
28201
24
INSPECTED X X X

COMMONWEALTH RLYS
TRANS-AUSTRALIAN RAILWAY
DINING CAR TICKET
CHILD—SECOND CLASS
4 YEARS & UNDER 14 YEARS
Not Transferable. [See back
0031

Dining in the Desert.
Waiting in the Wings.
Recalling travel in six
continents.

C 2762
Paramaribo-
Brownsweg
of omgekeerd.
2e Klasse
Enkele Reis
f 5.00

The JERSEY RAILWAYS Co. Ld.
DON BRIDGE
TO
BEAUMONT
SECOND CLASS.
B 479

453002
Quebec R'y
Light and
Power Co.
Gen. Mgr.
Good for One Fare

Rye and Camber Tramways
Company, Limited.
SECOND CLASS.
RETURN FARE 6d.
Williamson, Ticket Printer, Ashton-u-Lyne
A 1391

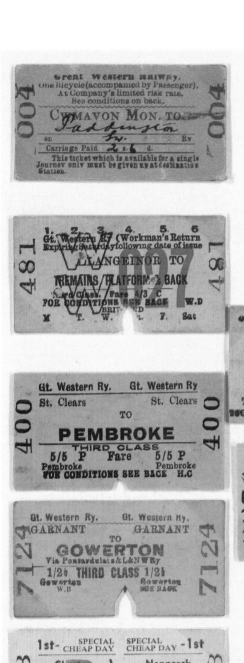

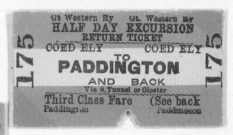

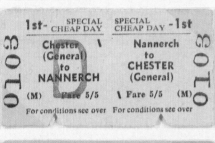

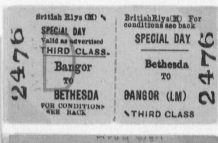
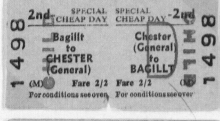
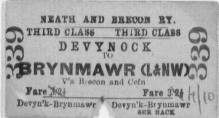

Long forgotten stations in Wales.

Holland Road Halt

Four new halts were opened between Brighton and Worthing on 3 September 1905, two of them in Hove. Dyke Junction halt, just short of the point where the main line and that to the Dyke parted company, is now Aldrington station. Holland Road halt was between Brighton and Hove, just 1½km from the latter. It had survived for half a century when the local evening paper claimed in an article that its receipts were less than half the salaries of its staff of two, who themselves spent part of their working day rug-making, apparently to a high standard. Whatever the truth of the matter, closure notices appeared within a few weeks and the last train called in May 1956. **519** was sold on 11 March 1950 and **520** on 2 April 1956.

The Wearhead Line

With the luxury of hindsight, one can so easily pour scorn upon the optimism of folk who expected financial rewards from the creation of country branch lines. No doubt some of those who paid for the Wearhead branch were hoping to open up an isolated valley while others had set their eyes on the minerals in the fells above. The route was not beset by engineering problems, it followed the upper reaches of the River Wear from Bishop Auckland for 40km until it reached a spot just short of the village of Wearhead, 300m above sea level. Beyond the terrain was too difficult for the train. This was a pity, since the rail head of Alston lay only 15km ahead, with connections at Haltwhistle to Carlisle, Hexham and the Border Country. In fact, the largest place served by the line was Stanhope, which at the time of closure to passengers in June 1953 boasted scarcely 5,000 inhabitants.

In its final years, its trains were clean and kept to time, its stations immaculate with gardens a blaze of colour and its station masters proud to display all their 'best kept stations' certificates. Only one element was lacking — passengers. We show two tickets from the once charming station of Westgate-in-Weardale: **521** was sold on 23 February 1906 and **522** on 17 June 1952. The Etherley specimen (**523**) was never issued but was supplied to a collector through the good offices of BR's Public Relations Department.

From a network of lines to the north, mainly concerned with goods, the stations of Tow Law and Crook maintained some passenger services until June 1956 and March 1965 respectively. **524** is the return half of a special excursion to Tow Law from Spennymoor, which had been closed to regular services in March 1952. The well-clipped **525**, which took someone from Crook to Oxford on 26 July 1943, is an example of the 'foreign' ticket used for journeys to destinations outside the LNER system.

The Climb to Middleton-in-Teesdale

Most that has been said of the Wearhead line applies also to that from Barnard Castle to Middleton-in-Teesdale. It was shorter, being just 14km, but climbed to a higher altitude as it followed the valley of the Upper Tees. It lasted 16 months longer although its largest village had just 1,600 inhabitants. One of them went into Barnard Castle to work and for some reason failed to surrender **526** as he arrived home on 17 June 1952. The Tees was the former boundary between County Durham and the North Riding and in the days trains were running Romaldkirk was a Yorkshire village. **527** is another ticket that remained when the branch closed.

The Lowland Routes of Mid-Durham

We conclude this chapter with a glance at some of the other lost railways of County Durham. The County was the very cradle of the public railway and not surprisingly, some of the closed lines

east of Bishop Auckland and Barnard Castle were far from being late-comers. The passenger-carrying railways remaining in County Durham were all laid down before 1850. They are the main line northwards to Edinburgh and southwards to King's Cross, the alternative coastal route through Hartlepool and Sunderland and of course the Stockton and Darlington line with its extension to Bishop Auckland.

We have selected nine tickets from closed routes in this area. **528** was purchased by a collector on 21 June 1952 in anticipation of the axe that fell the following January on Hetton and Pittington: **529** represents a genuine journey made on 16 February 1946. **530** was again a collector's purchase of 25 November 1964, five days before closure. **531** actually represented a journey made on 8 August 1955, when three years of service yet remained.

The line that ran southwest from Sunderland by way of Durham to Bishop Auckland became a Beeching casualty in May 1964. **532** was a collector's purchase of 18 June 1952; five days later he was at Brancepeth to acquire **533**. **534** marked the homecoming of a holidaymaker from Blackpool in July or August 1957. There were occasional through trains between Blackpool and the East Coast on Summer Saturdays. It is hoped that our traveller was fortunate enough to catch one of these, otherwise he would have arrived home more than a little weary. By leaving Blackpool Central at 10am and changing at Preston he may have arrived at Penrith at 1.13pm (the Tebay to Kirkby Stephen route being already closed), waited 64min and then spent the following 2hr travelling to Darlington, reached at 5.20pm. Then northwards to Durham for the final change and Penshaw with luck at 6.28pm. Mercifully further closures have made such a journey impossible today!

535 demonstrates that pre-standard returns in the North Eastern style were still in stock over 40 years after Grouping. It is undated and was probably sent in reply to a postal application just before closure.

The Coastal Line

Parts of the coast are now in either Tyne and Wear or Cleveland but we have ignored the new boundaries in this section. The Coastal Line still enjoys a good service but where steam trains once stopped for passengers, diesel units now rattle past derelict platforms. Ryhope East (**536**) closed in January 1960 (see also **69**); one would expect the journey into Sunderland to be a popular booking but LNER stock was still in use on 18 December 1959. Blackhall Rocks (**537**), a similar casualty, lay less than 2km from the colliery station and the village. Blackhall Colliery, Easington and Horden (**538** and **539**) remained until May 1964.

The lack of passenger interest in Single Tickets was largely the result of the policy of the very competitive Special Cheap Day return (**538** and **539**), usually at or below the standard single fare. **540** is an interesting demonstration of the effect of these fare bargains. In the early evening of August Bank Holiday 1954, two holiday-makers made their way from the beach to Blackhall Rocks station in time for the last train to West Hartlepool. They were refused the Cheap Returns as they would reach their destination after the last returning train had left. On examining expensive Singles sold to them, they immediately purchased a third to keep by way of souvenir. **540** offered an alternative destination in the shape of Hartlepool station, which had closed 15 years before. **541** was issued at Hartlepool station on 1 July 1925 while **542** is from BRB stock at the present Hartlepool station, which in 1954 was still known as West Hartlepool.

We saw in Chapter Seven a Monkwearmouth Platform Ticket spoof; **543** is a genuine one sold on 1 October 1955, 11 years before closure.

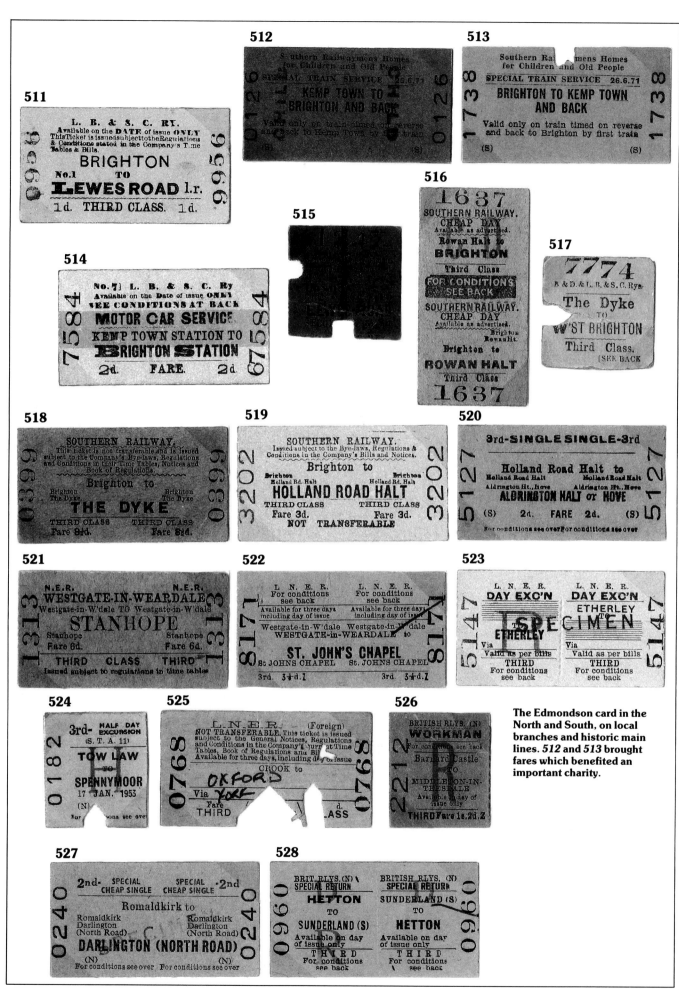

511

L. B. & S. C. RY.
Available on the DATE of issue ONLY
This Ticket is issued subject to the Regulations
& Conditions stated in the Company's Time
Tables & Bills.
BRIGHTON
No.1 TO
LEWES ROAD l.r.
1d. THIRD CLASS. 1d.

512

Southern Railwaymens Homes
for Children and Old People
SPECIAL TRAIN SERVICE 26.6.71
KEMP TOWN TO
BRIGHTON AND BACK
Valid only on train timed on reverse
and back to Kemp Town by first train
(S)

513

Southern Railwaymens Homes
for Children and Old People
SPECIAL TRAIN SERVICE 26.6.71
BRIGHTON TO KEMP TOWN
AND BACK
Valid only on train timed on reverse
and back to Brighton by first train
(S)   (S)

514

No. 7] L. B. & S. C. Ry
Available on the Date of issue ONLY
SEE CONDITIONS AT BACK
MOTOR CAR SERVICE
KEMP TOWN STATION TO
BRIGHTON STATION
2d. FARE 2d.

515

516

1637
SOUTHERN RAILWAY.
CHEAP DAY
Available as advertised.
Rowan Halt to
BRIGHTON
Third Class
FOR CONDITIONS
SEE BACK
SOUTHERN RAILWAY.
CHEAP DAY
Available as advertised.
Brighton
Rowan Ht.
Brighton to
ROWAN HALT
Third Class
1637

517

7774
B & D. & L. B. & S. C. Rys.
The Dyke
TO
W'ST BRIGHTON
Third Class.
[SEE BACK

518

SOUTHERN RAILWAY.
This ticket is not transferable and is issued
subject to the Company's Bye-laws, Regulations
and Conditions in their Time Tables, Notices and
Book of Regulations.
Brighton to
The Dyke   The Dyke
THE DYKE
THIRD CLASS   THIRD CLASS
Fare 8d.   Fare 8d.

519

SOUTHERN RAILWAY.
Issued subject to the Bye-laws, Regulations &
Conditions in the Company's Bills and Notices.
Brighton to   Brighton
Holland Rd. Halt   Holland Rd. Halt
HOLLAND ROAD HALT
THIRD CLASS   THIRD CLASS
Fare 3d.   Fare 3d.
NOT TRANSFERABLE

520

3rd-SINGLE SINGLE-3rd
Holland Road Halt to
Holland Road Halt   Holland Road Halt
Aldrington Ht., Hove   Aldrington Ht., Hove
ALDRINGTON HALT or HOVE
(S)   2d.   FARE   2d.   (S)
For conditions see over For conditions see over

521

N.E.R.   N.E.R.
WESTGATE-IN-WEARDALE
Westgate-in-W'dale TO Westgate-in-W'dale
STANHOPE
Stanhope   Stanhope
Fare 6d.   Fare 6d.
THIRD CLASS THIRD
Issued subject to regulations in time tables

522

L. N. E. R.   L. N. E. R.
For conditions   For conditions
see back   see back
Available for three days   Available for three days
including day of issue   including day of issue
Westgate-in-W'dale   Westgate-in-W'dale
WESTGATE-in-WEARDALE to
ST. JOHN'S CHAPEL
St JOHNS CHAPEL   St. JOHNS CHAPEL
3rd. 3½d.1   3rd. 3½d.2

523

L. N. E. R,   L. N. E. R,
DAY EXC'N   DAY EXC'N
ETHERLEY
SPECIMEN
Via   Via
Valid as per bills   Valid as per bills
THIRD   THIRD
For conditions   For conditions
see back   see back

524

3rd-   HALF DAY
EXCURSION
(S. T. A. 11)
TOW LAW
TO
SPENNYMOOR
17 JAN. 1953
(N)
For conditions see over

525

L. N. E. R.   (Foreign)
NOT TRANSFERABLE. This ticket is issued
subject to the General Notices, Regulations
and Conditions in the Company's Current Time
Tables, Book of Regulations and Bills
Available for three days, including day of issue
CROOK to
OXFORD
Via YORK
Fare
THIRD   CLASS

526

BRITISH RLYS. (N)
WORKMAN
For conditions see back
Barnard Castle
TO
MIDDLETON-IN-
TEESDALE
Available on day of
issue only
THIRD Fare 1s. 2d. Z

The Edmondson card in the
North and South, on local
branches and historic main
lines. *512* and *513* brought
fares which benefited an
important charity.

527

2nd-   SPECIAL   SPECIAL   -2nd
CHEAP SINGLE   CHEAP SINGLE
Romaldkirk to
Romaldkirk   Romaldkirk
Darlington   Darlington
(North Road)   (North Road)
DARLINGTON (NORTH ROAD)
(N)   (N)
For conditions see over   For conditions see over

528

BRIT. RLYS. (N)   BRITISH RLYS. (N)
SPECIAL RETURN   SPECIAL RETURN
HETTON   SUNDERLAND (S)
TO   TO
SUNDERLAND (S)   HETTON
Available on day   Available on day
of issue only   of issue only
THIRD   THIRD
For conditions   For conditions
see back   see back

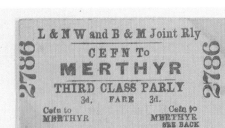

L & N W and B & M Joint Rly
CEFN To
MERTHYR
THIRD CLASS PARLY
3d. FARE 3d.
Cefn to
MERTHYR
Cefn to
MERTHYR
SEE BACK
2786 2786

COACH
Silver Jubilee Week
SWANSEA
TO LONDON PADDINGTON
AND BACK
SATURDAY 11 JUNE 1977
1952-1977
Inter-City 125

T.V.R. Return
Av'able day of issue only
Ilfracombe
TO
LLANTRISANT
(G.W.R. Junction)
Via Cardiff Docks
3rd Class Rail & any
part of Steamboat
In connection with the
Yellow Funnel Line Boats

T.V.R. (See Back)
ONE DAY EXCURSION
Llantrisant
(G.W.R. Junction)
TO
ILFRACOMBE
Via Cardiff Docks
3rd Class Rail and any
part of Steamboat
In connection with the
Yellow Funnel Line Boats
Av'able day of issue only
83 83

GREAT WESTERN RAILWAY,
BARRY PIER.
ADMISSION 3d.
This Ticket clears Pier Turnstile on day of issue
only, and must be given up on return, or the
Toll of 3d. paid. Issued subject to the conditions
and regulations set out in the Company's Time
Tables, Bills and Notices.
S.2 06995

Vale of Towy Joint Committee
Llanwrda Llanwrda
TO
LLANDILO
THIRD CLASS
1/2 C Fare 1/2 C
Llandilo Llandilo
FOR CONDITIONS SEE BACK. (W.L)
8423 8423

Cambrian Rys
Available on day of
issue or following day
RETURN HALF
CHILDS TICKET
THIRD CLASS
Portmadoc
TO
MINFFORDD

Cambrian Rys
Issued subject to the con-
ditions in the Co's Time Ta-
bles Books Bills & Notices
OUTWARD HALF
CHILDS TICKET
THIRD CLASS
Minffordd
TO
PORTMADOC
Revised Fare -/3½
209 209

B 0253
S.00
PRIVILEGE
SINGLE 2nd
Coryton Halt (Glam.) or
Whitchurch (Glam.)
to
CARDIFF (QUEEN ST.)
FARE 4d (W)
Cardiff (Queen Street)
For Conditions See Over
55—Williamson, Printer, Ashton

60190
CARDIFF GENERAL
British Railways
Board (W)
PLATFORM TICKET
Available
one hour on day
of issue only
Not valid in trains
Not Transferable
To be given up
when leaving
platform
FOR CONDITIONS
SEE OVER
1 2 3 4 5 6 7 8 9 10 11 12

WARRANT
ONE MOTOR CAR
Over 11 feet and up to 15 feet
with
Two Adult Passengers
Child Passengers
FISHGUARD to
KENSINGTON (OLYMPIA)
Car Reg. No. 889 DUB
Valid 1700 Train
Date 21 Sept 1965
Inclusive Rate £22.0.0
For conditions see over
W
No. 0932

Denbigh Ruthin & Corwen Ry
Issued subject to the conditions
in the Time Tables on the respective Co's
over whose Lines this Ticket is available
THIRD CLASS
RUTHIN To
RHEWL
RHEWL
2099

RHYL MARINE PARK & PLEASURE
PARK MINIATURE RAILWAY
RHYL (Marine Park)
AND
LAKESIDE
This Ticket is issued on the understanding that
the Company are not liable for any accident
which may occur to the passenger whilst on the
premises or train.
ADULTS Return Fare 4d.
Available at time of issue only.
2672

**Narrow gauge at Rhyl, and the
Great Big Trains of Wales.**

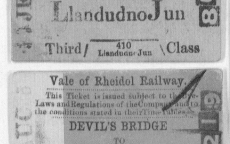

Issued by the L. & N.W.R.Co., subject
to the Company's regulations, and to the
conditions in their Time Tables.
Bettws-y-Coed To
Llandudno Jun
Third / 410 \ Class
Llandudno Jun
JE 88
8

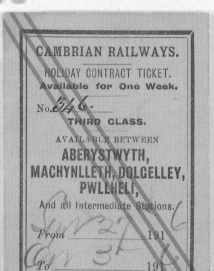

CAMBRIAN RAILWAYS.
HOLIDAY CONTRACT TICKET.
Available for One Week.
No. 346
THIRD CLASS.
AVAILABLE BETWEEN
ABERYSTWYTH,
MACHYNLLETH, DOLGELLEY,
PWLLHELI,
And all Intermediate Stations.
From 191
To 191
(TURN OVER)

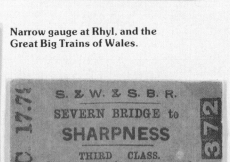

S. & W. & S. B. R.
SEVERN BRIDGE to
SHARPNESS
THIRD CLASS.
Issued subject to the conditions stated
on the Company's Time Bills.
Sharpness Sharpness
OC 17.75
372

Vale of Rheidol Railway.
This Ticket is issued subject to the Bye-
Laws and Regulations of the Company and to
the conditions stated in their Time Tables.
DEVIL'S BRIDGE
TO
CAPEL BANGOR
Fare 0s.4d. CHILD Single.
219

W.S 2092
M. T. W. Th. F.
Gt. Western Railway (Workman)
Available Friday following date of issue
PEMBROKE TO
PEMBROKE DK
AND BACK
Third Cls Revised Fare 1/5 See back
M. T. W. Th. F.
3601 3601

529

L. N. E. R.
CHILD
FOR CONDITIONS SEE BACK. Available for
three days, including day of issue.

PITTINGTON TO

SUNDERLAND

) CLASS Fare 10½d.C

0058

530

L. N. E. R. CHILD
FOR CONDITIONS SEE BACK. Available for
three days, including day of issue.

BARNARD CASTLE to

BROOMIELAW

Via
| Fare | S | s. 5 d. |
| FIRST | 3031 | CLASS |

6277

531

L. N. E. R.
FOR CONDITIONS SEE BACK Available for
three days, including day of issue.

COCKFIELD FELL to

EVENWOOD

| Fare | S | 5d.P |
| THIRD | 3110 | CLASS |
EVENWOOD

0226

532

BRIT. RLYS. (N)	BRITISH RLYS. (N)
SPECIAL RETURN	SPECIAL RETURN
PALLION	SUNDERLAND(S
TO	TO
SUNDERLAND(S	**PALLION**
Available on day of	Available on day of
issue only	issue only
THIRD	THIRD
For conditions	For conditions
see back	see back

0379

533

BRIT. RLYS. (N)	BRITISH RLYS. (N)
SPECIAL RETURN	SPECIAL RETURN
DURHAM	**BRANCEPETH**
TO	TO
BRANCEPETH	**DURHAM**
Available on day of	Available on day of
issue only	issue only
THIRD	THIRD
For conditions	For conditions
see back	see back

0292

534

L. N. E. R.
MONTHLY RETURN
BLACKPOOL LMS
TO
PENSHAW
Via TEBAY
Available for one month
from date of issue
Fare 28s.9d.C
RD / M.
For ditions
see b BLACK

0406

535

Valid for TWO ....
WILLINGTON
HUNWICK
Via
THIRD CLASS
Fare -/6
See back L.N.E.R.
CHILD

HUNWICK
to WILLINGTON
Via
THIRD CLASS
Fare -/6
SEE BACK L.N.E.R.

4257

536

L. N. E. R.
FOR CONDITIONS SEE BACK. Available for
three days, including day of issue.

RYHOPE EAST to

SUNDERLAND

| Fare | S | d.C |
| THIRD | 3442 | CLASS |
SUNDERLAND

7600

537

L. N. E. R.
FOR CONDITIONS SEE BACK. Available for
three days, including day of issue.

BLACKHALL ROCKS to

BLACKHALL COLLIERY

| Fare | S | 2d.C |
| THIRD | 3057 | CLASS |
Blackhall Coll'y

030

538

2nd SPECIAL	SPECIAL 2nd
CHEAP DAY	CHEAP DAY
	West
Blackhall	Hartlepool
Colliery	to
to	**BLACKHALL**
WEST	**COLLIERY**
HARTLEPOOL	
(N) Fare 1/6	Fare 1/6 (N)
For conditions see over	For conditions see over

SPECIMEN

9008

539

2nd SPECIAL	SPECIAL 2nd
CHEAP DAY	CHEAP DAY
HORDEN	Easington
to	to
EASINGTON	HORDEN
via	via
(N) Fare 8..	(N) Fare 8......
For conditions see over	For conditions see over

1127

540

L.N.E.R.	L.N.E.R.
For conditions	For conditions
see back	see back
Available for three days	Available for three days
including day of issue.	including day of issue.
BLACKHALL ROCKS to	
Blackhall Rocks	Blackhall Rocks
HARTLEPOOL OR WEST HARTLEPOOL	
HARTLEPOOL Etc	HARTLEPOOL Etc
3rd. 1s.2d.Z	3rd. 1s.2d.Z

2720

541

L. N. E. R.
PRIVILEGE TKT.
HARTLEPOOL
To
DARLINGTON
THIRD CLASS
Not transferable.

2860

542

CHEAP - 2nd
DAY
Leeds
to
HARTLEPOOL
(N)
For conditions se

2499

543

L. N. E. R.
PLATFORM. ADMIT ONE
MONKWEARMOUTH
THE HOLDER IS PROHIBITED
FROM ENTERING THE
COMPANY'S TRAINS.
NOT TRANSFERABLE.
FOR CONDITIONS SEE BACK.
d.
1

Closed stations in the North represented by tickets preserved
in the South. Transitional designs and now-impossible
journeys combine to create an archive.

CHAPTER 10

Colonel Holman F. Stephens' Railways

Between the beginning of the present century and his death in the autumn of 1931, Colonel Holman Fred Stephens, TD, AMICE (born 1866), was concerned with the management of several different marginally profitable minor railways. This is not the place to relate the stories of his 'do-it-yourself' and 'make-do-and-mend' system of running otherwise unprofitable lines on a shoestring. We are interested in his tickets and the background to their issue and use. The colonel was first and foremost an engineer and his main concern was to keep track and rolling stock in working order. On some of the railways he served as Engineer he was also General Manager and his influence on tickets as well as other matters of administration was strong. Below we consider some of the lines now associated with his name. We observed in the previous chapter that the last railways to be constructed tended to be the first to be abandoned. Many of the lines described here fall into this category.

Among the tasks undertaken at his headquarters in Tonbridge was the supply of tickets and these remain in sufficient numbers to encourage the enthusiast to build up a collection.

Welsh Highland Railway

This line had been established for three years when in 1925 he became its Chairman and Managing Director. His tickets differed only slightly from those previously supplied by Waterlow & Sons. **544** is a Tonbridge product, while **545** is by Waterlow. In some ways a more tangible souvenir is **546**, an unissued First Class Free Pass bearing the Stephens name.

Shropshire & Montgomeryshire Railway

Subsisted from 1911 until November 1933. Long before Stephens' time the line had once operated as the Potteries Shrewsbury & North Wales Railway (1866 to 1880) and it ended its days as a War Department training centre, a tramway and a railway. Its rolling stock included an old London County Council horse tram, a demonstration of the difficulty in drawing a distinction between light railways and tramways. **547**, issued in August 1933, is a typical print.

Hundred of Manhood & Selsey Tramway

For several years known as the West Sussex Railway, this enterprise served the Selsey Peninsula from 1897 until January 1935. **548** represents a pre-1914 journey over the full length of the line. It was printed before Col Stephens' days.

Weston Clevedon & Portishead (Light) Railway

Represented by **549**, this line was also born in 1897, and lasted until 1940. It was under the colonel's control during most of its existence. **550** is dated 3 July 193- (the final numeral being possibly a 1) while **551** is clearly dated 1 March 1939. **552** and **553** are both on thin card, undated and include the letters 'CAR' in their wording, three clear pointers to their having been issued on the train. The latter is unusual in that it carries no note of conditions, the back being completely blank. The Return Ticket (**552**) is further interesting for its mention of 'UP' and 'DOWN' on the coupons, as appropriate to each.

East Kent (Light) Railway

One of the two Stephens' lines that survived World War 2. The first stretch was opened in 1912 and it achieved its maximum passenger length of 22km, including a branch to within 1km of Sandwich, in 1925. The main line ran from Shepherdswell on the Canterbury to Dover line to Wingham, serving a number of collieries on the way. Its passenger service was slight, consisting of a morning and an evening mixed train in each direction. Passengers were few. The Sandwich-bound branch was open to passengers only from 1925 to 1928 and neither of the present writers have seen any tickets. An inspection of the derelict stations in 1938 suggested that they had been unstaffed. Until just before the withdrawal of all passenger services in 1948 most, if not all, of the main line stations were staffed and carried stocks of Edmondson cards. In addition the guards also carried a supply of thin card tickets and possibly in latter years Edmondson tickets also. Dating was by rubber stamp.

Ticket colours depended upon the destination station. **554** is salmon pink for Eythorne, while the umber of **555** indicates

544

WELSH HIGHLAND RAILWAY
NOTICE.—This Ticket is issued subject to the
conditions and regulations in the Company's
Time Tables, Books, Bills and Notices.

BEDDGELERT
TO
Portmadoc

THIRD CLASS FARE 1/-

3040

545

WELSH HIGHLAND RAILWAY.
NOTICE.—This Ticket is issued subject to
the conditions & regulations in the Company's Time Tables, Books, Bills & Notices.

SOUTH SNOWDON
TO
WAENFAWR

Third Class Actual Fare 8d.

659

546

WELSH HIGHLAND & FESTINIOG RYS.

FIRST CLASS TICKET

FROM _____
TO _____ AND BACK
ISSUED TO
Mr. _____
H.F.STEPHENS
Managing Director

480

547

SHROPSHIRE & MONTGOMERYSHIRE RLY.

FORD & CROSSGATES
TO
KINNERLEY JCT.

3rd. CLASS   Fare 9d
KINNERLEY JCT.   KINNERLEY JCT.

0397

548

HUNDRED OF MANHOOD & SELSEY
TRAMWAYS CO., LTD.

BETWEEN
CHICHESTER
AND **SELSEY.**

FARE, 7½D.

57069

549

W. C. & P. L. RLYS.
CLEVEDON
TO
KINGSTON ROAD
SECOND CLASS FARE 2d.
KINGSTON ROAD   KINGSTON ROAD

12 SEP 22   A 8610

550

W. C. & P. RLY.
DOG TICKET.
Weston-super-Mare
TO
Clevedon
or any Intermediate Station.
Fare 4d.

5574   5574

551

W. C. & P. RLY.
CLEVEDON
TO
PORTISHEAD SOUTH
SECOND CLASS.   FARE 3d
Portishead South   Portishead South

9293   9293

552

W. C. & P. RLY.   W. C. & P. RLY.
UP   DOWN
Day Excursion   Day Excursion
Available on day of   Available on day of
issue only   issue only
WESTON-S-MARE   HAM LANE
TO   TO
HAM LANE   Weston-S-Mare
(Ashcott Road)
2nd Class Return   Return Fare 8d

CAR B 3257   3257 CAR B

553

CAR
B-1 **1271**
W. C. & P. Rly.
SECOND CLASS
Ham Lane
TO
WORLE
Fare 3d
Williamson, Printer, Ashton
CAR
B-1 **1271**

554

EAST KENT RAILWAY
This ticket is issued subject to the Bye-laws,
Regulations and Conditions stated in the Com-
pany's Time Tables, Bills and Notices.
Available on day of issue only.

EASTRY SOUTH
TO
EYTHORNE
Third Class Fare 7½

0324   0324

555

EAST KENT RAILWAY
This ticket is issued subject to the Bye-laws,
Regulations and Conditions stated in the Com-
pany's Time Tables, Bills and Notices.
Available on day of issue only.

EASTRY SOUTH
TO
STAPLE
Third Class Fare 6d

0019   0019

556

EAST KENT RAILWAY
EASTRY
TO
SHEPHERDSWELL
10½d   THIRD   10½d
Shepherdswell   [SEE BACK]   Shepherdswell

1156

557

EAST KENT RAILWAY
TILMANSTONE COLLIERY
TO
SHEPHERDSWELL
WORKMAN'S   THIRD Fare 3d
TICKET
Shepherdswell   [SEE BACK]   Shepherdswell

9046

558

ROTHER VALLEY RLY.
BODIAM
TO
ROBERTSBRIDGE.
10d.   FIRST.   10d.

2954   2954

One man's empire — tickets to convey an impression of a
colonel's far-flung minor railways activity.

559

0027
KENT & EAST SUSSEX Ry.
MONTHLY RETURN
Available as advertised.
M
FRITTENDEN ROAD
Via S. Ry. and Headcorn
Third Class
FOR CONDITIONS SEE BACK.
KENT & EAST SUSSEX Ry.
MONTHLY RETURN
Available as advertised.
Frittenden Rd London
Frittenden Road to
LONDON
Via Headcorn and S. Ry.
Third Class
0027

560

9696 | 9696
KENT & EAST SUSSEX RAILWAY
HEADCORN JUNCTION
TO
ST. MICHAEL'S (Tenterden)
Third Class   Fare 1 3d
(SEE BACK)
St. M. T.   St. M. T.

561

3956 | 3956
Kent & E. S. Rly.
CHEAP.
Bodiam
TO
ROBERTSBRIDGE
JUNCTION
THIRD RETURN
Fare
Outward Journey
Kent & E. S. Rly.
CHEAP.
Robertsb'dge Jct
TO
BODIAM
THIRD RETURN
Fare 6d.
[SEE BACK]
Return Journey.

562

7157 | 7157
Kent & E. S. Rly.
ROBERTSBRIDGE
JUNCTION
TO
BODIAM
3rd. Return Fare 9½d.
Outward Journey
Kent & E. S. Rly.
BODIAM
TO
ROBERTSBRIDGE
JUNCTION
3rd. Return Fare 9½d.
Homeward Journey

563

0058
KENT & EAST SUSSEX Ry.
Issued subject to the Bye-laws,
Regulations & Conditions in the
Company's Bills and Notices.
Monthly as advertised.
M
Bexhill W. to BODIAM
Via S. Ry. & Robertsbridge
Third Class Fare 3/8
NOT TRANSFERABLE.
KENT & EAST SUSSEX Ry.
MONTHLY RETURN
Bodiam
Bexhill W.
Bodiam to
BEXHILL WEST
Via Robertsbridge & S. Ry.
Third Class. Fare 3/8
0058

564

0196 | 0196
KENT & EAST SUSSEX RAILWAY
Issued subject to the Bye-laws, Regulations &
Conditions in the Company's Bills and Notices.
Tenterden to
Rolvenden
Via   & Southern Rly.
First Class. Fare 9/-
NOT TRANSFERABLE.

565

0037 | 0037
SOUTHERN RAILWAY.
Issued subject to the Bye-laws, Regulations &
Conditions in the Company's Bills and Notices.
Tenterden Town to
Tenterden Town   Tenterden Town
Frittenden Rd.   Frittenden Rd.
FRITTENDEN ROAD
THIRD CLASS   THIRD CLASS
Fare 1/2½   Fare 1/2½
NOT TRANSFERABLE.

566

0079 | 0079
BRITISH RAILWAYS (S)
This ticket is issued subject to the Bye-laws,
Regulations and Conditions contained in the
Publications and Notices of and applicable to the
Railway Executive.
Tenterden Town to
Tenterden Town   Tenterden Town
Northiam   Northiam
NORTHIAM
THIRD CLASS   THIRD CLASS
Fare 1/1H   Fare 1/1H
NOT TRANSFERABLE

567

0273 | 0273
3rd-SINGLE   SINGLE-3rd
Tenterden Town to
Tenterden Town   Tenterden Town
Wittersham Rd.   Wittersham Rd.
WITTERSHAM RD.
(S) 9d. H   FARE   9d. H (S)
For Conditions see over For Conditions see over

568

7 | 8 | 9 | 10 | 11 | 12
0899 | 0899
KENT & EAST SUSSEX RLY.
JUNCTION ROAD
ADMIT ONE TO PLATFORM 2d
Available One Hour Not Transferable
FOR CONDITIONS SEE BACK
1 | 2 | 3 | 4 | 5 | 6

569

7 | 8 | 9 | 10 | 11 | 12
0264 | CHILD
THE ROTHER VALLEY RAILWAY
WITTERSHAM ROAD
ADMIT ONE TO PLATFORM 1d
Available on day of issue only and
for ONE HOUR. Not Transferable.
Issued subject to the Conditions
of the Company.
1 | 2 | 3 | 4 | 5 | 6

570

8759 | 8759
KENT & EAST SUSSEX RAILWAY
RETURN JOURNEY FROM
TENTERDEN TOWN
VIA
ROLVENDEN
ADULT FARE AS ADVERTISED
FOR CONDITIONS SEE OVER

Continuing the empire of
Col Stephens with ordinary
cards and thin pasteboards
together with prints by
nationalised British Transport.

571

0310 | 0310
KENT & EAST SUSSEX RAILWAY
DAY RETURN
Wittersham Rd. to   Tenterden Town to
**TENTERDEN   WITTERSHAM
TOWN   ROAD**
THIRD CLASS — Fare as advertised
Available on day of issue only
For conditions enquire ticket office
NOT TRANSFERABLE

572

B 4915
Rye & Camber Tramways
Company, Limited.
RETURN
SANDS
7d
Williamson, Ticket Printer, Ashton

Staple and **556** is green for Shepherdswell. Station-issued tickets were dated on the back by rubber stamp. **554** was sold on 18 April 1944 and **555** on 16 March 1945. There were also a number of Southern Railway printings for through journeys to SR stations but these are rarely seen. **557** is of interest as a maverick. Its colour is orange, elsewhere reserved for the Wingham station, it appears to be a Single and demands a fare of 3d for a little over 3km journey, which seems a little on the high side for workman's travel.[17]

Kent & East Sussex Railway

Happily this railway lived on until the dawn of the preservation movement. Before its equipment had finally rusted and crumbled, it was taken over by a skilful and dedicated band. Many of the unissued tickets and not a few used and surrendered specimens also survived and are available in moderate numbers to enthusiasts today. For this reason, it is worth spending a little time looking at the history of the line.

The Rother Valley (Light) Railway running between Roberts-bridge on the SEC and Rolvenden (then optimistically styled 'Tenterden Town' although almost 2km away) was opened on 2 April 1900. Colonel Stephens was Managing Director and Engineer from the outset. Some of its ticket stock, including **558**, remained unsold 54 years later. It changed its name to the Kent & East Sussex in April 1904. Construction of an extension to Headcorn had already begun and passenger services began in May 1905. The former northern terminus became Rolvenden and a Tenterden Town station worthy of its name was opened.

It never ran more than about half-a-dozen trains a day in each direction. Before World War 1 most trains ran from terminus to terminus but it gradually degenerated into two different services from Tenterden and Rolvenden, one to Headcorn and one to Robertsbridge. By the time of Nationalisation, services had dropped to four a day and the only through train was the 8.50am from Headcorn, which was scheduled to arrive at Robertsbridge, 40km distant, 101min later but rarely kept to time.

The Southern Railway began to print KES tickets (**559**) some years before Nationalisation. At that time, it became part of the Southern Region and for the next two years any tickets required were headed 'Southern Railway'. These were followed in 1950 by the pre-standard BTC prints. Closure for passengers came on 2 January 1954 (although there were some special excursions over the next few years) with no less than six distinct types of ticket in use. The unused tickets went to Southern Region Audit Office who at that time were making generous distributions of specimens to *bona fide*[18] collectors while many used items remained at the stations and eventually came into the possession of the Preservation Society.

The simple *Rother Valley* style has been illustrated above (**558**). **560** is pure Colonel Stephens' style on his favourite pink card and transported someone from Headcorn to St Michael's on 16 April 1943; **561** is a slightly later print and was sold at Bodiam on 25 July 1944. **562** is on thin card, white with red bands; it was in fact never sold. **591** is also of thin card and was printed at Manchester by Edmondson.

563 was unsold. **564** (a 'last day' collector's souvenir) was issued on 2 January 1954; it should be compared with **563** and souvenir **565**. To conclude this part of the story, the pre-standard item (**566**) was sold, unlike the standard one given number **567**.

As already indicated, this story has a happy ending. Although the track north of Tenterden to Headcorn was lifted, steam trains run further and further southwards as the restored section of track edges nearer and nearer to Robertsbridge. In 1966 there were no trains but the enthusiast could purchase Platform Tickets of a mock SEC style from former Southern Railway machine at Rolvenden station (**568**). The following year (still without traction) sets of 18 of a new style of ticket were on sale at Tenterden. Headed 'The Rother Valley Railway' they comprised 10[19] adult and eight child tickets representing the eight stations on the preserved section (**569**).

The advent of a train service produced a variety of tickets, two of which are reproduced. **570** took its holder on a trip to an unspecified spot beyond Rolvenden on 21 September 1975 while almost five years later on 20 September 1980, the user of **571** was able to achieve Wittersham Road.

Rye & Camber Tramway

This passenger line was in fact a narrow gauge railway. It was built and opened under the supervision of Col Stephens in 1895. At first it ran from the Cinque Port of Rye to Golf Course Halt. An extension to Camber Sands opened in 1908. Tickets gave no indication of a Stephens' interest. **572**, which was printed by Williamson, is typical and carries an advertisement for a Rye butcher on the back. The R&C closed in 1939.

Other lines in which the colonel took a direct interest, either as builder or administrator, included the Burry Port & Gwendraeth Valley Railway (opened in 1909 and taken over by the Great Western in 1922) and the Sheppey (Light) Railway (opened in 1901 and part of the South Eastern Railway after 1905). Colonel Stephens was also closely involved with rebuilding of part of the Plymouth Devonport & South Western Junction Railway which we illustrated with a ticket in Chapter 1 (**41**), and he supervised the Snailbeach District Lines.

CHAPTER 11

Preserved and Minor Lines

Even before the Beeching Axe[20], British Rail closed the country railway between Lewes and East Grinstead, leaving the wild flowers to flourish alongside a derelict track. Early in 1959 the mood of a public meeting in Haywards Heath, reflected a trend toward preservation already beginning to emerge throughout Britain, to the delight of enthusiasts and public alike.

The following year, the Bluebell Railway, formed as a direct result of the Haywards Heath meeting, reopened the line from Sheffield Park station, in a welter of publicity surrounding what was billed as a Living Museum. At first there were just two locomotives, two coaches and two hundred ideas. The railway grew steadily from those beginnings, and perhaps because it was one of the country's early standard gauge preservation ventures, caught the imagination of professional railwaymen and amateur public far beyond the borders of Sussex. Its Sheffield Park station, built in 1882, is carefully maintained in the Victorian style typical of its first owners, the London Brighton & South Coast Railway. The railway's northern terminus, 8km away at Horsted Keynes, is maintained in true Southern Railway fabric as a fairly impressive former junction building.

Before long the railway, in the care of its Preservation Society, was acquiring further locomotives, buying the right of way and mounting an ongoing publicity campaign. The result today is a firmly established tourist attraction which preserves a fine example of Victorian cross-country railway. There is currently talk of extending into East Grinstead where renewed connection with the national railways would assure future prosperity.

In the earlier years of the Bluebell, tickets were purposely designed in the likeness of LBSC days (**573**) including use of white and blue for First and Second Class Singles respectively and the altogether pre-Grouping device of lower-case repeat initial letters after the destination name (note 's.p.' in the illustration). Early Platform Tickets were fashioned after those of the LBSC, with their prominent red blob oval centrepiece, but were otherwise not very faithful representations. After two or three years, the variety of ticket categories increased greatly, while the colour scheme and choice of typefaces was allowed to wander

and collectors were gathering tickets now truly of Bluebell invention (**574**).

Preservation had started roughly 10 years earlier with the revival of Talyllyn Railway in Wales. The much-loved Festiniog Railway had followed soon afterwards with another contribution to preservation in Wales.

Signals were at 'go' and in the course of the next few years little trains got moving all over the country, from the Lincolnshire Coast Light in the east, to ventures on the Isle of Wight, at Seaton in Devon and Lochty and Strathspey in Scotland, to more of those Great Little Trains of Wales that we now cherish as a living heritage.

This scene engendered much that attracted the ticket enthusiast. In fact there are those who collect nothing else but tickets of minor tramways and railways. Others may include minor lines which cannot always be properly described as 'preserved' because they carried their passengers all through the Talyllyn-Festiniog-Bluebell era into the present time, in many cases without the ignominy of closure. To the cliff railways of Hastings (**588**), the pier tramway at Ramsey (**666-7**), the steep scenic tramway at Llandudno (**585**) and the preserved riverside tramway at Seaton may be added a family of little railways and tramways opened in more recent years, either by running over former company's tracks or by new building ventures. All tastes are assured of a well stocked hunting ground. Alderney, Bicton, Brecon, Crich, Llanberis, Longleat, Shane's Castle and Yorkshire Dales are names which act to excite the collector of passenger tickets. There are many more.

Perhaps the most imaginative intervention by a preservation group into the affairs of a former main line railway was that of the Torbay Steam Railway (**575**), later renamed Torbay & Dartmouth Railway. This is a line well known to the present writers. It is also the line that, even allowing for Wales (and Egypt!), provides their most abiding memories of scenery — just a glance is a holiday — and at the end of the run, a glorious trip into the architectural past with a ferry ride across the River Dart to historic Royal Naval Dartmouth.

Two long-lost railways which were obvious candidates for

573

BLUEBELL RY.
HORSTED KEYNES
TO
Sheffield Park S.P.
SECOND CLASS
[See Back
0622 0622

574

BLUEBELL RAILWAY
SHEFFIELD PARK
One Car Parked On Day of
Issue Only at Owners Risk.
Subject to Company's Bye-Laws
76988

575

Torbay Steam Railway
PLATFORM TICKET
NOT AVAILABLE ON TRAINS
ISSUED SUBJECT TO COMPANYS CONDITIONS
02290 02290

576

CLIFF RAILWAY,
ABERYSTWYTH
4d 4d
RETURN (UP) RETURN (DOWN)
Available day of issue only
51100 51100

577

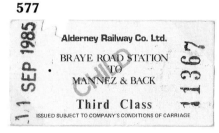

11 SEP 1985
Alderney Railway Co. Ltd.
BRAYE ROAD STATION
TO
MANNEZ & BACK
Third Class
ISSUED SUBJECT TO COMPANY'S CONDITIONS OF CARRIAGE
41367

578

BRECON MOUNTAIN RLY. CO. LTD.
PANT PONTSTICILL
TO TO
PONTSTICILL PANT
Issued subject to the Company's regulations and notices. NOT TRANSFERABLE
G. C. Frost & Co., Printers, Ashby

579

2nd - SPECIAL EXCURSION
27th August, 1972
Any S.W. Division station to
DISS AND BACK
INCLUDING ROAD TOUR TO
BRESSINGHAM AND ADMISSION TO
GARDENS AND STEAM MUSEUM
(S) For conditions see over
0209 0209

580

Sc 5770
10p
TRAM FARE
WAKEBRIDGE TO CRICH TOWN END
CRICH TOWN END TO WAKEBRIDGE
ADMISSION TO EXHIBITION
Available on car on which issued from point indicated by punch-hole. Issued subject to Bye-laws of the Tramway Museum and for transpolt entirely at risk of passenger, NOT TRANSFERABLE.
CRICH TRAMWAYS
TRAMS AND ROYALTY EXHIBITION
Bell Punch Co., Ltd., London

582

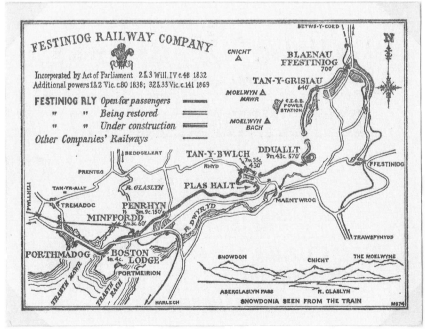

FESTINIOG RAILWAY COMPANY

Incorporated by Act of Parliament 2 & 3 Will. IV c.48 1832
Additional powers 1 & 2 Vic. c.80 1838; 32 & 33 Vic. c.141 1869

FESTINIOG RLY Open for passengers
" " Being restored
" " Under construction
Other Companies' Railways

BETWS-Y-COED
CNICHT
BLAENAU FFESTINIOG 700'
TAN-Y-GRISIAU 640'
MOELWYN MAWR
MOELWYN BACH
C.E.G.B. POWER STATION
TAN-Y-BWLCH
DDUALLT 9m 43c. 570'
RHYD
PLAS HALT
FFESTINIOG
MAENTWROG
BEDDGELERT
PRENTEG
TAN-YR-ALLT
R. GLASLYN
TREMADOC
PENRHYN 3m 9c. 150'
MINFFORDD 2m 3c. 60
R. DWYRYD
TRAWSFYNYDD
PWLLHELI
PORTHMADOG
BOSTON LODGE 1m 4c.
PORTMEIRION
SNOWDON
CNICHT
THE MOELWYNS
TRAETH MAWR
TRAETH BACH
ABERGLASLYN PASS
R. GLASLYN
HARLECH
SNOWDONIA SEEN FROM THE TRAIN
M974

581

DART VALLEY RLY
BUCKFASTLEIGH STATION
PLATFORM TICKET
3 d
NOT VALID ON TRAINS
Issued Subject to Company's Conditions
1656 1656

Some of the Great Little Trains
of Wales with items from
England and the Channel Isles.

583

FESTINIOG RAILWAY.
OBSERVATION CAR
EXTRA FARE 3d.
BETWEEN
PORTMADOC and
Station to which passenger is entitled to travel. Single journey on date of issue only.
5209

584

GREAT CENTRAL RAILWAY No.
LOUGHBOROUGH CENTRAL
PLATFORM TICKET
1/- For conditions see over 5p
Not transferable
Valid as advertised
489

touristik treatment, but which unfortunately were forced to close well before the vogue of preservation, were those formerly working in Jersey. It really would be a grand occasion if the track were laid and some iron hulk from a mainland cement works or ageing Spitzbergen tank could haul four-wheelers along the coastline to St Aubin and Gorey.

A mere fraction of the lines which we commend to the attention of collectors are surveyed below. Selected tickets are shown to emphasise the variety to be had across the country. Clearly this is a branch of the hobby which can be so easily advanced when one is holidaying or by systematic correspondence with collectors, companies and dealers.

Aberystwyth Cliff Railway
Opened in 1896 (**576**).

Alderney Railway
Opened in 1980. This enterprise employs a somewhat unusual colour scheme for its tickets, based upon a desire to account separately for each of the means of haulage: White (**577**) — Railcars, Yellow — Steam and Green — Diesel.

Bluebell Railway
Closed by BR 1958. Reopened privately 1960 (**573** and **574**).

Brecon Mountain Railway
Opened in 1980 (**578**).

Bressingham Railways
Illustration shows a through BRB(S) excursion ticket including admission to the steam museum (**579**). Four tracks each of a different gauge, operating for visitors to the Bressingham gardens at Diss, Norfolk.

Crich Tramways
Opened 1962 and operated by The Tramway Museum Society at Crich, Derbyshire (**580**).

Dart Valley Railway
A South Devon line closed by BR in 1962. Reopened privately in 1969 (**581**).

Festiniog Railway
Porthmadog, North Wales. Reopened in 1955 (**582**). Illustrated from pre-preservation days is **583**.

Great Central Railway (II)
Loughborough, Leicestershire.
Originally a section of the pre-Grouping Great Central company's line from Nottingham through Rugby to meet the Met & GC (Chapter 12). BR closed the line in 1969. Subsequently reopened by the Main Line Steam Trust Limited (**584**).

Great Orme Railway
Opened 1902. Municipalised 1948 (**585**).

Guernsey Railway
Opened as electric line 1892 (**586**). Replaced by buses 1934.

Gwili Railway
Opened in Southwest Wales 1978 (**587**).

Hastings West Hill Lift
Opened 1891. Municipalised 1947 (**588**). There is also a similarly ticketed East Hill Lift.

Isle of Wight Railway (II)
In 1975 the railway celebrated the hundredth year of the long-gone Ryde & Newport Railway (**589**).

Keighley & Worth Valley Railway
Former BR Oxenhope line closed 1961. Reopened privately 1968 (**590**).

Kent & East Sussex Railway
See Chapter 10. Reopened in 1974 by a charitable group named Tenterden Railway Company (**591** probably dates from Col Stephens' days).

Lakeside & Haverthwaite Railway
Reopened in 1973. (**592** is an uncommon Edmondson size. The company generally prefers thin cards of varying sizes.)

Lincolnshire Coast Light Railway
Built near Grimsby in 1960 (**593**).

Llanberis Lake Railway
North Wales line opened in 1971 (**594**).

Lochty (Private) Railway
A Fifeshire railway reopened 1967 (**595**).

Manx Northern Railway
Opened 1879. Taken over by Isle of Man Railway 1905 (**596**). Track abandoned in 1965. Also see Chapter 12.

Middleton Railway
Reopened 1960 (**597**).

Mid-Hants Railway
Former BR track reopened in 1977 by the Winchester & Alton Railway Company (**598**).

Nene Valley Railway
Line near Peterborough, formerly worked as part of BR and closed by them in 1972. Reopened 1977 (**599**).

Nidd Valley Light Railway
Opened 1907. Worked by Bradford Corporation. Closed 1929 (**600**).

North Norfolk Railway
At Sheringham, Norfolk, originally part of the Midland & Great Northern Joint Railway. Reopened 1976 (**601**).

North Yorkshire Moors Railway
Reopened 1973 (**602**).

Ravenglass & Eskdale Railway
Worked by preservation group since 1961 (**603**).

Romney Hythe & Dymchurch Light Railway
South Kent line affectionately known as the World's Smallest Public Passenger Railway (**604**). Opened in 1927. Refurbished and reopened 1947 following wartime use by the British Army.

585

GREAT ORME RAILWAY LTD.
VICTORIA STATION
TO
BLACK GATE.
1ᴰ
Issued subject to the Co's ... & Regulations.
D 4903

586

GUERNSEY RAILWAY COMPANY, LTD.
Please retain this Ticket for inspection on demand.
FARE 1½d.
Colley's Patents, Ltd., Printers, Saffron Hill, London.
B1960

587

CYMDEITHAS GADWRAETH RHEILFFORDD GWILI
THE GWILI RAILWAY PRESERVATION SOCIETY
SOCIETY DAY - 1979
SUNDAY, 30th SEPTEMBER
ROVER TICKET
This ticket is valid on all scheduled trains on the above date. Issued subject to byelaws, regulations, notices and conditions published in the company's bills and notices.
Nº 1680

588

County Borough of Hastings
West Hill Lift
Adult
FARE UP 4d
Williamson, Printer, Ashton
Q 04067

589

RYDE & NEWPORT RLY.
CENTENARY 1875-1975
Valid as Advertised on Day of Issue only from
HAVEN STREET
Not Transferable. To be Shewn On Demand
Unlimited travel at own risk permitted on date shewn on back hereof
I.W.R. Ltd.
8233

590

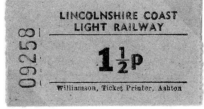

Keighley & Worth Valley Light Railway Ltd.
PLATFORM TICKET
KEIGHLEY
NOT VALID ON TRAINS
MAY BE RETAINED
Issued subject to the Co's Regulations
4040

591

S 6031
Kent & East Sussex Railway.
JUNCTION ROAD
to
Robertsbridge
Fare 4½d
THIRD CLASS
Edmondson, Manchester.

592

LAKESIDE AND HAVERTHWAITE RAILWAY
NEWBY BRIDGE
Platform Ticket
NOT VALID ON TRAINS
AVAILABLE ON DAY OF ISSUE ONLY
9 |10|11|12|13|14|15|16|17|18|19|20
4994

593

LINCOLNSHIRE COAST LIGHT RAILWAY
1½P
Williamson, Ticket Printer, Ashton
09258 09260

594

RHEILFFORDD LLYN LLANBERIS
DWYFFORDD
OEDOLYN
ADULT RETURN
LLANBERIS LAKE RAILWAY
Williamson, Ticket Printer, Ashton
2827

595

LOCHTY RAILWAY CO.
ONE PASSENGER — A
OUTWARD and RETURN
Subject to conditions of carriage as shown
Not Transferable
1516 Date of Travel.....AUG.....

More of Wales with an exceptional size from Mr Edmondson. The Isle of Man adding interest in the form of a three-coupon card ticket.

596

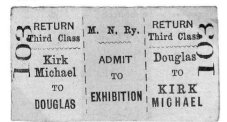

RETURN Third Class | M. N. Ry. | RETURN Third Class
Kirk Michael | ADMIT TO | Douglas
TO | EXHIBITION | TO
DOUGLAS | | KIRK MICHAEL
103

597

1758 MIDDLETON RAILWAY LEEDS
Tunstall Road to PARK HALT | Park Halt to TUNSTALL RD.
For conditions see over
11345

598

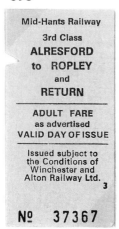

599

600

601

602

603

604

605

606

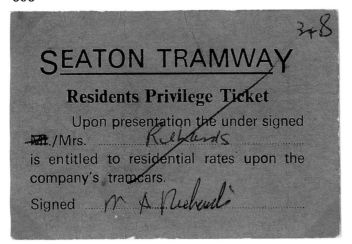

607

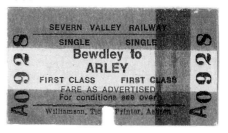

608

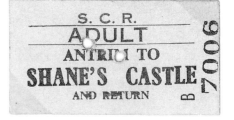

Tourism today and industrial feeders of yesteryear, with an
Irish private estate railway too. Note the minor railway's
'Parliamentary' travel.

609

Sittingbourne & Kemsley Light Railway Ltd.
SITTINGBOURNE to
KEMSLEY DOWN & RETURN
Available day of issue only
Issued subject to Co's regulations & conditions
COMPLIMENTARY
Williamson, Ticket Printer, Ashton

610

SNOWDON MOUNTAIN RAILWAY
Summit   Llanberis
TO   TO   **12/6**
LLANBERIS SUMMIT
The charge made for this Ticket includes entrance to the Company's Land on the Summit and Shelters at Stations. (Over)
Williamson, Ticket Printer, Ashton-u-Lyne

611

07 APR 1973
STRATHSPEY RAILWAY
DAY RETURN — PARTY RATE
**VALID FOR ONE
RETURN JOURNEY**
SECOND CLASS
Issued subject to Co's conditions
UP   DOWN
Williamson, Printer, Ashton   0536

612

TORBAY &
DARTMOUTH RLY
RETURN
Valid for one journey
within one month
**Paignton
or
Goodrington
to
KINGSWEAR**
For Dartmouth
AND BACK
For conditions of issue see
Company's Bye-laws
3 **7 7 1 5**

613

9076 **TUNNEL RAILWAY LTD.**
ADULT
SINGLE
Williamson, Ticket Printer, Ashton

614

Nᵒ   BRITISH RAILWAYS BOARD (M)   Nᵒ
VALE OF RHEIDOL NARROW GAUGE RAILWAY
LEIN FACH CWM RHEIDOL
DEVIL'S BRIDGE — PONTARFYNACH
PLATFORM TICKET 6d.   TOCYN GORSAF 6c.
2279   Available one hour on day of issue only. Not valid in trains. Not transferable.   2279
Mewn grym am awr ar y diwrnod yn unig. Yn ddi-rym ar y trenau. Ni ellir ei
drosglwyddo.
For conditions see over.   Gwler amodau ar y cefn.
| 1 | 2 | 3 | 4 | 5 | 6 | 7 | 8 | 9 | 10 | 11 | 12 |

615

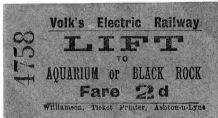

4758   **Volk's Electric Railway**
L I F T
TO
AQUARIUM or BLACK ROCK
Fare 2d
Williamson, Ticket Printer, Ashton-u-Lyne

616

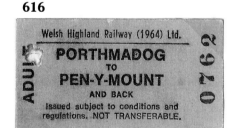

Welsh Highland Railway (1964) Ltd.
PORTHMADOG
ADULT   TO   2940
PEN-Y-MOUNT
AND BACK
Issued subject to conditions and
regulations. NOT TRANSFERABLE.

617

WELSHPOOL & LLANFAIR LIGHT
RAILWAY PRESERVATION CO., LTD.
ASSOCIATE MEMBER'S TICKET
AT SPECIAL RATE
to any WL Rly. Station **AND BACK**
Issued subject to the Coy's regulations
conditions and notices. NOT TRANSFERABLE
W191—Williamson, Ticket Printer, Ashton

618

001311   **West Somerset Railway Co.**   001311
Minehead   Blue Anchor
to   to
Blue Anchor   Minehead
ADULT   ADULT
Issued subject to Company's
conditions

619

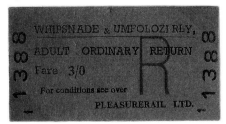

8813   WHIPSNADE & UMFOLOZI RLY,
ADULT ORDINARY RETURN
Fare 3/0
For conditions see over
PLEASURERAIL LTD.   8813

The Welsh language, the
Sussex seashore and a tenuous
South African connection (*619*)
add to a group of *touristik*
tickets.

620

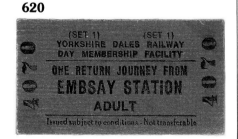

(SET 1)   (SET 1)
YORKSHIRE DALES RAILWAY
DAY MEMBERSHIP FACILITY
ONE RETURN JOURNEY FROM
4070   **EMBSAY STATION**   4070
ADULT
Issued subject to conditions - Not transferable

Seaton Tramway
Removed from Eastbourne, Sussex (**605**), to East Devon. Renamed and reorganised as a tourist tramway 1970 (**606**).

Severn Valley Railway
Railway in Shropshire (**607**). Part of an 1862 railway of the same name. Closed by Dr Beeching in 1963 and reopened by preservationists in 1970.

Shane's Castle (Light) Railway
Built in 1971 on the Irish estate of Lord O'Neill, northwest of Belfast (**608**).

Sittingbourne & Kemsley Light Railway
Short North Kent line established in 1970 (**609**).

Snowdon Mountain Railway
Llanberis to the summit of Snowdon, opened in 1896 (**610**).

Strathspey Railway
Southeast of Inverness. Reopened in 1977 (**611**).

Torbay & Dartmouth Railway
Ex-GW main line from Paignton to Kingswear, Devon. Purchased by the Dart Valley Railway Company in 1973 (**612**). **575** shows the first operating title.

Tunnel Railway
Closed at Ramsgate in 1965 (**613**).

Vale of Rheidol Railway
Steam-operated line in Central Wales. Formerly a private company (**67**) opened in 1902 and subsequently taken over by the Cambrian Railways in 1913, the GW in 1923, BTC and now BRB (**614**).

Volks Electric Railway[21]
Opened in 1883 (**615**).

Welsh Highland Railway (II)
Closed in 1937. Reopened privately in 1980 (**616**).

Welshpool & Llanfair Light Railway
Reopened in 1963 (**617**).

West Somerset Railway
Reopened in 1976 (**618**).

Whipsnade & Umfolozi Railway
Built in Whipsnade Zoo grounds in 1970 (**619**) and named to link the zoo with the South African home of many of its animals (where there is another narrow gauge railway, but no separate tickets).

Yorkshire Dales Railway
Opened in 1973 (**620**).

CHAPTER 12

Specialised Collections

It is neither practicable nor imaginative nor even satisfying to retain *every* ticket that comes one's way. Sooner or later the collector will begin to specialise. He may set himself the target of obtaining at least one ticket from each railway company past or present in a particular area. This presents little problem in the initial stages of building a collection but after the first few dozen titles have been obtained, further additions will become infrequent and often prove expensive. However, he will find that railway tickets, like postage stamps, command lower prices outside their country of origin. Accordingly, the collector will often obtain a bargain by purchasing from abroad while a foreign ticket attracting little interest in the UK may be highly prized in its country of origin.

Some collectors follow the philatelist in seeking sometimes minute variations in the general format of tickets. They find themselves with a surprising amount of scope. Even the **NCR 21** Single Ticket of British Railways Board's Southern Region, introduced in 1970, has appeared in seven distinctive types. The first to appear (**662**) had no wording to indicate that it was a railway ticket, the second brought in the BR logo and the wording 'British Rail(S)' (**661**) and the third omitted the two boxes that contained the fare and the issuing machine number (**660**). These appeared on both green and white card. Then followed a later style, on white card only, omitting the words 'British Rail (S)' but keeping the logo and printing the class of travel in bolder fonts. Since all these exist in both First and Second Class, full fare and half fare, tickets available for one day or three days, we have a possible 56 varieties of Single Tickets before turning our attention to Returns.

When a railway station is transferred from one administration to another or when its name is changed, there is rarely an immediate impact on the style of its tickets. A number of collectors discovered this hard fact early on a cold November morning in 1947 when Wood Lane station on London Transport's Central Line closed and was replaced by the new White City station. Arriving by various means in the hope of purchasing 'first tickets' they found that the Wood Lane stock had simply been moved during the night to serve White City! The only concession —

numbering in the automatic machines had been set back to zero. **621** was emitted from the 7d machine a little later that day for the benefit of a collector who had breakfasted before leaving home!

Changes come gradually and the first is usually the insertion of the new owner's name on existing printer's dies while a new ticket format is being settled and new dies cut. These hybrid tickets tend to be shortlived.

In 1923, the new Big Four companies put their names to their tickets with little delay. After Nationalisation in 1948, there was uncertainty and for two years the new BTC, acting through its Regional Executives continued to print tickets under the old company headings (**622**). One surprising result was that Marylebone station, which initially passed from the LNER to the Western Region of the new organisation, received a stock of Platform Tickets headed 'Great Western Railway'. It was a further two years before tickets in the standard British Railways style began to appear. Even then pre-Nationalisation conditions continued to appear while printed stock lasted.

There was indeed a false start in that a few tickets in the early days bore the heading 'The Railway Executive (Western Region)' (**623**). In the remainder of this chapter, we suggest some possible directions in which a ticket enthusiast's interest may be inclined to run.

Transition on the LNER
The tickets described in the following two paragraphs demonstrate this process of change during the two periods of transition that affected the London & North Eastern Railway.

The first transition. The new company's heading in a clearly Lancashire & Yorkshire Railway pattern for 'One Article' (**624**). A half-Edmondson that is so nearly a North Eastern Railway print that it would only be necessary to delete the 'L&' from 'L&NER' (**625**). Two green Third Class Singles. One of the former North British Railway (**626**), the other retaining its style but now headed for the new owners (**627**). Two blue Third Class Singles. One of the former Great Northern Railway (**628**), the other retaining its

621

'23 NOV

LT
WOOD LANE
7d to Liverpool St.
Elephant & Cas.
Holloway Road
Chalk Farm
Kentish Town
Angel
Borough
Oval
Aldgate
Aldgate East
W. Hampstead
or intermediately

WOOD LANE 7d

0 0 0 3 8

622

Gt Western Ry
Return Excursion
Jan 14, 1950
HALF DAY
East Dulwich to
OXFORD
Via S.R. London
& Didcot
Exclusive of conveyance
betw'n ...ton Termini
TH... CLASS
FO... ...ONDITIONS

623

The Railway Executive (Western Region)
Plympton   Plympton
TO
BITTAFORD Platform
THIRD CLASS
1/11 Z Fare 1/11 Z
Bittaford Platform Bittaford Platform
FOR CONDITIONS SEE BACK W.D
6187

624

FOR CONDITIONS OF ISSUE SEE BACK
L&NERy ONE ARTICLE under 2 CWTS
Accompanying the Passenger and conveyed at
Mileage Scale at PASSENGERS RISK
SHEFFIELD (Victoria) N
to   DARNALL
On .... Ry.
Description
of Article   DOG.
PAID ......8....d
This Ticket must be given up on arrival

625

HESSLE
J
To
HULL
THIRD CLASS
Fare 1s.3d.
SEE BACK. L.&N.E.R.
6195

626

N B R
THIRD CLASS
KIRKCALDY
No 1   TO   A
EDINBURGH (WAVERLEY)
Via Forth Bridge,
Not Transferable. See Conditions On Back
Fare   16
1/0   Edin...v y FB   OVER
4087
6 MR.18

627

L. N. E. R.
THIRD   CLASS
NORTH LEITH
TO
BONNINGTON
Not Transferable. See Conditions on Back
Fare   10
1d,   Bonnington   Over
586
2SP.3?

628

G. N. R.
Series C   Series C
HIGHGATE   to
HIGHGATE   HIGHGATE
CANONBURY
CANONBURY   CANONBURY
Fare 3½d. Third Class Fare 3½d.
SEE CON...TIONS ON BACK.
3531

629

L. & N. E. R.
Series A   Series A
FARRINGDON ST. to
FARRINGDON ST.   FARRINGTON ST.
HORNSEY
HORNSEY   HORNSEY
Fare 6d. Third Class Fare 6d.
SEE CONDITIO... ...N BACK
4612

630

LOCAL L.N.E.R.
THIRD CLASS
Rumbling Bridge
To
CROOK OF DEVON
Via ....
Fare ..... Over.
954

L.N.E.R. LOCAL
THIRD CLASS
CROOK OF DEVON
To
Rumbling Bridge
Via ....
Not Transferable.
954

631

P.S. 3609
LONDON & NORTH EASTERN RAILWAY
No. A 4512 Charge £ : 10. 0
PERIOD PARKING TICKET
NOT TRANSFERABLE
No. of MOTOR CAR/CYCLE
Marylebone Booking Office
XRC85
Date issued 11-9-49
Date of expiry 10-10-49
Signature of }
Depositor }
For Conditions see back

632

P.S. 3609 Spl.
THE RAILWAY EXECUTIVE
(EASTERN REGION)
No. B 5458 Charge £ —: 10. 0
PERIOD PARKING TICKET
NOT TRANSFERABLE
No. of MOTOR CAR/CYCLE HxR966
Issued at MARYLEBONE B.O.
Date issued 4-10-50
Date of expiry 3-11-50
Signature of }
Depositor }
For Conditions see back.

633

L.N.E.R.   L.N.E.R.
HALF DAY EXC'N HALF DAY EXC'N
KING'S CROSS   WEST HARTLEPOOL
to   to
WEST HARTLEPOOL KING'S CROSS
Via Doncaster   Via Doncaster
Valid as per Bills Valid as per Bills
THIRD ½ DAY THIRD
For conditions 3580 For conditions
see back. KING'S CROSS see back
5422

634

BRIT. RLYS. (N)   BRITISH RLYS. (N)
HALF DAY EXC'N HALF DAY EXC'N
NEWCASTLE   REEDSMOUTH
To   TO
REEDSMOUTH   NEWCASTLE
Valid as per Bills. Valid as per Bills
THIRD   THIRD
For ...nditions For conditions
...back   ...back
0068

Early days of Nationalisation
and earlier times of transition,
622 was printed for issue two
years after demise of the GW.

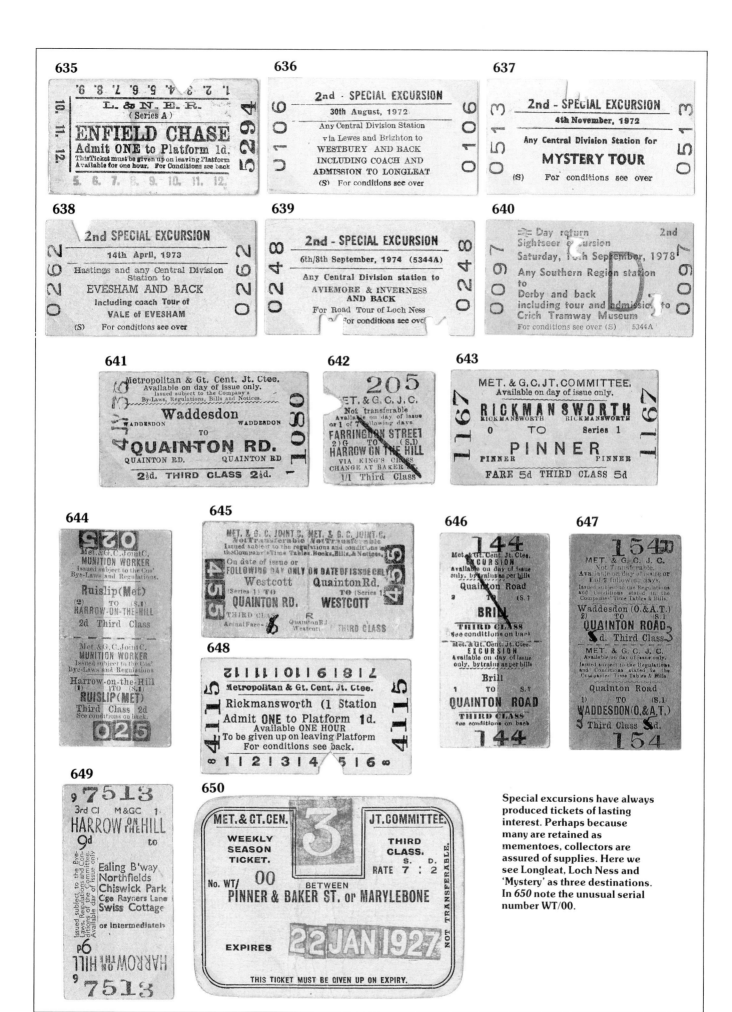

635

L. & N. E. R.
(Series A)

ENFIELD CHASE
Admit ONE to Platform 1d.
This Ticket must be given up on leaving Platform
Available for one hour. For Conditions see back

5294

636

2nd - SPECIAL EXCURSION
30th August, 1972
Any Central Division Station
via Lewes and Brighton to
WESTBURY AND BACK
INCLUDING COACH AND
ADMISSION TO LONGLEAT
(S)   For conditions see over

0106

637

2nd - SPECIAL EXCURSION
4th November, 1972
Any Central Division Station for
MYSTERY TOUR
(S)   For conditions see over

0513

638

2nd SPECIAL EXCURSION
14th April, 1973
Hastings and any Central Division
Station to
EVESHAM AND BACK
Including coach Tour of
VALE of EVESHAM
(S)   For conditions see over

0262

639

2nd - SPECIAL EXCURSION
6th/8th September, 1974 (5344A)
Any Central Division station to
**AVIEMORE & INVERNESS
AND BACK**
For Road Tour of Loch Ness
For conditions see over

0248

640

Day return   2nd
Sightseer excursion
Saturday, 16th September, 1978
Any Southern Region station
to
Derby and back
including tour and admission to
Crich Tramway Museum
For conditions see over (S)   5344A

0097

641

Metropolitan & Gt. Cent. Jt. Ctee.
Available on day of issue only.
Issued subject to the Company's
By-Laws, Regulations, Bills and Notices.
Waddesdon
WADDESDON   WADDESDON
TO
QUAINTON RD.
QUAINTON RD.   QUAINTON RD
2½d. THIRD CLASS 2½d.

1080

642

205
MET. & G. C. J. C.
Not transferable
Available on day of issue
or 1 of 7 following days
FARRINGDON STREET
2) G   (S.1)
HARROW ON THE HILL
VIA KING'S CROSS
CHANGE AT BAKER ST.
1/1 Third Class

643

MET. & G.C. JT. COMMITTEE.
Available on day of issue only.
RICKMANSWORTH
RICKMANSWORTH   RICKMANSWORTH
0   TO   Series 1
PINNER
PINNER   PINNER
FARE 5d THIRD CLASS 5d

1167 ... 1167

644

025
Met.&G.C.JointC.
MUNITION WORKER
Issued subject to the Cos'
Bye-Laws and Regulations.
Ruislip (Met)
(2)   TO   (S.1)
HARROW-ON-THE-HILL
2d Third Class

Met.&G.C.JointC.
MUNITION WORKER
Issued subject to the Cos'
Bye-Laws and Regulations
Harrow-on-the-Hill
(1)   TO   (S.1)
RUISLIP (MET)
Third Class 2d
See conditions on back.
025

645

MET. & G. C. JOINT C.   MET. & G. C. JOINT C.
NotTransferable NotTransferable
Issued subject to the regulations and conditions in
theCompany's Time Tables, Books, Bills, & Notices.
On date of issue or
FOLLOWING DAY ONLY ON DATE OF ISSUE ONLY
Westcott   Quainton Rd.
(Series 1) TO   (Series 1)
QUAINTON RD.   WESTCOTT
THIRD CLASS
Actual Fare—   Quainton Rd
Westcott
R

495 ... 495

648

2 1 1 1 1 0 1 1 6 1 8 1 2
Metropolitan & Gt. Cent. Jt. Ctee.
Rickmansworth (1 Station
Admit ONE to Platform 1d.
Available ONE HOUR
To be given up on leaving Platform
For conditions see back.
1 1 2 1 3 1 4 1 5 1 6

4115 ... 4115

646

144
Met. & Gt. Cent. Jt. Ctee.
EXCURSION
Available on day of issue
only. by trains as per bills
Quainton Road
2   (S.1)
BRILL
THIRD CLASS
See conditions on back
Met. & Gt. Cent. Jt. Ctee.
EXCURSION
Available on day of issue
only. by trains as per bills
Brill
1   S.1
QUAINTON ROAD
THIRD CLASS
See conditions on back
144

647

154
MET. & G. C. J. C.
Not Transferable.
Available on day of issue or
1 of 7 following days.
Issued subject to the Regulations
and Conditions stated in the
Companies' Time Tables & Bills.
Waddesdon (O.&A.T.)
2)   TO   (S.1)
QUAINTON ROAD
3d. Third Class.
MET. & G. C. J. C.
Available on day of issue only.
Issued subject to the Regulations
and Conditions stated in the
Companies' Time Tables & Bills.
Quainton Road
1)   TO   (S.1)
WADDESDON (O.&A.T.)
3 Third Class 3d.
154

649

9 7513
3rd Cl   M&GC   1.
HARROW ON THE HILL
9d   to
Ealing B'way
Northfields
Chiswick Park
Cge Rayners Lane
Swiss Cottage
or intermediately
P6
HARROW ON THE HILL
9 7513

650

MET. & GT. CEN.   **3**   JT. COMMITTEE.
WEEKLY
SEASON   THIRD
TICKET.   CLASS.
                    S.   D.
                    RATE 7 : 2
No. WT/ 00
BETWEEN
PINNER & BAKER ST. or MARYLEBONE

22 JAN 1927

NOT TRANSFERABLE

EXPIRES

THIS TICKET MUST BE GIVEN UP ON EXPIRY.

Special excursions have always
produced tickets of lasting
interest. Perhaps because
many are retained as
mementoes, collectors are
assured of supplies. Here we
see Longleat, Loch Ness and
'Mystery' as three destinations.
In *650* note the unusual serial
number WT/00.

style but now titled 'L.& N.E.R.' (**629**). An LNER Local Ticket in the style of the North British Railway (**630**).

The second transition. LNER and Railway Executive Period Parking Tickets — **631** and **632**. LNER and British Railways (N) Half-Day Excursion Tickets (**633** and **634**), the latter still a Railway Executive issue but now with a revised heading and omission of the snip panel removed by the issuing clerk when sold for a child; the LNER ticket is dated 14 August 1955 — ie seven and a half years into the Nationalisation regime. An old style LNER Platform Ticket (**635**) of a kind still on sale at a few stations as late as 1954.

Indian Summer

Some collectors concentrate on interesting excursion tickets. They are specially printed to meet particular needs and show marked differences in wording and layout. The special excursion train enjoyed a brief heyday in southeast England between 1972 and 1974. In the summer of 1972, Southern Region of British Rail ran a number of well-advertised special trains from south coast stations to Westbury, where motor coaches were waiting to take the passengers to Longleat House (**636**). The fare of £2 included admission to the house, the lion enclosure and also the services of a courier. The trains were filled and the experiment was followed by a series of Saturday trips to places difficult to reach by regular services. The coach trip, the courier and the £2 fare were retained.

These trains also were well patronised, with casual trippers soon becoming loyal regulars. A comaraderie developed as friendships were made and seats saved for companions who were to join the train towards the end of the catchment area. Photographs were taken on one trip and shown around on the next. The regulars seemed ready to go wherever British Rail decreed, even on mystery tours. That of 4 November 1972 (**637**) took the North London Line to Stratford and on to Colchester, with a coach trip around Constable Country. The time allocated to the road tour had been based on experience in summer when many lanes are jammed with sightseers. On that November day the excursionists saw the beauty spots at speed and in comfort and arrived back in Colchester almost 2hr early, permitting further sightseeing in the town.

The excursions continued throughout 1973 (**638**) and 1974 although in the latter year it became clear that the number of possible destinations was finite. As earlier trips were repeated support began to wane. Trains were no longer fully booked. Sunday workings were tried and the £2 fare abandoned to enable more ambitious tours to be planned (**639**). Eventually excursionists were offered travel by any train to the London terminus, coach from there to the terminus of another region and a guaranteed seat on a scheduled train to some provincial centre, often with a coach tour (**640**). Still good value for money but now the inconvenience of changing trains frightened away the less hardened travellers. The Indian Summer had ended.

The Met & GC to Brill

Other collectors specialise in the tickets of a particular area or railway. We have considered Brighton and County Durham in Chapter 9. Here we look at some other areas.

The Metropolitan & Great Central Joint Committee was formed on 2 April 1906 to take a lease on hitherto pure-Met lines north of Harrow, Middlesex. This facilitated working over the GC's London extension which had opened in March 1899 and was part of a bold strategy to run trains to the Channel Ports. Harrow-on-the-Hill formed the Committee's southern limit to

their new Chesham and Brill territory, and Verney Junction its most northerly.

Being a legally separate entity (registered at the Stock Exchange and in every respect the owner of its fabric), it lasted until Nationalisation of Britain's railways in 1948. This was 15 years after its Met partner had been drawn into the London Passenger Transport Board (LPTB) in 1933. The GC partner had meantime been grouped into the LNER in 1923, who managed the Committee from 1932. Management had previously alternated between the Met and the GC partners.

Prior to 1918 most prints were Met in appearance. A few GC prints were still being used on the little-visited Quainton Road to Brill branch when it closed on 30 November 1935. Waddesdon station on the branch was always distinguished by the addition of the suffix 'O&AT' to avoid confusion with the station on the main line which once had the same name — Waddesdon (**641**). The initials O&AT meant the Oxford & Aylesbury Tramroad Company (it never got nearer than 17km from Oxford!) which took over the earlier Wotton (Brill) Tramway in October 1894. The Joint Committee took control from the Met after its formation and closed the line on the expiry of its lease on 30 November 1935.

A few tickets issued at the LNER agency (Code A602) in Harrow for journeys from Harrow or Pinner, were in post-Grouping LNER styles and headed either 'Met & G.C. Joint' or '. . . Joint Railways'. From 1937 tickets to London Transport points south of Harrow were of the Scheme type. That is to say, the FARE and STATION OF ISSUE were in large print followed less conspicuously by a list of alternative destinations which could be reached for the same stated fare. A Rickmansworth to Watford example **Rolltic** (Chapter 2) is also known. First Class travel was withdrawn on 6 October 1941 except on LNER trains to points outside the London area.

A selection of tickets representing this former Joint Committee is illustrated as follows (all of Met-style unless otherwise mentioned):

1 Return half-Edmondson issued a few days after formation of the Committee in April 1906 (**642**).
2 Standard Single Ticket issued in 1907 (**643**) and a further Single dated 1936 (**641**).
3 **644** is a Munition Worker's ticket dated about 1916. It will be noted that the word 'fare' has been omitted. The wording of the conditions of issue is typical of prints rather later than 1910. Clearly this ticket would not have been produced before the outbreak of World War 1 in 1914.
4 A GC-influenced style issued on the final day of Wescott, November 1935 — at least 12 years after it was printed (**645**).
5 A 1935 Excursion Ticket for the O&AT's full length (**646**).
6 Another Brill line item issued on the final day — note the '(O&AT)' suffix to the name of Waddesdon, which places the printing before October 1922 when the name Waddesdon Road came into use, as also does the printed '(S.1)' for the original series-one pattern (**647**).
7 Ordinary Platform Ticket dated July 1936 (**648**).
8 LPTB-style Scheme Ticket dated October 1946 (**649**).
9 Standard Weekly Season Ticket of a type current until about the second half of 1927 (**650**).

Corringham

Sometimes the collector will feel that one small group of tickets merits a special display or that a number of such groups can be written up and kept in a separate album. There are times when a visitor asks to see a portion of the collection and it is clear that the

651

CORRINGHAM LIGHT RAILWAY

An independent railway in Essex, which ran from Corringham near Stanford-le-Hope, to Coryton (or Kynochtown) near Thames Haven.

Open from June 1901 to March 1952.

The four Edmondson cards, overstamped with a Week Letter, represent types in use in 1936 – blue, violet, green and pink. White paper tickets were also used. The two shown with a 1½d fare are from an earlier period. The single fare in 1936 was 2½d and the weekly fare 2/6d (22½p). Weekly tickets were issued in sequence as follows: 'A' through each of four colours, then 'B' through each and so on.

C. L. R.
THIRD CLASS
WEEKLY SEASON TICKET
PRICE:
ONE SHILLING AND THREE PENCE
NOT TRANSFERABLE
22516

C. L. R.
THIRD CLASS
WEEKLY SEASON TICKET
PRICE:
ONE SHILLING AND THREE PENCE
NOT TRANSFERABLE
22436

C. L. R.
THIRD CLASS
SINGLE BETWEEN KYNOCHTOWN
And CORRINGHAM
FARE - 1½d.
32424

C. L. R.
THIRD CLASS
WEEKLY SEASON TICKET
PRICE:
ONE SHILLING AND THREE PENCE
NOT TRANSFERABLE
23156

C. L. R.
THIRD CLASS
WEEKLY SEASON TICKET
PRICE:
ONE SHILLING AND THREE PENCE
NOT TRANSFERABLE
24023

C. L. R.
THIRD CLASS
SINGLE BETWEEN CORRINGHAM
And KYNOCHTOWN
FARE - 1½d.
32027

Corringham Station

Coryton Station

Level Crossing on line.

Three further views of Corringham.

Taken directly from an album, this page of tickets is brought into steam with the addition of several snapshots. Timetables, maps, local scenery sketches and leaflets are other 'props' helpful in displaying tickets.

request springs from courtesy to a host rather than unbridled enthusiasm. On such an occasion this would be the album to produce. We illustrate an A4 page (**651**) taken from a 'showpiece album' relating to the tickets of the Corringham Light Railway and go on to introduce particularly cherished parts of the wider collection. It will be seen how the addition of a map and several pictorial prints provides further pleasure for the viewer.

Wimbledon to West Croydon (A personal appreciation)

I am thrilled by the railways of Fort William and Mallaig and to Oban but mainly from awe at the engineering skills of the men who built them and the strength and determination of those who continue to operate them in the worst conditions that Britain can provide. There is only one railway line I can claim to love. It is almost 10km long and runs from Wimbledon by way of Merton Park, Morden Road, Mitcham, Mitcham Junction, Beddington Lane and Waddon Marsh to West Croydon. Its sole engineering feature is a bridge about 3m long across the River Wandle. I lived about 3km from Wimbledon and discovered the line in 1933. I was 12 and well into O-gauge Hornby Trains. I felt an immediate affinity for something I could relate to and even reproduce at home on the sitting room floor. Its operation was simple enough for an unsophisticated youngster to understand.

It shared a platform at Wimbledon with the Holborn Viaduct trains. It was double-tracked as far as Merton Park, where another line departed mysteriously to the left, then single-track to Mitcham, double to Mitcham Junction, single to Waddon Marsh and finally double to West Croydon, where it again shared accommodation with London-bound trains. Operation was simple: trains left the two termini at the same time, passed each other between Mitcham and Mitcham Junction and arrived at the opposite end 17min later. If Hornby had sold trailing points in those days, I could have worked it single-handed!

Not only was the line attractive; so were the fares. Besides the Cheap Day Returns after 10am there were also Cheap Day Singles. Travelling half-fare, my cheapest option for a joyride was a penny Return to Morden Halt (now Morden Road). At Merton Park began the novelty of travelling on a single track and watching the ceremony of the handing over of the staff that permitted the driver to take his train along the reversible track. An interesting alternative was a penny Single to Mitcham and if pocket-money had run out, spending the rest of the afternoon walking home. This way, one could be sure of a visit from the guard. Some stations were unstaffed and the train, called a Rail Motor Car, consisted of two coaches, each having an open way beside the seats, along which the guard walked with a rack of punch-type tickets, enquiring whether anyone needed a ticket and usually giving me a friendly word or nod. The incongruity in those days of railway guard playing tram conductor was part of the magic of this line.

Just beyond Morden, we ran beside the River Wandle, through water meadows where cattle grazed. At Mitcham Junction — 2½d (today's 1p) Return — Mitcham Common began. People said you could still smell the aroma of Mitcham lavender in those parts. I never did but the nearby hamlet of Mill Green seemed a rural paradise to a young town-dweller. Once I managed to raise fivepence (2p) for the full return trip to the far terminus, only to find that Croydon was just another town.

I learned the history of the line many years later. It had opened in 1855 with stations at Mitcham and Beddington. Morden and Merton Park (once Lower Merton) came during the next 15 years, as did the mysterious route from Merton Park. Actually it went to Tooting Junction (now Tooting) by way of Merton Abbey and was

closed as a war economy in 1917. They reopened it in 1923 but traffic had already passed to the electric tramcar and its passenger life finally ended in 1929. The big upheaval came in 1930 when my line was electrified and Waddon Marsh Halt built. The excitement had been just three years too early for me to enjoy.

It was struggling to pay its way in 1933 and the much publicised Cheap Tickets were a desperate attempt to attract passengers. Since Nationalisation, it has appeared on one closure list after another yet survived every time. Over the years industrial estates have grown up all along the route — at Morden Road, the once rustic Mill Green, at Beddington Lane and at Waddon Marsh, places where an acute shortage of parking space makes public transport attractive to the most committed motorist. Closure of a railway is rarely authorised if there is no alternative transport facility. The already overcrowded A236 road runs almost a kilometre to the north of the section between Mitcham Junction and West Croydon but there is no feasible omnibus route that could connect the remaining stations.

Half-a-century after my acquaintance and courtesy of a Senior Citizen Railcard, I again took a joyride to West Croydon at half-fare and recaptured my memories. Happily, very little apart from the scenery had changed since the days of King George V. The site of the Tooting Branch was built over and the junction at Merton Park neatly turfed. It was perhaps the most rural part of the line, Mitcham Common only excepted. The trains were still of two coaches, they left the termini at the same time and still took 17min. The guard was friendly although about 40 years my junior. The staff was no longer passed to the driver; they changed to colour-light signalling around 1982. The station buildings at Morden Road and Mitcham were demolished and tiny portable booking offices put in their place. The fares were different. The adult Off Peak Return along the whole line was once 10d (4p) and in 1984 was £1.10.

Tangible reminders of the line remain in tickets preserved by collectors. **652** is half a Parliamentary Return of Victorian Days (its condition alone tells that!), long before my story commenced. **653** was sold in 1933 and would have cost 5d (2p). By 1939, the year of **654**, Cheap Day Tickets were printed on green card. It would have cost one penny and the passenger could have travelled for one station from Mitcham Junction in either direction. **655** and **656** are **Bell Punch** products on stout paper held in a rack by the guard during the 1930s and clipped by him to indicate the journey for which issued and, in the case of **655**, a Return, the day of issue. **657** and **658** are Returns of the 1950s sold by the guard but printed on card by British Railways, held in a more advanced rack and intended to be clipped to indicate not the journeys but the day or month of issue. **658** includes journeys to stations that could be reached by means of a change at Mitcham Junction. **659** is a normal Railway Executive pre-standard printing of the early 1950s while **660** to **664**, all from **NCR 21** machines, indicate the fares of more recent years; 1976 to 1984 inclusive.

An Isle of Man collection

One of the attractions of studying an island is that because its limits are fixed and its area is finite, so the scope of one's investigations is firmly settled. A substantial bonus for the ticket enthusiast who selects the Isle of Man is the plentiful supply of specimens. We must content ourselves with a consideration of the Manx Electric Railway, the various steam railways and a brief mention of the tramways and the Steam Packet Company.

Before World War 2 there were tramway services in Douglas and southwards to Port Soderick. Original tickets are rarely seen but photographic reproductions may be found (**665**). Trams still

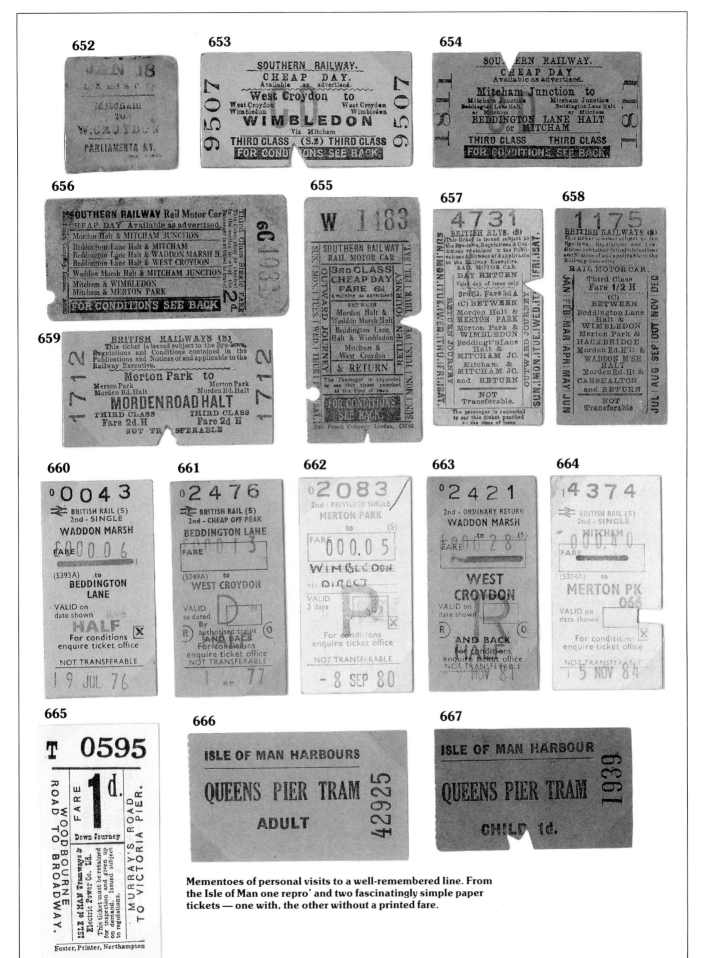

652

JAN 18
L.B. and S.C. Ry.
MITCHAM
TO
W. CROYDEN
PARLIAMENTA RY.

653

SOUTHERN RAILWAY.
CHEAP DAY.
Available as advertised
West Croydon to
West Croydon
Wimbledon
WIMBLEDON
Via Mitcham
THIRD CLASS (S.2) THIRD CLASS
FOR CONDITIONS SEE BACK

9507

654

SOUTHERN RAILWAY.
CHEAP DAY.
Available as advertised.
Mitcham Junction to
Mitcham Junction
Beddington Lane Halt
or Mitcham
BEDDINGTON LANE HALT
or MITCHAM
THIRD CLASS   THIRD CLASS
FOR CONDITIONS SEE BACK

656

SOUTHERN RAILWAY Rail Motor Car
CHEAP DAY Available as advertised
Morden Halt & MITCHAM JUNCTION
Beddington Lane Halt & MITCHAM
Beddington Lane Halt & WADDON MARSH H.
Beddington Lane Halt & WEST CROYDON
Waddon Marsh Halt & MITCHAM JUNCTION
Mitcham & WIMBLEDON
Mitcham & MERTON PARK
FOR CONDITIONS SEE BACK

655

W 1183

SOUTHERN RAILWAY
RAIL MOTOR CAR
3RD CLASS
CHEAP DAY
FARE 6d
Available as advertised
BETWEEN
Morden Halt &
Waddon Marsh Halt
Beddington Lane
Halt & Wimbledon
Mitcham &
West Croydon
& RETURN
FOR CONDITIONS
SEE BACK

657

4731
BRITISH RLYS. (S)
This ticket is issued subject to the Bye-laws, Regulations & Conditions contained in the Publications & Notices of & applicable to the Railway Executive.
RAIL MOTOR CAR
DAY RETURN
Valid day of issue only
3rdCl. Fare 3d A
(C) BETWEEN
Morden Halt &
MERTON PARK
Merton Park &
WIMBLEDON
Beddingt'nLane
Halt &
MITCHAM JC.
Mitcham &
MITCHAM JC.
and RETURN
NOT
Transferable.

658

1175
BRITISH RAILWAYS (S)
This ticket is issued subject to the Bye-laws, Regulations and Conditions contained in the Publications and Notices of and applicable to the Railway Executive.
RAIL MOTOR CAR
Third Class
Fare 1/2 H
(C)
BETWEEN
Beddington Lane
Halt &
WIMBLEDON
Merton Park &
HACKBRIDGE
Morden Rd.Ht &
WADDON M'SH
HALT
Morden Rd. Ht &
CARSHALTON
and RETURN
NOT
Transferable

659

1712
BRITISH RAILWAYS (S)
This ticket is issued subject to the Bye-laws, Regulations and Conditions contained in the Publications and Notices of and applicable to the Railway Executive.
Merton Park to
Merton Park   Merton Park
Morden Rd. Halt   Morden Rd. Halt
MORDEN ROAD HALT
THIRD CLASS   THIRD CLASS
Fare 2d. H   Fare 2d. H
NOT TRANSFERABLE

660

0 0043
BRITISH RAIL (S)
2nd - SINGLE
WADDON MARSH
FARE 00.06
(5393A) to
BEDDINGTON
LANE
· VALID on
date shown
HALF
For conditions
enquire ticket office
NOT TRANSFERABLE
19 JUL 76

661

0 2476
BRITISH RAIL (S)
2nd - CHEAP OFF PEAK
BEDDINGTON LANE
FARE 0013
(5349A) to
WEST CROYDON
VALID
as dated
By
authorised trains
AND BACK
For conditions
enquire ticket office
NOT TRANSFERABLE
1 77

662

0 2083
2nd - PRIVILEGE SINGLE
MERTON PARK
to (S)
FARE 000.05
WIMBLEDON
via DIRECT
VALID
3 days
For conditions
enquire ticket office
NOT TRANSFERABLE
- 8 SEP 80

663

0 2421
2nd - ORDINARY RETURN
WADDON MARSH
FARE 00 28 (S)
to
WEST
CROYDON
VALID on
date shown
AND BACK
For conditions
enquire ticket office
NOT TRANSFERABLE
NOV 81

664

1 4374
BRITISH RAIL (S)
2nd - SINGLE
MITCHAM
FARE 000.40
(5374A) to
MERTON PK
066
VALID on
date shown
For conditions
enquire ticket office
NOT TRANSFERABLE
15 NOV 84

665

T 0595
FARE
1d.
Down Journey
WOODBOURNE
ROAD TO BROADWAY.
MURRAY'S ROAD.
TO VICTORIA PIER.
ISLE of MAN Tramways &
Electric Power Co. Ld.
This ticket must be retained
for inspection and given up
on demand. Issued subject
to regulations.
Foster, Printer, Northampton

666

ISLE OF MAN HARBOURS
QUEENS PIER TRAM
ADULT
42925

667

ISLE OF MAN HARBOUR
QUEENS PIER TRAM
CHILD 1d.
1939

Mementoes of personal visits to a well-remembered line. From the Isle of Man one repro' and two fascinatingly simple paper tickets — one with, the other without a printed fare.

668

V88 6635
2d. STAGE 2d.
From Derby Castle to Broadway.
DOUGLAS CORPORATION TRAMS.
Ticket must be retained for inspection and given up on demand.
Issued subject to Bye-laws.
From Broadway to Derby Castle.
LUGGAGE. DOG.
AUTO-TICKET LTD. BIRKENHEAD

669

G62 1757
5d STAGE 5d
From Victoria Pier to Broadway
Douglas Corp. Transport
Ticket must be retained for inspection and given up on demand.
Issued subject to Bye-laws.
From Broadway to Victoria Pier
Luggage
Williamson, Printer, Ashton

670

Nb73 1566
FARE 8p
TO Victoria Pier
FROM Victoria Pier
FROM Summerland M.E.R.
Douglas Corp. Transport
Ticket must be retained for inspection and given up on demand.
Issued subject to Bye-laws.
TO Summerland M.E.R.
Luggage
Luggage
Williamson, Printer, Ashton

671

05904
Douglas Corporation Transport
80th Anniversary
HORSE TRAM CARS
7th August, 1956
SOUVENIR TICKET
56
From Victoria Pier to Derby Castle
Fare 6d
From Derby Castle to Victoria Pier
AUTO-TICKET LIMITED. BIRKENHEAD

672

Ga 0580
DOUGLAS CORPORATION
A TRANSPORT 83
HORSE TRAMS
TO Victoria Pier
FARE STAGE 25p ADULT
FROM Victoria Pier
Ticket must be retained for inspection & given up on demand. Issued subject to Bye-laws.
CONTROL SYSTEMS LTD.

673

Issued in accordance with the Conditions & Regulations shewn on Co's Time Tables &c. I.O.M. Ry.
FIRST CLASS
DOUGLAS
TO
CASTLETOWN
AVAILABLE ON DAY OF ISSUE ONLY
DOUGLAS
CASTLETOWN
A420 326

674

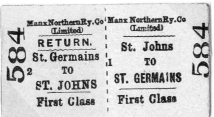

584
Manx Northern Ry. Co (Limited)
RETURN.
St. Germains TO ST. JOHNS
First Class
Manx Northern Ry. Co (Limited)
St. Johns TO ST. GERMAINS
First Class
584

675

Isle of Man Ry. Co., Limited.
RAMSEY
TO
BALLASALLA
FIRST CLASS.
203

676

Issued in accordance with the Conditions & Regulations shewn on Co's Time Tables &c.
I. O. M. RLY. SECOND CLASS
DOUGLAS
TO
SODERICK
AVAILABLE ON DAY OF ISSUE ONLY
DOUGLAS
SODERICK
5276

677

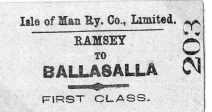

ISLE OF MAN RAILWAY
Issued in accordance with the conditions and regulations shewn on Time Tables etc.
BRADDAN
TO
DOUGLAS
Available on day of issue only
0191

678

ISLE OF MAN VICTORIAN STEAM RAILWAY CO. LTD.
DOUGLAS PORT ERIN OR ST. MARY
SINGLE
Issued in accordance with the conditions and regulations shewn in the Railway timetables etc.
AVAILABLE ON DAY OF ISSUE
15154

679

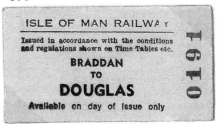

ISLE OF MAN VICTORIAN STEAM RAILWAY CO. LTD.
DOUGLAS PORT ERIN OR ST. MARY
RETURN
Issued in accordance with the conditions and regulations shewn in the Railway timetables etc.
AVAILABLE ON DAY OF ISSUE
46837

680

ISLE OF MAN RAILWAY CO.
OPERATING CENTENARY
SUNDAY, 1st JULY, 1973
TO
DOUGLAS CASTLETOWN
SEE NOTICE ON BACK
0980

All from the Isle of Man and dated 1934 to the 1970s. Note the 1973 print to commemorate a centenary.

681

ISLE OF MAN RAILWAY
You may retain this ticket as a Souvenir

Douglas to Port Erin/Port St. Mary

RETURN

N° 10046

20 JUL 78
VALID ON DAY OF ISSUE ONLY

ADULT

A

682

ISLE OF MAN RAILWAY Co. 1939
FOUR 3/9 GO-AS-YOU
DAYS CHILD PLEASE
Issued in accordance with general regulations
Not transferable. Must be given up on expiry.
Available 3rd. Class between ALL STATIONS
on any 4 days (need not be consecutive) within
7 days from date of issue.

Sun	Mon	Tue	Wed	Thu	Fri	Sat

0934

683

X 9773

684

MANX ELECTRIC RAILWAY
3d
Williamson, Printer, Ashton
L 7 1 4 2

685

MANX ELECTRIC RAILWAY
Single Journey
2/4
Williamson, Printer, Ashton
M 2 6 1 9

686

MANX ELECTRIC RAILWAY
Single Journey Exchange Ticket
D 3506

687

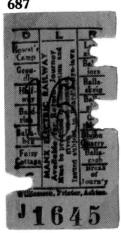

MANX ELECTRIC RAILWAY
J 1 6 4 5

688

SINGLE
Derby Castle to LAXEY
LAXEY to RAMSEY
MANX ELECTRIC RAILWAY
Available for One Single Journey
SINGLE JOURNEY
Williamson, Printer, Ashton
L 2 0 8 7

689

DERBY CASTLE
LAXEY
MANX ELECTRIC RAILWAY
Return Journey
Williamson, Printer, Ashton
A 7 7 7 9

690

MANX ELECTRIC RAILWAY
ROVER TICKET
TWO DAYS TRAVEL
(See other side)

Thurs.	Fri.	Sat.	SNAEFELL One journey

10106

**Further Manx items including
the untitled Falcon Cliff issue
(692).**

691

MINIATURE RAILWAY
DOWN or UP
Single Journey 6d
Monday
7306

692

2d
4299
Williamson, Ticket Printer, Ashton

run on Ramsey Pier but the information on the ticket is meagre (**666** and **667**).

Douglas has a summer service of horse trams between Victoria Pier and the Derby Castle terminus of the Manx Electric Railway. Apart from a lapse into machine issues between 1979 and 1983, tickets have remained punch-types An interesting feature of these tickets is that the year of issue always appears somewhere in the design. **668** was printed for the 1938 season, **669** for 1962, **670** for 1973, **671** for 1956 and **672** for 1983. It will be noted that in 1973 the Derby Castle terminus had become 'Summerland'. This was an enclosed and covered leisure park intended to cater for holidaymakers in inclement weather. It was the scene of a disastrous fire in 1974 with tragic loss of life. Tickets from 1975 onwards mention only Victoria Pier (**672**). The Isle of Man Steam Packet Company Limited carried a large and varied stock of tickets mainly for journeys between Liverpool and Douglas but also some from Fleetwood or Heysham to Douglas, and others including rail travel on the mainland.

Unused 19th century railway tickets are available in large numbers. There were two companies. The Isle of Man Railway Company opened in 1873, eventually running between Douglas and Port Erin and Douglas and Peel. The Manx Northern Railway came six years later and ran from St John's to Ramsey, with a short-lived line to Foxdale. It was first worked by the IoM company and later absorbed by it. However, it was in control of its own affairs from 1880 to 1905 and issued tickets. The format and colours of the tickets of the two companies are the same. Colours were white for First Class and blue for Second Class (redesignated Third in 1878). **673** and **674** are representative of the two companies while **675** is for a journey from the Manx Northern system to a station on the IoM and probably printed in 1879. **676** was sold on 15 September 1957 just after Third Class had reverted to Second. Dating was generally by dry stamp.

The company ceased running trains on 13 November 1965 and the tracks lay idle until leased to the Marquis of Ailsa. He reopened the Ramsey line on 3 June 1967 and reached Port Erin in 1969. **677** is one of his printings. He surrendered the lease in 1972, whereupon the original company resumed operations over part of the system. Tickets were headed 'Isle of Man Victorian Steam Railway Co Ltd'. **678** is a Single dated on the front while **679**, although a one-coupon Return, has the serial number at each end and so is dated on the back.

On 1 July 1973 came the centenary of the IoM and the day's celebrations included the printing of special tickets (**680**). More recently, the company has produced pictorial tickets intended to be retained as souvenirs (**681**). The collector will also find Holiday Runabout Tickets and Two-, Three- or Four-Day Tickets (**682**).

Manx Electric Railway (ME) tickets are plentiful for the simple reason that they are not collected at the end of the journey. Let it be explained at the outset the service is one of tramcars, some enclosed and some of toast rack type, running along and beside the A2 East Coast Road between Douglas and Ramsey with an interchange at Laxey (about midway) to the Snaefell Mountain Line (620m) which runs across moorland with only one intermediate boarding point at 'Bungalow' where the line crosses a public road. Built in stages between 1893 and 1899, it has also seen business crises — in 1900 some of the company's members were imprisoned for fraud — but changes have made little difference to the style and wording of the tickets. **683** is a particularly early and rare specimen carrying the early title. Unusually, it is dated — 12 June 1899.

684 was issued on the car to a passenger travelling the final short distance into Douglas and **685** is a 24p conductor's issue that became redundant as a result of a fare change. **686** is not quite what it seems. Described as a 'Single Journey Exchange Ticket' it was given in exchange for a voucher purchased in advance by a regular traveller. The back carries the words 'Not available for break of journey'. Careful inspection of **687** will reveal it to be a Return.

Booking office issues are quite different. Single tickets carry the word 'SINGLE' at the opposite end to the serial number while Returns utilise the spot by summarising the journey. **688** is a Single from Ramsey to Douglas while **689** is a Return from Douglas to Laxey. Tickets of the ME are generally not dated: **690** is an exception as it is necessary to ensure that the second day of travel is not taken more than a week after issue; it will be noted that it permits one journey only on the mountain track.

At Groudle the short 0.610m gauge Groudle Glen Railway operated from 1896 until 1962, and issued several quite distinctive tickets. There were titled roll-types printed by Williamson, and several untitled of unidentified source. The latter carry advertisements for the nearby Glen Hotel. A colour scheme was operated at certain times by which each day's tickets were of a different colour and day named. A typical 'Monday' ticket (**691**) was purple and a similar 'Saturday' print was pale green. At other times the line used untitled anonymous roll tickets from a stationer's Ivy Series not unlike the Williamson product illustrated for the Falcon Cliff Hotel cliff railway (**692**), but alas also untitled. This installation was opened at Douglas in 1927 as a means of improving access to the Falcon Cliff Hotel. An earlier cliff lift on the opposite side of the hotel was closed and moved away in 1927.

CHAPTER 13

The Story of a Famous Collection

The Grantham Railway Ticket Collection was started by William Wilson Grantham KC (1866-1942) in the late 1870s, when he and his younger brother were growing up with their parents at Barcombe Place, a few kilometres to the north of Lewes, Sussex.

It is believed that Barcombe was the only village in England to have been served by two railway stations on the same Company's metals. The first station to serve the village was on the Lewes-Uckfield line of the London Brighton & South Coast Railway and was called Barcombe; a second station was later provided on the Lewes-East Grinstead branch. This second station was initially called New Barcombe and the name of the earlier one was changed to Old Barcombe. Before long, however, both stations were again renamed — the first became Barcombe Mills and the second simply Barcombe (**693**[26]). They retained these names until closure in 1969 and 1955 respectively. Each of the two stations were within easy walking distance of young Mr Grantham's home and the repeated changes of name were strongly represented in his collection.

Initial progress seems to have been slow. His tally of tickets on 20 April 1901 was just 723, of which 69 were from the Barcombe stations. The remaining items were mainly of the Metropolitan, and District Railways and the main line companies with termini in London (**694**[26]). Only 63 'various' and 85 'foreign' fell outside these categories. The collection was now a regular exhibit at the annual Barcombe village fête and so received the attention of the local Press. These were the years before any in-depth studies had been conducted by collectors (see entry for 1908 in Chapter 16). The Press evidently unchallenged, were frequently equating 'Parliamentary' with Third Class.

In 1917, his son, Mr W. Ivor Grantham, returned from World War 1 wounded and temporarily immobilised. By way of therapy father handed to son the control and management of the collection. It grew rapidly with the help of many members of a large family and of a wide circle of friends and acquaintances together with unexpected aid from Fleet Street, which continued to regard the father as the true owner.

The father was a well known figure, being a King's Counsel, a prominent London County Councillor as well as the son of a High Court judge, and his eccentric hobby received much amused comment from the National Press. On his side he carefully retained the cuttings concerning himself together with unique records and comments on tickets. One article in a Russian newspaper circulating in Paris in 1932 placed his name among three other prominent Englishmen and one American with unusual hobbies — H. G. Wells (playing with tin soldiers), Lord Grey (Foreign Secretary at the outbreak of World War 1 — bird watching), Winston Churchill (landscape painting and bricklaying) and Henry Ford (collecting old gin bottles).

The value of the publicity afforded by both Local and National Press cannot be over-estimated. In 1925 a village schoolmaster of Belford, Northumberland wrote to offer some North British Railway waybills and tickets of 1846 (Two such tickets are illustrated in Chapter 3 (**164** and **180**) and further specimens are held by the Science Museum in London's South Kensington). From the schoolmaster's letter we learn that passengers from Newcastle to Edinburgh completed their journey by train and their tickets were collected in the ordinary way. However, passengers from Edinburgh arrived at Newcastle on the stage coach and the tickets were handed to the driver.

Collected tickets were wrapped inside the waybills and retained by the coach proprietors for accounting purposes. When the railway was complete and the coach link ceased, tickets and waybills were bundled and stored at the offices of the coach operator at Belford until about the turn of the century when all but one bundle was burned. The contents of the surviving bundle (waybills and tickets of the autumn of 1846) were presented to the schoolmaster. He kept them for many years until selling them to various dealers and collectors during the 1920s. One waybill purchased by Mr Grantham included the name of a peer of the realm, travelling 'First Class and Inside', a gentleman, perhaps his butler, travelling 'Second Class and Inside' and a soldier who was exposed to 'Third Class and Outside'.

A further letter surviving from this period is one from a well known firm of booksellers in Great Russell Street, London, offering William Grantham the following item for the princely sum of 5s (25p).

693

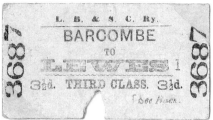

694

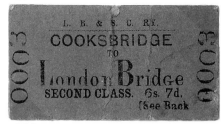

695

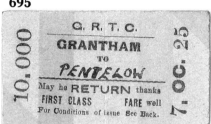

696

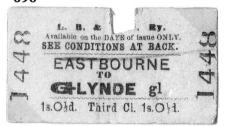

697

Illustrating Chapters 13, 14 and 15: *above* three fine Singles attributed to the 'G.R.T.C' or Grantham Railway Ticket Collection; *at left* the railway contract which demanded provision of a chartered bus, and *below* the *reverse* of three unusual specimens showing features of added interest — the commercial advertisement can be helpful both as a pointer to probable vintage and as light relief.

698

699

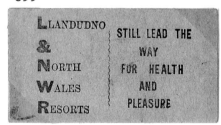

700

'BOLTON AND LEIGH RAILWAY: A sheet of Eight Tickets from Bag Lane on blue paper, complete with counterfoils. These tickets are in blank to be filled up with destination, fare, time of train, etc'.

In January 1930 a lady living in Sydenham read an article about Mr Grantham in the London *Evening News* and wrote to send him an eight-page 15-day Season Ticket for the whole of the Polish National Railways network that she had purchased the previous July when visiting an exhibition in Poznan. The lady recalls paying 150.10 zloty (then £3 15s 0d now £3.75) for this blue and white gem complete with her *fotografja*. Papers within the Grantham archive shed further light on the railway disaster of the night of 28 December 1879, when the Tay Bridge collapsed and at least 76 persons were drowned (See Chapter 16 and Appendix 3).

A total of 10,000 tickets was reached on 7 October 1925, when 100 'mock' railway tickets (**695**) were printed to record that fact and to serve as acknowledgements of contributions. Acquisitions continued steadily and in 1928 these included the collection of the Rev Bacon Philipps. The now enlarged collection boasted such choice issuing companies as the Busby, Delhi-Durbar, Shanghai & Nanking, Uganda, West Clare and Wick & Lybster Railways. In 1932, the collection reached 20,000 and continued to add the local stations (**696**[26]) as well as specimens from further afield. Mock tickets were again distributed.

Just before his death in 1986, Mr Ivor Grantham related an amusing conversation of 1935 which should be memorised by every would-be collector. He found himself late one summer's afternoon in Baghdad awaiting a flight to Cairo the following morning. With time on his hands he found his way on foot to Baghdad East railway station and presented himself at the booking office to obtain a ticket for the collection. The exchange of words went something like this:

One ticket, first class, please, to Baghdad West.
There is no train to Baghdad West.
Never mind, I would like one ticket, please. How much?
There will be no train to Baghdad West until tomorrow evening and you can walk there in half-an-hour.
Tomorrow I will be in Cairo, and I do not want to walk to Baghdad West today.
Then you do not want a ticket.
Yes, I do. I collect railway tickets from all over the world — from beautiful cities like Baghdad, Paris and London (where I live). Here is a photograph of many tickets and not one from your beautiful Baghdad'.

(Turning to a colleague beside him and tapping his forehead with a wink.)
'Two and a half piastres, please'.
(Both parties retire with triumph and dignity.)

Soon after the end of World War 2, Mr Ivor Grantham removed to a smaller house and the collection, by now 40,000 strong, was occupying too much space and time. He presented it to the Stephenson Locomotive Society in London, who themselves disposed of it by public auction in lots in the early 1950s. Some photographic records of part of the collection remain.

Among the press cuttings is one from a Westminster local paper of 1881, reporting the tragic story of the disgrace of a chief ticket inspector at Grosvenor Road[22] station — a married man with four working under him and earning 25s (£1.25) a week.

'At the Westminster Police-court, before Mr Partridge, George H . . ., late Chief Ticket Inspector with the London Brighton & South Coast Railway at Grosvenor Road station, was charged with stealing 134 tickets. He was taken into custody on the platform early on the morning of the 1st of April. He had in his possession 134 tickets issued that morning from York Road to Victoria and was about to leave for York Road, the inference being that he intended to resell the tickets there, they being available by any Parliamentary train during the day, and unclipped. In the presence of the Station Superintendent at Victoria, the prisoner begged to be forgiven and implicated a clerk and porter at Battersea Park as having received the tickets for re-issue. The tickets represented 11/2d (56p) in money if all re-issued. He was to lose his position with the railway and his £10 accrued investment in the Superannuation Fund.'

Here the story tantalisingly ends. Was the cutting saved purely for the railway interest or was a member of the Grantham family professionally involved?

Mr William Wilson Grantham started to collect these transient documents of railway history a mere 40 years after their invention by Thomas Edmondson, and while John Edmondson was still active in business, and so preserved them for posterity — something most fortunate in the annals of our hobby. Mr Ivor Grantham was shocked when he first learned that a collection built up over three-quarters of a century had been broken but he consoled himself with the thought of the pleasure and knowledge the individual tickets must have brought to the countless unknown and unknowing enthusiasts that have received them.

CHAPTER 14

The Ticket as a Contract

It is generally realised that once a prospective traveller has paid his fare and received his ticket, the railway company has contracted to convey him to his destination. Similarly, the passenger has agreed to use the railway company's services, usually subject to certain conditions. It is arguable that if a person represents himself as a *bona fide* passenger but then instead of boarding a train, goes away and places the ticket in an album, he has broken a contract but it is difficult to envisage the company bringing an action against him[23], if only for the reason that it has incurred no loss as a result of such eccentricity.

Nevertheless, the passenger might abuse the right he has purchased, perhaps by accepting one part and rejecting another. By way of example, until fairly recently Day Excursions were sometimes offered at weekends for less than the normal single fare. Tickets could be purchased in advance and a person taking a week's holiday might make a saving by buying two and foregoing the return journey on the first and the outward journey on the other. The pattern of Sunday Excursions between County Durham and London's King's Cross during the 1950s was one of several that lent itself to this practice (**633**).

Another aspect is that of the transferability of tickets. It is a basic principle of English and Scottish Law that if one party has a right to receive something from a second, he may transfer that right to a third, either by gift or sale. When our Sunday excursionist arrived at King's Cross from West Hartlepool (as it was then known) he possessed a right to be transported back later that night. It would be difficult to argue that there was anything wrong or illegal, in passing that right to some other, stranger or friend, and remain in London. It costs the railway no more to carry one passenger than another. Only if the second traveller intended to make the journey to West Hartlepool anyway would it lose revenue. For this reason it is normal railway practice to impose a condition that no ticket shall be transferable, not even a Single or a Return at precisely twice the single fare. More important than any of these considerations is that of the company's liability to the passenger in the event of accident or loss of goods. In general, the railway has an obligation to get the passenger and his property safely and expeditiously to the agreed destination and it is responsible for

negligence by an employee or any other person connected with the enterprise.

Against this background, it has always been possible for passenger and company to agree that the former shall pay a little less for his fare and the latter shall not be liable if something goes wrong. A similar bargain is usually struck with the issue of a Platform Ticket. For such a contract to be valid, both passenger and company must be absolutely clear as to the exact terms they have agreed. The railway usually ensures this by setting out the conditions on the ticket or else telling him on the ticket that there are conditions and where he may study them before he sets out on his dangerous way. A typical form of words is 'For conditions, see Company's Regulations at the Booking Office' although an excellent wording is that printed on the back of a Romney Hythe & Dymchurch Railway ticket of 1928 (**29**) which reads 'This special rate ticket is issued subject to the Regulations governing the operation of the Company and as may be stated in their Bills, Notices or Timetables, and also to the special condition that the R.H.D.Lt.Rly.Co. shall not be liable to the holder or any other person for injury, damage, loss or delay, however caused' (see however, the West Ham case below).

When there is an accident and injury or worse, there can be doubt as to whether the passenger has known and therefore accepted the conditions. How should the railway company safeguard its position? As long ago as 1869, in the Court of Queens Bench, Chief Justice Cockburn tried to settle the matter once and for all. When the South Eastern Railway Company was sued by an injured passenger, he found in the company's favour on the grounds that 'when a man takes a ticket with conditions on it, he must be presumed to know the contents of it and be bound by them'. However, six years later in an appeal from the Scottish Court of Session, the House of Lords found that there is no simple rule and all cases must be decided on their merits as a matter of common sense. Two years after this, Lord Justice Mellish held in the High Court in another case involving the South Eastern Railway that the question to be decided was whether or not the company did what was reasonably sufficient to give notice of the conditions to the passenger. Since then, cases have been decided upon their particular facts rather than any further doubt as to the law.

The legal position was examined in 1894 in a steamship case. A lady named Richardson travelled steerage from Philadelphia to Liverpool and suffered injuries on the way. The company had issued her with a ticket containing a condition restricting their liability to $100 American. It had been handed to her folded in such a way that the writing was not visible. A British Court decided that the condition had not been brought to her notice and she recovered damages in excess of the conditional liability.

Armed with this precedent, the lawyers who represented Mrs M. E. Thompson against the London Midland & Scottish Railway must have felt confident of success. She had travelled on an Excursion Ticket from Darwen to Manchester on 21 January 1928 returning around 10pm. Her coach pulled up at the end of the platform where the ramp begins and stepping down in the darkness, she slipped and injured herself. Her Excursion Ticket had cost 2/7d (13p), half the normal fare, and of course it referred the holder to the conditions shown in the company's timetables. Timetables cost 6d (2½p) each and contained the normal Excursion Ticket condition that the company should not be liable for any injury to the passenger however caused. But her ticket had been bought for her by a niece and moreover Mrs Thompson was unable to read. She admitted that she knew she was getting an Excursion Ticket. A Manchester jury awarded her damages but the Court of Appeal overturned their decision on the grounds that the LMS had done all that was reasonable to bring the conditions to her notice and she must be bound by them.

The unpredictability of the outcome of such actions was demonstrated by the West Ham Corporation Tramways case. In 1907, the Corporation were charging their passengers less than the fares authorised by their Act and accordingly sought to restrict their liability to any passenger at £25. They displayed appropriate notices to this effect on all their cars and referred to the matter on each ticket. On the face of it, they were doing everything right. On 20 July, a Mr Clarke, who by coincidence had worked for the Corporation as a motorman some time before, boarded a car in the Barking Road, climbed to the upper deck, touched the trolley standard as he made his way to a seat and received a serious electric shock. Of course, he had not received his ticket at this stage but he agreed that he was well aware of the conditions as a result of his service with the Corporation and so they did not have to be brought to his notice by way of a ticket. The High Court held that although the Corporation was genuinely charging less than the fare authorised by statute, they were wrong in making no provision for passengers to pay full fare — no fares other than those being charged were displayed. Although it was open to the railway or tramway company to charge a lower fare and limit their liability, they could not do so without giving the passenger the option of travelling at the company's risk. The only option being offered to the passenger in this case was not to travel at all and the

Corporation was bound by statute to afford reasonable facilities for passengers. Mr Clarke received £500.

Mrs Nunan was confronted in 1922 by the particularly harsh condition that was attached to Workman Tickets restricting compensation to £100 even in the case of death. On 21 August, her husband purchased a Workman's Ticket for return from Charing Cross to Milton Range halt near Gravesend and so accepted the condition. Unusually for that time of year, it was foggy when the train arrived at Milton Range and while the passengers were crossing the line to leave the station, a light engine suddenly appeared and ran into their midst.

There were seventeen casualties in all — five, including that of Mr Nunan were fatal. When the widow sought compensation for the loss of her husband, she was immediately reminded of his contract with the company. However, the Court held that the only two parties affected by the contract were Mr Nunan and the company. Since Mrs Nunan had not been a party to it, she was not bound by its conditions. She was awarded £800.

Almost contemporary with Mrs Thompson's case was that of Mr Penton. He travelled from Earlsfield to Waterloo on 10 October 1929, having simply asked for a 'Waterloo Return'. In fact he had been given a cheap ticket with the usual non-liability conditions and put it in his pocket without looking at it. He was injured at Waterloo. He recovered no damages as he was held to be bound by the conditions.

An occurrence in Sussex in 1962 did not lead to litigation as the British Transport Commission made speedy and handsome amends. However, it was well reported in the local evening Press. A lady shopkeeper in St Leonards felt a nostalgic desire to visit Midhurst, a town she had known in prewar days. She attended Warrior Square station on 18 June and the booking clerk, being unable to find any current Cheap Return to Midhurst, issued her with a three-monthly Return Ticket, calculating the fare on distance at 37s (now £1.85), routeing her via Ford and Pulborough. On arrival at Ford she learnt that Midhurst station had closed on 7 February 1955. Rising to the occasion, the management arranged for her to travel by special bus between Pulborough and Midhurst and also to retain her ticket as a souvenir (**697**). She later presented it to its current owner.

In Victorian and Edwardian days, a prudent passenger would often insure himself for the journey for a penny or two with the Railway Passengers' Assurance Company of Cornhill, London. Although he purchased the insurance policy (contained on an Edmondson card) from the booking office at the same time as he obtained his travel ticket, the insurance contract was made between passenger and assurers; the railway were not concerned beyond the function of premium collection agents.

In conclusion, it should be mentioned that British Rail rejected the practice of their predecessors in dodging responsibility to excursionists and others. Cheap tickets in Britain no longer carry these oppressive conditions of yesteryear.

CHAPTER 15

Keeping Tickets in Good Health

With 14 chapters foregoing, each in some way expounding the high ideals(!) of acquiring and understanding passenger tickets, it will be no surprise that consideration is now given to the physical well-being of the collection. Tickets are ephemeral by nature; their care and conservation should not be so. The proper treatment and housing of a collection should be perpetual.

Every kind of ephemera will benefit from the application of certain basic common sense methods and each separate hobby has its variations upon any established procedures. Recommendations here are straightforward. Avoid the use of poor quality paper, inferior plastic pockets and strong sources of light. Above all, avoid chemically-based adhesives and fancy 'instant' aids and mounts.

Conservation is highly recommended whereas restoration of tickets is both unwise and for the most part unnecessary. If one is lucky enough to acquire a travel ticket of the early 1800s but finds it age-hardened and somewhat brittle, with a corner creased or broken away, keep it that way. Ensure that it does not deteriorate further while resisting all temptation to restore it to what would be a presumed original appearance and substance. It may be just about reasonable to open a creased portion that is folded well down — this point is covered later. Any treatment necessary to hold together failing fragments of a rare ticket should not disguise its true state or hide printed or other characteristics. Even for a recently issued and seemingly commonplace ticket (tomorrow's rarity), a stain or prominent blemish should not be tampered with unless this is vital to identification and understanding of the specimen.

For many purposes the commercial stamp album leaf is an excellent railway ticket page. Remember however, that this hobby starts with a disadvantage in regard to mounting of specimens. Weight-for-weight the philatelist can deal with 50 to the billetelist's one or two. Even the very finest philatelic leaf will tend to be in need of reinforcement at the binding holes (more on that later). To guarantee a constant flow of suitable pages for tickets it is suggested collectors purchase a plain crisp bond paper of between 85 and 200gm/sq m substance. A heavy page is important for the mounting of a full complement of 16 or 18 Edmondson cards for example. The best brands available will offer material which retains its clean and crisp appearance, accepts reinforcement and ticket additions well and turns nicely without distortion.

Where it is deemed *essential* to use an adhesive, only water-soluble 'old-fashioned' flour paste is likely to give a good adhesion with no long-term adverse effect. It is emphasised that this is recommended only for the absolutely essential occasion where no reasonable alternative can be found. During many years of active collecting the writers have not found a single instance of essential use of adhesives. Far superior is the transparent photocorner for Edmondson and medium-large cards, and clear cellophane strips cut to requirements for larger and flimsy subjects. For example: see Chapter 6, where 24 half-Edmondsons, each with two photocorners, are shown mounted — nothing is directly affixed to the tickets although secure gummed corners hold the specimens to their page. The other extreme is the almost-A4 size ticket which demands a page of its own. For this three 20mm-wide strips of clear cellophane are suggested; two vertical over the entire page and turned over top and bottom to be gummed on the reverse and one similarly placed across the centre. This creates a neat 'cage' effective in keeping the ticket central and vertical. Where the ticket is floppy the corners may be further restrained by either a photocorner or a short strip placed at 45° and gummed on the reverse of the page. Alternatively, the whole ticket may be housed in a clear-fronted pocket itself affixed to the page. These are obtainable in a variety of sizes from commercial centres, but it should be remembered that while the clear front is not likely to do any long-term harm, the opaque backing will almost certainly be composed of acidified paper which *will* be harmful sooner than later. The over-riding consideration must always be that although the tickets should be held secure and flat, no substance likely to begin an irreversible process is used in direct contact with the ticket specimen.

Bulky Season Tickets and heavy metal passes can be kept in place by specially home-tailored clear pockets gummed to the page as necessary. These may be formed of folded cellophane material made to suit each ticket or by cutting away and retaining the lower two-thirds of a standard window envelope (use only the finest ultra-clear quality). Such methods should secure an excellent enclosed fixing coupled with full ventilation to avoid trapping damp and thereby encouraging mould. Clear cellophane pockets are also commercially available. With these the seams and lower folds usually appear unsightly unless the whole pocket capacity is occupied by the contents.

The use of photocorners is most popular. They are effective and easy to handle and free of all but the most unlikely disadvantages when confined to one standard ticket size on each page. It must be indicative of the suitability of the photocorner that, when asked what methods he uses, a collector in a foreign country recently reported back that he purchases his supplies (of photocorners) from Britain. Recommended transparent loose photocorners are sometimes difficult to obtain from stationers, no doubt because photographic enthusiasts are making greater use of self-adhesive corner-plates and concealed patent sticky devices of various sorts. Substitute transparent photocorners mounted on a dispenser roll in gangs of 1,000 are also on the market. These are just as effective in the short to medium term, but in the longer term are inclined to lose their tacky backing and emigrate. A number of collectors are known to have consolidated their individual orders to create more attractive batches for the manufacturer. Disappointment is rare.

Fixing standard tickets by only the two corners nearest the binding edge of the page enables some rearrangement when, say a 4d blue ticket arrives to be placed between its fellow 3½d magenta and 4½d green pagemates. This method also handles well when the page is turned during inspection.

The observation ward
Albums are the most widely used means of grouping together pages of mounted tickets. A large number of collectors were first philatelists, perhaps giving up that hobby from disenchantment at its commercialisation and the realisation that virtually any stamp may be obtained at the appropriate price, greatly eroding the satisfaction that should follow from acquisition. Naturally the first thought of a suitable medium for the storage and display of the new collection will be a loose-leaf (stamp) album. Whatever choice is ultimately made for binding, the stamp album page will continue to serve well.

There are tried and tested commercial patterns freely available in most areas. The international A4 is a very suitable choice and albums to accept this are readily obtainable. Ring binders are considered best because of the ease with which they permit rearrangement and addition. Those based upon 8cm centres are the most satisfactory if one is to rely upon just two punched holes per page. Also with 8cm centres and widely used, are standard lever-arch files. These have the advantage of being capacious and durable, with really easy access, but when bought in ordinary office decor can be obtrusive in domestic surroundings. It is suggested these be purchased in quantity, when one may select an appropriate covering, colour and texture and the term 'file' may properly become 'album'.

Other binders include various four-, six- and multi-ring patterns, some freely obtained internationally, others tied to the territory of manufacture. The advantage of the two-ring or ordinary 8cm-centre binder is that it requires no more than an ordinary inexpensive two-hole perforator to adapt the pages. These pages therefore can, if necessary, be of any material that is to hand. Patterns with more rings are often very pleasing in appearance and certainly retain their content quite parallel to their cover, but they also demand special punches or the purchase of

ready-drilled pages of proprietary dimensions. These factors make the choice expensive in the longer-term and sometimes promise difficulties later on when the national or international stationery specification changes or certain branded products become less freely obtainable.

All albums should be stored flat rather than upright. If the tickets rest flat there will be no pressures to distort the albums and their contents. Two-ring albums are completely satisfactory and do not require any additional support when kept flat. Stored this way they are also less likely to trap dust and suffer bookshelf fatigue. Each ticket will lightly compress and protect the one on the next page immediately below it.

Although a limited number of albums may be safely stored in a box, as the size of the collection increases it is better to keep each album separately in its own cubicle-shelf. This need not involve huge expense. If divisions of fairly precise dimensions can separate each album and if the shelves are closely spaced, dust will largely be excluded and the overall appearance enhanced.

The constant movement of pages on rings in an album causes heavy wear and tear unless each hole is reinforced. The reinforcement could be either a proprietary gummed ring of paper, plastic or, better still, linen or else something devised for the purpose at home. The use of individual gummed rings is quite neat and an effective method but it can be a real tedium. Rings with self-adhesive backs available on dispenser rolls are unsatisfactory in the longer-term. Eventually the adhesive decomposes to release the ring and leave a staining deposit. Only rings gummed and requiring moisture can be relied upon to stand the passage of time.

The handyman may prefer to make up a supply of 20mm-wide strips of linen or stout paper ready gummed and to cut them into suitable lengths to place over the area to be reinforced. For a page that holds extremely heavy displays such as Season Tickets or metal Directors Passes, a second strip will prove helpful.

The neatest method is to provide a 20mm guard reinforcing the entire length of the page down its binding edge and then to punch the required holes through both guard and page. This may be reserved for a small collection to be made to high standards of presentation, perhaps for public showing in a library or at a meeting.

The so-called 'magnetic' photograph albums that first appeared in the shops in Britain in the late 1970s are useful provided certain dangers are avoided. One should never place any ticket directly on to the sticky surface; any specimen can be irrevocably damaged when it comes to removal for further examination or rearrangement. Tickets must be mounted on a thin sheet of bond paper (see earlier regarding quality), perhaps by a single photocorner and the whole placed under the transparent cover. Again this is an option best used for showpiece occasions. The covering films may well contain compounds injurious in long-term contact with an ageing railway or tramway ticket. Having said that it should also be mentioned that there is no evidence at present that the cheaper brands are any less reliable than the more expensive. A further disadvantage with these 'magnetic' albums is their unit-weight. In relation to the number of tickets which may reasonably be mounted within, each is very heavy and tends therefore to be out of proportion with the needs of the hobby.

A few collectors purchase the plastic stamp wallets used by philatelists to display mint specimens they do not wish to mark with a stamp hinge. These are helpful for temporary storage and for carrying tickets about to meetings and exhibitions, but would prove both expensive and extravagant in their demands for space if used on a larger scale. Such wallets are excellent for the transmission of ticket selections by post. Typical use would be an exchange circuit or two collectors conducting a special postal study which entails scrutiny of many specimens.

Patients need a bed

The loose storage of tickets in racks, trays and boxes is not recommended except for transient stock such as exchange items. Any form of loose storage, even in meticulously prepared divisions is bound to lead to unnecessary fingering and handling and trapping of dust, all injurious to the life of the very susceptible passenger ticket. It is also devoid of any real visual appeal, both for the collector and his most tactful visitor. In an active and beneficial collection frequent consultation and periodic revision is inevitable. This is the more so because the hobby is not graced with any comprehensive catalogue which might otherwise direct tickets into a virtually permanent page or album siding.

If, however, loose storage is thought to be worth trying, possibly because it is the only method for which sufficient space can be found in the home, then the wear and tear factor should be minimised as far as possible. If the collection is to engender its full complement of pleasure and release facts at a moment's notice, each ticket must be found in a minimum of search time. This should be aided by inserting a liberal supply of markers or header cards showing the salient divisions — Countries, Companies, Singles, Platforms, etc — or highlighting the principal periods — pre-Grouping in Britain, new currency in India, Showa Era in Japan — and so on. Such dividers may alternatively carry a single sequential code letter or numeral to be referred to elsewhere in an explanatory index. Whatever the mechanics, the aim should be to *touch* the tickets as infrequently as possible but also to find each item as expeditiously as can be devised.

There is one redeeming factor in favour of loose storage — the backs of tickets may be examined just as easily as their fronts. Seen commensurate with the proportion of back-printed tickets this is, however, not to be over-rated. In a long running series of standard tickets the conditions of issue shown on the backs may not have changed and therefore in an album ONE representative specimen may be mounted face down to suffice. In another preference the conditions of issue or other narrative can be quoted in full as an annotation on the album page. Where there are exceptional features, such as the story of a mariner's achievements (on the reverse of **742**), a helpful map (**698** from Holland's Geldersche Tram) or the often entertaining advertisements on the backs of tickets (**699** and **700**), specimens may be mounted upon an under-size aperture cut into the page. Otherwise, they can be placed on a transparent panel affixed over a full-size window. In the case of a group of tickets which have narrative, dates and important features on both sides, there is a case for mounting them on a wholly transparent page. For this, only the use of fine quality acid-free material will be entirely trouble-free. A clear cellophane sheet reinforced at its holes and corners will serve quite well, but note that the photocorners and their additives will also be seen throughout the reverse side.

Very fortunately, such methods are rarely necessary. If just two corners of a ticket are fixed or each specimen is in its own pocket, occasional inspection of the back may be effected with the aid of a pair of tweezers. When removing a ticket held by more than two adjacent corners, always destroy one corner mount so as to avoid all risk of creasing the ticket.

Before about 1930, many collectors would glue or paste tickets directly to album sheets. They took no account of the substance and make-up of the page material. Mercifully, this practice declined and has since *almost* ceased. Before condemning it, it should be recalled that until the advent of the photocorner there was no real alternative to adhesive and collectors of all small paper throw-aways were given to the lingering Victorian vogue for scrapbooks and album filling on a rather haphazard basis. In Europe people were collecting for their own satisfaction items of what is now recognised as historic ephemera of purely nominal value. Only the most recent generations have set themselves up as guardians of pieces of social history to be passed on for posterity. For a collection of passenger tickets to be systematically broken up and dispersed would have been unthinkable in the first 60 years of railways. Yet when that has been said, the sad fact is that perhaps two-thirds or more of the earliest tickets now circulating show signs of having been gummed down to a Victorian after-dinner scrapbook, so often obliterating the date or other important feature. These specimens give rise to thoughts of cleaning and restoration, options which have already here been dismissed as unwise or unnecessary.

Intensive care

Unlike the postage stamp, which is a single-ply slip of paper, Edmondson and many larger card tickets are three-ply products. Usually an absorbent board is sandwiched between thin laminated surface papers. Any immersion or nearness to water will accelerate the normal deterioration of the substance used to hold these plies together. Often when a ticket becomes damp its surface paper will part company as it dries out. Worse still, those tickets printed with bright rich hues tend to become discoloured and spoil. The modern British Season Ticket is composed of two lightweight boards which incline to separate following a dose of dampness. Even single-ply papers react badly to water and require careful drying, preferably slowly and under slight pressure.

Any attempt to wash tickets is unwise. For those collectors with a compelling need, there are specialist processes which command professional fees. A little first aid may be all that is advisable.

It is sometimes possible to remove small fragments of paper adhering to the back of a ticket by carefully painting the fragment with water. The fluid should be accurately confined to the offending material and left only long enough to penetrate through to the adhesive. When the piece has been lifted — use a fine needle — the residual adhesive may be painted once more with water and **promptly** and **entirely** removed by use of white blotting paper or a highly absorbent domestic cloth. Care must be taken not to rub or disturb the ticket surface and to confine this second application to the area of the original fragment. Unless the adhesive is a water-soluble variety, no entirely satisfactory process is open to amateur conservators. A rusty staple embedded in a ticket is best removed before the rust attacks the structure of the paper or leather. The careful use of a sharp needle will help to raise the staple ends and to control the material around them.

Coming to the aid of a creased ticket is important. In due course, a crease causes the fibres of the paper to fail and a portion of the document will be lost. Many older products, particularly those with a high rag content, are durable and successful in coping with a crease over a long period, but then tend to fail suddenly. Short of enlisting the help of a professional conservator, it is best simply to gently open the crease and to return the specimen to its correct flat state. It is then **imperative** — because the material has once more been subjected to stress at the crease — to ensure the ticket is never again folded. This demands proper mounting and care in its album home. In a majority of cases a ticket which has earlier suffered prolonged creasing and is now returned to the flat state will recover with time. The crease will always be present but it may lose much of its 'insistence'. Furthermore, when the ticket is properly mounted and in company with supporting items alongside, a crease or two will be far less prominent. In short, open a crease but do not try to remove or conceal it. Above all, shun damping and hot ironing and similar drastic measures.

Grease-marked tickets are a real problem. If the stain is not too old it is often possible to remove it by slowly warming the surface of the paper and then placing it between heavy coverings of white blotting paper and hot-ironing the sandwich — precisely the opposite treatment recommended for a mere crease. Just as this is not recommended for creases, so here too there is a good deal of risk. The process can remove parts of the printed text or diminish the richness of the colouring. It is wiser to tolerate the stain and hope to obtain a better specimen in due course; a policy which, incidentally, applies equally well with other damage, such as faded colours, tears and staple punctures.

Occasionally, two like-numbered halves of a two-coupon ticket remain in company and reach the collector together. It is natural that one should wish to place these together in the collection and where the subject is made of stout board or heavy material with a noticeable thickness to want to effect some sort of rejointing of the pieces. If the broken edges of each half are not different in their alignment and precise shaping one from the other, then clearly the two will 're-marry' well. A clean and sparingly applied flour-paste will be all that can be advised. No tapes or bridging materials of any kind are recommended, back or front. When both portions are accurately pressed together and the whole is kept flat and under a dry weight until secure and solid, there will be an acceptable degree of repair. An alternative and altogether wiser practice is to mount the two portions separately side-by-side, or one above the other, merely to resemble the original two-piece ticket. In this way conservation is practised and restoration is avoided.

CHAPTER 16

A Chronology

In this final chapter we set out a brief table of events selected as probable markers in the incidence and progress of tickets and matters broadly related. The concept that a throw-away document of today can become the archive of tomorrow is a 20th century one; the Victorian Age was chiefly concerned with replacing the old with something newer and more advanced. For the lesser documents of its everyday life we relied very much upon the family scrapbook, professional conservators, and latterly the achievements of a few dedicated collectors.

This chronology is meant to be suggestive of ticketing occurrences and occasions rather than exhaustive of any one individual aspect. Sometimes a special excursion or single event has been noted. These will include cases believed to be typical of the thought or the practice of their time. This chapter is by no means a history of tramway or railway development. Events such as the inauguration of the first main line electric service on 1 January 1933 are of great moment to the engineer. However, tickets between London and Worthing were unchanged by it and we make no mention. Later in the year the formation of the LPTB had little effect on Underground passengers but it resulted in a major change of tickets and we include it.

It is hoped to show how collectors may look upon every one of the last 160 years as a potential source of archival and highly collectible tickets. Every day of railway and tramway operation demands the issue of vast quantities of ordinary tickets — the Singles, Returns and many special categories which reflect the equally large number of travellers — but extraordinary tickets are also created by unique occasions in the life of every area served by a train or tram. Inaugural journeys, new stations, disasters, festivals, regional administrative changes, visits of dignatories and many more, all play their part. Alongside the utilitarian operation of transport there exists an array of publications and activities which produce more dates of direct influence upon the hobby.

In Chapter 1 parallels were drawn with the ubiquitous postage stamp. Just as the philatelist can determine from his catalogues the earliest date upon which stamps were first postally used in each territory, so in this hobby there are commencement dates for the humble travel ticket, alas not very thoroughly recorded even

today. These dates are not accorded the same status as the First Day of Issue is for stamps, since some are approximate and others are unproven.

A minimal sprinkling of trans-Atlantic and other foreign affairs is included merely to demonstrate how the British practice had spread while generally encountering local modifications or competing alternatives. Because railway and tramway operators are the prime source of the historic throw-away ephemera this book is about, some opening dates are included as guidelines.

1825
First regular passenger trains operated on the Stockton & Darlington Railway.

1830
Opening of the Liverpool & Manchester Railway, attended by William Muir (1808-1888) who later became a very supportive partner of Thomas Edmondson at Manchester. See also 1930 and 1980.

1831
Population of Britain 16 million, with a total of 2,700km of railway.

1832
Leicester & Swannington Railway opened and using brass fare tokens; a few still held by collectors. Commemorative opening day tickets also survive.

1834
Leeds & Selby Railway opened.
Ireland's first public railway opened with the title Dublin & Kingstown Railway. See **80** in Chapter 1.

1835
Opening of the Newcastle & Carlisle Railway, the company which a year later employed Thomas Edmondson.
First, Second and Third Classes of travel now routinely available by many railways.

1836

First section of the London & Greenwich Railway opened.

Beginnings of the 'Railway Mania'.

1837

Thomas Edmondson, working at Milton, Cumberland (now Brampton, Cumbria) and beginning his process of invention.

Britain's first trunk railway, the Grand Junction Railway, opened with First and Second Classes only available.

The Leeds & Selby Railway introduced its Third Class facility.

1838

Opening of first section of the Great Western Railway from Paddington to Maidenhead.

First steamship services across the Atlantic, soon to be carrying ticket supplies from Manchester to the early United States railroads.

Edmondson gave public exhibition of his inventions.

Opening of first section London & Southampton Railway, later renamed London & South Western Railway.

London & Birmingham Railway opened throughout.

Dundee & Arbroath Railway opened.

1839

Whitby & Pickering Railway provided cheap Excursion Tickets for travel to Grosmont church bazaar on 7 and 8 August — probably the first printed railway excursion tickets.

Eastern Counties Railway reached London (Mile End).

London & Croydon Railway opened.

The Manchester & Leeds Railway opened. Employed Thomas Edmondson immediately before he set up his printing business.

Edmondson's first ticketing patents.

The London & Greenwich Railway introduces its Third Class facility.

First publication of *Bradshaw's Railway & Steam Navigation Guide*, the much-prized reference volume.

1840

The Durham & Sunderland Railway (opened in 1836) offers one of the earliest stagecoach-railway through bookings.

First section London & Brighton Railway opened.

London & Blackwall Railway opened (See **366**).

1841

Thomas Cook (1808-1892) organising his early excursions to Leicester. Tickets at first referred to 'Mr Cook'. Cook went on to found the international Thos Cook & Son Ltd group of companies. The company soon expanded into all six railway continents. **701** shows a much-endorsed specimen from Iraq 108 years later. Also see **706**.

Organised public excursions operated by the Midland Counties Railway, following isolated earlier experiments by the Whitby & Pickering Railway in 1839 (qv), the Newcastle & North Shields Railway (1840) and others.

1842

Establishment of the Railway Clearing House. The RCH not only regulated passenger rates and inter-company administration, but also issued its own tickets valid over specified lines. **702** shows an 1869 specimen valid over the Lancashire & Yorkshire Railway.

Queen Victoria made first royal train journey.

1843

Stagecoaches now suffering severe competition from the railways.

1844

Stockton & Darlington Railway makes its first use of the standard Edmondson card.

Formation of the Midland Railway.

Dublin & Drogheda Railway opened (**703**).

The Regulation of Railways Act takes effect to give Britain its so-called Parliamentary Class of travel. Third Class must now include seats and a roof. Children may now travel for half-fare.

1845

Railways Clauses and Lands Clauses Consolidation Acts passed by Parliament to speed up the process of obtaining powers to build railways.

1846

'Railway Mania' in Britain, with 272 Acts of Parliament for new railways.

Formation of the LBSC and LNW Railways.

1847

Establishment of the Lancashire & Yorkshire Railway.

Approximately 74 railways now using the Edmondson card in Britain.

1848

Opening of the Great Northern Railway, which company introduced a Fourth Class in the year.

London & South Western Railway extended into Waterloo.

The Irish Railway Clearing House is founded.

1850

Robert Stephenson's tubular bridge over the Menai Strait is available for public trains, thus completing the route to Ireland. See under 1972.

1851

Prince Albert's Great Exhibition in London stimulates traffic.

Death of Thomas Edmondson (b1792).

1853

Death of George Bradshaw (b1801).

First publication of *The ABC Rail(way) Guide*

1854

Several railways in the United States buying tickets direct from John Edmondson of Manchester.

Great North of Scotland Railway opened and offering only First and Third Class travel.

Australia's first public steam railway opened from Flinders Street, Melbourne.

1855

Aberdeen Railway one of the early lines to experiment with discontinuance of Second Class travel.

Foundation of the General Passenger & Ticket Agents Association in the United States to regulate inter-company ticketing affairs.

1856

First known production of tickets by William Rand, afterwards senior partner in Rand McNally & Company. See entry for 1868.

1859

Completion of the Royal Albert Bridge at Saltash in Cornwall. See entry for 1959.

701

Bd. No. ....0129....

COOK - WAGONS - LITS
World Travel Service.

IRAQI STATE RAILWAYS.

Available for one Single journey

From BAGHDAD to AL-MA'QIL

FIRST CLASS   FILS 2,560

Available for Three days from   13 MAR 1949   including date of issue.

Series 9583

NOT TRANSFERABLE

The journey may be
Issued subject to a'

BAGHDAD WEST 15 MAR 1949

703

JY 29. 61

GLASGOW
TO
DUBLIN
Via Ardrossan
First Class
& Cabin
Not Transferable

702

No. **17610**
RAILWAY CLEARING HOUSE.

LANCASHIRE AND YORKSHIRE RAILWAY COMPANY.

HORSE, CARRIAGE, AND DOG TICKET.

8.50am o'Clock Train   DCC. 22nd 1869

From *Bromley Cross* to *Chatburn*

Hunter

	RATE.	PAID ON.	TO PAY.	PAID.
Horse	8/8			8 8
4-wheel Carriage				
2-wheel Carriage		*Return*		
Dog				

Name *Pass*   *WB.*   *Booking Clerk.*

N.B.—This Ticket is issued subject to the Owner's undertaking all risks of Conveyance whatsoever, as the Company will not be responsible for any injury or damage (however caused) occurring to Horses, Carriages, or live Stock of any description travelling upon the LANCASHIRE AND YORKSHIRE RAILWAY, or in their Vehicles, or in, or upon any of their Stations or Premises.

THIS TICKET MUST BE GIVEN UP WHEN REQUIRED.

704

Volunteer Review.
Maryhill
To
Alexandria
3rd Class.
3 AUG. 1861.
Volunteer in Uniform.

705

A
G. E. R.
DOWNHAM & STOKE FERRY LINE
THIRD CLASS
4D Fare 4D
This Ticket is issued subject to the Regulations of the Company. It is available for ONE single journey only and in the direction indicated by the punch. It must be produced or given up when required by the Conductor or other Official of the Company.

DENVER to ABBEY   ABBEY to DENVER

706

P. R.
Series 5553
0795 ✳

COOK'S TOURS
سياحات كوك تَיִירֵי קוק

PALESTINE RAILWAYS
سكه حديد فلسطين   רכבת פלשתינה

JERUSALEM (1) TO HAIFA
القدس الى حيفا   ירושלם לחיפה

1st CLASS FARE L.E. 1.405 MIL
درجه ١ الاجرة جم م ١.٤٠٥   מחלקה א' המחיר ל.מ. 1.405

Date Stamp of Issuing Office

NOTE: This part to be kept by Passenger and given up at arrival station.

ملاحظة على المسافر ان يحفظ هذا الجزء ويسلمه لمحطة الوصول
הערה החלק הזה נשמר בידי הנוסע ונמסר ע"י תחנת היעוד.

707

M.S. & L.R.
HULL
TO
BRIGG
ON DATE OF ISSUE ONLY
THIRD CLASS PARLY
Hull   Hull
Brigg   Brigg
28.MY.83   976

Early days in Scotland, a fragment from England (705) and travels in the Middle East — even a horse by the '8.50 a.m. o'Clock'.

In the United States George M. Pullman (1831-1897) operates his first sleeping cars.
Death of Isambard Kingdom Brunel (b1806).

1860

America's Baltimore & Ohio Railroad using the first machine-numbered strip tickets.

1861

Population of Britain now 23 million, with 14,800km of railway.
The Glasgow Dumbarton & Helensburgh Railway issues special tickets for 'Volunteer in Uniform' travelling to the annual Volunteer Review (**704**).

1862

Formation of the Great Eastern Railway.

1863

Metropolitan Railway opened the world's first underground passenger service from Bishop's Road, Paddington to Farringdon Street (now Barbican).

1864

First London area Workman Tickets introduced by the Metropolitan Railway (3d Return).

1865

In Wales the Festiniog Railway collects its first fares from passengers.

1868

Foundation of the international Chicago printing company Rand McNally & Co, since renowned for their production of passenger tickets. McNally was an Irish émigré.

1869

In the United States, the Union Pacific and Central Pacific Railroads met at Promontory Point, Utah, to create a through trans-continental railway[24]. See entry for 1969.

1870

Third Class now representing 75% of all railway travel in Britain.
Tramways Act allowed for eventual purchase of all private tramways by municipalities.
Inaugural passenger train on the Jersey Railway.

1872

First use of Edmondson-type tickets in Japan.
Midland and Great Eastern Railways introduce Third Class facilities for all their trains.

1873

First publication of *Cook's Continental Timetable* which became a reliable sourcebook for travellers and collectors. See entry for 1892.
Opening of the Isle of Man Railway.
Inaugural train on the Jersey Eastern Railway.

1874

Legislation required GE to offer 2d rides into the London suburbs for 7,000 persons displaced by extension of its tracks toward Liverpool Street.
Midland Railway runs the first Pullman cars using vehicles owned by the Pullman Palace Car Company of America.

1875

Second Class travel abolished and most reductions on Return Tickets removed by the Midland Railway.

1878

Formation of the Bell Punch Company and first appearance of bell-punched pasteboard tickets.
One of the hobby's earliest accomplished adherents, William Wilson Grantham, now establishing his collection — see Chapter 13.

1879

The Fall of the Tay Bridge. William Friend the Ticket Collector and Alec Inglis the Porter at St Fort on the North British Railway, collected tickets from passengers riding the ill-fated evening Burntisland northbound train. The major railway bridge of the day tragically failed during a severe gale just as the laden train was crossing the Tay. At least 76 persons lost their lives. See Appendix 3.

1882

Formation of the British Pullman Car Company.
Great Western Railway discontinues Express as a separately specified class of travel.
Opening of Downham & Stoke Ferry Railway (GE) 11km line from Ely, closed in 1887 (See fragmented **705**).

1883

Opening of Volk's Marine Electric Railway at Brighton — the first public electric railway in the country.

1885

Now approximately 350 public railway companies operating in Britain.
Foundation of the International Railway Congress Association and the beginnings of inter-company ticketing regulation throughout Europe (first London meeting 1895).
The Great Northern Railway abolished Second Class travel on many main services.

1886

First passenger services through the Severn Tunnel.

1887

Death of John B. Edmondson, son of the famous ticket originator.
Golden Jubilee of Queen Victoria through whose reign Britain's railways grew and prospered.
Express Class abolished by the LBSC.

1889

Regulation of Railways Act required that fares be shown on all ordinary Single and Return Tickets from commencement of 1890.

1890

Beginning of electrification of tramways.
Third Class now available on all trains of the Great Western Railway.
Opening of the City & South London Railway as the world's first electric underground passenger railway.

1891

Population now totalling 33 million, with approximately 28,000km of railway.

Globe Ticket Company founded in Philadephia. The company went on to produce tickets for many companies in overseas British territories.
Great Northern Railway abolished remaining Second Class travel, except in London area.
Manchester Sheffield & Lincolnshire Railway abolished Second Class on main line trains.

1892

Great Western Railway introduced corridor trains and with them numerous Dining Car Bills and Tickets.
Death of Thomas Cook (b1808), the travel organiser and agent. Cook's card and paper tickets are issued in all six continents. Rare to some extent are examples from North China, Central Africa and lesser lines of South American republics. **706** shows a tri-lingual item from the former Palestine Railways (now Israel Railways). Also see entries for 1841 and 1873.
Remaining Manchester Sheffield & Lincolnshire Second Class travel abolished.

1893

Introduction of first British Platform Tickets then mostly valid for just half an hour.
GE, NE and most Scottish lines abolish Second Class travel.
First section of Liverpool Overhead Railway opened.

1896

Opening of Snowdon Mountain Railway.
Opening of the electric sea-going 'Daddy Long Legs'. See **444** in Chapter 6.
Glasgow underground railway opened and closed the same day due to an accident. Reopening came on 21 January 1897.
Passing of Light Railways Act, enabling promotion of many railways without the need for individual Acts of Parliament.

1897

The *Railway Magazine* first published (see entry for 1966).
Renaming of the Manchester Sheffield & Lincolnshire Railway to Great Central Railway; **707** shows a Single of the former and **708** a 'British Emigrant' of the latter, from 1883 and 1907 respectively.

1898

First publication of *The Railway Year Book* in London. Now entitled *Railway Directory & Year Book*.
Opening of the Lynton & Barnstaple Railway — **709** is dated August 1922.
Waterloo & City Railway opened.

1899

Foundation of The Railway Club, the oldest British group for railway enthusiasts. See also entry for 1908.
Final year of personalised George Pullman's Palace Car Co. The pattern of ticket illustrated as **710** remained unchanged for a few more years.
LCD and SE Companies agreed upon a joint Management Committee which served until the end of 1922. Tickets at first were headed 'S.E.&C.&D.Rys' before settling down to 'S.E.&C.R.', colloquially the 'Slow, Easy and Comfortable'.
GW and LSW Railways commenced a joint steamer service to the Channel Islands.

1900

Paris Metropolitan Railway introduces ticket-issuing machines.

Opening (July) of the Central London Railway — The 'Tuppenny Tube'. There had been at least one public 'trial train' with suitably endorsed tickets, in the month before.

1902

Third Class Season Tickets introduced on LSW.
Whitechapel & Bow Railway opened for passengers.
Wholly new through service opened by the Great Central and Great Western companies from Newcastle to Bournemouth. Tickets were by the Great Central Railway.
North London Railway introduces its first Season Tickets for Third Class travel.
Manx Electric Railway opened.
Opening of the Vale of Rheidol Railway in Central Wales.

1903

Mersey Railway introduces Third Class Season Tickets.
A committee of the Midland Railway took control of the Belfast & Northern Counties Railway, establishing the title Midland Railway Northern Counties Committee, later LMS NCC.
Opening of the Invergarry & Fort Augustus Railway — **711** is an early unissued Single overstamped by the LNER after 1923.
Cambrian Archaeological Association meeting at Porthmadog, was preceded by special vouchers. These were exchanged for travel tickets endorsed 'Voucher'. Each voucher was marked 'Railway' perhaps suggesting there were similar documents for other modes of travel.
Pressure by Local Authorities for the Great Western Railway to introduce Third Class Seasons and Workman fares on London services.
Great Central Railway starts through coaches from Manchester to Dover via the South Eastern & Chatham Railways. Tickets were by the Great Central.

1904

Opening of the New Ross & Waterford Extension Railway (**712**).
Great Northern & City Railway opened from Moorgate.

1905

London motor buses in direct competition with railways.
GW started to withdraw its Second Class facilities.

1906

Automatic ticket machine installed at Farringdon Street on the Metropolitan Railway.
Opening of the Baker Street & Waterloo Railway.

1907

Waterloo & City Railway taken over by LSW.
Dublin Wicklow & Wexford Railway renamed Dublin & South Eastern.
George Pullman's (1831-97) British interests sold.

1908

Introduction of the all-Pullman 'Southern Belle' by the LBSC.
The highly accomplished collector, G. W. Potter, organising the Railway Club's meetings and distributing the first hobbyist study papers of tickets of the GE, GN and NE Railways.

1910

SEC introduces Pullman cars on certain boat trains.
Metropolitan Railway introduced Pullman cars.
Formation of London Electric Railway.

708

GREAT CENTRAL RAILWAY
Issued subject to the printed conditions
and regulations of the Company
BRITISH EMIGRANT CHILD
LONDON (Marylebone)
(AGENCY 154) TO
LIVERPOOL (CENTRAL)
Via SODLEY JN.
THIRD CLASS
FARE 6/3

709

Lynton & Barnstaple Ry
MARKET TICKET
Barnstaple Tow (S.
TO
WOODY BAY
See 3rd Class
Over Revised fare

MARKET TICKET
Woody Bay
TO (S.?)
BARNSTAPLE TOWN
See 3rd Class
Over Revised Fare

710

PULLMAN'S PALACE CAR CO.
Passenger's Check.

THIS CHECK IS GOOD FOR THIS TRIP ONLY.

PASSENGER TO RETAIN THIS CHECK.

The Conductor is required to furnish a Check to each person entitled to a Berth or Seat, one Check to a Berth, Section or Drawing Room, whether occupied by one or more persons, if paid for by one person. One person is not permitted to occupy a Whole Section, if there are others desiring Berths. The Conductor will punch out Date, Amount Collected, for fractions of one dollar, from 1 to 0, Kind of Tickets or Passes, No. of Persons and Cash, Tickets, or D. H. for a Free Pass.
Baggage, Wearing Apparel, Money, Jewelry or other Valuables taken into the Car will be entirely at Owner's Risk, and employes of this Company are forbidden to take charge of the same. Passengers are requested to report any neglect of duty or incivility on the part of employes and forward this Check with such report to any of the Superintendents of this Company, or to
GEO. M. CRAY, General Ticket Agent, CHICAGO.

711

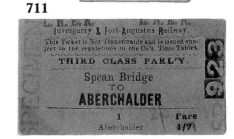

L. N. E. R.
Invergarry & Fort-Augustus Railway.
This Ticket is Not Transferable and is issued subject to the regulations in the Co's. Time Tables.
THIRD CLASS PARL'Y.
Spean Bridge
TO
ABERCHALDER
1 Fare
Aberchalder 1/7½

712

D&SE &NR&WER. D&SE &NR&WER.
Available within SIX Months from date of issue
FIRST CLASS
See conditions on back
Issued subject to the conditions & regulations in the Co's Time Tables
REVISED FARE
1st Class 5s 6d
Dun Laoghaire Waterford
TO TO
WATERFORD DUN LAOGHAIRE
via New Ross & W.E. Ry Via New Ross & W.E.Ry
53(R) 0023 0023

713

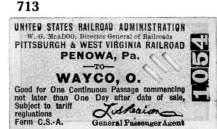

UNITED STATES RAILROAD ADMINISTRATION
W. G. McADOO, Director General of Railroads
PITTSBURGH & WEST VIRGINIA RAILROAD
PENOWA, Pa.
TO
WAYCO, O.
Good for One Continuous Passage commencing not later than One Day after date of sale, Subject to tariff regulations
Form C.S.A. General Passenger Agent
1054

714

London Electric Ry
(available day of issue ONLY)
Member (L.N.E.)
EXHIBITION STN.
TO
PICCADILLY CIR
Change at...
Not Transferable
B.E.E. ADULT
THIRD CLASS
(See Back)
9796

715

SOUTHERN RAILWAY
WATERLOO STATION.
Exhibition of Locomotives
"GLADSTONE" & "LORD NELSON"
ADMIT ONE PERSON TO PLATFORM NO. 12
on MAY 14th, 1927.
Available for ONE VISIT ONLY.
Charge - Threepence.
FOR CONDITIONS SEE BACK.
0014

716

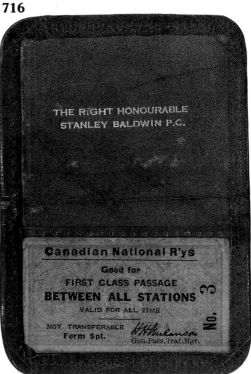

Baldwin next to *Gladstone*, **war days in America and travels in Ireland and Scotland — that is the diversity of this hobby.**

THE RIGHT HONOURABLE
STANLEY BALDWIN P.C.

Canadian National R'ys
Good for
FIRST CLASS PASSAGE
BETWEEN ALL STATIONS
VALID FOR ALL TIME
NOT TRANSFERABLE
Form Spl. Gen. Pass. Traf. Mgr.
NO. 3

717

L. M. & R.
Admit to Exhibition
OF 2001A
"ROYAL SCOT" ENGINE
6,7,8,9,10&11th, February 1928
NO 10 PLATFORM MANCHESTER (VIC.) ST'N
IN AID OF
PROCEEDS LOCAL HOSPITALS (ADULT) 6d
VALID FOR ONE OCCASION ONLY
6756

718

RAILWAY CORRESPONDENCE AND TRAVEL SOCIETY
RAILWAY AND CANAL HISTORICAL SOCIETY
Middleton Colliery Railway
BICENTENARY RAIL TOUR
Saturday, 7th June, 1958
For conditions see notes for passengers

719

SOUTHERN RLY. "Golden Arrow"
PULLMAN CAR TICKET. Issued subject
to the Bye-laws, Regulations & Conditions in the
Company's Bills & Notices, & to the Pullman Car
Company's Notices, as displayed in Pullman Cars
London to
DOVER
(S.1)   OR VICE-VERSA
Available for one journey on day of issue only,
when accompanied by Second Class Railway Ticket
(Issued by
Three Shillings.   NOT TRANSFERABLE

6170   6170

720

Railway Centenary
Celebration
LIVERPOOL & MANCHESTER RY. **1830**
LONDON MIDLAND & SCOTTISH RY. **1930**
(A) Admit to view Engines
ADULT -/6

753

721

SOUTHERN RLY.   "Brighton Belle"
PULLMAN CAR TICKET. Issued subject
to the Bye-laws, Regulations & Conditions in the
Company's Bills & Notices, & to the Pullman Car
Company's Notices, as displayed in Pullman Cars
Victoria to
BRIGHTON   **11.0**
A. M. TRAIN
Available for one journey on day of issue only
when accompanied by First Class Railway Ticket
...T TRANSFERABLE.   CHARGE 3/-

9552   9552

722

L. N. E. R.
THE SILVER JUBILEE
Car............   Seat No............
KING'S CROSS (S. M)
TO
NEWCASTLE CENTRAL
Available for one journey only when
accompanied by a THIRD CLASS
Rail Ticket.
Supplement Fare 3s.

1910

723

SPECIMEN

SOUTHERN RAILWAY.
This ticket is issued subject to the Company's
Bye-laws, Regulations and Conditions in their
Time Tables, Notices and Book of Regulations.
French Line.   S.S. "Normandie"
(451) Southampton Docks to (451)
Southampton Docks   Southampton Docks
Waterloo   Waterloo
WATERLOO
FIRST CLASS   FIRST CLASS
Fare 16/6   Fare 16/6

0000   0000

724

London Passenger Transport Board.
Issued subject to the Bye-Laws, Regulations and
advertised Conditions of the Board.
12th MAY, 1937.
Available only by Special Train
leaving at **9** a.m. from
High Street (Kensington)
to WESTMINSTER
Fare 3d.   Not Transferable.

953   953

725

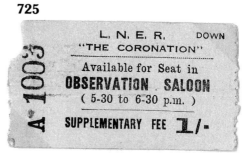

L. N. E. R.   DOWN
"THE CORONATION"
Available for Seat in
OBSERVATION SALOON
(5-30 to 6-30 p.m.)
SUPPLEMENTARY FEE **1/-**

A 1003

726

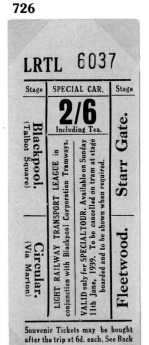

LRTL **6037**

Stage	SPECIAL CAR.	Stage

2/6
Including Tea.

Blackpool.
(Talbot Square)

Circular.
(Via Marton)

LIGHT RAILWAY TRANSPORT LEAGUE in
conjunction with Blackpool Corporation Tramways.
VALID only for SPECIALTOUR. Available on Sunday
11th June, 1939. To be cancelled on tram at stage
boarded and to be shown when required.

Starr Gate.   Fleetwood.

Souvenir Tickets may be bought
after the trip at 6d. each. See Back

727

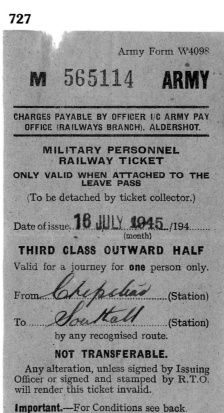

Army Form W 4098
M 565114 ARMY
CHARGES PAYABLE BY OFFICER I/C ARMY PAY
OFFICE (RAILWAYS BRANCH), ALDERSHOT.
MILITARY PERSONNEL
RAILWAY TICKET
ONLY VALID WHEN ATTACHED TO THE
LEAVE PASS
(To be detached by ticket collector.)
Date of issue..**16 JULY 1945**../194......
(month)
THIRD CLASS OUTWARD HALF
Valid for a journey for **one** person only.
From....*Chepstow*........(Station)
To.......*Southall*........(Station)
by any recognised route.
NOT TRANSFERABLE.
Any alteration, unless signed by Issuing
Officer or signed and stamped by R.T.O.
will render this ticket invalid.
Important.—For Conditions see back.
[P.T.O.

728

THE HARTON COAL COMPANY, LIMITED.
South Shields, Marsden & Whitburn Colliery
Railway.
Bicycle or Perambulator Ticket
Perambulator by Passenger 2d
Perambulator unattended by Passenger 4d
SINGLE JOURNEY ONLY
...t subject to Regulations.

4327

729

THE HART...
South Shields, Marsden, and Whitburn
Colliery Railway
NCB
shields
TO
MARSDEN
THIRD CLASS—FARE 4d
Issued subject to the Company's
Printed Conditions & Regulations
NOT TRANSFERABLE

9149   9149

**A khaki uniform, silver jubilee
and golden arrow mix with a
centenary, a coronation and
colliery to create further
fascinating ticket finds.**

Great Western Railway completes withdrawal of Second Class facilities.

1911
Baker Street & Waterloo Railway tries out early Scheme Tickets. Birmingham receives its first **Regina** ticket machine.

1912
Second Class facilities withdrawn on LNW, L&Y and NS Railways.
Metropolitan Railway issues its first Limited Season Tickets to wives of regular Season Ticket holders.
London Tilbury & Southend Railway taken over by the Midland Railway.
LBSC withdraws Second Class except on certain continental services.
At sea, SS *Titanic* is sunk with loss of 1,500 lives. Railway tickets inscribed 'Sold on board SS *Titanic*' were from stock intended for supply to the vessel had it returned to Britain.

1914
Railways under control of a Railway Executive Committee (REC).
Scheme Tickets now issued by the City & South London Railway.

1917
Reduced fares withdrawn and most ordinary fares raised 50%.
Order in Council ensures 'all Season Tickets to be shown for every journey'.

1918
Major railroads in the United States subject to United States Railroad Administration (USRA) which proceeded to add its title above that of individual issuing companies (**713**).
'Railway Season Ticket Order' increasing rates and changing conditions of use.
All Irish railway fares raised 50%.
LSW discontinued Second Class facilities.

1919
All major United States railroads adopt a newly standardised pattern of commuter's ticket required by the USRA, but not enforced after 1920.
LBSC reopens its London-Paris daily service.

1920
Third Class travel now accounting for 85% of all British railway passenger traffic.
Decline of tramways begins.
SEC reopen their Dover-Calais route.
L&Y and NE Railways reopen Hull-Zeebrugge services to the Continent.

1921
Population now 43 million with 32,600km of railway.
Railways decontrolled after recent war.
Weekend Tickets restored on many railways.

1922
L&Y and LNW companies working as one.
GW and LSW companies inaugurate a through Cardiff to Brighton service via the Severn Tunnel.
Railway Clearing House membership immediately prior to Grouping — 57 companies, and the Irish RCH — 49.

1923
The Grouping of 123 of Britain's railway companies to form the 'Big Four' — GW, LMS, LNE and SR. Certain jointly-owned railways, example: Cheshire Lines Committee, Midland & Great Northern Joint and Somerset & Dorset Joint, continued independently.

1924
British Empire Exhibition held at Wembley into 1925 (**714**).
Members of Parliament now allowed Free Passes for railway travel.

1925
Major reorganisation created the Great Southern Railways Co in Ireland (see **86** in Chapter 1).
An important collection of North British Railway tickets came up for sale and went on to form the earliest representation of that company many collectors have known.

1927
An exhibition of locomotives is held at Waterloo Station. Special tickets allowed admittance — (**715**).
Opening of the world's smallest public passenger railway, the 381mm gauge 21km Romney Hythe & Dymchurch Railway. See **29** in Chapter 1.
Opening of New Union Station, Toronto, Canada. British Royalty and Prime Minister attend the opening. Special tickets issued to dignitaries — Serial Nos 1 and 2 to the Royal personages and Nos 3 and 4 to Mr Stanley Baldwin PC (**716**), and Mrs Baldwin.

1928
The world's longest non-stop passenger train run inaugurated by the LNER from King's Cross to Edinburgh (632km) (first express run held in 1862). The train was named the 'Flying Scotsman' and accorded a number of special ticket prints.
The LMS company's 'Royal Scot' had earlier made the journey a little faster and was later exhibited at Manchester, when **717** allowed admission.
Foundation of the Railway Correspondence & Travel Society. **718** shows a 1958 colliery tour ticket mentioning the society.
GW, LMS and LNER companies introduce Third Class sleeping cars.

1929
The 'Golden Arrow' all-Pullman train made its first through run to Paris after an initial service operating Calais to Paris opened in 1926. See entry for 1946 and illustration **719**.

1930
100th Anniversary of the opening of the Liverpool & Manchester Railway. **720** shows a commemorative issue by the LMS. Also see 1830 and 1980.

1933
GW commenced first British railway air service, between Cardiff and Plymouth.
Formation of London Passenger Transport Board.

1934
Formation of Railway Air Services Ltd by the Big Four railway companies.
The 'Southern Belle' is renamed the 'Brighton Belle'. **721** shows a typical ticket for an 11am train from London. See also entry for 1908.

1935

Jubilee of HM King George V. Numerous special trains. Variety of colourful tickets.

First run of the LNER 'Silver Jubilee' train. **722** is a typical Supplementary Ticket displaying the name.

The French Line's SS *Normandie* crossed the Atlantic Ocean in a record 107½hr. The vessel is here represented by undated **723**, printed for issue on board.

Centenary of the Great Western Railway.

1936

Inauguration of the Dover-Dunkirk train ferry and London-Paris through services.

1937

Annual hop picking season in south eastern England. Special trains bring casual pickers from the Capital. Tickets sold by selected stations, and by hop farmers on an agency basis.

Coronation of HM King George VI. Special trains operated by LPTB and tickets as **724** issued.

First run of the LMS 'Coronation Scot' and of the LNER 'Coronation'. **725** was for a seat in an Observation Saloon on the latter train.

1938

Foundation of the Light Railway Transport League for enthusiasts. The society, issued **726** jointly with Blackpool Corporation Tramways and has since produced many other interesting items, including special convention issues in Rotterdam in 1964. The society was renamed The Light Rail Transit Association in 1980.

1939

Commencement of World War 2. Government control of railways by a second Railway Executive Committee. The 'Big Four' and their subsidiaries and joint lines, together with the East Kent, Kent & East Sussex, Mersey and other companies taken under a unified administration.

Sharp increase in the issue of Navy, Army and Air Force ticket forms, including some printed for 'Visiting Forces'. One nostalgic form is shown as **727**.

Evacuation of 1¼ million Londoners and southern women and children. Issue of tickets such as 'Evacuee's Visitor'.

Seat Reservation facilities discontinued.

1940

London Transport abolished First Class travel facilities on lines of former Met and Met District companies.

Reintroduction of many reduced fare facilities. Fares generally raised 10% above prewar levels (May) and 17% (December).

1941

Remaining London local First Class facilities discontinued.

1945

Formation of the Irish Transport Co (CIE).

1946

Nationalisation of coal mining meant change of ownership for the South Shields, Marsden & Whitburn Colliery Railway — see **728** of 1938 and **729** overstamped 'NCB' (National Coal Board) in 1952.

Foundation of The Ticket & Fare Collection Society, which was reorganised in 1964 (qv).

The 'Golden Arrow' train service re-established. See also entry for 1929.

Main line fares now 55% over prewar levels.

A representative of South African Railways & Harbours visited Britain and was given **730** for all-stations free travel expiring 31 May.

Foundation of the Irish Railway Record Society in Dublin.

1947

Completion of the series of papers published in parts since 1939 entitled *Passenger Tickets* by Lionel Wiener. See Footnote to the Introduction for greater detail.

Introduction of the 'Devon Belle'.

1948

Nationalisation of British main line railways and creation of the British Transport Commission. See Chapter 5 for details.

Volk's Electric Railway reopened after eight years of disuse.

Cheshire Lines committee absorbed into London Midland Region of British Railways (November).

Foundation of the American Vecturist Association, Boston. This well-established group publishes *The Fare Box*. The association and its journal are of particular interest to collectors of transport tokens. A number of companies used tokens alongside or even interchangeable with less durable ephemera.

1949

Formal dissolution of the Southern Railway (June) and GW, LMS and LNE Railways (December).

Former London Tilbury & Southend line transferred to Eastern Region of British Railways.

Transfer of Gravesend Ferry Stage to Southern Region and the Tilbury Stage and Ferry Services to Eastern Region.

Chicago Railroad Fair (**731**).

1950

Various transfers from Railway Executive to London Transport Executive and readjustment of other Regional boundaries.

London area Workman Tickets redesignated 'Early Morning Return'.

1951

Population of Britain now 49 million, with 32,000kms of railway.

The Festival of Britain, a massive and brilliant celebration of the Great Exhibition of 1851 and a device to give the people a much needed postwar fillip in trade and culture. For the ticket devotee were specimens from the Emett Railway mentioned in Chapter 2. There were also special tickets taking excursionists to view the Festival Ship *Campania* which toured the coast of Britain.

1952

Ordinary Third Class fares **reduced** from 2.44d to 1.75d per mile. Workman Tickets outside London area renamed Early Morning Returns. Only Liverpool Overhead Railway retained the former term, until its closure in 1956.

London's last tram operated between Victoria Embankment and Woolwich.

1953

Coronation of Queen Elizabeth II. Special tickets by the Talyllyn Railway (**732**), the Railway Executive (**733**) and others. The Executive item was for travel in connection with a Coronation Cruise of the SS *Caronia*. Note the similarity in style between **732**

730

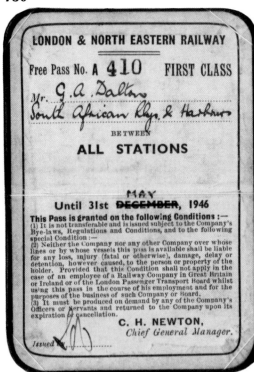

LONDON & NORTH EASTERN RAILWAY

Free Pass No. A 410   FIRST CLASS

Mr. *G. A. Dalton*

South African Rlys. & Harbours

BETWEEN

ALL STATIONS

~~MAY~~
Until 31st ~~DECEMBER~~, 1946

This Pass is granted on the following Conditions :—
(1) It is not transferable and is issued subject to the Company's Bye-laws, Regulations and Conditions, and to the following special Condition :—
(2) Neither the Company nor any other Company over whose lines or by whose vessels this pass is available shall be liable for any loss, injury (fatal or otherwise), damage, delay or detention, however caused, to the person or property of the holder. Provided that this Condition shall not apply in the case of an employee of a Railway Company in Great Britain or Ireland or of the London Passenger Transport Board whilst using this pass in the course of his employment and for the purposes of the business of such Company or Board.
(3) It must be produced on demand by any of the Company's Officers or Servants and returned to the Company upon its expiration or cancellation.

C. H. NEWTON,
Chief General Manager.

Issued by

732

TALYLLYN RAILWAY

CORONATION OF
Her Majesty Queen Elizabeth II

SPECIAL TICKET, Available for
TRAVEL BETWEEN TOWYN (WHARF)
& ABERGYNOLWYN & RETURN OR
INTERMEDIATE STATIONS.

Subject to Co's. Regulations.

0286

734

0264

1   LONDON TRANSPORT   1
UXBRIDGE LINE
50th ANNIVERSARY Pty
4th JULY 1954
UXBRIDGE

BAKER ST.
via South Harrow
& High Street (Kens.)
3rdCl. Not Transferable
For Conditions see back

LONDON TRANSPORT 1
UXBRIDGE LINE
50th ANNIVERSARY Pty
4th JULY 1954
BAKER STREET
To
UXBRIDGE
via Harrow-on-the-Hill
3rdCl. Not Transferable
ForConditions see back

1   0264

733

2nd JUNE 1953
DAY EXCURSION
Cook 1193 Agency
S.S.'Caronia'CoronationCruise
OPTIONAL TOUR No 33
AVAILABLE FOR ONE JOURNEY FROM
SOUTHAMPTON DOCKS   TO
LONDON (VICTORIA)   AND BACK
BY SPECIAL PULLMAN TRAIN
FOR CONDITIONS SEE OVER   FARE 87/6 H CM
TRAIN No I

154   154

731

A SOUVENIR OF
Chicago Railroad Fair 1949

CHICAGO
RAILROAD
FAIR

1949

ADMIT ONE

25¢

EST. PR. .21
FED. TAX .04

ESTABLISHED PRICE .21¢, FEDERAL TAX .04¢, TOTAL   25¢

16943   16943

L.R. Lohr President
The Chicago Park District, as Lessor, does not assume responsibility for this Fair or for its Exhibitors, Licensors or Permittees.

735

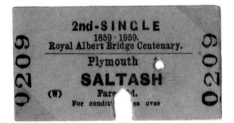

2nd-SINGLE
1859·1959.
Royal Albert Bridge Centenary.

Plymouth
to
SALTASH
(W)   Fare   d.
For conditions see over

0209   0209

736

LONDON TRANSPORT   1

LAST DAY OF STEAM SHUTTLE
OPERATION
11th SEPTEMBER, 1960

Chesham
to
CHALFONT & LATIMER
2nd Cl.   Fare 10d
For conditions see over

0441   0441

Between 1946 and 1964 celebrations in London, Cornwall, Wales and Chicago, Illinois, have occasioned the issue of this ephemera.

737

S O U V E N I R

British Railways Board
Western Region
CARDIFF (Gen)
PLATFORM TICKET 1/-

FLYING SCOTSMAN

Visit of
locomotive No. 4472.
'Flying Scotsman'
on March 18th 1964.

4472

S O U V E N I R

738

STEAMING
THROUGH A
CENTURY
1865 to 1965

739

SOCIÉTÉ NATIONALE DES CHEMINS DE FER FRANÇAIS
THE RAILWAY MAGAZINE
2eCl.
THE SOMME RAIL TOUR.
DIMANCHE 15 MAI 1966
ALLER ET RETOUR
CALAIS (MME) — NOYELLES
via Boulogne — Etaples
Voir au verso — See over
0020

740

British Railways Board
SOUVENIR TICKET
3rd September 1966.
GLASGOW Buchanan St. to
ABERDEEN & BACK
Fare 40/- 2nd Class
Last public run of A4 Pacific Class Loco
366

741

10月6日(金)――――18日(水)
大英国展
西武百貨店　7階＝特別催事場
各階＝特設会場
英国王室展
主催＝毎日新聞社
8階＝特設会場
SEIBU西武
西武鉄道
（西武鉄道）　No 9859
椎名町 ―→ 池袋
通用／昭和42年10月18日まで
2等　20円下車前途無効
椎名町駅発行

742

British Rail | Western Region

SIR FRANCIS CHICHESTER'S RETURN

Special Souvenir Ticket

to PLYMOUTH and back

AVAILABLE ON THE DAY "GIPSY MOTH IV" ARRIVES
AT PLYMOUTH AND FOR RETURN SAME DAY

Issued subject to the British Railways Board's Standard Conditions

743

MIDLAND & GREAT NORTHERN JOINT RAILWAY SOCIETY
SOUVENIR TICKET 6d
Sheringham Station
Arrival of locomotives and rolling stock
June 4th 1967
This is not an admission ticket: no public liability

744

British Railways Board (M)
This ticket permits the holder to view the
"FLYING SCOTSMAN"
at Morecambe Station
on 17th September, 1967
by courtesy of Alan Pegler, Esq.
Charge 6d. (including admission to the Platform)
This ticket may be retained
For conditions see over
0917

Japan's Seibu Railway flies the Union Jack in a unique
commemorative railway ticket. Back home, other events lead
to specially printed passenger tickets.

and the prewar **724**.
Abolition of the Railway Executive. *See* Chapter 5.

1954

British Transport Commission purchased the Pullman Car Company.
BTC introduce the Special Shopping Ticket, and later the Business Travel Season Ticket. The latter was available to employers for periods of between three and 12 months over customer-selected routes in First or Third Class.
50th anniversary of the Metropolitan Railway's Uxbridge Branch — illustrated is **734**, a Third Class Cheap Return of London Transport Executive (I).
Foundation of the Railway & Canal Historical Society. *See* **718** for 1928.

1955

Third Class fares again on increase.

1956

Third Class travel is redesignated as Second Class on British Railways' network (June) and in Northern Ireland (October).

1957

First operation of Trans-Europ-Express ('TEE' on many tickets).
Seat Reservation charge of 1/- (since 1905) doubled.

1958

The charge for an ordinary Platform Ticket raised to 2d (two old pence) — the first nationwide change for over 40 years.

1959

Centenary of the Royal Albert Bridge between Devon and Cornwall. **735** shows a BTC specially printed centenary ticket for the short trip over the bridge.

1960

Wedding of The Lady Pamela Mountbatten and running of special all-Pullman trains to the family seat of Romsey. Special tickets by BTC.
Foundation of The International Society of Transport Ticket Collectors, a group absorbed in 1964 by the Transport Ticket Society.
The 'Last Day of Steam Shuttle Operation' on the Amersham-Chesham and Rickmansworth line of the London Transport Executive (**736**).
In Manchester, closure of the J. B. Edmondson company's only remaining works. See also 1981.
Britain's Royal Family no longer required to pay railway fares.

1961

Exceptional consignment of railway tickets from the 1880s blew from a lorry crossing the Thames: see Chapter 3 illustration **169**.
Final publication of the British *Bradshaw's Guide*.
Early Morning Return tickets abolished by British Rail.

1962

Centennial journey of the 'Flying Scotsman' between London and Edinburgh. The name lives on in the preservation of the locomotive No 4472 and issue of souvenir Platform Tickets (**737**) and private run travel tickets.
Glasgow's last tramway service; only Blackpool was left with a municipal 'system' of any note.

1963

British Railways Board takes control of nationalised railways from the British Transport Commission.

1964

Formation of the Transport Ticket Society. *See* 1946, 1960, 1971 and Appendix 1.
Long Island Rail Road, New York State introduced the first magnetic-strip tickets and London Transport experiments with similar devices.

1965

The Talyllyn Railway marks 100 years of its incorporation. **738** shows this on the reverse of an ordinary Single.

1966

The Somme Rail Tour is sponsored by *The Railway Magazine* (**739**). See also entry for 1897.
The last year in which BRB operated the 'A4' Pacific class locomotive for public runs (**740**).
The Great Britain Exhibition is held in Japan. Seibu Railway Company is one of several to issue commemorative tickets similar to that of **741** — note the Union Jack.
Inter-City marketing concept introduced by BR, with unique ticket ranges — example **506**.

1967

The return of Sir Francis Chichester (1902-1972) to Plymouth. Tickets as **742** provided for travel to witness the home-coming. In 107 days from 27 August 1966 Sir Francis completed the single-handed voyage to Australia via the Cape of Good Hope.
A prominent preservation society commemorates arrival of additional locomotives — see **743**.
Special Platform Tickets issued by BRB(M) allowing admission to an exhibition of the *Flying Scotsman* (**744**).

1969

The Pullman Company's operation of America's sleeping cars transferred to individual user railroads.
Centenary of the Union Pacific Railroad's completion[24] of its United States trans-continental link (**745**).
Investiture of HRH The Prince of Wales. Special 'Investiture' versions of the Wales Travelmaster tickets (**746**).

1970

Introduction of **NCR21** (Chapter 2) vertical-format tickets by the Southern Region of BRB. Contemporary railway reports read like the epitaph of the half-Edmondson.

'Southern Region is to abandon one of the railway's most time-honoured devices — the tear-in-half return ticket. The new type ticket will simply name the destination, adding "And Back". It will also be overprinted with the letter "R". The ticket will be clipped at the platform barrier when the first journey is undertaken, and handed-in complete at the end of the return trip. These new tickets, the same size as the old ones, are designed to be issued by the cash registers now installed at more than 550 of the region's stations. These machines print the price and date on the front and have already done much to simplify accounting.'

The IX British Commonwealth Games held in Edinburgh. Unique 90mm diameter tickets, as in **747**.

745

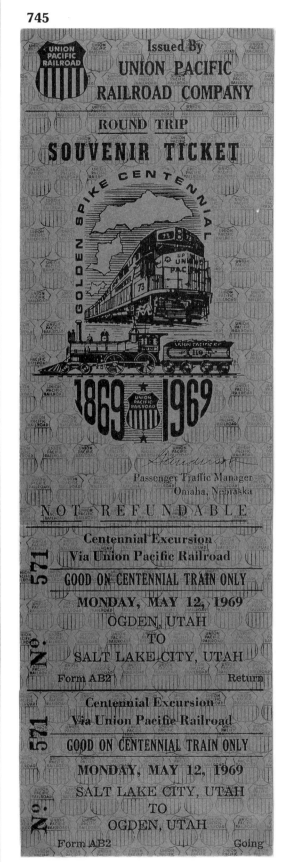

Issued By
UNION PACIFIC
RAILROAD COMPANY

ROUND TRIP

SOUVENIR TICKET

GOLDEN SPIKE CENTENNIAL

1869 1969

Passenger Traffic Manager
Omaha, Nebraska

NOT REFUNDABLE

Centennial Excursion
Via Union Pacific Railroad

GOOD ON CENTENNIAL TRAIN ONLY

MONDAY, MAY 12, 1969

OGDEN, UTAH
TO
SALT LAKE CITY, UTAH

Form AB2   Return

No. 571

Centennial Excursion
Via Union Pacific Railroad

GOOD ON CENTENNIAL TRAIN ONLY

MONDAY, MAY 12, 1969

SALT LAKE CITY, UTAH
TO
OGDEN, UTAH

Form AB2   Going

No. 571

746

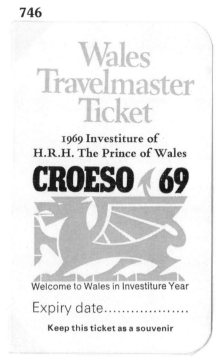

Wales Travelmaster Ticket

1969 Investiture of
H.R.H. The Prince of Wales

CROESO 69

Welcome to Wales in Investiture Year

Expiry date...................

Keep this ticket as a souvenir

747

IX BRITISH COMMONWEALTH GAMES · EDINBURGH · 16-25 JULY · 1970

GAMES ROVER TICKET

1 ST CLASS CHILD

SEE OVER FOR CONDITIONS
OF ISSUE & AVAILABILITY

748

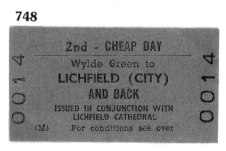

2nd - CHEAP DAY
Wylde Green to
LICHFIELD (CITY)
AND BACK
ISSUED IN CONJUNCTION WITH
LICHFIELD CATHEDRAL
(M)   For conditions see over

0014   0014

749

TRANSPORT TICKET
SOCIETY
296 1 13
1ST CL.
VALID ONLY FOR
THE PRESIDENTIAL
WEED-END
PARIS-
BIENVENÜE
TO OUR BRITISH FRIENDS

10226

745 marks an historic date in the history of North American railroading. *747*, as a circular card, is virtually unique amongst modern railway tickets. *749* is perhaps the nearest the hobbyist has come to his own privately commissioned ticket.

750

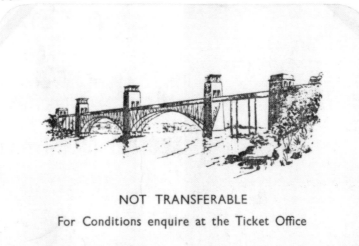

NOT TRANSFERABLE

For Conditions enquire at the Ticket Office

751

Don't forget to visit the exhibition of historical railway items on the Mezzanine Floor, also the photographic display on the main Concourse. Admission free.

125 PADDINGTON

Nº 0332

10p

Souvenir Platform Ticket

VALID ON 1 MARCH 1979 ONLY TO VISIT DISPLAY OF
EX. GREAT WESTERN RAILWAY STEAM
LOCOMOTIVES AND PASSENGER COACHES TO
CELEBRATE THE 125th ANNIVERSARY OF
PADDINGTON STATION

Not valid in trains –
Not transferable
For conditions see over

Four special occasions led to four special tickets.

752

Commemorative Pass
October 5, 1979

POPE JOHN PAUL II

F 16770

753

LONDON TRANSPORT SPECIAL TICKET
commemorating The Marriage of The Prince of Wales and Lady Diana Spencer

The
Royal Wedding
Warrant

On Wednesday 29th July, 1981
On this day
this ticket is available
for unlimited travel on all

London Transport
buses and the Underground,
except as shown on the reverse.

CHILD PRICE **50p**   **CHILD**

754

2

VENICE
SIMPLON
ORIENT~EXPRESS

Please see important notice and the conditions
of contract printed inside this ticket. They affect
your legal rights.

Voir l'avis important et les conditions du contrat de
transport imprimés dans le présent billet.
Ils concernent vos droits.

Si prega di leggere l'importante "avvertenza" e
le clausole contrattuali riportate nell'interno del
biglietto in quanto concernenti i vostri diritti
stabiliti per legge.

PASSENGER TICKET

755

2nd British Railways Board (H) 2nd
PAPAL VISIT 1st JUNE 1982
To CORKERHILL
From
DUMFRIES
OUTWARD & RETURN

0329   0329

756

JUBILEE RAIL TOUR

LONDON TRANSPORT
50
1933 1983
GOLDEN JUBILEE

09 OCT 83

On the same day, also available for unlimited
travel on any other LT trains, except
as shown on reverse

The highly acclaimed and beautifully refurbished Orient
Express produces tickets unlike all others. A Papal Visit to
Scotland and a Fiftieth Year in London complete a range of 884
railway and tramway passenger tickets.

1971

Decimalisation of the currency in Britain and Ireland. Large numbers of old currency tickets issued late into the new system, dual-currency prints with curious errors in conversion, and a variety of differences in the way that fares were expressed: example: 14p, 0.14p, £0.14p and in rarer instances 14np. Reduction in the price of Platform Tickets from six old pence (2½p) to two new pence (2p) to facilitate acceptance of the new Two Pence coin.

Formation (by virtual nationalisation) of the National Railroad Passenger Corporation in the USA trading as AMTRAK (acronym for AMerican TRAcK), to operate over tracks of 20 independent railroad companies.

Cheap Day tickets made available by BRB to Lichfield Cathedral for those attending a performance of Son et Lumière, a 20th century art form first seen in France in 1952 (**748**).

The Transport Ticket Society's 25th anniversary celebrated with a Presidential Week End in Paris. Members received specially prepared tickets as **749**.

The Railroadiana Collectors' Association incorporated in the United States.

1972

750 shows Robert Stephenson's Britannia Bridge, which was closed by fire damage in 1970. This is the reverse side of a special 'Preview Special Train' ticket.

1973

Centenary of the Isle of Man Railway.

1975

Introduction by BRB of Senior Citizen Railcards.

1977

Change in ticket colours by BRB. Standard became red print on white card for tickets at standard fare and normally available throughout the day. For tickets at reduced fares, where there would be some likelihood of times of travel being restricted, the standard became black on red card.

1979

Introduction of the Family Railcard by BRB.

125th anniversary of London's Paddington Station, when specially issued Platform Tickets enabled visits to a display of locomotives (**751**). Special tickets mark the 'First High Speed Train' excursion from Sheffield Division of BRB.

Pope John Paul II visits Chicago, Illinois (**752**).

1980

Oban Station 'Centenary Week' tickets issued 29 June to 5 July.

Opening of Tyne & Wear Metro.

150th anniversary of the Liverpool & Manchester Railway — commemorative Platform, Excursion and Exhibition tickets. See entries for 1830 and 1930.

1981

INTIS machine (Chapter 2) put into service at Gatwick Airport and Slough.

Wedding of HRH The Prince of Wales and The Lady Diana Spencer. Unique tickets by London Transport (**753**) and British Railways Board.

Alfred Williamson Ltd, the Ashton-based ticket printers taken over by Henry Booth Ltd of Hull. Williamson had 20 years before taken the goodwill of John B. Edmondson Ltd of Manchester.

1982

First run of the 'Venice Simplon Orient Express' — a refurbished and privately organised revival of the famous Orient Express (**754**).

Visit of Pope John Paul II (**755**).

1983

Introduction of London Transport's wholly new concept, the Travelcard. See Chapter 4.

Jubilee Rail Tour over London Transport Lines. Special 'Golden' tickets with drawing of stock used and a suitable logo (**756**).

1984

London Transport Executive (II) reorganised as London Regional Transport.

1985

Introduction of London's Capitalcard facility.

NCR24 machine (Chapter 2) introduced at Newhaven Town Station and soon followed by Basingstoke, Tunbridge Wells and other locations on BRB's Southern Region.

Formation of London Underground Limited.

1986

Introduction of One Day Capitalcard.

Creation of Network SouthEast.

Reopening of Groudle Glen Railway. See **691** in Chapter 12.

Introduction of Network Card. See Chapter 8.

British Rail accelerated the substitution of APTIS for the Edmondson system. At some stations, PORTIS saw temporary service. See Chapter 2.

An Act of the Irish Parliament separates railway services of CIE to be managed (from 1987) by newly established Iarnrod Eireann (IE) — Irish Rail.

Appendix 1
Societies for the Collector

1   The Transport Ticket Society (TTS)
Membership Secretary, Robert Davis
42 Hillview Avenue, Orpington
Kent BR6 0SF
Facilities include Postal Library and Exchange schemes, Monthly *Journal* and specialist Occasional Papers. Active membership in 10 countries. Regular meetings in Britain.

2   American Transit Collectors' Association (ATCA)
8304 Sixteenth Street, Silver Spring
Maryland 20910, United States
All transport tickets, with emphasis upon North American issues and the transfer fare form in particular. Bi-monthly journal *The Collectors' Item* and specialist information exchange.

3   The Club of Ticket Collectors (CTC)
The Club of Ticket Collectors (CTC)
Organising President: Raimund Schnitker
Hans-Böcklerstrasse 13, D-4700 Hamm 4, Germany
Railway tickets generally, with emphasis upon German and Continental European specimens. English language used.

4   American Vecturist Association (AVA)
Membership enquiries
PO Box 1204, Boston
Massachusetts 02104, United States
All world tokens and passes, with emphasis upon North American transportation issues. Catalogues and lists offering the finest readily available detail. Publishes *The Fare Box*.

5   Railroadiana Collectors' Association Inc (RCA)
Box 365, St Ignatius
Montana 59865, United States
Collectibles from railways generally. Special attention to American material. Some facility for the collector of passes and tickets.

6   The Ephemera Society (Ephsoc)
12 Fitzroy Square   124 Elm Street, Bennington
London W1P 5HQ   Vermont 05201, United States
Conservation and study of all printed ephemera. Bi-monthly *The Ephemerist*. Pre-eminent in its field.

7   Australian Ticket Collectors' Association (ATCA)
Enquiries to PO Box 292, Hamilton, New South Wales 2303.
All passenger tickets, with emphasis upon Australia. Publishes *Ticket News*.

Appendix 2
Suggested Further
Reading and Reference

In addition to those publications mentioned in footnotes earlier, the works below are fully recommended. Some are excellent sourcebooks of direct benefit to the collector of tickets. Others provide the essential final piece in the jigsaw of many ticket queries. Recommended reference also includes a vast and ever increasing array of formal material such as catalogues, timetables and maps. Ordinary promotional ephemera telling the public of travel opportunities and facilities is frequently a unique and important source of information at stations and travel agencies.

1   Cecil J. Allen *Railways of Britain*. Thomas Nelson & Sons 1958

2   John Allwood *The Great Exhibitions*. Cassell & Collier Macmillan, London 1977. ISBN 0-289-70792-7.

3   Francois Bédarida *A Social History of England 1851-1975*. Methuen & Co, London 1979. ISBN 0-416-85910-0.

4   G. M. Beedle *Travel Themes* (late *Platform Ticket Quarterly*). Graeme Beedle Enterprises Ltd, London 1983 onwards. ISSN 0951-0168.

5   W. H. Bett *The Theory of Fare Collection on Railways & Tramways*. Railway World Limited, London 1945.

6   G. Body & R. L. Eastleigh *Cliff Railways*. David & Charles 1964.

7   Maurice Bray *Railway Tickets Timetables and Handbills*. Moorland Publishing Co Ltd 1986. ISBN 0-86190-163-0.

8   *The Collectors' Item*. The American Transit Collector's Association (ATCA).

9   E. L. Cornwell *The Pictorial Story of Railways*. Hamlyn Publishing, London 1972. ISBN 0-600-33972-6.

10   Dr Edwin Course *London Railways*. B. T. Batsford 1962.

11   W. J. Davis & A. W. Waters *Tickets and Passes of Great Britain & Ireland*. Spink & Son, London 1922.

12   Marius Dujardin *Les Tickets des Enterprises de Transport de Voyageurs*. La Vieux Papier, Paris 1905.

13   G. H. I. Fairchild *A World of Tickets*. G. H. I. Fairchild, Brighton 1972. ISBN 0-9502400-0-1.

14   Michael Farr *Thomas Edmondson Transport Ticket Pioneer*. M. G. D. Farr, Whitchurch 1979.

15   D. G. Geldard *The First Fifty Years (The Early Development of the Railway Ticket)*. The Transport Ticket Society, Luton 1984. ISBN 0-903209-09-8.

16   John C. Hanbach. *In Good Company*. J. C. Hanbach. Privately published, Illinois 1970.

17   Geoffrey Hoyle *World Railways*. G. Hoyle. Privately published, Dundee 1965.

18   David Kay & Ian Cormack *Trams & Trolleybuses*. Spurbooks Ltd 1978. ISBN 0-904978-11-7.

19   C. Klapper *The Golden Age of Tramways*. David & Charles 1961.

20   Charles E. Lee *Sixty Years of the Bakerloo*. London Transport 1966.

21   Charles E. Lee *Passenger Class Distinctions*. The Railway Gazette. London 1946.

22   John Lewis *Collecting Printed Ephemera*. Cassell & Collier Macmillan, London 1976. ISBN 0-289-70393-X.

23   John Lewis *Printed Ephemera*. W. S. Cowell Ltd, Ipswich 1962.

24   John Marshall *Guinness RAIL-The Records*. Guinness Superlatives Ltd 1985. ISBN 0-85112-447-X.

25   O. S. Nock *Encyclopedia of Railways*. Octopus Books 1977. ISBN 0-7064-0604-4.

26   Robert C. Post *Manuscript Sources for Railroad History*. Bulletin 137. The Railway & Locomotive Historical Society. Boston, Massachusetts 1983. ISSN 0090-7847.

27   *Railway Directory & Year Book*. Transport Press Ltd, London 1985. ISBN 0-617-003-89-0.

28   Specialist works published by the Transport Ticket Society intermittently, of which item 15 is one excellent example.

29   *Steam Passenger Service Directory*. Empire State Railway Inc, New York. Annually. ISSN 0081-542X.

30   *Stock Exchange Official Year Book*. Macmillan Publishers, London 1983. ISBN 0-333-31563-4.

31   J. T. Howard Turner *The London Brighton & South Coast Railway*. B. T. Batsford, London 1978. ISBN 0-7134-1198-8.

32   Ben Weinreb & Christopher Hibbet *The London Encyclopaedia*. Macmillan, London 1984. ISBN 0-333-32556-7.

33   P. B. Whitehouse *Railway Relics & Regalia*. Country Life, London 1975. ISBN 0-600-37572-2.

Appendix 3
The Tay Bridge Disaster Tickets

Note: 12 persons retained their tickets (including two Season Ticket holders). Five employees also perished.

All 59 listed tickets are printed for destination DUNDEE.

See entry for 1879 in Chapter 16

Serial number	Journey from	Class of travel	Notes
	Great Northern Railway (GNR)		
237-8	King's Cross	Parly Third	Single
	North British Railway (NBR)		
1899	Unclear	Second	**Note 1**
232	Unclear	Uncertain	**Note 4**
331-2	**Note 2**	Parly Fourth	Left half
1903	**Note 3**	Parly Third	Left half
5163	Cupar	Parly Third	Left half
7131-7	Cupar	Parly Third	Single
508	Dysart	Parly Third	Single
9917	Edinburgh	Second	Right half
451	Edinburgh	Parly Third	Left half
464	Edinburgh	Parly Third	Left half
504-5	Edinburgh	Parly Third	Left half
518	Edinburgh	Parly Third	Left half
723	Edinburgh	Parly Third	Left half
6661-3	Edinburgh	Parly Third	Single
7387-9	Edinburgh	Parly Third	Right half
911	Kirkcaldy	Parly Fourth	Left half
1020-1	Ladybank	Parly Third	Single
100	Leslie	Parly Third	Left half
5585	Leuchars	Parly Third	Left half
4071-6	Leuchars Junction	Parly Third	Single **Note 5**
1490-1	Newburgh	Parly Third	Right half
2062-8	Newburgh	Parly Third	Left half
010-1	Perth	Uncertain	Right half
722	Perth	Parly Third	Left half
961	Perth	Parly Third	Right half
1461-3	Perth	Parly Third	Single
8132	St Andrews	Parly Third	**Note 4**
4253	St Fort	Parly Fourth	**Note 6**

Notes
1. Blank card ticket. Left half.
2. Possibly Abernethy.
3. Possibly Dairsie.
4. Has three vertical stripes. Left half.
5. 4072 was bisected to create two half-rate Singles.
6. Possibly serial number 4233. Left half.

Appendix 4
A New Railway Game

(By kind permission, reprinted from The *Daily Mail*[25])

The craze for 'collecting' things seems to become more widespread every day. The articles of common use now included in the category of things prized by collectors have become well-nigh countless. From birds' eggs and butterflies to postage-stamps and Jacobite relics the gamut runs, and the latest of these hobbies is ticket-collecting.

Ticket collecting, for pay and as a duty in life, has been known in this country ever since the advent of railway companies. It remained for an undergraduate of Cambridge University — a Trinity man — to invent the new science of 'billetely'. A *Daily Mail* reporter has secured an interview with this first of 'billetelists', who, contrary to expectation, proved to be a young man of considerable intelligence, a fine chess player, and no mean athlete.

'Yes', he said, 'my cousin and I started the hobby ('craze', if you like) some little time ago, and great sport we have had out of it. I should say that we despise omnibus and tramway tickets — unless they are foreign ones — as being common, and as presenting no difficulty in their collection, since passengers are not required to give them up at the end of the journey. What we go in for are railway tickets, and I can assure you that the collection of these requires a considerable amount of tact, ingenuity, and not a little 'cheek'. For instance, on alighting at a country or suburban station, one has to practice all sorts of ruses to escape the necessity of delivering up one's ticket. I have crossed the line before now and scrambled through the palings of the opposite platform. I have gone straight to refreshment rooms, where such exist, and waited there — at considerable expense — until the coast was clear. Several times, after boldly passing the barrier, a vigilant porter has given chase to me, and sometimes caught me, when I have had the satisfaction of disappointing his detective instincts by coolly handing over the ticket. I have been successful in a more wholesale way. My greatest coup was at Gower Street, where tickets are collected at the top of the stairs. I took my stand at the bottom and collected a trainful of them, passing up last and handing my own to the man at the top in order to mystify him the more completely'.

'But', objected the *Daily Mail* representative, 'I don't see how you could have done so bold a thing without detection. Were there no porters about, and did not the official at the top of the stairs suspect something when he found all the passengers without tickets?'

'No; you see there is very seldom more than one porter on a Metropolitan platform like Gower Street, and he was at the end furthest from the gate. The man upstairs when the passengers loudly protested that they had already given up their tickets below stairs had no option but to believe them, and probably concluded that an extra ticket inspector had alighted from the train, and (as frequently happens, I believe) collected them at the platform gate. His surmise was right; I was certainly an "extra" collector, but not one in the pay of the company. Probably so outrageous an explanation as that a passenger was collecting the tickets would never occur to the average railway employee'. Noticing that the reporter still looked incredulous, the 'Billetelist' remarked quietly, 'You don't believe me. Well, here are the proofs. Here are about 40 tickets from different stations to Gower Street, all dated the same day and of different classes'.

'And how many tickets have you in your collection?'

'Upwards of 1,500', replied the Billetelist; 'here they are'.

In a handsome cabinet next to the fireplace were arranged these treasures, neatly and systematically, in drawers, by countries, railways, classes, returns, singles, clipped and unclipped. Among the foreign specimens were an unusual number of German tickets.

'But are not the German officials strict in the matter of tickets?'

'They are. But a friend of mine got these for me in a curiously simple way. He handed his own ticket to a collector at the next station to Trier-am-der-Mosel; then he asked in broken German if the man would give it him back. The official looked at him suspiciously, laughed, and walked away; but, evidently struck by the novelty of the request, returned as the train was starting and thrust all the tickets he had collected into my astonished friend's hands, muttering something graceful and appropriate about "these mad Englishmen".

'And which are your most valuable specimens?'

'Well, probably this one; a First Class Paris (Lyons) to Monte Carlo; but I have also a local Spanish one here, and a German "Fourth Class" by the Mosel-Valley Line. Here are also some short-journey Swedish, several Swiss, and this "Ecternach-Luxembourg" is not common'.

'You have collected these mostly yourself?'

'Yes. But I have a great many "correspondents" who help me'.

'Gratuitously?'

'Oh! yes. They do it for the fun of the thing at first, then it becomes a passion with them. It is a species of sport, you know, enjoyed always from the hare's point of view. And then, of course, there is no danger; for if detected slipping through the gates you simply produce your ticket, and *voilà tout!* By the way, if you are going to publish an account of this interview, it will put the companies on the alert and make the sport more difficult to follow, like wire-fencing does fox-hunting. But I don't care. I've got the record collection, so far, and I don't bother so much about it as I used. But I warn you it will prove a most fascinating sport to others. On your head be all the blood shed in the pursuit of this hobby'.

Notes to the Text

1. *Passenger Tickets* by Lionel Wiener. Bulletins of the International Railway Congress Association, Brussels 1939-47. Partly published by the *Railway Gazette* London 1940, partly unpublished.

2. Further excellent reading — *Stagecoach* by John Richards. Watmoughs Limited, 1976, ISBN 0 903775 04 2.

3. The 1889 jubilee booklet of Hollandse IJzeren Railway stated the Edmondson card was introduced that year.

4. *History of the Railroad Ticket* by Robert Gardiner 1898. American Antiquarian Society, Boston, Massachusetts. Gardiner was personally acquainted with John Edmondson and well placed in railway circles at Boston and New York.

5. *Philadelphia Bulletin* 1856. By permission.

6. Facts regarding early Japanese practice have been elusive. Very little of substance is known at the time of writing.

7. *Ephemera of Travel & Transport* by Janice Anderson and Edmund Swinglehurst. New Cavendish Books, London 1981, ISBN 0 904568 27 X.

8. Vancouver's newest equipment accepts certain foreign currency as well as Canadian funds, and then issues or endorses the required ticket, after giving any necessary change.

9. The Transport Ticket Society, in its 1985 *Journal* illustrates one of only two discovered examples.

10. Further profuse illustration and fine reading: *The Ultimatic Machine and Its Use by BR* by B. P. Pask, The Transport Ticket Society, 1984, ISSN 0261 2798.

11. One wonders if this was simply typographical inertia!

12. This ticket is less of a rarity than the reader might imagine. Its full story is told in Chapter 13.

13. Paul E. Garbutt. *London Transport and the Politicians*, Ian Allan Limited 1985, ISBN 0 7110 1478 7.

14. Recommended is an Occasional Paper *Ticket Dating Schemes of the L&NW, Midland, Furness, North Eastern & LM&S Railways* by John Britton. Published by The Transport Ticket Society, ISSN 0261 2798.

15. Was it thought that long-established staff who would recall previous procedure, would now be too elderly for military service?

16. See reference to charities at the commencement of this book.

17. Until the closure of Senghenydd Station and Windsor Colliery Halt (Mid Glamorgan) in April 1964, British Rail had a 2d fare from the former to the Colliery Halt; the ticket was the shade of grey associated with the Workman Ticket but headed '2nd Special Single'.

18. It is recalled that one of the writers was considered to be *bona fide* by having been found named on the list of members of an American collectors' association. The regular practice had been to permit specimens to be posted only to members of inland groups.

19. Rolvenden and Tenterden each had two different adult tickets.

20. Dr Richard Beeching PhD(Lond). Appointed Chairman of British Railways Board 1 June 1961. His policy of rationalisation for the country's railways involved substantial cut-backs and closures, leading to the notion of his wielding an axe.

    One of the nicest stories told about him with a ticketing flavour was that soon after his appointment to British Rail, he was found travelling on his morning train from East Grinstead to Town with neither ticket nor his free pass. The travelling inspector, Mr John Hogan, demanded the 15/3d fare. Not only did the Doctor pay up but he complimented the inspector. (*Anonymous Reporter* acknowledged).

21. Further reading: *Tickets of Volks Electric Railway, Brighton* by Peter Wootton. The Transport Ticket Society 1984, ISSN 0261 2798.

22. Grosvenor Road was mainly a ticket-collecting stop shared by LBSC and SE trains serving the old Victoria station. Its platforms were on the river bridge. The LBSC premises were closed during April 1907 and the SEC in October 1911. Tickets for journeys to the newly rebuilt Victoria station were then collected at the terminus.

23. It is worth noting however, that certain companies have tended to disregard this aspect by selling travel tickets at their proper fare-value through the post in the full knowledge each is to become part of a private collection.

24. Story recounted by Dee Brown in *Hear That Lonesome Whistle Blow*. Chatto & Windus Ltd 1977, ISBN 0 7011 2232 3.

25. The precise date of the original article is uncertain but the Editor believed it to have been written between 1901 and 1910.

26. The history of **693-4** and **696** since the early 1950s is entirely consistent with their having been part of the collection but following the elapse of 40 years Mr Ivor Grantham was unable positively to identify them as having belonged to him.

Index

Standard figures refer to text.
Illustrated pages are denoted by
Italics for black & white and **Bold** for colour

People

General

G.H.I.F.